CONSTRUCTING AND IMAGINING
LABOUR MIGRATION

Constructing and Imagining Labour Migration
Perspectives of Control from Five Continents

Edited by

ELSPETH GUILD and SANDRA MANTU
Radboud University Nijmegen, The Netherlands

Routledge
Taylor & Francis Group

LONDON AND NEW YORK

First published 2011 by Ashgate Publishing

Published 2016 by Routledge
2 Park Square, Milton Park, Abingdon, Oxfordshire OX14 4RN
711 Third Avenue, New York, NY 10017, USA

First issued in paperback 2016

Routledge is an imprint of the Taylor & Francis Group, an informa business

British Library Cataloguing in Publication Data
Constructing and imagining labour migration : perspectives
   of control from five continents.
   1. Emigration and immigration--Government policy.
   2. Emigration and immigration--International cooperation.
   3. Labor mobility. 4. Foreign workers--Legal status, laws, etc.
   I. Guild, Elspeth. II. Mantu, Sandra.
   344'.0162-dc22

Library of Congress Cataloging-in-Publication Data
Guild, Elspeth.
   Constructing and imagining labour migration : perspectives of control from five continents
/ by Elspeth Guild and Sandra Mantu.
      p. cm.
   Includes bibliographical references and index.
   ISBN 978-1-4094-0963-2 (hardback) -- ISBN 978-1-4094-0964-9 (ebook)
1. Foreign workers. 2. Emigration and immigration--Government policy. 3. International
relations. I. Mantu, Sandra. II. Title.
   HD6300.G85 2010
   331.6'2--dc22

                                                                        2010024655

ISBN 13: 978-1-138-25199-1 (pbk)
ISBN 13: 978-1-4094-0963-2 (hbk)

Contents

List of Figures

List of Tables

Notes on Contributors

Didier Bigo is Professor of International Relations at Sciences Po Paris, professor at King's College London and researcher at CERI/FNSP. He is co-editor with Rob Walker of the new ISA journal *International Political Sociology*. He is also Director of the Centre for Study of Conflict and editor of the quarterly journal *Cultures & Conflits* published by l'Harmattan and edited once a year in *Alternatives* (Lynne Rienner ed.). Didier Bigo works on critical approaches to security in Europe and the relation between internal and external security, as well as on sociology of policing and surveillance. He analyses the relations and tensions between international relations, politics and sociology.

Alexandra Délano is currently a post-Doctoral Fellow at the New School. Her research interests are mainly Mexico–US migration policies, international migration, immigrant integration and Mexico–US relations. She is Mexican (from Mexico City) and did her BA in International Relations at El Colegio de Mexico. She recently completed her PhD in International Relations at Oxford University. The title of her dissertation was *Sending States' Emigration Policies in a Bilateral Context: Mexico's Transition from Limited to Active Engagement (1982–2006)*. Her recent publications include, The Politics and Business of Immigrant Integration, *Americas Quarterly*, 2008; Del Congreso a los suburbios: Iniciativas locales para el control de la migración en Estados Unidos, *Revista Migración y Desarrollo*, 2008; The Mexican Government and Organised Mexican Immigrants in The United States: A Historical Analysis of Political Transnationalism (1848–2005), co-authored with Gustavo Cano (Columbia University), 2007 *Journal of Ethnic and Migration Studies*, 33(5), 695–725; De la 'no intervención' a la institucionalización: La evolución de las relaciones Estado-diáspora en el caso mexicano, in *Relaciones Estado-Diáspora: perspectivas de América Latina y el Caribe*, edited by Carlos González Gutiérrez. México DF: Miguel Ángel Porrúa 2006.

Anaïs Faure Atger is a Researcher at the Centre for European Policy Studies in Brussels. She holds a BA in English and German law from the University of Kent, Canterbury (UK) and Phillips Universität, Marburg (D) and a Masters degree in Humanitarian aid and applied Human rights from the Université Paul Cézanne, Aix-en Provence (F). Her latest works include *Education and Political Participation of Migrants and Ethnic Minorities in the EU: Policy Analysis* (CEPS Special Report) and *Implementation of Directive 2004/38 in the Context of EU Enlargement: A Proliferation of Different Forms of Citizenship?* (CEPS Special Report) together with Sergio Carrera.

Christina Gabriel is Associate Professor in the Department of Political Science, Carleton University (Canada). Her specific research interests focus on citizenship and migration, gender and politics, regional integration and globalization. She is the co-author of *Selling Diversity: Immigration, Multiculturalism, Employment Equity and Globalization* (2002) and is the co-editor of *Governing International Labour Migration* (2008). She has contributed chapters to various edited collections focusing on issues such as gender and migration, border control and North American regional integration.

Blanca Garcés-Mascareñas graduated from the University of Barcelona with degrees in History and Anthropology. In 2004 she obtained an MA, cum laude, in Ethnic and Migration Studies at the International School for Humanities and Social Sciences at the University of Amsterdam. In her MA thesis she compared guest worker programmes in the United States, Western Germany, Malaysia and Kuwait. In 2005 Blanca Garcés worked as a Junior Researcher at IMES (University of Amsterdam). She did research on trafficking and forced labour among West African migrants in the Netherlands as part of the ILO's Action Programme against Trafficking and Forced Labour in West Africa (PATWA). As a member of IMISCOE, she has also written about immigration and integration policymaking in the Netherlands. She is currently finishing her PhD (at IMES) on the regulation of labour migration in Malaysia and Spain. The main questions considered are how the Malaysian and Spanish states responded to the huge demands on foreign labour and how they attempted to solve the underlying trilemma between markets, citizenship and rights.

Laura Griffin is currently completing her PhD at the University of Melbourne. Her interdisciplinary thesis is a case study of Basotho migrant domestic workers in South Africa, examining the impacts of migration regulation on women's lives. With degrees in Sustainable Development and Law (with honours in human rights law), Laura's research interests include: borders, labour migration, human rights, human development, globalisation, citizenship and transnationalism.

Elspeth Guild is Professor of European migration law at the Radboud University Nijmegen (The Netherlands). In 2009 she has been awarded a Jean Monnet Chair *ad personam* at the Radboud University Nijmegen. She is also Senior Research Fellow at the Centre for European Policy Studies in Brussels and a partner at the London law firm Kingsley Napley. She is a Visiting Professor at the LSE London and teaches in the Department of War Studies at Kings College London. In 2008 she was awarded a Doctorate Honoris Causa by Lund University in recognition of her work in the area of migration. She has acted as Special adviser to the House of Lords and is a member of the European Commission's expert group on the policy needs for data on crime and criminal justice. Prof. Guild is the author of numerous books and articles on the development of the EU, particularly in the area of justice and home affairs and the creation of an area of freedom, security and justice. Her latest monograph is *Security and Migration in the 21st Century* (Blackwell Publishers, 2009).

James Jupp is Director of the Centre for Immigration and Multicultural Studies in the Research School of Social Sciences at the Australian National University. Dr Jupp has published widely on immigration and multicultural affairs and has acted as a consultant for the Office of Multicultural Affairs, the Department of Immigration and other public agencies. His publications include *Arrivals and Departures* (1966), *Ethnic Politics in Australia* (1984), *The Challenge of Diversity* (1989), *Immigration* (1991), *Nations of Immigrants* (1992), *The Politics of Australian Immigration* (1993), *Exile or Refuge?* (1994) and *Understanding Australian Multiculturalism* (1996). The second edition of *Immigration* was published by Oxford University Press in 1998. His study of recent immigration policy, *From White Australia to Woomera*, was published in 2002 and his *The English in Australia* in 2004, both by Cambridge University Press. Dr Jupp's recent publications include the edited collection *Social Cohesion in Australia*, Cambridge University Press, 2007 and the 2009 updated version of the *Encyclopaedia of Religions in Australia*, which he has edited. In 1989 he was elected as a Fellow of the Academy of the Social Sciences in Australia and was its Executive Director from 1992 until 1995. He is an Adjunct Professor of the RMIT University in Melbourne. He was awarded membership of the Order of Australia (AM) on Australia Day 2004 for services to immigration and multicultural studies.

Melody Chia-Wen Lu is Research Fellow at the Asia Research Institute (Asian Migration Cluster), National University of Singapore. She received her PhD in Anthropology and Chinese Studies at Leiden University, the Netherlands. She has co-edited *Asian Cross-border Marriage Migration: Demographic Patterns and Social Issues* (Amsterdam University Press, 2010), guest-edited for the *Journal of Comparative Family Studies* (Special Issue on *Transnational Families in the South*, March 2010), and published several journal articles and book chapters. Her current research projects include comparative studies of migration regimes in Taiwan and South Korea, cross-border marriage migration in Singapore and Malaysia, and Chinese migrants in Southern Africa. Prior to joining ARI, she was a research fellow at the International Institute for Asian Studies, the Netherlands where she coordinated a research program Gender, Migration and Family in East and Southeast Asia, and taught at the University of Amsterdam, the Netherlands. She was an activist and worked in several Asian regional NGOs in Taiwan, Hong Kong and the Philippines on the issues of gender, migrants, and sex work/ers.

Sandra Mantu is currently working on her PhD at the Centre for Migration Law of the Radboud University in Nijmegen, the Netherlands. Her PhD examines state practices of citizenship deprivation in a selection of Member States of the European Union and is part of a Framework VII project called Enacting European Citizenship.

She holds an LLM in European and International Law from the Radboud University and her research interests are in European citizenship, free movement and human rights. Her master thesis has been published as *The Boundaries of European Social Citizenship* (Nijmegen: Wolf Legal Publishers 2008).

Carolina Moulin Aguiar holds a PhD in International Relations, McMaster University, Canada. She is currently Assistant Professor, Institute of International Relations, Pontifical Catholic University of Rio de Janeiro, Brazil where she teaches courses in the area of critical IR Theory and the relationship between human mobility and cosmopolitanism. Her research interests revolve around the international politics of human mobility, especially in relation to borders, sovereignty and claims to citizenship. She is currently working on the politics of protest among refugees and non-status communities in Brazil, focusing on how they reframe the debate about the international politics of management and protection of mobile groups writ large.

Mark Nyandoro is an Economic History Lecturer in the History Department at the University of Botswana and a research associate in the Niche Area for the Cultural Dynamics of Water (CuDyWat), School of Basic Sciences, North-West University (Vaal Triangle Campus). He is a PhD history graduate of the University of Pretoria and an MA, BA Spec Hons, BA history and economic history graduate of the University of Zimbabwe and he has specialized in the socio-economic history of irrigation agriculture, land, water and environmental conservation. Nyandoro is currently engaged in irrigation and water research. He has diverse interests in development studies focusing on potable water, water for irrigation (agriculture), industrial water, water-borne diseases especially cholera, including wastewater treatment, sanitation and migration issues. He also researches on climate change in arid and semi-arid environments; public policy, governance, democracy and human rights and has published academic papers and a book on irrigation.

Midori Okabe is currently an Associate Professor with the Faculty of Law, Sophia University, Tokyo. She received her BA in Sociology (1994), MA in Area Studies (1996), and MA in International Relations (2000) from the University of Tokyo. Prof. Okabe has also been a Visiting Scholar (Ushiba fellow) at the Centre of International Studies, University of Cambridge, UK; an Academic Programme Associate in the Division of Peace and Governance Programme at the United Nations University headquarters in Tokyo; a Centre of Excellence Research Fellow at the International Christian University in Tokyo; a Special Advisor to the Japanese Ministry of Foreign Affairs at the embassy in Luxembourg; and a research fellow for Nomura Research Institute Ltd. Her research interests include international and global migration studies and international relations, including European Union studies.

Lilia Ormonbekova is a PhD candidate at the Centre for Migration Law of the Radboud University of Nijmegen, the Netherlands. Her thesis explores the development of labour migration policies of Central Asian states and their relations with Russia and Kazakhstan in the area of migration. Migration from international relations' perspective is of her particular interest, as well as comparative regional studies (European Union, CIS). Lilia has a Master of Arts Degree in European External Politics from the Free Brussels University and a Bachelor of Arts Degree in Regional Studies from the Moscow State University of International Relations.

Mónica Serrano is Executive Director of the Global Centre for the Responsibility to Protect at the Graduate Centre at City University New York. Since 1992 she has been a Research Professor at Colegio de México and has been directing research projects on North America, Regional Security and the Human Rights Regime in Latin America. Ms. Serrano has written and lectured extensively on international, regional, and national security issues. She completed her doctorate at Oxford University in International Relations and has maintained both a teaching and research role there as well. Her more recent works include *Transnational Organised Crime and International Security: Business as Usual?* (2002) with Marts R. Berdal, and *Regionalsim and Governance in the Americas: Continetal Drift* (2005) with Louise Fawcett.

Acknowledgments

This book is the result of a workshop that took place in February 2009 in New York. We would like to thank the International Studies Association for the generous grant that they have given us to conduct research on the topic of control of labour migration and to organize the workshop. Also, we are indebted to Martin Heisler and Kamal Sadiq for their contribution to the success of the initial workshop. Finally, we would like to thank the Centre for Migration Law of the Radboud University Nijmegen for its support and to Hannie van de Put for all the time and effort she has invested in the editing of the book.

Introduction

Elspeth Guild and Sandra Mantu

The aim of this book is to launch a long-term re-assessment of the interaction between states regarding labour migration and shifting paradigms of control regarding movement of persons. Despite the fact that only a small percentage of the world's population actually lives outside the country of birth or nationality,[1] migration is high on the political agenda of many countries world wide. This phenomenon challenges the view of the world as divided into neat, territorially exclusive, national states exercising sovereignty over their clearly demarcated territories and homogenous populations. States increasingly view the movement of persons across borders as something they need to control and constrain, mainly by castigating certain types of movement and putting into place mechanisms designed to control movement.

Migration, in general, and labour migration, in particular, have generated an impressive body of literature that has looked at migration-related issues from various perspectives, trying to understand, for example, what drives labour migration, what informs state policies, how to measure the effectiveness of these policies and predict future trends. This book tries to look beyond how migration is controlled on a national basis and the experiences of one geographic region by shifting the attention to 'the global politics of labour migration'[2] and the possibility of conceptualizing labour migration control from a comparative perspective. We have particularly chosen to use the concepts of *construction* and *imagination* of labour migration control in order to avoid reverting to repertoires that attempt to criminalize certain types of migration and impose a monopoly of underlying truth and knowledge about how migration takes place and how it is controlled. Our objective is to examine states' claims about control, its need, its effectiveness and its purposes against the realities which exist. As such, the interaction between states' claims and the manner in which individuals experience controls holds the key to understanding how control mechanisms shape policies, experiences and identities.

The book shows how labour migration control is in itself a complex concept whose definition should be enlarged beyond external or internal controls in order to capture the experiences of illegality and deportability which inform the

---

1 The percentage is about 3% according to Cornelius and Tsuda, in Cornelius et al. 2004.

2 Geddes 2007.

migration experiences of many individuals, regardless of their actual location in developed (the so-called receiving countries) or less developed (the so-called sending countries) countries. The blurring between external and internal control and the increasing use of surveillance practices point to changes in the governance of migration and a growing emphasis on the disciplining of migrants via social control. One of the important issues which arises in all chapters is the capacity of the state to allocate the status of 'illegal' with important consequences for the individual concerned, mainly in terms of the diminution of his/her economic capacity and access to rights. The negotiation of identity between states and migrants shows the ease with which the border between legal and illegal migrants, between labour migrants and unwanted migrants can be crossed, even by categories of migrant workers, such as the highly skilled, which are supposedly enjoying a privileged position (see the chapters by Gabriel and Lu).

Thus, beyond identifying the mechanisms that states deploy in controlling migration and in creating the appearance of control, all chapters pay special attention to the impact of such mechanisms for the individuals involved. By looking at migration experiences over five continents, we wanted to establish a framework that can help understand better the impact of state policies on labour migration. The interactions between the policies of states that tightly control migration and those with light controls need further theorizing. How can one understand and theorize connected yet asymmetrical control problems? The diversity of practices and interests involved leaves room for conflicting or uncoordinated solutions. It is a logical conclusion that if one border is not controlled or summarily controlled this will have an impact upon a tightly controlled border. This seems to be the case in several geographical areas. In Europe one can observe this phenomenon in the interplay between tight controls in core Member States and a less strict policy in newer ones. Looser controls by Mexican authorities and tighter controls, at least in the rhetoric, of US borders suggest similar issues. How is this phenomenon affecting the policies employed at a wider, global scale?

While the movement of persons across borders for the purpose of working or seeking employment has become a matter that states around the world increasingly consider that they should control, the extent and purpose of state control, the manner in which it is actually carried out and its intensity differ substantially from state to state. For example, in some developed countries such as Japan, labour migration is perceived as an important and relatively rare exception to the homogeneity of the national labour market. In the EU labour migration among nationals of the Member States (an ever growing number due to enlargement) has ceased to be a matter of state control, while the common mechanisms for labour migration from outside the EU are a matter of divergence between various Member States that have different interests on the subject. It can thus be argued that at the level of the EU we are already witnessing a new type of control paradigm that transcends the national dimension. Various chapters engage with this issue and explore whether this is a singular experience determined by the uniqueness of the EU project and its transnational style governance.

In order to understand what state contentions are regarding the control of labour migration, it is indispensable to examine the position of the individual migrants as the objects, but also actors in a dialectic with state authorities. How are their personal experiences and projects influenced and transformed as a result of the state practices involved? How does the relationship between the country of destination and that of origin influence their situation? In other words, to whom does the migrant belong? After he or she has crossed a border, is he or she no longer a citizen? There seems to be a dynamic and on-going process of status determination since once crossing a state border the individual may no longer be a citizen but a migrant depending on the power relationship between his or her country of origin and that of destination. For instance, US nationals are rarely described as immigrants, their US citizenship status follows them throughout the world, whereas Mexicans or Moroccans almost always are described as immigrants even if they are students or visitors in their host state. Consequently, one region's citizens may be another region's labour migrants. The perspectives of control and relations between states are influenced by the individual who moves to take up work. In all regions however, some migrants are caught in the politics of control of the labour market. For instance, Australian migrants to the EU or most EU labour migrants to Canada barely cause any worries on the central landscapes while others, Mexicans in the US or Moroccans in Spain, are highly visible and targeted as 'unwanted'.

Labour migration as a term presupposes a particular relationship between the migrant and the economic system. The migrant will be a worker, a term redolent of claims for workers' rights and trade unionism. The term employee conjures up fewer images of struggle and is preferred by those who examine highly skilled migration. But the relationship is still one embedded in a certain image of migration where the individual is in a relationship of subordination. The problem with this image is that it precludes other forms of economic migration – the self-employed who may be in need of protection as well. The movement of business people to places where they hire local workers also constitutes economic migration, though more rarely questioned. Even service providers and recipients, like tourists count as economic migration. Once one uses the less laden term, the ubiquity and normalcy of economic migration becomes apparent.

The interplay between labour migration and other types of migration is also relevant in as much as it overlaps with family reunification or forced migration, for example. States have the capacity to create the categories of labour migration (highly skilled, low-skilled migrants etc.) and make them more or less attractive for individuals who may claim one status over another in the expectation of obtaining a residence status or being tolerated. Depending on the nature of the state's claim to control identity and presence on the territory the status may be very fixed or highly negotiable. All the chapters tease out the gaps between law and policy, on one hand, and their practical implementation and enforcement, on the other hand. These gaps depend on the resources that a state has at its disposal and its willingness to implement its regulatory framework. Closely related to this, is the state's capacity to blur its presence and obscure its visibility from the market generating irregularity and vulnerability for migrant workers. The privatization of labour and the state's invisibility, which is touched upon by several chapters in the book, bear witness to this trend. In this context it becomes more appropriate to talk about narratives of control, some states being more successful than other in propagating an appearance of control.

The book is divided into three sections based upon underlying assumptions about the intensity of control exercised by the state. All authors have tried to map out the changing landscape of migration control and point towards emerging patterns as well as dynamics and correlations that can be made between existing paradigms. The book has a diverse geographical coverage, spanning over five continents. Furthermore, it brings together a mix of scholars from various disciplines, all sharing a keen interest in migration and the construction of controls around borders and the mobility of persons.

The first section is titled 'Uncertain Borders, Empty Control Claims: Labour Migration Regimes with Weak Control Claims'. It brings together geographically distant countries that nevertheless share similar issues around discrimination and its vital function in structuring identity. The first chapter by Laura Griffin looks at the labour migration experiences of Basotho domestic workers in South Africa and makes it clear that state power and legal instruments are only part of the migration control picture. The chapter outlines South African labour migration and policy and contrasts them with the realities of women's movements and employment in order to demonstrate the failure of the border and of border controls to achieve their purpose – the exclusion of migrants from the territory or the labour market. The chapter uses a distinct definition of the border as a socio-legal mechanism involving a variety of actors and bordering mechanisms that shape migrants' experiences and their self-reflection. As such, the understanding of the border as a social reality and its embedded-ness in a larger context of labour governance illustrates the constitution of illegality despite the actual technical legal status enjoyed by domestic workers and their constitution as an exploitable work force.

The chapter by Carolina Moulin Aguiar studies Bolivian migrants in Brazil in the context of processes of zoning. The labour agreement between Brazil and Bolivia ratified in 2004 has transformed the border between the two countries in a space of free movement for labour migrants while at the same time creating a new juridical figure, the *fronteiriço* or the trans-border dweller. By reading the labour agreement from the perspective of zoning practices, Aguiar argues that it is both a response to the mobilities engendered by trans-local connections and a mechanism of enabling flexibility in contexts of growing economic linkages and disruptions. The concept of zoning becomes a helpful tool in analysing the (dis)connections between statist claims regarding the control of labour migration and the everyday practices involved in the mobility of migrant workers within and beyond the territorially circumscribed spaces of border zones. The type of special economic zones, like the one created between Brazil and Bolivia, tend to tolerate modes of existence and forms of mobility that are not otherwise present in the traditional territories of the nation-state. They suggest a different reading of state sovereignty in the context of the regulation of labour migration within the border zone and simultaneously articulate a logic of control/discipline and solidarity/ inclusion. As such, Aguiar argues that the border zone leads to flexible notions of citizenship, neither resident, neither migrant, neither citizen, neither alien. Yet, the distance between law and everyday life is great because through local practices and policies of containment and control the *fronteiriços* end up being forced to occupy spaces of informality and exclusion from the local community thus suggesting that the gap between legal improvement of status and de facto integration remains a challenge for Bolivian migrants in Brazil.

Blanca Garcés-Mascareñas looks at labour migration in Malaysia through the lens of the theory of high numbers, low rights. According to this theory there is a relationship between the number of migrants employed in low-skilled jobs, the rights accorded to them and the categorization of the country in question as democratic or not. Democratic countries are supposed to allow a smaller number of migrants but award them a high level of rights, where as non-democratic countries, such as Malaysia, tend to allow large number of migrants but give them only a temporary status and limited rights. The Malaysian state, bearing in mind the failure of the guest worker programmes initiated in Europe has sought to limit the rights enjoyed by migrant workers by placing a limit on their total period of residence in the country, tying them to their employers and thus immobilizing their position in the labour market and limiting the social and economic rights they can access. Malaysia's migration policy is informed by the idea that the presence of migrants is temporary and that it should not endanger the ethnic composition of the country, leading to the interplay between labour migration regulation and national security concerns. The chapter shows how despite this rigid policy, the reality is much more complex as the state must meet the demands of the market and ensure the viability of the economy. The implications of this type of policy are problematic: legal labour migration is expensive; the privatization of labour and the increasing role of recruitment agencies have led to the vulnerability of workers that is further enhanced by their immobilization in the labour market. While the official line of policy is to make sure that what are imported are 'workers' and not 'migrants', migrants themselves start to challenge these policies, sometimes with the aid of the recruiting agencies and under the blind eye of the state, by resorting to illegality, which at least ensures their mobility within the labour market.

The chapter by Melody Chia-Wen Lu reviews labour migration policies and practices in several East Asian states with a particular emphasis on Taiwan. Despite different approaches to labour migration, the East Asian states import large numbers of workers from neighbouring states in Asia while, at the same time developing policies to prevent the low-skilled ones from becoming citizens or long-term residents. Taiwan is an interesting case study as the chapter captures its rapid move from fairly loose labour migration controls to extremely efficient and stringent ones in a short period of time. The discussion of the mechanisms of control in Taiwan is based on Foucault's concepts of biopower and governmentality, which in this context take the form of a specific technique of control, 'the governing at a distance via recruitment agencies and employers' and the control of the body and of sexuality (mainly in the case of the low-skilled female workers). From the perspective of the state's policy and goals, Taiwan can be considered a success story as it has prevented the settlement of migrant workers but this policy is pursued at the cost of harsh working conditions and living experiences of migrant workers, whose basic human rights are ignored and who are subjected to multiple surveillance mechanisms. While the state's restrictive policies have not gone uncontested, the power of individual employers and migrants in influencing government policy and public discourse has remained limited.

The last chapter of this section, by Mark Nyandoro looks at the impact of irregular migrants and refugees from Zimbabwe into South Africa and reveals major immigration policy limitations on the part of the state, regional actors and intergovernmental agencies. The analysis of the relationship between Zimbabwe and South Africa reveals the complexities of labour migration patterns in the region as well as the tensions that have risen in South Africa as a result of a relatively lightly controlled border with Zimbabwe. Contested control claims and the failure to regulate labour migration on a bilateral basis are superposed over the interests of part of the employers who find the fluidity of controls to be in their advantage. The circularity of migration patterns in South Africa challenges underlying assumptions about migration as a permanent phenomenon and brings to the table the issue of regional free movement regimes as a possible way forward.

The second section of the book 'The Appearance of Control: Examining Labour Migration Regimes with High Control Claims', looks at countries that manage to construct and project a narrative according to which they operate tight controls over labour migration. James Jupp opens the section with a chapter analysing labour migration in Australia, a country that due to its particular history and colonial connection with Britain has mainly seen migration in terms of permanent settlement. Thus, by viewing immigrants as potential citizens, an attitude shared with Canada, the state is very much interested in micromanaging who is allowed to enter the country as a permanent settler as a way of controlling the composition of the citizenry. Jupp traces the shifting paradigms of control by pointing out the increased reliance on visas and the oscillation between free migration and arranged schemas which also suggest the changing understanding of the type of labour migrants allowed to enter. Temporary labour recruitment has been on the rise as the need to fill up labour shortages in rural areas and certain industries has become an important issue. Despite Australia's rejection of guest worker programmes similar to the ones operated in Europe in the 1960s and its use of the points-based system that is supposed to select migrants on the basis of their skills, education, language facility and employability, the government is facing similar problems to other industrial countries in the world. As such, it has been forced to attract more un-skilled temporary labour with the downside that the gap between the treatment of this category and that of highly-skilled is increasing. The long-term implications of these shifts in control remain yet to be clarified.

Christina Gabriel's chapter looks at the Canadian claims of migration control. She argues that the state's recent immigration direction can be read as part of a dominant national imaginary that constructs Canada as a nation that is welcoming of migrants, that offers the promise of citizenship to all and is the pioneer of a multicultural model of integration. At the same time, Canada operates within a particular neo-liberal paradigm that favours certain types of labour migration, and more recently places more emphasis on the ability of the migrant to adapt to the economy rather than to society. The success of Canada's points-based system is questioned especially in light of the labour market experiences of more recent migrants and the expansion of the category of temporary workers. Similar to other developed countries, there is an emphasis on employer driven programmes that import a flexible, immobile migrant workforce to respond to market needs. Gabriel underlines the shift in scope of migration policy, as whereas in the past people were recruited under various categories to build the 'new' nation, currently the skills of migrants are seen as a means to allow the nation to compete in a globalizing world. This process is coupled with an increasing dichotomy between the highly skilled migrants who enter on a permanent basis and the low-skilled ones who seem to have no place in imagining the nation. Her conclusion is that the increasing volume and fragmentation of the temporary migrant category and the differentiated social inclusion that it brings along point towards the shortcomings of the points-based system, underscore the need for low-skilled migrants and raise broader questions about social justice.

Anaïs Faure Atger's chapter looks at labour migration control towards third country nationals at the level of the European Union. It shows the complexities of EU and Member State labour migration systems, which are highly elaborate and give a very strong impression of control and direction. The chapter first gives an overview of national policies on labour migration within the EU Member States, after which it discusses the attempts to develop an EU labour migration policy. Within the EU, the national regimes applicable to labour migration do vary, but there seems to be a common logic, i.e. the state's desire to protect the local labour market while satisfying its economical actors. National policies are characterized by a high level of state control whose practical implementation is left to employers, at the expense of an approach based on the rights and security of individual migrants. While the EU has progressively sought to gain competence and initiative in this area, the Member States have shown increasing resistance and managed to block up to now the development of an independent EU policy regarding all aspects of labour migration of third country nationals, including the right of first entry. The emerging European policy towards labour migration has moved away from the development of a comprehensive policy defining common rules for access to any employment across the EU, towards sector-specific rules according to the type of activity to be pursued by the migrant worker. The conclusion of the chapter is that the position of individual migrant workers remains weak as a fragmented and inefficient set of European labour migration rules has emerged at the expense of a rights-based approach.

In the last chapter of the section, Midori Okabe discusses labour migration policy in Japan and how claims regarding control over labour intersect with claims about human rights. The underlying issue seems to be that the Japanese government exercises a tight control over migration as it allows only for highly skilled workers to enter the country and tries to prevent the permanent settlement of those migrants that do enter. The government's initial reluctance to recruit foreign labour runs counter the realities of the economy that demands more un-skilled and temporary labour. Despite increasing concerns regarding Japan's capability to compete with other developed countries in attracting highly skilled migrants, this concern is not the main pillar of the current migration policy or recruitment strategy. Conversely, security concerns in the region do play an important part in the formulation of policies. Labour migration, unlike other countries in Asia, fits very much into an international agreement framework. Japan's 'isolationist' policy and the government's claim to control migration run against the fact that Japan has become a *de facto* country of immigration mainly through the back door. Thus, while labour migration is presented as less of an important issue for public debate, the state's claim to control labour migration has been mainly challenged in the form of human rights claims and equality juxtaposed with the 'fallacy' that Japan is still a country of non-immigration.

The last section titled 'Equivocal Claims: Examining Labour Migration Regimes with Ambivalent Control Claims' investigates state authorities whose claims about controlling labour migration are tempered by the fact that these states have entered into regional agreements who exclude groups of persons from control.

The first chapter of this section is by Elspeth Guild and it examines claims about labour migration regimes in the European Union, a particularly dynamic area that also shows deep cleavages in perceptions and meanings of control. The chapter stresses that regarding free movement of workers, the EU experience shows that abolishing controls on labour migration based on reciprocity even among countries with very different standards of living, minimum wages, standards of social benefits and unemployment rates does not result in significant movement, a reduction of social solidarity nor a rise in xenophobia. Contrary to the free movement of workers logic, the EU's approach to TCNs (discussed in more depth in the chapter by Faure Atger) which no longer has a reciprocal basis shows much greater fears of foreign workers which results in a restrictive approach and less rights. While the power to control labour migration has shifted from state borders and sovereign decisions to EU mechanisms, the burden of carrying out controls has also shifted towards carriers and employers, and more generally towards the private sector. While security claims around traditional state borders have lost much of their appeal in the EU, new security claims have fuelled the development of supranational electronic control systems and large-scale databases filled with personal data on people on the move. Based on the EU's experience, the future seems to bring an increasing irrelevance of state borders for the movement of labour migrants and an increase of electronic surveillance detached from specific territorially symbolic places in a renewed disciplining effort.

The chapter by Sandra Mantu looks at European citizenship as a mechanism to cease control on labour migration by state authorities. The EU framework on free movement of workers has always relied on the assumption that those over whom the Member States had ceased to exercise control were nationals of the Member States. At the same time that the Member States were relinquishing control over their borders in the name of the requirements of a free and internal market, the possibility of giving up control over nationality issues was never considered seriously. Yet challenges to this last bastion of state sovereignty, in the context of an ever closer Union that ultimately started to escape its economic dimensions, came in the form of European citizenship and its promised destiny as the fundamental status of the nationals of the Member States. It remains to be seen if the rethinking and reworking of state sovereignty along the lines of EU citizenship will recapture the possibility of free movement for all those living on the territory of the EU regardless of nationality.

Alexandra Délano and Mónica Serrano analyse Mexico–US labour relations from the perspective of the North American Free Trade Agreement (NAFTA) and the 9/11 events. The chapter first describes the impact of NAFTA on the wider efforts to regulate regional economic integration and intensified cross-border flows, including the movement of people. Unlike the EU, NAFTA was mainly interested in the promotion of free trade and dealt with free movement of persons as a security issue. The 9/11 events have further diminished the impact of NAFTA and inscribed a security approach to regional border controls and the broader regional environment in which labour migration takes place. Migration and drugs were swept into counter-terrorism efforts, as in a very brief space of time the same arguments that prior to 9/11 had been marshalled to justify the tightening of the border to stop the flow of illicit drugs were articulated together to validate US responses against undocumented migration from Mexico. Despite the allocation of impressive resources, the US have not managed to stop illegal crossings but only to push more people into illegality and create a market niche for people smugglers. Also the circular pattern of Mexican migration to the US has been replaced by settlement and the creation of an important Mexican diaspora, for whom the Mexican government has started to take a stand. As migration and the growing diaspora in the US became foreign policy priorities, the relationship between the two countries became more complex.

In the next chapter, Lilia Ormonbekva discusses labour migration in the Central Asian region which is a fairly new political region. She describes the change from the USSR system of labour migration to the systems developed by the new states (Kazakhstan, Tajikistan, Kyrgyzstan and Uzbekistan) after they have gained their independence. Attempts at developing a regional system of labour migration, the CIS agreement of 1994, have failed mainly because of security concerns in the area. Unlike most of the countries discussed in this book, the Central Asian republics are not liberal democracies and the extent to which human rights arguments or the international framework for the protection of migrant workers are actually relevant seem to vary from state to state. The initial approach of most of the countries discussed here has been to encourage ethnic labour migration, while labour migration dominated by economic incentives started to emerge only at the beginning of the 21st century. The migration dynamics of this region are not yet stabilized and seem to be influenced by political as well as socio-economic factors. Most Central Asian states have not yet invested heavily in claiming control over labour migration while the poorer countries in the region are overtly encouraging emigration.

Didier Bigo closes the book with a chapter that questions control mechanisms in the EU and shows the tensions between a legal system predicated on openness and a groundswell of security-driven rhetoric justifying coercive and ostracizing practices against foreigners. Bigo argues that in spite of growing interest in all sort of control mechanisms and technologies and the proliferation of laws on immigration that label some forms of migration wanted and some unwanted, the political will to curb immigration has had next to no impact in terms of effective control of cross-border practices in market-economy regimes whose borders have to remain open to goods, services and capital if those regimes are to remain viable. Similar to the conclusions of Seranno and Delano, he also cautions against prohibitionist policies which do not solve any problems in terms of fraud but allow for its professionalization. Thus, instead of attempting to import the exceptionalism that informs American policy, the EU should continue along the lines of free movement and devise a labour migration policy that provides for decent conditions of family unification, equal wages, pension rights and cross-border movement.

The survey of control claims regarding labour migration in a variety of places around the globe suggests the failure of paradigms build around theories of control and security. Thinking of labour migration in terms of flows that need to be managed in an orderly fashion has failed to deliver the results promised by the same policies, i.e. allowing only wanted labour migrants to enter. The fallacy between the needs of the economy and the frameworks designed by states is increasingly problematic as control paradigms build around the conceptualization of migration as a security issue, ignore the human aspect of the phenomenon. The capacity of the state to brand certain categories of labour migrants as illegal and the very fluidity of the legally designed space between legality and irregularity question the very legitimacy of control claims.

Bibliography

Cornelius, W.A., Martin, P.L. and Hollifield, J.F. 2004. *Controlling Immigration: A Global Perspective*. Stanford: Stanford University Press.

Geddes, A. 2007. The Europeanization of What? Migration, Asylum and the Politics of European Integration, in *The Europeanization of National Policies and Politics of Immigration: Between Autonomy and the European Union*, edited by T. Faist and A. Ette. Basingstoke: Palgrave Macmillan.

SECTION I
Uncertain Borders, Empty Control Claims: Labour Migration Regimes with Weak Control Claims

Elspeth Guild and Sandra Mantu

This first section brings together the experiences of countries, who in spite of their diverse geographical location on the African, Asian and South American continents, share similar issues around discrimination and its vital function in structuring identity. All chapters capture the deployment of irregularity as a mechanism of labour migration control and as the principle structuring experiences of exploitation and exclusion from social security. Irregularity arises again and again as a source of fascination – it seems to fulfil all sorts of different functions – from being an inherent part of labour migration (Griffin), a by-product (Aguiar), a disciplining move by the state (Mascareñas) or a by product of the state's attempt to establish a monopoly over residence on the territory (Lu). The main mechanism through which the state disciplines migrants and makes them available for economic exploitation is related to its monopoly over the attribution of legal status and its capacity to blur the line between legal/irregular, wanted/ unwanted migrants. In spite of migration taking place under various headings, the underlying issue is labour migration which is tied with the state's willingness to admit the necessity of this type of movement. Lu and Mascareñas' chapters highlight the disjunction between the labour market and the state, and although the other chapters are less clear about this, the privatization of labour control is an underlying issue in all of them. The state's presumed absence from the regulation and control of labour migration is tied in with its capacity to obscure its presence. Strict regulations and even, over-regulation are characteristic of these countries' formal labour migration policies and yet, irregularity, be it in a formal, legal sense or as a subjective mode of identification, informs the every day experiences of many migrants. National security plays a part in some areas (Asia) while in Africa the chapter by Nyndoro illustrates the ambivalence of state politics and migration and the constitution of migration as a subject of international relations. Finally, the spatial and temporal experience of migration seems fluid as the state's capacity to construct and negotiate identify within these fields varies. The chapter by Aguiar illustrates how proximity or distance to the border can be deployed as a safety net against exploitation or as a mechanism favouring it. The chapters by Griffin, Lu and Mascareñas focus on the state's desire to control the temporality of migration by instituting categories of migrants based on the length of their residence.

Chapter 1

When Borders Fail:
'Illegal', Invisible Labour Migration
and Basotho Domestic Workers
in South Africa

Laura Griffin

Summary

This chapter examines the 'failure' of laws and state controls to regulate labour migration, by focusing on a specific case study: domestic workers in South Africa who are Basotho (i.e. who have migrated from Lesotho). It examines state power and legal instruments as elements within a larger, more complex regulatory apparatus: the border. The chapter applies a novel conception of the border by focusing on the experiences and strategies of migrant workers themselves. This exposes the blurred lines between state and non-state, legal and illegal, in the regulation of migrants' movements and their employment. Ultimately the 'failure' of state measures effectively to control Basotho women's labour migration is seen to produce a number of specific effects. In particular, the border apparatus, resting on a complex system of documentation and operating through a range of agents, constitutes migrant workers as 'illegal'. This 'illegality' undermines the efficacy of labour protections, distinguishing Basotho women as a supply of exploitable, expendable and invisible labour for South African homes.

The chapter begins by outlining a conceptual framework for the study of labour migration based on a conception of migration control regimes, or 'borders', which extends beyond state or legal controls. The perspective of the labour migrant herself is considered particularly crucial in this framework. The remainder of the chapter comprises such an analysis of Basotho domestic workers in South Africa, including: a brief introduction to the case study group; an outline of South African labour migration law and policy (contrasted with the realities of women's labour migration); migrants' experiences of 'illegality' as produced by the border's surveillance and disciplining processes; and most crucially, the effects of this 'illegal' subjectivity in terms of the domestic service labour market and the concealment of this particular migration flow.

'Our problem is that we are not here legally; almost nobody has the right papers.'
– Mosotho migrant domestic worker

Introduction

African states face a complex and difficult task in attempting to control or 'manage' cross-border labour migration. Indeed, state power and legal instruments represent only part of the migration control 'picture'. The state and the non-state, the legal and the illegal, compete and intersect in constituting the 'labour migrant' as a unique subject. This chapter outlines and analyses state regulation and experiences of Basotho[1] migrant domestic workers in South Africa. It examines their production as 'illegal' migrants and the implications of this status for workers' lives and employment. Particular attention is paid to the role of the host state South Africa, and its legal instruments. As this chapter explains, the South African state ultimately fails in its attempts effectively to regulate women's labour migration from Lesotho. However, the 'failure' of border controls to achieve their ostensible purpose – the exclusion of migrants from territory or the labour market – itself produces a number of specific and systematic effects. In particular, the constitution of Basotho women as 'illegal' migrants leads to their exploitation and invisibility within the host country.[2]

This chapter begins by outlining a conceptual approach to the study of labour migration control, examining the nature of migration control regimes, or borders. This section attempts to locate in general terms the role of states in the control of labour migration more generally. This leads to a consideration of the perspective of the labour migrant herself, discussing how her viewpoint and experiences may advance our understanding of labour migration control. Following this more general background section, the remainder of the chapter comprises the analysis of Basotho domestic workers in South Africa, building upon extensive qualitative data gathered in Lesotho and South Africa in 2008–2009. Building on a brief introduction to the case study group, the chapter outlines South African labour migration law and policy, contrasting these with the realities of women's movements and employment: hence the 'failure' of the border as constructed by the state. Migrants' experiences of 'illegality' are also considered, and how these are produced by the surveillance and disciplining apparatus of migration control. The chapter then outlines the implications of this 'illegal' subjectivity in terms of the domestic service labour market, and migrants' employment experiences.

---

1   Lesotho is a country in Southern Africa, occupied almost entirely by members of the Basotho people (singular: Mosotho), whose language and traditions are known as Sesotho. Although 'Basotho' and 'Mosotho' are technically nouns, for the sake of convenience they are used here – as in many other scholarly accounts – as adjectives.

2   I have briefly discussed these effects in Griffin (2009), divorced from any discussion of border theory or migrant 'illegality'.

The invisibility of migrant workers (and their employment) is also discussed as an effect of the border. The chapter ends with a brief conclusion, and a note as to the case study's relevance to the study of other labour migration flows and their regulation.

Conceptualizing Migration Control: The Border

A comprehensive review of the various conceptualizations of migration control is obviously beyond the scope of this chapter. However, it is fruitful to consider briefly the ways that scholars understand the role of the state, and its laws, in regulating or 'controlling' labour migration. Most analysis of migration regulation rests upon several problematic assumptions. First, 'the state' is taken as a discrete institution which acts and interacts in certain ways (including through immigration policy) to further its interests and to respond to identifiable political or economic pressures (see for instance Massey 1999). It is therefore usually portrayed as a single entity with a unified goal and strategy. In contrast, recent anthropological studies of states have demonstrated that 'the state' itself is a multilayered and contradictory ensemble of institutions and practices (see Sharma and Gupta 2006).

Second, migration law/policy is assumed to represent a state's dispassionate and unified strategy – ignoring the legacy of history[3] or domestic politics, and the reality of conflicting laws on different levels or within different state branches. A third common assumption, to which legal scholars are particularly prone, is that of legal efficacy: that social realities and processes, including labour migration, can in fact be effectively and coherently influenced and 'controlled' through the use of legal instruments. Proceeding as it does from these assumptions, much migration literature reproduces this dominant discourse, re-creating a mythical image of the state and law; reaffirming the capacity and legitimacy of states in seeking to control migration, and law as *the* mechanism by which to do so. This is reflected in the common disappointment or frustration (even alarm) at the failure of states and their laws to command migration flows.

In contrast, this chapter argues that control mechanisms enacted or wielded by the state must be viewed within a broader context/system of labour migration governance. Any conception of 'migration' or 'migrant' rests on the idea of an international territorial border.[4] A border is a line that is drawn on the ground (and/ or upon a map) and actualized through continual processes of identification and designation; practices of distinguishing and separating citizen from foreigner, local from 'other'. I therefore refer to the 'border' as the larger socio-legal apparatus by

---

3 Having said this, there is insufficient space in this chapter to consider the rich history of South African immigration regulation (including the restriction of Basotho women's movements across the border).

4 This chapter does not consider 'internal' labour migration flows, as they fall beyond the scope of this book.

which this is achieved, comprising a complex assemblage of various 'bordering' mechanisms which make the borderline a social – rather than merely legal – reality. This border apparatus comprises mechanisms or practices that:

- involve both state and non-state actors (such as private companies, employers, migrants, transport operators, and community groups);[5]
- may be legal or illegal, or a combination of both (such as payment of bribes, forgery or fabrication of documentation);
- may conflict and contradict each other (such that the system is neither coherent nor stable);
- occur at a range of sites throughout the host country territory and sometimes beyond;[6]
- both include and exclude migrants, often simultaneously;[7]
- produce different types of 'subject' (such as 'tourist', 'migrant worker' or 'citizen') in particular ways and at different times;[8] and

---

5   This is one aspect of border controls (or migration regulation) that is often overlooked. When analysts ask 'Who controls?' (Bigo 2004, 68), the answer is always assumed to be some agent of the state – or, when the actor is not the state, it is assumed that the state once exercised such control but has since devolved it elsewhere. In contrast, my conceptualization is not limited to states' conscious and deliberate 'outsourcing', 'exporting' or 'externalization' of border enforcement and labour migration control (e.g. Guild, this volume). Rather, it includes regulation of migration/migrants by other entities where such a responsibility or role may not be granted by the state, but is assumed by force or simply by default – such that these processes may even be illegal or in resistance of state control. An interesting example is provided by Mosselson (2009), wherein South African community members involved in xenophobic attacks speak of the need to re-assert differential treatment of citizens and non-citizens, in response to the state's failure to do so.

6   International frontiers are important, but not *sole*, sites of bordering. If a territorial frontier was the *only* site of a border (i.e. if access to territory was the only form of inclusion/ exclusion) then an individual's mere presence within a country's territory would be a sufficient indicator of her legal presence; there would be no mechanisms for identifying or expelling foreigners within the host country. Regarding the 'functional mobility' of borders, see Weber 2006; the de-territorialization of borders is fast becoming a common theme in migration and border literature, as scholars attempt to trace states' strategies 'to shift the US–THEM line from the border of the nation to within the nation, wherever it is required' (Dauvergne 2004).

7   Indeed, a principle function of borders is the simultaneous inclusion of migrants into territory and their exclusion, for instance from citizenship, rights, membership, belonging, etc. For instance see the discussion by Gabriel (this volume).

8   Much of the migration literature describes how the categories created under migration regulation regimes defy simplistic distinctions between 'citizen' versus 'non-citizen'. For example Weber (2006) speaks of the 'personalised' border.

• discipline these subjects, operating as technologies of surveillance and control.[9]

This border apparatus relies primarily upon a system of documentation and data management, which enables surveillance throughout the constellation of sites involved. State power is therefore merely one form of power that is exercised, and legal or law enforcement processes never account for the working of the entire system – these are therefore more fruitfully considered as parts of a greater, more complex whole. This helps to expose, for instance, how stricter entry controls may redirect migrants to informal/illegal channels such as people-smuggling, or how specific documentation systems are manipulated by forgers. To dismiss such practices as beyond (or against) the scope of migration control precludes a more realistic, nuanced understanding of how migration processes are patterned or regulated. It also takes the state as the only agent – and state power as the only form of power – involved in the construction of borders, the control of migration, and the production of migrants as subjects. In contrast, I argue that employers, people-smugglers and forgers do not simply avoid or ignore the state's legal migration regime. Rather, by strategically engaging with it, their own policies and practices form a part of the larger set of social practices that *is* the border.

This approach also sheds greater light on the nature and persistence of borders' perceived failure: not merely in terms of the reasons why states' construction of borders continue to fail (such as state incapacity, corruption, etc.), but in understanding why states attempt to construct or enforce such controls in the face of continued failure. More broadly, we could ask: why do borders, as more complex socio-legal institutions, persist if they consistently fail to achieve their ostensible functions? I argue that in order to understand a border's persistence and indeed its nature, it is necessary to examine the border's successes: the actual lived effects that the border *does* achieve, continually and systematically. This methodology builds upon Merton's (1957) distinction between manifest and latent functions, and follows such institutional studies as Foucault's (1977) examination of the prison, or Ferguson's (1990) ethnography of a rural development project. Inevitably, a border's effects – and its very mechanisms or practices – vary across countries and across migrant groups.[10] As border practices are invariably gendered,[11] raced and

---

9   This aspect of the conceptual framework in particular builds upon other considerations of 'technologies of control' (e.g. Pickering and Weber 2006) and Foucauldian theorizations of the border as comprising – or connected to – a surveillance apparatus (such as by Bigo 2004; 2007; Marx 2005; Lyon 2005).

10   As Bigo (2004, 62) notes: 'The controls are always differentiated and sometimes have contradictory effects.'

11   See Dodson 2001 for a critique of the 'marked' lack of gender concern and analysis regarding development of migration policy and law in post-apartheid South Africa. More generally, the role of gender in border controls and dynamics has now been widely noted (for instance see Segura and Zavella 2007).

classed, they constitute different migrants differently, producing different effects on those migrants' lives.

The Role and Experiences of Labour Migrants

As migrants engage with and experience a border in very different ways, the migrant herself provides the key to understanding the mechanisms and complexity of this migration regulation system. As the preceding section illustrates, it is not merely monolithic 'states' with which individual migrants must negotiate and engage, in navigating the labour migration system. Indeed, adopting a ground-level view of migrants' strategies, encounters and experiences, unearths the more dynamic and complex border apparatus. For instance, migrants' everyday experiences of 'illegality' and deportability[12] demonstrate how bordering and disciplining processes occur not only at territorial frontiers but in sites such as workplaces, government offices, medical clinics, and even on street sidewalks. Such a view may also trace where the interests and projects of state entities and labour migrants diverge or conflict; expose the inefficiencies or failures of state policies and tactics; and interpret the impacts of official policy or law on the lives and strategies of migrants and their families (or conversely, the impact of migrants' and others' practices upon the law and its enforcement).

The migrant's perspective also highlights the material practices of borders and migration control, and the effects produced thereby. This emphasizes the everyday technologies of surveillance, which are often otherwise invisible to migration scholars – owing either to their ubiquity in everyday life or to their distance from the 'law on the books'. For instance, labour migrants are acutely aware that legal migration regimes inevitably depend upon manipulable systems of documentation (passports, stamps and stickers) and data collection/storage (computer profiles of migrants' biographical details, their bodies and their movements). Labour migrants in particular are also attentive to the intersections of migration law and labour law, and the ways that migration policy shape labour market dynamics. Identifying a particular border's actual effects, as explained above, also requires us to examine how it is lived and experienced by migrants. In this respect, legal scholars' understandings of migration law, and migration governance more generally, could profit immensely from further ground-level, ethnographic studies of specific migration regulations and borders.[13]

---

12   Regarding scholarly inquiry into the production of migrant 'illegality', and its impacts in migrants' everyday lives, see De Genova (2002, 2004). Excellent examples of such qualitative studies of 'illegality' can be found in the Special Issue of International Migration on 'Illegal' and 'Irregular' Migrants' Lived Experiences of Law and State Power (2007) 45(3).

13   See for instance Kyle and Siracusa 2005, Wight 2004, and Coutin 2003. More generally, for a useful summary of legal ethnographic literature and approaches, see Darian-

Basotho Women as Cross-Border Labour Migrants

This chapter is based upon such a specific case study: Basotho migrant domestic workers in South Africa, and the ways that the border impacts upon their movements and their employment. Before moving on to examine the host state's legal framework governing this labour migration pattern *vis-à-vis* migrants' everyday practices, it is necessary to consider the context and patterns of this migration flow itself. Labour migration in Southern Africa[14] has recently undergone several significant changes. Rural and 'labour reserve' communities have faced mass retrenchments of men (both citizens and foreigners) from the South African mining industry.[15] This has occurred alongside a broader shift towards informalization, externalization and casualization in the sub-regional labour market (see Fenwick et al. 2007). Combined with the devastating impacts of HIV/AIDS throughout the sub-region, these factors have led to a greater reliance on women's migration for waged employment as a survival or livelihood strategy.

Lesotho is an extreme example of this trend. As an enclave state completely surrounded by the region's economic giant (South Africa), Lesotho's economy and families became heavily dependent on remittances from male mining migration throughout the 20th century.[16] More recently, Basotho women have taken up waged work in the various textile factories in urban areas within Lesotho, or have sought work opportunities across the border in South Africa. Data on women's cross-border work opportunities are scant, but they are known to engage primarily in farming and domestic work.[17] Aside from the obvious impact of gender on migrants' sector of employment, there is a key difference between the traditional migration of Basotho men for mining work in South Africa, and Basotho women's migration – particularly in the case of domestic service. That is the question of legality and regulation. Whereas for decades Basotho men have laboured under a

---

Smith 2004.

14   This brief discussion only considers recent trends of labour migration within Southern Africa, but many working migrants to South Africa travel from further afield, such as West Africa or the Horn of Africa.

15   For an account of the impact of mineworkers' retrenchment in the Eastern Cape province of South Africa, see Ngonini 2007.

16   The dependence of Basotho households on mining remittances in the 20th century has been widely documented (e.g. Murray 1981; Ferguson 1990; Gustafsson and Makonnen 1994). The number of Basotho men working in South African mines has steadily declined since the early 1990s: from 101,262 (1996), to 68,604 (1999), to just 52,450 (2005); over this time Lesotho has been 'facing a difficulty of re-absorbing the retrenched mine workers in the local market' (Bureau of Statistics 2005, 5; see also Bureau of Statistics 2009, 67–9).

17   For a study of Basotho women engaging in farmwork, see Ulicki and Crush 2000 and Johnston 2007. According to Table 2 in Ulicki and Crush 2000, the number of Basotho women migrants in South Africa engaged in domestic service is double that engaged in farmwork (though the source of these data is only vaguely defined).

highly regulated system of official recruitment, yearly contracts, work permits for migration, and automatic remittances, Basotho women cannot easily obtain work permits for South Africa. This obstacle does not itself prevent women seeking and entering waged work across the border, but it does generate a host of other important repercussions for their migration and their working lives.

The following sections outline the legal framework – including both migration law and labour law – as an important element of the more complex 'border' system governing such labour migration in South Africa. The legal framework is contrasted with the everyday realities of migrants' border-crossing and employment. The analysis also reveals the effects of the state's 'failure' to regulate or exclude migrant workers. In particular, state agents' attempts to enforce migration law – and not the applicable labour law – lead to an 'illegal' subjectivity as experienced by migrants. This experienced 'illegality' undermines the efficacy of labour protections, creating the conditions for migrant domestic workers' exploitation and their silencing or concealment.

South African Labour Migration: Law versus Reality

South African labour migration legislation is similar to that of other popular 'destination' countries like Australia or Canada. The Immigration Act[18] prioritizes highly-skilled immigrants, and allows for the issuance of work permits under s19 based upon either:

1. A gazetted list of work categories and quotas therefore; or
2. Sponsorship by a prospective employer, in which case the salary and benefits must not be 'inferior to those prevailing in the relevant market segment for citizens and residents' (s2(b)).

This reflects the common approach of issuing work permits to foreigners only in sectors of employment where local labour is deemed insufficient, such that foreigners do not compete with citizens for jobs. There are many professionals from Lesotho working in South Africa. But in terms of un- or semi-skilled labour migration from Lesotho, this legal framework effectively means that work permits are available only for seasonal agricultural work (e.g. in asparagus and cherry farms along the Lesotho borderline) or mining work. According to the most recent official figures adult unemployment in South Africa is 24.3% (Statistics South Africa 2009), making work permits for other less-skilled jobs – like domestic service – generally unattainable for migrants.

The state's task of enforcing these provisions, and regulating the presence or behaviour of foreigners accordingly, is distributed across a several agencies.

---

18   No. 13 of 2002, as amended by the Immigration Amendment Acts, No. 19 of 2004, and No. 2 of 2007.

The Department of Home Affairs is responsible for issuing temporary residence permits, including work permits. This department also detains and deports foreigners when they are found to be staying or working in South Africa 'illegally'. The South African Police Service (SAPS) lends support at the Lesotho frontier, and in identifying deportable foreigners within South Africa.[19] The South African National Defence Force also carries out operations along the Lesotho borderline, to prevent smuggling of *dagga* (marijuana), cattle or grazing theft, and 'illegal' border-crossings.

In reality there is an abundance of foreigners working in South Africa without work permits, including many Basotho.[20] Therefore, to consider only the legal framework, and only the state's role, is to miss the true picture of labour migration into South Africa. In a country where corruption and the state's inefficiency or lack of resources is an everyday reality, labour migration practices challenge and undermine the Immigration Act in a number of ways. These are revealed by an account of the ways in which Basotho domestic workers engage with the official system.

Negotiating the Lesotho–South Africa Border Gates

A Mosotho woman intending to engage in domestic service in South Africa first locates a job opportunity through social networks, *before* crossing into South Africa. Once she has obtained a Lesotho passport – by lodging forms and paying official fees in Lesotho (perhaps accompanied by a bribe) – she can prepare her things and approach the border. Leaving Lesotho presents little or no obstacle, but entering South Africa at the other end of the border-gate bridge can be a more complicated (and stressful) affair. Under the legal scheme outlined above, there is no possibility of obtaining a work permit for domestic service. However, citizens of Lesotho are normally able to acquire a visitor's permit simply by approaching the South African Home Affairs desk at the border-gate. As common practice, Basotho visitors are granted visitors' passes for periods of up to 30 days. To be

---

19   Weber (2006, 57) notes that the 'border policing effort in South Africa has increasingly depended upon particularly problematic internal policing practices that extend the border into the South African state'. For a discussion of migration policing in South Africa see Klaaren and Ramji 2001. Police xenophobia and harassment of foreigners for bribes is well documented in South Africa. As noted in Lefko-Everett (2007, 48), such practices are so common that many women migrants in South Africa 'have come to expect harassment and abuse in everyday exchanges with police officers patrolling the streets'.

20   Estimates of the total population of 'illegal' foreigners in South Africa are notoriously problematic and controversial. Most recently, in response to the xenophobic attacks of May 2008, the South African Institute of Race Relations estimated the total population of 'illegal' immigrants at 3 to 5 million, commenting that '"illegal" immigrants are a permanent feature of South Africa's population' (SAIRR 2008).

granted the full 30 days a Mosotho domestic worker may have to hide her intention to work, for instance by carrying less luggage, and/or by saying that she is visiting relatives or attending a funeral. Once she has a visitor's permit, the migrant must be sure to return to Lesotho within the number of days specified on the green sticker: otherwise she may face penalties, both official and unofficial (e.g. payment of hefty fines or bribes) and – if she cannot pay these – potential destruction of her passport (which is itself an illegal practice among immigration officials).

If a woman does not hold a passport, she must avoid the border-gates completely. This is not difficult: in many places, depending on the season, the Lesotho–South Africa border is a dry or shallow stretch of the Caledon River, easily crossed on foot. Where the frontier line does not trace the river, it is evidenced by a mere wire fence at the edge of farmland (hence the practice of 'paqama': literally 'lying face down', as in slipping under a fence). Although this is an easy task, it is usually resorted to only when the option of crossing at the border-gate is precluded by a lack of funds or papers.

Why would migrants opt for the stressful, deceitful and potentially expensive encounter at the border-gate? First, there is the convenience of using taxis and buses available to/from border-gates, as these are the major transport hubs between Lesotho and South Africa. Second, a border-gate offers the legitimacy of a Mosotho's presence on South African soil, as evidenced by a green sticker on her passport. This is valuable to migrants only because they are subject to continued surveillance throughout South African territory – at random roadblocks, in medical clinics, when approached by police on the street, etc. Like other border systems, the South African migration regulatory apparatus necessarily rests upon a system of documentation, involving passports, forms, stickers, and stamps. The key to navigating this multi-sited system is possessing documentation. Even where a more powerful document (such as a work permit) is unavailable, a visitor's pass is still useful for what little legitimacy or protection it may afford under such a system.

A Mosotho migrant domestic worker therefore prefers to present herself at official border-gates, and to lie to or bribe Home Affairs officials working there. However, in doing so she must incur substantial expenses (in terms of both time and money) to ensure that she returns to the border-gates within her allocated 'days', in order not to over-stay her visitor's permit. The documentation that is procured provides evidence of her legal *presence* in South Africa, and therefore helps her to negotiate the various other sites of 'bordering' and surveillance throughout South Africa (without which, such documentation would arguably be redundant). However her repeated and tense efforts, to confront the borderline and have her movements documented, do not enable full compliance with the legal framework, as she is never able to secure a work permit. This explains the apparent paradox that despite repeated and meticulous documentation of their migration, Basotho domestic workers constantly refer to themselves as 'illegal' migrants.

'We are Illegal': Failing Borders and the Creation of 'Illegal' Migrants

The movement and employment of Basotho domestic workers expose the ambiguities of distinctions such as 'legal' versus 'illegal' migrants, or categories such as 'visitors' versus 'labour migrants'. The legal framework and accompanying state practice in South Africa – the official creation of the Lesotho border – fails to achieve its ostensible purposes. First, the erection of border fences and gates does not exclude Basotho from South African territory. In fact, it is ironically easier to walk across the Caledon – to cross 'illegally' – close to the border-gates, because all the state officials in those areas are busy at the gate itself (versus crossing 50 kilometres along the river, where Defence Force personnel may be lying in waiting). Second, the denial of work permits to Basotho labour migrants who do not fit the Immigration Act's categories does not exclude such migrants from South Africa's labour market. Basotho domestic workers always secure a job in South Africa before they approach the border-gates, and as the following sections explain, workplace surveillance is minimal in the case of domestic service.

However, the 'border' apparatus, as negotiated by Basotho domestic workers, does achieve distinct effects. Most visibly, it ties Basotho migrants to a disciplinary/ surveillance system of South African documentation, such that their movements can be restricted and regulated (for instance by forcing women to return to the frontier each month to have their visitors' permits re-issued). Less obvious but incredibly significant is the function of such documentation by constituting Basotho women not as *legal* but as *illegal* subjects within South Africa. During the in-depth interviews carried out with Basotho domestic workers for this study, interviewees consistently referred to themselves as 'illegal'[21] migrants. This experienced subjectivity was not a result of ignorance of the law. Rather, it was seen as a direct function of documentation: the women claimed that they themselves – rather than their employment – were 'illegal' because they did not possess either work permits or South African identity documents (ID books).

This particular group of migrants challenges the frequent, almost universal, scholarly conflation of 'illegal' with 'undocumented' migration/migrants.[22] As

---

21 The use of the term 'illegal' is not used here to refer to migrants' technical status under law, which inevitably fluctuates according to their movements back and forth, periods of non/employment, etc. (as per the definition of 'illegal foreigner' in the Immigration Act (s1)). This term is used to echo the language and labels used by migrant domestic workers themselves. Out of concern not to contribute to prevailing (criminalizing) discourse regarding 'illegal' migrants, the use of inverted commas is intended to question the category's existence, and emphasize the label itself as a subjective experience of the migrants in this study.

22 This is related to the assumed nature of 'illegal migration' as involving 'illegal' frontier-crossing; 'illegal' migration is often assumed to refer to unauthorized territorial access, rather than behaviour, such as employment, that is not documented or authorized. For instance Walters (2008) discusses the EU's official preoccupation with territorial borders as the site of 'illegal' immigration, despite the prevalence – even dominance – of

a Mosotho woman's 'illegal' subjectivity is reinforced each time she returns to the border, it does not result from a *lack* of engagement with the state or with documentation/surveillance, but from *routine and repeated* interactions with the state's regulatory apparatus (and its repeated apparent failure). The migrants are still 'undocumented' in the sense that they do not possess work permits; hence their *employment* is still unrecorded by the state. Most analyses of 'illegality' do not distinguish between presence and employment – and the distinctive legality or recording/documentation of each. The case of Basotho domestic workers highlights this distinction, as these migrants' movements are repeatedly documented – in particular through frontier-crossings – even while they remain in an 'illegal' status. Repeated documentation and sanctioning by officials, rather than easing their stay and their status, operates as a tactic of extortion, intimidation and therefore disciplining; instead of endorsing women's migration, these officials effectively *reinforce* (or re-produce) migrants' 'illegality'.

For Basotho migrant women, the impossibility of obtaining a work permit or a South African ID book itself shapes their choice to enter domestic service. ID books are more likely to be required for retail or factory work in South Africa, so without one, a less-educated or less-skilled Mosotho woman seeking (urban) job opportunities across the border is effectively restricted to domestic service. Similarly, Basotho women choose their destination town or city in South Africa based on the expense and time taken in constantly returning to the border every 30 days. Therefore, it is not only the explicit legal framework which shapes labour migrants' work/location choices and oscillation across the frontier, but the *failure* of such laws, the practices of state officials (both licit and illicit), and the surveillance mechanisms of the border as a more complex system. Despite (and even through) the failure of the host state effectively to regulate labour migration according to its legal framework, the more complex border apparatus still successfully constitutes migrant workers themselves as 'illegal'. The experience of being an 'illegal' migrant is characterized by a constant fear of detection and deportation, and consequently a fear of state officials. Many aspects of migrants' life in South Africa are shaped by this 'illegal' subjectivity and ongoing sense of deportability. For a Mosotho woman, the most significant consequence of this experienced 'illegal' status is her exploitability in the domestic service labour market.

'internal' processes of 'illegal' migration, such as through migrants' violation of the terms of their residency or remaining in the country after their visas expire. He also contests the 'sharp line' drawn between legal versus 'illegal' status or migration, highlighting instead the nature of the legal/illegal binary as 'a normative distinction embedded in a particular political project', which 'functions as a site of power relations' (2008, 55–6).

'She is Cheating Me': Basotho Women in the Domestic Service Labour Market

Many of the migrants who participated in this study described an experience of being 'cheated' by their employers. According to these domestic workers, their employers (usually other black women, sometimes also from Lesotho) saw their lack of work permits or ID books as an opportunity to take advantage of them by paying them lower wages and/or forcing them to work longer hours under worse working conditions. And many of the participants did indeed receive wages that were shockingly low, even less than half the legal minimum.[23] The workers saw that there was little they could do to change this situation: for them, the only option was to accept the conditions and pay on offer or 'pack my bags and head home to Lesotho'.[24] Migrants explained that this exploitation was a result of their 'illegality', which according to them, also meant that they had 'no rights' in South Africa.

Under South African law, migrant workers do indeed have rights. First, under its impressive Constitutional Bill of Rights,[25] the South African state guarantees a wide range of human rights to 'everyone'. The only provisions expressly reserved for citizens are: s19 (political rights), s20 (the right to citizenship), s21(3–4) (freedom to enter and reside, the right to a passport), s22 (freedom of trade, occupation and profession). Importantly, under s23, 'everyone has the right to fair labour practices.' Labour legislation in South Africa is based upon the Labour Relations Act (LRA),[26] which typically applies to 'every employee'. Nonetheless, as discussed by Bosch (2006), South African courts traditionally held that since migrants working 'illegally' lacked a legal employment contract, they were unable to enforce employment rights under the relevant legislation. However, a recent turnaround in 2008 by the Commission for Conciliation, Mediation and Arbitration[27] saw the institutional mechanism for labour disputes and rights-claiming officially open to migrants working 'illegally' in South Africa.

---

23   It is not suggested here that all Basotho domestic workers in South Africa are paid wages below the legal minimum or suffer ultra-exploitation. However, the *potential* for such exploitation always exists, due to the migrant worker's legal or structural position, as explained in this section. Those migrant domestic workers who receive relatively high pay and/or work under favourable conditions therefore do so at the whim of their employers.

24   Finding alternative employment in South Africa was often not an option, or was seen to be difficult and/or time-consuming. It also involved returning home to Lesotho, most likely empty-handed, to enquire after (or wait for) any other job opportunities.

25   Constitution of the Republic of South Africa, No. 108 of 1996, Chapter 2: Bill of Rights.

26   Labour Relations Act, No. 66 of 1995 (amended in 1996, 1998 and 2002).

27   The Commission for Conciliation, Mediation and Arbitration (CCMA) is the independent dispute resolution body established by the Labour Relations Act. It is the forum for workers seeking to resolve disputes with their (present or former) employers. The CCMA may refer cases to the South African Labour Court.

Immediately following this, the South African Labour Court (itself referring to Bosch's analysis (2006)) confirmed that a foreigner working without a work permit can indeed be considered an 'employee' under the LRA, and is therefore entitled to certain basic work rights, including fair dismissal.[28]

As with the LRA, the Basic Conditions of Employment Act (BCEA)[29] applies to 'all employees and employers' (with specific exceptions, as listed in s1). Chapter 8 of the BCEA allows the Minister of Labour to make Sectoral Determinations establishing basic employment conditions for employees in various sectors (s51). In 2002 Labour Minister Mdladlana pronounced Sectoral Determination 7,[30] which applies to 'the employment of all domestic workers in the Republic of South Africa' (s1(1)).[31] It stipulates wage levels,[32] working hours, overtime, leave, etc. Among its Annexures, the Sectoral Determination also provides templates for the 'Written Particulars of Employment', 'Payslip' (BCEA 4) and 'Certificate of Service' (BCEA 5) to be completed by the employer. The latter two contain spaces where the employee's 13-digit ID number must be written. Similarly, under the Unemployment Insurance Contributions Act,[33] 'every employer and employee' – including domestic workers and their employers[34] – are required to make regular contributions to the Unemployment Insurance Fund (UIF).[35] However, the form by which such contributions can be made for domestic workers in particular (Form UI.19D) requires that the employee's South African ID number be provided.[36]

These identity numbers, and correlating identity 'cards' (more commonly known as IDs or ID books) are only available to, and by law are required for, South African citizens and permanent residents.[37] Basotho domestic workers typically do not hold South African ID books. Many of the women interviewed for this study remarked that if they did have an ID – as many Basotho living and/or

---

28   *Discovery Health Limited v Commission for Conciliation, Mediation and Arbitration and Others* (JR 2877/06) [2008] ZALC 24; [2008] 7 BLLR 633 (LC).

29   Basic Conditions of Employment Act, No. 75 of 1997 (amended in 2002).

30   Sectoral Determination 7: Domestic Worker Sector, South Africa, No. R. 1068, 15 August 2002.

31   In addition, for all domestic workers and their employers covered by the Sectoral Determination, the BCEA applies in respect of any matter not regulated by the Sectoral Determination (s1(4)).

32   The Sectoral Determination was amended on 1 November 2003, such that under s3(1), wage levels were required to increase by at least 8% on 1 November 2003 and 1 November 2004. Minimum wage levels were again officially increased on 1 December of 2005, 2007, and 2008.

33   Unemployment Insurance Contributions Act, No. 4 of 2002.

34   After a one-year delay from the Act's coming into force (s4(2)).

35   The UIF was established under the Unemployment Insurance Act, No. 63 of 2001.

36   Interestingly, this is an explicit contrast with the general form (UI.19), which allows an employee's ID number *or passport number* to be supplied.

37   Identification Act, No. 68 of 1997.

working in South Africa do – they would seek work in other sectors and attempt to exit domestic service. Without IDs, although the national legislation and regulations may technically apply to them and their employment in South Africa, Basotho domestic workers are effectively blocked from exercising their legal rights, by the requirement to supply an ID number on forms. The requirement for such an ID number suggests either the intended exclusion of non-South Africans from the application of the regulations/laws (though this would conflict with their expressed broad application), or simply a failure to acknowledge that non-citizens could be employed in domestic service in the country (as discussed in the following section). Either way, there exists a tension between the progressive, inclusive spirit/letter of South African national labour laws, and the institutional mechanisms for accessing or enforcing those labour rights – to the effective exclusion of foreign domestic workers.

While South Africa's laws regulating domestic service may be ambiguous towards migrant domestic workers, Basotho migrants themselves experience no ambiguity as to their rights in South Africa: they simply state that as 'illegal' foreigners, they have none. They see that without the proper documentation – ID books or work permits – their employment in South Africa is 'illegal', they *themselves* are 'illegal', and consequently they have no access to legal protections or avenues of complaint. Again, this is not due to ignorance about the law. Even interviewees who were aware of the minimum wage and rules about overtime for domestic workers in South Africa, when asked what they could do to get those wages, or improve their working conditions, simply said there was nothing they could do. As they stated, their employers could summarily dismiss them ('send them packing' home to Lesotho), or even call the authorities and have them deported.[38]

Of course, by employing foreigners as domestic workers, employers are also breaking the law: s38 of the Immigration Act specifically targets employers, expressly prohibiting the employment of: (a) an 'illegal foreigner' (as defined in s1), or (b–c) a foreigner whose status does not authorize him or her to be so employed. In this section the state even attempts to shift or outsource its responsibility for surveillance and exclusion of foreigners from the workforce, by assuming the employer's knowledge that the employment is a violation of the Act (s38(3)). In *law*, then, the South African state holds the employer as responsible, if not more responsible, than the foreigner working 'illegally'. But in *practice*,

---

38 The threat of deportation as a disciplinary technique by employers has also been well-documented in other studies of migrants' working lives (for instance Stasiulis and Bakan 2003). This dynamic even operates in circumstances of legal employment, where migrants are 'tied' to their employer: as Mezzadra (2004, 274) describes it: 'bound to the power of personal mood of the private entrepreneur with whom he signs the employment contract, the 'regular' migrant is daily and *explicitly* exposed to the *instability* of his condition, to the threat of falling back to 'clandestinity' and thus becoming 'expellable' at any moment' (emphasis in original).

the burden of 'illegality' is borne primarily by the migrant worker. As an 'illegal' migrant, she has little or no bargaining power *vis-à-vis* her employer. In countries like South Africa, where corruption is widespread, employers are also far more likely to wield the financial and other means to navigate bureaucracies and buy their way out of legal action or penalties.

As a result of these dynamics, Basotho women have gained a reputation in South Africa as workers who are cheap, submissive, and dismissible (not least because they are also deportable). This can be seen as a consequence of the South African state's failure effectively to enforce migration law and/or labour regulations. Returning to the conceptualization of 'border' outlined above, it can be seen that larger bordering processes and mechanisms operate not only at the territorial frontier, and not merely through the exercise of state authority or power. Rather, the Lesotho border is continually and repeatedly created through the South African domestic service labour market and employer–employee relations therein.[39] The Mosotho domestic worker is continually identified and engaged with as foreign: her 'illegal' subjectivity is constituted by the border's technologies (particularly documentation and repeated frontier-crossing), reinforced by the practical and institutional barriers that effectively exclude her from official rights-claiming mechanisms, and reproduced by her exploitation at the hands of an employer who is 'generous' enough to offer her a job 'illegally'. Her constitutional and legislative rights have little influence on her migration experience or her position in the labour market; such laws hold little reality or protection for her. These specific effects are consistently produced by the border apparatus, even as it fails to achieve its ostensible aims – the exclusion of Basotho women from South African territory and from the South African labour market. This complex border dynamic does not rely on extensive state targeting of Basotho domestic workers: in fact, just the opposite.

'I Stay Indoors': Labour Migrants' Invisibility and Imprisonment

As cross-border migrants, Basotho women prefer to secure 'live-in' domestic work, where they stay at the employer's house (either inside the house, or in a small building in the back yard). This saves them time and money that would otherwise be spent renting another home – most likely in the nearby township – and commuting to work each day. It also helps them to avoid the attention of, and potential extortion/deportation by, state officials such as police officers. 'Staying inside' is therefore an important strategy by which migrant domestic workers attempt to make themselves invisible or undetectable to threatening state

---

39 This dynamic even operates when the employers involved are non-citizens themselves. The participants in this study observed that ironically, Basotho employers are likely to pay lower wages and demand longer hours of their workers than, for instance, white South African employers.

authorities. Their employers may also restrict their movements out of a similar concern, for instance by forbidding them from leaving the premises during the week, or by personally driving them to central transport stations (or even to the Lesotho border) for their trip home each month.

This pattern or strategy is therefore unique to domestic service, and is a deeply gendered difference between the experiences of migrant domestic workers – who are almost all women – and migrants working in other sectors. Domestic service presents an opportunity to work clandestinely, in stark contrast to other (highly visible) jobs popular with migrants, such as street trading or car guarding. However, live-in domestic service is associated with a high degree of dependence upon the employer, and living under her demands or control. In addition, social interaction or networking is crucial for domestic workers: it is how they gain moral support, discover labour market conditions in the area (going wage levels, working conditions, etc.), learn strategies of negotiation with employers, and make contacts who could find alternative jobs for them in case of dismissal or resignation. Social isolation thus makes a worker less informed, with less avenues of support, and lowers her bargaining power *vis-à-vis* her employer. For these reasons, migrant domestic workers' 'imprisonment', whether chosen or enforced, has significant implications for their working lives and their position in the labour market.

This also adds to the stress of frontier-crossing, as each monthly return to the Lesotho borderline draws Basotho domestic workers out of 'hiding' and into direct confrontation with state officials. As mentioned above, in these encounters, the fact of their employment is still concealed, for instance through light luggage, the hiding of salaries, lying and bribery. Of course, if they held South African ID books, these migrant women would still make regular visits home to visit family in Lesotho. However, their movements – both within South Africa and through the border-gates to/from Lesotho – would be freed up,[40] and there would be no need to deceive or bribe border guards. Recognizing the risks, costs and hassle of physically returning to the frontier each month, some migrant women simply pay taxi[41] drivers heading to the Lesotho frontier, to take their passports and bribe officials to validate them. While her documentary 'shadow' shows a circular migration pattern, in fact a women may stay concealed at her employers' home. This practice involves corruption, but also the use of official stamps/stickers (as opposed to forgery or a lack of documentation altogether); thereby demonstrating

---

40 They would have the freedom of staying in South Africa for longer periods of time, rather than spending considerable portions of each monthly wage on transport. The global migration literature often casts cross-border mobility as a sign or axis of power or status (for instance see Pickering and Weber 2006), whereas in the case of this migrant group, constant mobility is a sign of unfreedom, as migrants' circulation is dictated by their documentation.

41 Mini-bus taxis (an alternative to commercial buses) are a very popular form of shared transport, both within and between cities/towns throughout South Africa and Lesotho.

the blurred line between legal and 'illegal', state and non-state. By strategically engaging with the border's surveillance regime of documentation, these workers contradict the common equation of migrants' invisibility with a lack of papers or stamps. Although their movements are meticulously and repeatedly documented, these migrant women and their employment remain hidden.

Interestingly, this invisibility is not simply a result of migrants' (or employers') strategies to avoid state power or agents. Rather, it is produced by the larger, more complex border mechanism, involving both state and non-state actors. On a personal level, officials within the South African Department of Home Affairs and Labour Department recognize and admit to the circular, 'illegal' migration of domestic workers from Lesotho. Some even employ such workers in their own homes. But in official terms, there is no acknowledgement of these women's existence or their employment. There are no government statistics on migration from Lesotho into South Africa for the purposes of domestic service employment: because of this deception and bribery at the border, all documented entries/exits from South African territory are recorded as mere visits, such as for shopping or visiting family. Similarly, although there are extensive statistics within South Africa on domestic service, there are no figures for non-citizen domestic workers: as there is no work permit for domestic service, officially speaking there shouldn't *be* any foreigners working in the industry.[42] The non-acknowledgement of Basotho workers is replicated in the failure of institutions such as the South African domestic workers' union,[43] the CCMA,[44] and Legal Aid offices, to record users' nationality – though all admit to low or negligible Basotho women clientele. Similarly, the Lesotho government has barely ceded any official acknowledgement of Basotho women's labour migration across the border into South Africa.

Thus it can be seen that state and non-state, host and sending country agents, and both legal and illegal processes, all seemingly conspire to conceal Basotho women's labour migration. That is, the border apparatus constructs these migrant workers as invisible – both physically (as they hide within and behind employers' homes) and institutionally (through official silence about their employment). The principal means by which this effect is produced are the regime of documentation, and migrants' subjectivity as 'illegal'. On the one hand, this works to migrants'

---

42   A 2005 study of domestic workers in Johannesburg (Peberdy and Dinat 2005) did reveal a sizeable portion of foreigners (and roughly half of these were Basotho), but this was not a government study, and did not prompt any official response from government bodies either in South Africa or Lesotho.

43   The South African Domestic Service and Allied Workers' Union (SADSAWU). Basotho workers' relations with this union are discussed further in Griffin (2009).

44   This is the case at least within the Free State province, which neighbours Lesotho and is a popular destination for Basotho labour migrants. The CCMA did represent the migrant working 'illegally' in the 2008 labour court case cited above, but this did not involve a domestic worker. The shift in the CCMA's attitude to migrant workers is therefore yet to be evidenced in respect of foreign domestic workers.

advantage, as they are able effectively to 'slip through the cracks'; to navigate the system and secure employment in contravention of migration law. However, their circumstances and struggles are also rendered invisible, as they are silenced and their access to legal representation or protection is hindered. Basotho women's fearful experience of being 'illegal' migrants taints their relationship with the host state South Africa, rendering inaccessible – and even irrelevant – the laws that (on paper) empower or protect them.

Looking to the Future: International Instruments

Millions of migrants throughout Southern Africa regularly cross borders: these movements are both crucial for many families' survival, and practically impossible for states to control effectively. In response to this situation, the Southern African Development Community (SADC) approved in 2005 a Draft Protocol on the Facilitation of Movement of Persons.[45] Article 3 of the Draft Protocol lists its specific objectives as the facilitation, in relation to every citizen of a State Party, of:

- entry, for a lawful purpose and without a visa, into the territory of another State Party for a maximum period of ninety days per year for bona fide visit and in accordance with the laws of the State Party concerned;[46]
- permanent and temporary residence in the territory of another State Party; and
- establishment of oneself and working in the territory of another State Party.

As the region's economic powerhouse and largest welfare state, South Africa has long served as an attractive destination for labour migrants from other SADC countries. As these aims sit in tension with South Africa's current immigration law and policy, it may be this country's concerns – and bargaining position – which have hindered the Draft Protocol's progression to binding law.[47] However, South Africa has taken steps to deal with Lesotho on a bilateral basis. In 2007 the governments of South Africa and Lesotho signed a bilateral Agreement on the Facilitation of Cross-Border Movement of Citizens. Its ratification and coming into force have been delayed, for 'political reasons'. If implemented, this Agreement would ease

45 Approved and signed by six member states in August 2005. The protocol is yet to be ratified by the requisite number of states (9) to come into effect.

46 While this first objective corresponds with the most generous of current South African law, even for South Africa to extend this status to *all* SADC countries would constitute a significant shift in its immigration policy.

47 For a general discussion of this protocol and its predecessor, see Williams and Carr 2006.

border-crossing for citizens of Lesotho or South Africa, eliminating the need for visitor's permits.

Both the SADC Draft Protocol and the bilateral Agreement aim to facilitate migrants' cross-border movements, but are silent as to the requirements or avenues for migrants to work legally. That is, neither of these instruments would change the 'illegality' of domestic service for migrant Basotho women. As one South African Home Affairs official explained to me, if implemented, the Lesotho–South Africa Agreement would alleviate the problem of congestion and long queues at the Lesotho border-gates. This would then allow greater allocation of departmental resources to workplace raids and other in-country surveillance measures aimed at locating and deporting migrants working 'illegally' in South Africa. (Thus, even those delayed international political compromises regarding Basotho migrants' access to territory seem to reflect South Africa's concern with border-gate congestion, rather than any difficulties faced by cross-border migrants in their migration experience.) Official failure, with its continual production and policing of 'illegal' migrants in South Africa, would therefore continue and even intensify. As explained in the preceding section, live-in domestic workers are rarely subject to workplace inspections or other forms of state scrutiny while staying in South Africa. As such, the implementation of the Agreement may still advantage migrant domestic workers, particularly compared with migrants working in other sectors. However, it remains to be seen when and how exactly these legal instruments will be implemented.

Conclusions

As this chapter has demonstrated, the relationship between 'illegal' migrant workers and their host state is dynamic and complex. As the regulation of migrants and their lives often defies dichotomies of legal versus illegal, or state versus non-state, these relations are best understood within the context of a larger socio-legal apparatus: the border. As illustrated in this study of Basotho domestic workers in South Africa, this larger border system operates not simply in terms of state agents enforcing laws, but through a much wider range of actors and processes. The state's lack of control, or the non-enforcement of laws – such as the practical inaccessibility of migrants to institutional avenues for exercising their rights, or the endemic payment of bribes in frontier-crossing and documentation checks – could simply be understood as a 'failure' by the host state to regulate labour migration effectively. However, rather than take these processes at face value, we may be prompted to question not only *why* the regulatory system fails, but *how*, and *to what effects*. Of particular concern are the effects of such a regulatory failure on migrant workers themselves.

If we adopt the perspective of migrants and their strategies or experiences,[48] an alternative understanding of migration regulation becomes apparent. In the case of Basotho migrant domestic workers, an in-depth analysis of their movements and working lives reveals several interesting dynamics. Most critically, we see that the 'failure' of the host state South Africa to enforce migration and labour laws, leads to migrants' constitution as 'illegal' subjects in the host territory. This 'illegality' is neither a mere reflection of migrants' technical status under South African law (which is inevitably more complicated and shifting), nor a result of lack of documentation. Rather, these migrant workers and their movements are repeatedly and meticulously documented by state officials; what is more, this routine of documentation serves to *reinforce* migrants' experienced subjectivity as 'illegal'. In this way, granting 30-day visitors' passes to Basotho migrants, rather than preventing them from engaging in waged work in South Africa, becomes a mechanism for their discipline and surveillance. Migrants' own experience of 'illegality' then refers not only to the mere unauthorized nature of their employment, but pervades and defines their lived identity within South Africa.

This production of migrants' 'illegality' also generates other concrete effects in their lives. Most significantly, it constitutes Basotho women as a different class of domestic worker: workers who can be paid less, forced to work longer hours, and dismissed without notice or compensation. Employers therefore play a critical role as agents of the border, by identifying Basotho women as 'other' in the labour market, and reinforcing their subjectivity as 'illegal' migrants. The ultimate result of these dynamics is the concealment of Basotho domestic workers, both physically/spatially and institutionally. As explained above, the 'invisibility' of this migrant group is produced not only by workers themselves but also employers, host and sending state governments, legal institutions, etc. The border apparatus, operating through a range of actors and a variety of both legal and extra-legal processes, therefore constitutes Basotho women as an invisible, exploitable labour force within South African homes.

The applicability of this case study to other border systems is a problematic question. Ultimately, only other ethnographic accounts of state-migrant relations, and the role of law in regulating labour migration, would facilitate comparative analyses, by exposing the commonalities and variations between labour migration regimes in different countries or regions. In that sense, the most widely applicable aspect of this chapter is the conceptual framework outlined above, whereby it is possible to examine a state's (and law's) role in regulating labour migration, within a larger and more complex apparatus: the border. This approach is most

---

48   As indeed we should, if borders and labour migration regimes operate differently for different groups or categories of migrants. Although migration scholars admit the fact of migrants' differential regulation, subjectivity and experiences, there are surprisingly few in-depth studies of migration regulation which focus on a particular migrant cohort, examining how migration law operates *in practice* to shape and discipline particular migrants' lives, movements and work.

likely to unearth a nuanced understanding of migration regulation where controls are seen to 'fail'. This certainly includes many borders on the African continent, where state incapacity is common (for instance in the form of corruption, lack of resources, artificiality of international frontiers, lack of coordination between various 'arms' of the state, etc.). However, migrants everywhere navigate regimes of documentation, and increasing numbers of them are constituted as 'illegal': thus, 'failing' borders and labour migration laws extend to every corner of the globe. As this case study has demonstrated, rather than the closure of analysis, such failure or incapacity in itself may provide a starting point for fascinating paths of inquiry into how migrants' lives are shaped and regulated in practice.

References

Bigo, D. 2004. Criminalisation of 'Migrants': The Side Effect of the Will to Control the Frontiers and the Sovereign Illusion, in *Irregular Migration and Human Rights: Theoretical, European and International Perspectives*, edited by B. Bogusz, R. Cholewinski, A. Cygan and E. Szyszczak. Leiden: Martinus Nijhoff, 61–91.

Bigo, D. 2007. Detention of Foreigners, States of Exception, and the Social Practices of Control of the Banopticon, in *Borderscapes: Hidden Geographies and Politics at Territory's Edge*, edited by P.K. Rajaram and C. Grundy-Warr. Minneapolis and London: University of Minneapolis Press, 3–34.

Bosch, C. 2006. Can Unauthorised Workers be Regarded as Employees for the Purposes of the Labour Relations Act, *Industrial Law Journal*, 27, 1342.

Bureau of Statistics, Kingdom of Lesotho. 2005. *Labour Statistics Report*. Available at: www.bos.gov.ls/New%20Folder/Copy%20of%20Demography/Labour_Statistics_Report_2005.pdf [accessed 26 February 2010].

Bureau of Statistics, Kingdom of Lesotho. 2009. *Statistical Yearbook 2008*. Maseru: Bureau of Statistics.

Coutin, S.B. 2003. *Legalizing Moves: Salvadoran Immigrants' Struggle for U.S. Residency*. Michigan: University of Michigan Press.

Darian-Smith, E. 2004. Ethnographies of Law, in *Blackwell Companion to Law and Society*, edited by A. Sarat. Oxford: Blackwell Publishing, 545–68.

Dauvergne, C. 2004. Sovereignty, Migration and the Rule of Law in Global Times, *Modern Law Review*, 67(4), 588–615.

De Genova, N. 2002. Migrant 'Illegality' and Deportability in Everyday Life, *Annual Review of Anthropology*, 31, 419–47.

De Genova, N. 2004. The Legal Production of Mexican/Migrant 'Illegality', *Latino Studies*, 2(2), 160–85.

Dodson, B. 2001. Discrimination by Default? Gender Concerns in South African Migration Policy, *Africa Today*, 48(3), 74–89.

Ferguson, J. 1990. *The Anti-Politics Machine: "Development", Depoliticization, and Bureaucratic Power in Lesotho.* Cambridge and New York: Cambridge University Press.

Foucault, M. 1977. *Discipline and Punish: The Birth of the Prison (Surveiller et Punir; Naissance de la Prison.* Gallimard, Paris 1975). Translated by A. Sheridan. London: Penguin.

Griffin, L. 2009. 'To be a Slave in South Africa': The Hidden Lives of Basotho Migrant Domestic Workers, *South African Labour Bulletin*, 33(4), 4–6.

Gustafsson, B. and Makonnen, N. 1994. The Importance of Remittances for the Level and Distribution of Well-Being in Lesotho, *Journal of International Development*, 6(4), 373–97.

Johnston, D. 2007. Who Needs Immigrant Farm Workers? A South African Case Study, *Journal of Agrarian Change*, 7(4), 494–525.

Klaaren, J. and Ramji, J. 2001. Inside Illegality: Migration Policing in South Africa after Apartheid, *Africa Today*, 48(3), 36–47.

Kyle, D. and Siracusa, C.A. 2005. Seeing the State like a Migrant: Why so Many Non-criminals Break Immigration Laws, in *Illicit Flows and Criminal Things: States, Borders, and the Other Side of Globalization*, edited by W. van Schendel and A. Itty. Bloomington and Indianapolis: Indiana University Press, 153–76.

Lefko-Everett, K. 2007. *Voices From the Margins: Migrant Women's Experiences in Southern Africa*, Southern Africa Migration Project, Migration Policy Series No. 46. Cape Town: IDASA.

Lyon, D. 2005. The Border is Everywhere: ID Cards, Surveillance and the Other, in *Global Surveillance and Policing: Borders, Security, Identity*, edited by E. Zureik and M.B. Salter. Cullompton: Willan, 66–82.

Marx, G.T. 2005. Some Conceptual Issues in the Study of Borders and Surveillance, in *Global Surveillance and Policing: Borders, Security, Identity*, edited by E. Zureik and M.B. Salter. Cullompton: Willan, 11–35.

Massey, D.S. 1999. International Migration at the Dawn of the Twenty-first Century: The Role of the State, *Population and Development Review*, 25(2), 303–22.

Merton, R.K. 1957. *Social Theory and Social Structure.* Glencoe, Illinois: Free Press.

Mezzadra, S. 2004. The Right to Escape (translated by T. Rajanti), *Ephemera*, 4(3), 267–75.

Mosselson, A. 2009. *'There is no difference between citizens and non-citizens anymore': Understanding the Xenophobic Attacks: Citizenship, the Politics of Belonging and the State of Exception in Post-apartheid South Africa.* Paper presented at SASA (South African Sociological Association) Congress, Making Sense of Borders: Identity, Citizenship and Power in Comparative Perspective, 28 June–2 July 2009, University of the Witwatersrand, Johannesburg.

Murray, C. 1981. *Families Divided: The Impact of Migration Labour in Lesotho.* Cambridge and New York: Cambridge University Press.

Ngonini, Z.A. 2007. Anxious Communities: The Decline of Mine Migration in the Eastern Cape, *Development Southern Africa*, 24(1), 173–85.

Peberdy, S. and Dinat, N. 2005. *Migration and Domestic Workers: Worlds of Work, Health and Mobility in Johannesburg*, Southern Africa Migration Project, Migration Policy Series No. 40. Cape Town: IDASA.

Pickering, S. and Weber, L. 2006. Borders, Mobility and Technologies of Control, in *Borders, Mobility and Technologies of Control*, edited by S. Pickering and L. Weber. Dordrecht: Springer, 1–19.

SAIRR. 2008. *'Illegal' immigrants are a permanent feature of South Africa's population*. South African Institute for Race Relations, 13 May. Available at: www.sairr.org.za/press-office/archive/201cillegal201d-immigrants-are-a-permanent-feature-of-south-africa2019s-population-13th-may-2008.html/ [accessed 26 February 2010].

Segura, D.A. and Zavella, P. (eds) 2007. *Women and Migration in the US–Mexico Borderlands: A Reader*. Durham and London: Duke University Press.

Sharma, A. and Gupta, A. 2006. Introduction: Rethinking Theories of the State in an Age of Globalization, in *The Anthropology of the State: A Reader*, edited by A. Sharma and A. Gupta. Oxford: Blackwell Publishing, 1–41.

Stasiulis, D. and Bakan, A. 2005. *Negotiating Citizenship: Migrant Women in Canada and the Global System*. Toronto: University of Toronto Press.

Statistics South Africa. 2009. *Latest Key Indicators*. Available at: www.statssa.gov.za/keyindicators/keyindicators.asp [accessed 26 February 2010].

Ulicki, T. and Crush, J. 2000. Gender, Farmwork, and Women's Migration from Lesotho to the New South Africa, *Canadian Journal of African Studies*, 34(1), 64–79.

Walters, W. 2008. Anti-Illegal Immigration Policy: The Case of the European Union, in *Governing International Labour Migration: Current Issues, Challenges and Dilemmas*, edited by C. Gabriel and H. Pellerin. London and New York: Routledge.

Weber, L. 2006. The Shifting Frontiers of Migration Control, in *Borders, Mobility and Technologies of Control*, edited by S. Pickering and L. Weber. Dordrecht: Springer, 21–43.

Wight, E. 2004. *Challenging Deportation under Changing Laws: An Ethnographic Perspective on the Deportation of Undocumented Immigrants*. Paper presented at the annual meeting of the American Sociological Association, San Francisco, CA, 14 August 2004. Available at: www.allacademic.com/meta/p_mla_apa_research_citation/1/0/9/9/9/p109999_index.html [accessed 26 February 2010].

Williams, V. and Carr, L. 2006. *The Draft Protocol on the Facilitation of Movement of Persons in SADC: Implications for State Parties*. South African Migration Project, Migration Policy Brief No. 18. Cape Town: IDASA.

Chapter 2

(In)hospitable Border Zones: Situating Bolivian Migrants' Presence at Brazilian Crossroads

Carolina Moulin Aguiar

Summary

This chapter aims to articulate the construction of border zones from the standpoint of multiple, and usually conflictive, sovereign perspectives. I argue that the paradoxical combination of more hospitable normative and diplomatic interventions in border areas and the (often exclusive) daily negotiations over their terms among different social groups is central to an understanding of the complexity of migrants' experiences, particularly in the context of peripheral societies. I illustrate this argument with an analysis of the contemporary construction of the border zone between Brazil and Bolivia (in the twin cities of Corumbá and Puerto Suarez), especially in relation to the regulation (and regularization) of a transborder status for border dwellers. I focus on ethnographic research conducted with migrant groups, NGOs and government officials in the region and how they (re)produce particular notions about the modes of (mobile) presence to which border communities are entitled. In sum, I discuss how certain inter-subjective discursive practices about the regulation of migration help to constitute border zones not only as rites of passage for migrants, but as spaces of life itself.

It seems we live in a world of paradoxes, especially in what concerns the regulation of labour migration. On one hand, special regional agreements are facilitating the movement of migrants (either through the creation of common spaces such as the EU or the recently formalized free residence agreement between countries of Mercosur). On the other, new barriers, walls and border controls are making the movement, especially from those coming from the global peripheries, increasingly difficult. More than that, it has become harder to define where these peripheries are currently located and even more difficult to precisely pinpoint who their inhabitants are. In important respects, this chapter addresses the connection between the construction of such peripheries through zoning practices and their impact on the regulation of labour migration. Zoning strategies have been central to the operation of borders (and bordering activities) in these regions of the world. As such, the concept of zoning might help one to analyse the (dis)connections between statist claims regarding the control of labour migration and the everyday practices involved in the mobility of migrant workers within and beyond the territorially circumscribed spaces of border zones. Aihwa Ong (2006) defines zoning strategies as a mechanism of adaptation by sovereign power – as a response to profound changes in the global structures of capitalist accumulation and circulation – in which states adapt to the new demands of global capital. Consequentially, sovereign authorities devise zones as sites where the regulations, rights, restrictions, administrative processes and services are designed to secure development, prosperity and freedom for those outside of it. Special economic zones tend to tolerate modes of existence, and forms of mobility, that are not otherwise present in the traditional territories of the nation-state. The border in these cases bends to 'flexible notions of citizenship', neither resident, neither migrant, neither citizen, neither alien. It also bends to flexible or graduated notions of sovereignty by allowing governance structures to incorporate the interests and de facto power of important players in the global capitalist order.

> Zoning technologies encode alternative territorialities for experiments in economic freedom and entrepreneurial activity. The logic of the exception fragments human territoriality in the interests of forging specific, variable and contingent connections to global circuits. The resulting pattern of graduated or variegated sovereignty ensures that the state can both face global challenges and secure order and growth. It is also crucial to note that these strategies produced through the logic of the exception are free of the "enlightenment" package of free-market ideology, modern political liberalism and participatory citizen-subjects. While the state retains formal sovereignty, corporations and multilateral agencies frequently exert de facto control over the conditions of living, laboring and migration of populations in special zones (Ong 2006, 19).

Ong provides an interesting approach to how sovereign power rearticulates itself in the face of globalization processes. In her analysis, flexible or graduated notions of citizenship and sovereignty are conveyed in an attempt to trace these transformations and to illustrate alternative mechanisms of responding to a world increasingly marked by fluidity and transversal connections. Zoning technologies carry with them a highly ambiguous connotation. They are embedded in new structures of discrimination and new forms of exploitation, especially from the standpoint of displaced groups. For migrants, special zones present themselves as a permanently impossible gateway to equality and justice, as flexible mechanisms of inclusion place them into a transient zone where they are neither 'proper' migrants, 'potential' citizens or otherwise. These groups and individuals are somewhat tangentially incorporated into a logic of being that never fully realizes itself, and that is constantly subjected to the volatile interests of multiple sovereign authorities. Moreover, zoning practices entail highly selective mechanisms of partial inclusion, opened to a group of marginal, yet privileged, few who have the abilities and 'desired' identities sought by those who control the exercise of graduated sovereignty. Practices of zoning as such do not alter the dynamics of exclusion inherent in the control of labour migration, but they can certainly minimize them. For example, zoning strategies can create mechanisms of inclusion that allow for migrant workers to circumvent some of the restrictions imposed by prioritizing a national, territorially exclusive notion of community membership. One might say that there are elements that present the border zone as a more hospitable site than the one individuals left behind (access to public services, informal jobs, better chances of social mobility and so on). But there are also elements that compose a more precarious condition of living, such as submission to degrading work standards, discrimination on the part of the hosting community, restrictions on mobility rights, difficulties in language and integration etc. Therefore, the balance between abjection and protection is always dependent on the evaluation and effect of these zoning strategies on mobile groups (and on the responses they provide to the problems they face in this new environment).

Zoning strategies demonstrate how flexible mechanisms of management of migrant workers serve to reproduce a peculiar form of sovereignty performance, that articulates simultaneously a logic of control/discipline and of solidarity/ inclusion. The concept of zoning also demands an analysis of how different actors, usually disconnected from state-run institutions, operate as crucial gatekeepers of the borders labour migrants have to cross in order to integrate into host societies.

Reflecting upon this theoretical discussion, the chapter discusses the contemporary agreement on labour migration between Brazil and Bolivia ratified in 2004. This agreement transformed the border into a space of free movement for labour migrants and created a new juridical figure: the transborder dweller or *fronteiriço*. Portrayed by public officials of both countries (and in the media) as a cooperation effort aimed at improving the living conditions of border dwellers, and thus of advancing an understanding of the border as a hospitable zone, this chapter tries to elucidate the multiple aspects of life at the border that make this claim both possible and unattainable. It draws on ethnographic research conducted in Corumbá and Puerto Suarez, twin cities on the border zone, in order to discuss the (im)possibilities of the condition of *fronteiriços*. It also illustrates the difficult conciliation between a hospitable border zone in an inhospitable country, especially in what regards Bolivians presence within urban spaces in Brazil. This is particularly salient in relation to the situation of Bolivians in Brazil largest metropolis, São Paulo. The chapter is organized in three sections. In the first section, I briefly describe some of the tensions crisscrossing Brazil–Bolivia relations and advance a particular understanding of the everyday negotiations of fronteiriços in the border zone. In the second section, I move towards a description of the situation of Bolivian migrants in São Paulo and, in the third, I conclude with some reflections on the consequences of this particular case for contemporary labour migration regulations.

Welcome to the Border Zone

Brazil has borders with ten countries along an area that encompasses 27% of the national territory in 11 provinces. The almost 16,000 kilometres (out of which 3,000 are with Bolivia) encompass 588 municipalities and are inhabited by more than 10 million people. Brazilian legislation establishes a border strip, or *faixa de fronteira*, that envelops 150 kilometres alongside the territorial line. Corumbá, in the Province of Mato Grosso do Sul, occupies 200 kilometres of the border. Alongside the Paraguay River, the city is connected by land to the Bolivian villages of Arroyo Concepcion, Puerto Quijarro and Puerto Suarez. Corumbá is known as the capital of Pantanal, the entry point to a vast tourist region recognized by its biodiversity and unique natural landscapes. During the dry season, the wetlands become a haven for fishermen and tourists, who come to experience the biodiversity of one of the world's largest freshwater wetland systems. But Corumbá is also an important entry point for other mobile groups. The railway and road connections to Bolivia make it one of the routes for entering Brazilian territory for Bolivians and also other Andean communities. The bi-oceanic corridor that crosses the region from Santa Cruz to Corumbá 'articulates the Brazilian South-East to the Peruvian and Chilean harbors in the Pacific' (Souchaud and Baeninger 2007). It has been praised as an important stepping stone in the process of South American integration.

The Bolivian presence in Corumbá has its historical roots in the first efforts of integration, reflected in the construction of the railroads connecting the two territories. Many Bolivian descendents residing in Corumbá were born out of this immigration process. Corumbá can be seen as a hub in a network of overlapping policies and infrastructure projects which have shaped the relationship of the two countries and the patterns of migratory flows. The economic inequalities between the two countries have impacted the socioeconomic dynamics of mobility in the region, with Bolivians crossing the border to work in Corumbá, notably in informal trade and domestic work, and to have access to public services not available to them in their hometowns. For many years, the only way of having access to Brazilian public services was by entering the territory and applying for migratory status as either permanent residents or citizens; both procedures were difficult and costly for many of the impoverished families who arrived at the border. Many of these restrictions stem from a strictly economic and geopolitical emphasis on the diplomatic relationships of the two countries, largely ignoring the human dimension of these processes in the social landscape of the border zone. From the first treaties on the demarcation of the border in the mid-1800s to the 1955 Roboré Accords, the emphasis was mainly given to negotiations on transport infrastructure and supply of energy resources.

Corumbá is located in the border with *Departamento de Santa Cruz*.[1] One of the richest provinces in the country, Santa Cruz holds the bulk of energy resources and has a productive and highly concentrated agribusiness sector. Mining companies, usually supported by foreign corporations, many of them Brazilian, are also an important source of income and jobs in the region. In the past decades, the lowlands of Bolivia have started to receive increasing numbers of indigenous *campesinos* from the Andean region in search of employment and better living conditions. The growing ethnic tensions between the *Qullas* (or *Collas* in the Hispanic appropriation of the term), peoples of indigenous origin from the Bolivian plateaus, and the *cambas*, the Spanish descendent groups from the lowlands (*mestizos*), have started to mark the everyday life of the region. This is in part due to the growing migration of *Qullas* to Santa Cruz, notably alongside the railway and the infrastructure projects built there which have attracted workers. These tensions have also sparked conflict over the terms of land occupation and appropriation. Small and subsistence farmers are faced with growing pressure from

Figure 2.1 View of Corumbá and Pantanal with the railroad on the bottom corner (Author's Personal Archive, 2007)

1 While I was conducting research in the region, in November 2007, Santa Cruz was one of the four provinces which opposed the central government of Evo Morales. In fact, the oppositionist movement in Santa Cruz had a central national role, especially due to economic and social predominance of the Province in the Bolivian landscape.

large commercial farmers to leave their properties, as price speculation escalated and the terms of land ownership became increasingly contested. Changes in the Central Government's policies, notably in an effort to assure more rights to indigenous groups, have led to violent clashes in Santa Cruz. During my stay in the region (November 2007), the border between Brazil and Bolivia was closed for three days by oppositionist protesters, some of whom were defending the total autonomy of Santa Cruz, and even an eventual separation, from the rest of the country.

This border area has recently been the focus of major media coverage and intense debate in both countries. In Bolivia, this is the result of the aforementioned position of Santa Cruz, as both an economic centre and an oppositionist enclave to Evo Morales' government. In Brazil, these clashes have shaken regional diplomatic relations, as the economic interests of major Brazilian corporations, like Petrobras and Vale do Rio Doce, are put in jeopardy and as agreements between governments become less stable. Throughout Corumbá's central avenue, everyone sees the signs of one of the most important, and therefore contentious, projects involving the two countries: the gas pipeline Brazil–Bolivia (GASBOL). Financed in large part by Petrobras, the pipeline is responsible for providing energy to important industrial and residential sectors in other parts of Brazil. Recent efforts on the

Figure 2.2   **Border Brazil–Bolivia on the Bolivian side (Author's Personal Archive, 2007)**

part of the Bolivian Government to nationalize the refineries and the economic exploitation of natural resources have raised doubts about the future of this almost US$ 2 billion project (including construction investment in both the Brazilian and Bolivian sides). As of May 2008, the Bolivian Government had increased taxation of foreign companies exploiting energy in the country from 18% to 82% (in taxes and royalties). Petrobras and its subsidiaries, installed in 1995 in Bolivia, are responsible for almost 20% of Bolivia's gross national product and for 25% of the country's tax revenues. As Brazilian corporations start to amplify their regional presence, they also start to reinforce the image of Brazil not only as a hegemonic regional power, but also as the new face of predatory multinational corporations (Domingues 2008). Recent interventions have, for example, revived a narrative of Brazilian 'imperialism' in the region or have stated, in the words of Rubens Ricupero (2007), former UNCTAD head, that for many of Brazil's neighbours, the 'yankees are us'. Especially from the 1980s onwards, Bolivian history has been marked by clashes between social movements and multinational corporations, perceived as predatory exploiters of Bolivian national resources and sponsors of neoliberal projects. In great part, Morales' election is the result of a discourse that equates the retaking of state control over natural resources, particularly in the mining and energy sectors, with more inclusive policies towards indigenous groups, expropriated and impoverished after decades of cultural, social and economic marginalization.

This brief digression attempts to illustrate the convoluted context in which the treatment given to human mobility, particularly in relation to Bolivians in Brazil, is taking place. As foreign policy clashes start to invade the daily lives of people, they also help to structure perceptions or even accentuate mistrust and suspicions about migrant communities (and within them). In the imaginaries of the border, the perception of Brazilian corporate interests with multinational strategies of exploitation is very salient. During fieldwork, it was common to hear Bolivian migrants stating that Brazilian mining companies were 'invading' Bolivian territory to exploit resources that were later on brought and sold in Brazil without any sort of control or compensation. The crisis over gas and mining practices feeds the perceptions of the Bolivian community in Corumbá that Brazil's interests are not only rapacious, but also highly unjust.

Despite the growing tensions between the two countries, in 2004 Brazilian and Bolivian authorities signed an Agreement on Transborder Movement. Following the zoning delimitations established in the early 1980s, the Agreement established a new status for transborder dwellers. Transborder dwellers or *fronteiriços*, those residing in the 150-kilometre perimeter along the borderline, would be allowed free movement and rights of residence. *Fronteiriços* would also be allowed to work on both sides and would acquire all the rights associated with it, like pension funds' entitlements and workers' rights. Transborder residents and their children would also be entitled to attend public and private educational institutions. The agreement has, in a sense, recognized the right to participate in the everyday life of the city for its residents, regardless of whether they are of Brazilian or Bolivian origin. The condition of *fronteiriço* depends on the issuance of a special document by either the Brazilian Federal Police or the Bolivian National Migration Service. Applicants must submit a valid identity card, along with proof of residence in one of the municipalities. The transborder status is granted for five years, and can be renewed for an equal period. After the renewal, the condition can be granted for an indeterminate period of time. Some limits nevertheless apply. Applicants must not have a criminal record and the transborder status can be cancelled in case of a criminal conviction or the loss of Bolivian or Brazilian citizenship. The status is only valid within the spatially delimited border zone (the 150-kilometre strip) and for those residing in specific towns, namely in the municipalities of Brasileia-Cobija, Caceres-San Matias, Guajaramirim-Guayeramirim and Corumbá-Puerto Suarez. It excludes then some rural areas outside of the municipal limits of these cities, as well as other less populated regions.

The agreement attempts to regularize the intermittent flow of transborder mobility, where residents of Arroyo Concepcion, Puerto Quijarro and Puerto Suarez commute daily to the Brazilian side to sell goods or work, mostly without any access to legal rights, in Corumbá. Given the absence of control on transborder movement (except for those from Corumbá who take the highway to Campo Grande, the Provincial Capital), commuters have always been a constant feature of the social and economic landscape of the region. Most of these families faced significant constraints because their access to rights had to be fixed on the basis of territorial, national attachments. However, their lives were characterized by complicated negotiations between multiple and transient levels of engagement with where they worked, where they resided, where they studied, where their children were born and so on. These multiple attachments were then not easily met by the legal procedures in effect. As such, acquiring the status of *fronteiriço* would help ensure and regularize a condition of *being* characterized by ongoing mobility and a relational and instrumental usage of public and private services offered in the border zone. As one of the migrants in Corumbá stated, the transborder status represents an initial step, 'it is the start for later requiring permanent residency. It is usually given to those who live in the region and work as vendors in the produce fairs [...] it is a means to make them feel safer in their jobs. But they have to pay and present a whole list of documents. Only then, they are free to work' (Interview 2007).

It is interesting to read the transborder agreement from the perspective of zoning practices as both a response to the mobilities engendered by translocal connections but also as a mechanism of enabling flexibility in contexts of growing economic linkages and disruptions. The *fronteiriço* emerges as the paramount mobile subject in the ordering produced by zoning strategies. Despite the necessity of citizenship attachments, *fronteiriços* are no longer fully constrained by the triad citizen–nation–territory as the sole conveyor for rights entitlements. They are no longer just citizens, neither migrants, nor 'undocumented', 'irregular' crossers. They are the subject of this newly founded territory that constitutes the border zone as a site where multiple and overlapping mechanisms of governance are put in place. They are subject and subjected to constraining spatialities, as their movement is restricted to the limits of the border zone demarcation. This demarcation is also restricted to the particular spaces of selected cities and thus involves the implementation of these rights on the part of local structures of authority, like the municipalities, administrators of educational institutions and local employers. They are also subjected to new modes of temporalities, since the *fronteiriço* status is given based on some temporal connections to the border zone (as such they must prove previous residential attachments to the cities) and is granted also on a temporal basis (five years, initially). In a sense, the zoning strategy conveyed in the agreement recognizes a mode of existence that is somehow located in the past; it does not create or produce the transborder movement but rather recognizes its previous presence and engenders new openings for border crossers in these contexts. This is one example of the regimentation of mobile life in transnational settings, through the creation of zones that evinces possibilities for inclusion, for access to equal opportunities and rights even if the documentation and requisites imposed for the recognition of *fronteiriços* might prove burdensome for many. It is interesting to note that in this particular case, the international negotiations that produce this 'trans'national zone of the *fronteiriço* gives rise to, at once, a logic of enclosure but also of insertion into a framework of rights, once reserved to those with exclusive citizenship status. The states that enact the border zone present themselves as actors working for the inclusion of the demands of transborder dwellers.

This is obviously not a simply altruistic act. After all, the condition of *fronteiriço* would permit companies, many of them Brazilian corporations who depend on low-skilled workers, to circulate within these spaces of capitalist expropriation without the constraints of national legislation and restrictions over mobility between their territories. But, first, it is important to note that border control within the region has always been precarious to say the least. The Federal Police (PF) office, responsible for border control on the Brazilian side, had a handful of employees to patrol 200 kilometres. As stated in an interview with one of the PF's agents, their focus was not the border, but the bus station and the highway that connects Corumbá to inner urban centres. Every bus that leaves Corumbá is thoroughly searched for drugs and undocumented passengers. The journey that usually takes five to six hours extends itself to nine to ten hours, resulting from several patrols set along the way (Interview 2007). The situation might change in the near future as construction work is underway at the border post and a new building will host both the PF agents and the Brazilian Revenue Agency. Second, the job market is extremely restricted for locals, Brazilian or Bolivians. Except for low-skilled jobs, the majority of the workers come from other Provinces of Brazil, notably from the South-East region in Brazil, thus feeding the service sector of the city, as hotels are constantly full, even in the low season for tourism. Thirdly, this zoning strategy also aims to prevent transborder dwellers from entering further inside Brazilian territory, especially in the case of Bolivians, as their movement is always regarded as a unidirectional one towards São Paulo (I will return to the case of Bolivians in the metropolis in the next section).

Additionally, it is important to read how the logic of migration control is put in practice within the context of the everyday life of *fronteiriços*. In the same way in which the agreement attempts to incorporate the transborder dweller into the framework of citizenship entitlements within a transnational zone, it fails to tackle the 'informal' mechanisms of exclusion that are pervasive for *fronteiriços*. Therefore, it is possible to identify important gaps between the conceived *fronteiriços* as transborder citizens and the perceived and lived *fronteiriços*. This difference is developed by Dean (2007), borrowing the insight from Lefebvre, in the context of border encounters and in relation to the representation of space. I draw on this distinction here to demonstrate these three moments of encounter, not just in terms of processes of spatialization, or of zoning, but also in relation to how these discrepant representations of *fronteiriços* are intertwined in the processes of inclusion/exclusion to which they are subjected.

The conceived representation is formally articulated in the agreement through the construction of a *de jure* figure named *fronteiriço* with a set of rights and duties, regarded in relation to the spaces they inhabit and to the temporalities of their relationships to residence and mobility. This conceived *fronteiriço* enables in its turn a particular reading of the space of the city; in this case of transborder settings, as a site of hospitality, openness and inclusion for those who dwell in it. It recognizes, in a sense, a mode of 'dwelling-in-motion' (Urry 2008) that has long been an important trait in the landscape of the border. The perceived representation of the *fronteiriços* is reflected in the ways in which local communities, authorities, national officials dispatched to the area, and migrant communities themselves interpret the signs and modes of presence of transborder dwellers. As will become clear in the following paragraphs, constructed and perceived representations have not only symbolic, but highly material impacts on the lived moments of *fronteiriços* and as such help us unveil how diverse zoning, and consequently, (de)bordering practices proliferate and make more complex the ambivalent, complicated and tenuous mode of being of transborder dwellers. It is to these perceived and lived representations of the Bolivian *fronteiriço* community in Corumbá that I turn my attention now.

In interviews with local merchants and those working with Bolivian migrants in this border zone, it seemed clear that the majority of those with *fronteiriço* status were residents of the villages of Arroyo Concepcion and Puerto Quijarro (poor, rural communities within the control of the Municipality of Puerto Suarez), notably *campesinos* who farmed small tracts of land for subsistence and for local trade. Most of them worked in the itinerant fairs, or *feirinhas*, where local residents come to buy local produce and small, ordinary products. The *feirinhas* are mobile and each day of the week they take place in a different neighbourhood, both on the Bolivian and Brazilian sides. In my visits to the itinerant fairs, I could notice that the majority of the street vendors were women, many of them with typical Bolivian clothes indicating their indigenous background. Under the scorching heat, these women told me their routine. They would wake up at 4 am and get the products ready to transport. They usually walked to the border line and from there took the bus to Corumbá. The fairs operate from early morning to mid-afternoon. Around 4 pm, they would start the journey back to their homes and get ready for working the land and taking care of the house and their family members. Many of them worked seven days a week in the fairs, but in recent months Corumbá's Municipal authorities have forbidden the *feirinhas* to open on Sundays. This decision reflects the growing pressure of local businesses to restrict what they perceived as an unfair competition. According to labour legislation, contractors are obliged to grant their employees one day off per week or pay extra hours; a cost many local business owners are unwilling to absorb.

Most of the Bolivians working at the itinerant fairs have the transborder document. Apart from that, all vendors have to be registered in Corumbá's City Hall. The authorization to participate in the fair also involves paying a small fee that is collected daily by a municipal employee. The fee during my visit was one real (approximately 50 cents US$) per day. For many of the *fronteiriços* these fees can amount to 10% of their total monthly income. Another place where Bolivian migrants, *fronteiriços,* permanent residents and some undocumented persons congregate is the *Feira Brasil–Bolivia,* known by the locals as *BrasBol.* Contrary

Figure 2.3   Itinerant fair in Corumbá/MS: One of the zones inhabited by *fronteiriços* (Author's Personal Archive, 2007)

Figure 2.4   *BrasBol* Fair: View from one of the corridors (Author's Personal Archive, 2007)

to the other fairs, this one is permanent and trades in a more diversified set of products, from clothes to kitchen supplies. Many of the products are bought at the *Zona Franca*, a commercial centre with duty free exemptions on imported goods in Puerto Aguirre. M., the president of *BrasBol*, told me that initially the fair occupied an abandoned terrain close to downtown. Bolivians and Brazilians had their tents and the local population was used to buying their products, usually cheaper and aiming at low-income customers. But some store owners started to complain about the fair and accused the vendors from disturbing local commerce and from occupying a space without any sort of regularization. The Municipal authorities then negotiated with members of *BrasBol*. M. described with great anxiety those days as the future of their livelihood was in jeopardy, given the threats to shut down the fair and to prevent them from selling their merchandise. An agreement was reached in which the Municipality granted a site for them where they could operate, even though the new location, M. said, was not as 'good for business' as the previous one (Personal Notes, 2007).

Even though the transborder agreement was supposed to open up the possibilities for access to work and services for *fronteiriços*, we see how other repertoires of authority impact the mobility and inclusion of migrant communities at the local level. *Fronteiriços*, despite the guarantees provided to them through diplomatic accords, face important restrictions to their mobility and to the daily exercise of their rights. Through local policies of containment and control, they end up being forced to occupy informal working spaces in reserved sites, allocated to them by municipal authorities. This explains the 'pasteurized' image of Corumbá in relation to the Bolivian presence, since it is very difficult to notice the Bolivian community that resides and works in town except for these localized concentrated regions distributed in the landscape of the city. The Municipal Policy of control and containment is evidenced in the regulation of the fairs and in the establishment of rules and restrictions about how migrants, both residents, *fronteiriços* and 'undocumented', can inhabit the border zone.

This micro-politics of exclusion has deep consequences for the ways in which migrant communities relate to and perform their own identities. One of these consequences is a certain refusal to show or portray a Bolivian identity and a strong drive towards the assimilation of language and cultural traits of Brazilian life. As D., a Bolivian descendent residing in Corumbá stated, 'the majority of the population here in Corumbá descends from Bolivians. You go to the stores and ask whether they are Bolivian and they promptly reply: "no, of course not … I am just a Bolivian grandson". The grandson is filled with hatred towards the Bolivian identity, he is angry, but this is also because he sees that his ancestors and other descendents have rejected their origins' (Interview 2007). This refusal is also a response to, or the development of a survival strategy within a context of widespread suspicion against Bolivians. Many refer to this sense of discrimination in their ordinary life activities. Some have stated that Bolivians are perceived as 'criminals' and 'drug dealers', as having 'illegal' money and so the local economy treats them in a different way. One of the participants gave a clear example of how this practice takes place:

> Bolivians are very suspicious, because of the drug trafficking. They are afraid of police officers, of having connections or of possibly creating problems. Look, for example, let's talk about our experience: if we, my husband and I, go here downtown to buy a fridge. There is a Brazilian who comes and asks the price and the salesman says 1200. If we come and ask for the same product he will look at us, and say 2500. It has happened. And this is because there is a stereotype of Bolivians, they assume we are all involved in the drug dealing and so we have money to spend. They think we are all loaded with dollars (Interview 2007).

Bolivian migrants also explain this feeling and perception of inferiority as an induced process prompted by Brazil's hegemonic presence. This presence is deepened by the recent crises in the relationship between the two countries and by how locals interpret these events. For Brazilians at the border, the new changes in Bolivia's Federal policies show the unreliable nature of Bolivian culture and thus, in order for them to be included in the community, it is expected that they will somehow choose to not indicate their 'foreignness'. Bolivians feel a huge anxiety about these identity representations. It is hard for them to navigate a transborder condition of living. Reflecting on these ambivalences, C., a Bolivian migrant residing in Corumbá since 1986, stated that:

> Corumbá is a pasteurized border, one can't feel the other here, the language and the currency…our currency was never accepted here. On the other side, they take everything. I think Brazil is a hegemonic country, including in education. In Bolivia, we studied the histories of our neighbours and we were asked about them with equal expectations. Here, we only study Brazilian geography, Brazilian history, Brazilian this and that…people don't know anything about others.[2] This is a more closed country culturally speaking. It is a very hospitable country but it also demands that you absorb its culture. Brazilians are proud of their culture, they never renegade it. When we arrived they told us, you can't speak Spanish or they will arrest you. But if you do not speak your maternal language, you lose your identity; it creates a rancor, a rage, many people feel ashamed of speaking *castellano*. In a sense, I feel that patriotism enforces itself in the uprooting, *what we are, is what we brought from there* (Interview 2007).

With rampant discrimination on the part of the local community to hire Bolivian *fronteiriços,* many of them resort to 'illegal' activities and use their ability to easily cross the border to enter with drugs. C., also a member of the pastoral, works with migrant women detained in Corumbá's penitentiary. She describes in some detail the realities and difficulties faced by migrant detainees in Corumbá.

> One third of the prisoners are foreigners and they all spoke Spanish. The social worker invited me to work with this group. Some of them knew me from before, because I was a high school teacher in Quijarro. The first day they were 50 to 60. They said they were alone, they had no family, they felt left out. The only solution for them is to be sent back. The work we did was of a confessional nature, we created a space for conversation and we also made contact with their families. Mostly, they complained about discrimination inside the prison system, they were used for the worst sort of jobs – cleaning toilets and so on. We talked to the managers and explained to them about the prisoners' rights, we also met with the judge who was very sensitive to the issue and he supported our work and helped implementing changes in the system. They couldn't find work and working is very important because it reduces the amount of time they are supposed to stay incarcerated. We also tried to change the regime [it is possible to request a progression, in which detainees can combine time inside and outside the detention centres] so that they

---

2   The reading of Brazilian education provided here might not be accurate, since border areas do have bilingual schools and since most of the curriculum is established through federal policies. But, nevertheless, her statement reflects how perceptions on issues of identity impact on the general 'world view' of transborder dwellers in relation to their hosting community and to their own origins.

could work outside and sleep in. But we couldn't make it because no one would want to take the responsibility for them [detainees in a progression regime should have a person responsible for them, a type of tutelage]. One thing we did manage to get was to guarantee that prisoners were sent here to be closer to their families [those in other cities of the province]. All of the prisoners were there for drug trafficking. Very few, in earlier times, were arrested for false documents and for being undocumented. Most of them were caught in the bus, the line that connects the border with São Paulo. [This bus is known for being systematically checked by the police: no one passes unnoticed; there are anonymous calls telling them that some are carrying drugs. C. says that they were checked in their last trip for an hour and a half. But C.'s husband also tells me that most of these calls are just about the "small fish" – to divert police attention from the large shipments that are sent to the Brazilian territory through the roads]. The jail comports 120 women but now holds 250 people. They are all crowded. Last year we had 12 children born in the jail and eight were Bolivians. Based on their children, we managed, with the partnership of the local judge, to expedite their expulsion to Bolivia. What happens is that they are sent back to the other side of the border, handed back with their documents to the Bolivian authorities and they are prohibited from entering Brazil for five years. But some do come back before that (Interview 2007).

After these convictions, legislation prevents individuals from applying for *fronteiriço* status. These zoning practices then create a vicious circle, since the logics of containment and the more 'informal' restrictions presented by local authorities and by the overall discrimination against them ends up reducing the choices for some (that then resort to illegal activities and who are later caught and end up being formally prevented from having access to the rights to which they were initially entitled). This situation feeds into the perceived portrayal of *fronteiriços*, and Bolivian migrants in general, as carriers of drugs and therefore as dangerous trespassers. The perceived representation of Bolivian *fronteiriços* becomes, in a sense, a self-fulfilling prophecy as it imposes important restrictions in the lived spaces of these communities.

To complicate matters even further, the increasing arrival at the border of indigenous Bolivian groups, in what was otherwise a mainly Cruceña community, has prompted the overall ethnic tensions present in the Bolivian context to also affect the relationship between Bolivian migrants in Corumbá. The experiences of violence and radicalism, which have led to growing social divisions and political instability in Bolivia, start to be replicated in the microcosms of the *fronteiriço* community. Therefore, it is possible to witness divisions and tensions which have dislodged any idea of a homogeneous and unified Bolivian community in the city. C., the member of Pastoral, and a descendent of Cruceños herself, talks about her perceptions of the impasses and difficulties in the relationship between Collas and Cambas in the transborder context. She recalls in our interview a moment in which these ethnic cleavages abruptly interfered in the lived reality of migrants. In a sense, she speaks about these events from the standpoint of her own *fronteiriço* condition:

> I've travelled a lot with the Pastoral. And I see, for example, the indigenous losing their quechua, their maternal language. This is what our president is trying to change, 200 years of submission. Earlier, you would never hear a word in quechua or aymara. I always thought that if you lost your original language, you lose yourself, you lose everything. When they come here, they are adamant about speaking Portuguese. I find this process of acquiring a new nationality, with the implication of forgetting one's origin, very problematic. The consequences are sad. In my last visit to São Paulo, I was amazed. The way he speaks [Evo Morales] is very nice, because he is giving value to the indigenous that have been always submissive. But we're talking about 500 years, and so they come with everything, in anger, resentful. Instead of looking for those who placed them at those conditions in the first place (Interview 2007).

It is interesting to note how the empowered recovery of indigenous language and culture is perceived as both necessary, as an exercise of remembering one's origins, and as deleterious, because it is associated with a vengeful attitude in relation to colonial impositions and social/cultural marginality. The ambivalent position stated by C. exemplifies the difficult negotiations between Cambas and Collas in the search to maintain one's identity, of becoming oneself again, while, at the same time, facing important constraints from the hosting community. This position is in part due to the impossibility of reconciling this becoming, this identity transformation, with a condition of *being* always read in terms of 'appropriate' behaviour. This impossibility involves the inability to retain a certain dialogue capacity with other groups for whom being indigenous is associated with a rebellious, unlawful, improper attitude. This impossibility of translation, their inability to read and accept indigenous identities in terms other than the ones established through a colonial mentality, is then transposed into a threat to 'Cambas' social and economic position. The ascendance of indigenous groups is perceived as a menace to Bolivia's own development project, since the rise of Collas means, necessarily, a decline of Santa Cruz as the epicentre of the country's economy. Another interviewee stressed this sense of threat in relation to Cruceños' position in the national projects:

> Evo Morales said that they [the indigenous] are the land owners... They are snobbish now. We, white like this, do not have rights to anything anymore. This is a mechanism of deterring development; they want us to fight amongst each other. This resentment now is turning against the region that is the richest, which is Santa Cruz. He says that Cruceños are an oligarchy, and he is somewhat right but these are the groups that produce something (Interview 2007).

The point here is not to discuss the longstanding grievances and problems between ethnic groups in Bolivia that resulted from years of colonial impositions on indigenous peoples and a highly unequal developmental strategy, influenced by oligarchic interests and neoliberal frameworks. Rather, I want only to point out how these perceptions and tensions are inserted in the context of transborder relations and how they impact on the strategies of inclusion and mobilization, making it difficult to speak about Bolivian migration as a unidirectional and cohesive whole. These tensions help unveil some aspects of the dynamics of Bolivian migrant groups that are reflected, for example, in the lack of dialogue between Collas and Cambas in the fair zones, the separations and difficulties of assistant workers to engage in dialogue and foster community organization and participation. Moreover, we see how these important divisions and inequalities within Bolivian society allow for transnational modes of exploitation in which Bolivian migrants themselves are the primary agents responsible for the construction of zones of intolerance within the larger framework of bordering practices. In the following section, I illustrate this trend through an analysis of the Bolivian presence in São Paulo and the neo-slavery conditions to which they are subjected in the megalopolis.

Between the *Eldorado* and the Camp: Bolivians in São Paulo's Border Zones

Bolivians constitute the largest group of migrants in São Paulo, a city with an estimated population of 18 million people. Pastoral do Migrante in São Paulo estimates that, in the city alone, 200,000 Bolivians live undocumented. As Souchaud and Baeninger remark, 'even if these numbers are overestimated, this means that the number of undocumented Bolivians would be seven to ten times larger than the total number of Bolivians accounted for in the 2000 census; this number represents 22%–29% of the total of foreigners residing in Brazil and 1.81%–2.42% of the total population of Bolivia in 2001' (2007, 5). São Paulo's Province alone is responsible for 33% of the Brazilian GNP and attracts workers from other provinces and also immigrants who see the metropolis as a promise land for attaining a better life. 'If for many Brazilians, Brazil is no longer the land of opportunities, for Bolivians it still is. This is the reason why thousands of them leave the country annually, to escape poverty and a subsistence economy and, consequentially, to catch a glimpse of any possibility of social mobility' (Silva 2006, 158).

The image of Brazil as an *Eldorado* of economic opportunities (Silva 2006), common to the fantasies of many immigrants who arrive in the country, is abruptly disrupted by the proliferation of bordering practices that, at once, make it extremely difficult for them to regularize their permanence in these new territories of estrangement and that reproduce zones of confinement and of social/cultural abjection. This is the situation of many Bolivians working in sweatshops in

São Paulo, some of them run and owned by Bolivian migrants themselves. The pervasive exploitative conditions to which these migrants have been subjected in the sewing shops have been described as a form of neo-slavery and servitude. Accusations of labour exploitation and human rights violations against Bolivian migrants in the sweatshops have led to the establishment of a Parliamentary Inquiry Commission (CPI) with the mandate to investigate and punish such practices in the city. The final report of the CPI describes how the Eldorado fantasy transforms itself into a nightmare for Bolivians, whose journey usually starts in Santa Cruz de La Sierra, where they are recruited and transported by *aliciadores*, with promises that are never fulfilled. The recruiting process is the initial step for imposing slave-like labour conditions on migrants, as they are forced to work to pay their initial debts.

> The recruitment of Bolivians through radio and newspapers hides a trap that is the starting point for slave-like labour conditions in São Paulo. Many of the Bolivians who reply to the job offers do not have enough resources to pay for the journey to Brazil; they receive a cash advance to be paid through their work once they arrive in the sweatshops. As the costs of the trip are overcharged and the payment they receive is insignificant, many Bolivians end up working for months without receiving payment so that they can liquidate their initial debts. The specific case of Bolivians has an additional difficulty. Throughout the years, some migrants manage to flourish in their businesses and are able to open their own sewing factories, where they start to hire the next generation of Bolivians. A vicious circle is installed: the employers reproduce with the newcomers the same conditions to which they were subjected when they first arrived. Because of family ties or even because of their compatriot situation, the newcomers feel uneasy to protest against their employers. Moreover, they feel grateful for those who offered them jobs and housing and believe that they own them, not only money but also fidelity (CPI 2006, 24; Author's translation).

The working conditions become even more restraining for Bolivians, who once absorbed into the labour circuit of the sweatshops, find themselves subjected to degrading and inhumane treatment. These restrictions range from the retention of documents and threats based on their lack of 'proper' documentation to unhealthy housing and food, an inability to relate to the Brazilian community and a series of restrictions to regularization, as rights of residence and work are circumscribed to those who have children born in national territory or who have married a Brazilian spouse. Lack of information is also omnipresent as many Bolivian migrants register their children (even the ones born in Brazil), under the name of relatives who are documented in the country, for fear that they will be deported if they resort to local authorities (Silva 2006, 162). This situation is amply described in the CPI report:

Once employed, there are numerous ways of restricting their liberty. In many cases, their documents are retained by their employers, supposedly for security reasons. Because they find themselves in situations of irregularity, with an inadequate visa (tourist), expired or even without any visa, Bolivians are afraid to go to the streets and get arrested – a risk that is stressed and exaggerated by the employers, who sometimes threaten to hand them over to the police in case the migrants leave their jobs. All in all, as they do not learn how to speak Portuguese and do not have time or opportunity to leave their working place, many are afraid of getting lost in the city and prefer not to take the risk. The housing offered to the seamstresses is the factory floor; after working the whole day they place their mattresses underneath the sewing machines, where sometimes children are left asleep the whole day. They also have their meals there. The buildings are precarious, with inadequate electric connections, combustible material near the wires and the constant danger of accidents – without mentioning the fact that they are all exhausted after long working hours […] Since many of the sweatshops work without authorization or have several irregularities, they keep the windows closed – sometimes even walled with woods or bricks. This heightens the feelings of discomfort and, without proper ventilation, the possibility of diseases being transmitted, like tuberculosis which has a high incidence among Bolivians, increases […] To disguise the noise of the machinery, some employers turn on loud Bolivian music, which also fulfills another purpose: to prevent seamstresses to talk with one another (fearing that communication might lead to organization and to some sort of rebellion or uprising) and to create a forced atmosphere of familiarity; by transposing an element of their native culture to this new address. For all these reasons, the neighbours of the sweatshops where Bolivians live and work say that they resemble *refugees*; they quickly enter their homes, they keep doors and windows shut and they do not talk to Brazilians (CPI 2006, 25–26; Author's translation).

The sewing shops operate as 'informal' labour camps, as 'reservation zones where the rights of subjects can be suspended as a first step in stripping away their status as political subjects in order to render them as abjects' (Isin and Rygiel 2006, 197). They spatially confine Bolivian migrants and deprive them not only from having rights, but also from the ability to claim any rights. Several mechanisms are put in place to ensure that migrant workers will follow the logics of these labour camps; mechanisms that resemble Foucault's *panopticon*. The *panopticon* is a structure of power that operates through discipline. In the case of the sweatshops, discipline comes with the imposition of long working hours and pressure to produce as many pieces as possible since wages vary accordingly. It also involves restrictions on mobility and liberties, through the retention of documents, the confinement of their lives to their working space, the inability to communicate with the outside world and with each other. These disciplinary mechanisms prolong themselves in time since indebtedness and lack of documents perpetuate a condition of absolute dependency for migrant workers. But disciplinary mechanisms are only effective, as Foucault (2007, 66) aptly remarks, because they are internalized and interpreted as being a necessary and forceful part of the lives of those subjected to the *panopticon* structure. In these 'informal' labour camps, internalization of disciplinary mechanisms takes place, for example, through the construction of fear (when employers exaggerate the penalties to which workers might be subjected because of their undocumented condition and the likelihood of a potential deportation), the production of hope (that one day they might become the employers and thus move up on the social ladder), the creation of a 'familiar atmosphere' (where workers might feel closer to a reality they already know), the enactment of bondages (of fidelity and gratitude towards those who have 'hosted' them), and the implementation of an environment in which such restrictions are normalized and considered to be ordinary in the daily routine of most Bolivians in the city.

It is precisely through this combination of disciplinary and normalizing mechanisms, of containment and abjection, that the sweatshops can be compared to the camp. The perception of neighbours, described in the report, that Bolivians working in the sweatshops *resemble refugees* reflects the process of political abjection and social ostracism to which they are subjected. Moreover, it reflects a conflation of the normalized image of the migrant as a worker and that of the speechless, victimized refugee. The immigrant is converted into this moving 'inexistence', whose presence is confined to closed buildings where their body is appropriated as a piece in a long production chain that involves not only sewing shop owners but also large retail shops. In fact, the Commission found out that most of the clothes produced in the sweatshops were sold to large retail corporations, including multinational stores like the Dutch C&A.

The camp mentality, associated with the working situation of many Bolivians, is also accompanied by other mechanisms of containment and practices of zoning. The delimitation of spaces within the urban landscape where the Bolivian presence is tolerated responds to the difficult negotiations between the lived and perceived dimensions of migrants' modes of existence. One example is given by the establishment of Kantuta Square, currently the meeting point of Bolivians in the city. As Silva describes,

> The growing presence of young migrants, most of them undocumented, has
> generated an increase in the offer of entertainment sites for Bolivians in the
> neighbourhood of Pari. The problem acquired new dimensions due to increasing
> violence, resulting from excessive consumption of alcohol, leading the locals
> to organize a petition to obstruct the use of the neighbourhood central square
> by the migrants. According to an old resident, the square was known as "square
> of the roses", and had suddenly been transformed by the migrants into a
> place of disorder, drug dealing, and immorality (Silva 2003, 231–2; Author's
> translation).

Figure 2.5   **Bolivian women looking through pictures of cultural and religious events in search of acquaintances – Kantuta Square (Author's Personal Archive, October 2007)**

The solution to the impasse was provided by São Paulo's City Hall, which granted Bolivians a different venue for their Sunday gathering in Canindé, a place known as Kantuta Square. It is important to note that, even within the constraints provided by an almost forceful reterritorialization of their presence in the megalopolis, these border zones also provide for an opportunity to contest the traditional portrayal of Bolivians as either exploited migrant workers or as unlawful, disturbing individuals. The dynamics of the Sunday meetings at Kantuta give the migrant community an opportunity to articulate and organize their presence. Bolivians count with several cultural associations and important festivities, which range from sport tournaments to religious celebrations. In Kantuta, they have managed to construct a space of tolerance, of sharing and exchange. They have also managed to articulate a forum for Bolivian migrants to get to know each other, interact with other groups and even with Brazilians, who are now starting to discover Kantuta. Therefore, one possible mechanism found by the Bolivian migrant community to respond to the proliferation of border zones and spaces of abjection in the urban landscape was precisely to reinforce and promote their cultural presence, to try to bridge regional and ethnic divisions among the group and attempt to change the perceived image of Bolivians in the city.

> There is growing consensus among Bolivian Associations in the city [...] that it is time for the group to surpass regionalisms and differences of a social, cultural, and ethnic order, in search of a possible integration. An example of this trend is the proposal to create FURBRA [Central Federation of Bolivian Residents in Brazil]. Another concern is with changing the generalized negative image that the large majority of Brazilians have about Bolivia and Bolivians [...] The Bolivian Consulate took some steps, like relocating their headquarters from downtown to an upscale neighbourhood (Jardins), airing tourism campaigns of Bolivia in a local TV channel and hosting an adjunct Consul to deal with the problems of disfavoured compatriots (Silva 2003, 30–31; Author's translation).

Among the several proposals put forward by the CPI the establishment of specific public policies towards migrants, notably focusing on health assistance, access to education for migrants' children and changes in federal and municipal legislation to guarantee work rights even for those with an irregular status in the country. The CPI has also attempted to increase the control over sweatshops and suggested the creation of a reception centre that could host workers dislodged by these operations. The results of these policies are, at most, scarce. There is evidence that the sweatshops are now relocating to the interior, therefore outside the jurisdiction of the Municipality of São Paulo, and it is still too soon to tell whether the legislative changes will be approved and how they will impact on the ability of the Bolivian community to find more hospitable conditions. Nevertheless, the battle over the border, as the Bolivian case illustrates, depends not only on transforming the juridical framework on migration, but mostly on changing the *perceived* and *lived* modes of existence of migrants, informed, first, by the fact that borders are concomitantly idealized and internalized and, second, by the 'tendency of borders, political, cultural, and socioeconomic to coincide' (Balibar 2002, 84).

Zones, Camps and the Border as a Site of (In)hospitality

I have attempted to show how zoning and bordering practices come hand in hand in terms of defining the spatial and temporal locations of mobile subjects. Zoning practices, whether those which create new territories of inclusion, as is the case of *fronteiriços*, or those which, in more subtle but no less powerful ways, work to contain and confine the 'others' presence in the landscape of the city, the border strip, the working space, grant flexibility to borders' strategies and are thus central to defining what is involved in statist claims to regulate labour migration. Borders are therefore composed of a myriad of representations, of moments of presence and also of absences, formed through a complex combination of legal, material, cultural, social and economic frameworks that stem from states, international and transnational agreements, local arrangements, municipal policies and also from public assumptions and migrants' responses.

The situation of Bolivians in Brazil attests to the fact that any transversal experience is accompanied by transitions between different modes of existence. There are moments in which their migrant worker status prevails, moments of being like a refugee, moments of abjection and moments of transnational citizenship performances. The movement of Bolivians across these multiple, and more often than not divergent, sites of inclusion/exclusion shows how border zones can, at once, be territories of hospitality, but also abruptly convert themselves into internment camps. The gap between the Eldorado and such spaces of abjection, symbolically so distant, is strikingly reduced in the terrain of the square, the fair, and the duty free with dire material consequences for migrant groups. An analysis of practices of zoning allows for an incorporation of these 'informal', capillary structures of power as central features to understanding how this moving 'inter' condition is enacted through the border encounter. And these encounters, especially in the context of periphery countries, happen routinely no longer at the border.

As Bonnie Honig (2001, 54) aptly highlights, the foreigner is always this 'undecidable' figure, this polysemic subject, both friend and enemy, both refugee and migrant, both citizen and alien and sometimes none of the above. These moments of presence depend on how one conceives, perceives and lives through these border zones. And the struggles over these moments, the fact that sometimes they diverge or converge, that they tend to be diachronic rather than synchronic are what constitutes border politics. The battle over the border (Rodriguez 1996), and thus over how difference is constructed and dealt with, takes place sometimes at the territorial line, but more often than not in the bus, in the fair, in the working space, in the public square. And these sites have conventionally been disregarded by International Relations as not having any significant relevance to its 'analytical economy'. As Cynthia Enloe puts it, 'there is a serious flaw in this analytical economy [...] it presumes that margins, silences and bottom rungs are so naturally marginal, silent, and far from power that exactly how they are *kept* there could not possibly be of any interest to the reasoning, reasonable explainer' (2004, 23). In a sense, and following Rosello's analysis of the enactment of forms of postcolonial hospitality, these zones become a 'place of forgiveness and of punishment at the same time. Or, put another way, a form of forgiveness that implies exile is what constitutes punishment' (2001, 156). In the case of Bolivians in border zones, both as *fronteiriços* and as urban dwellers, their forgiveness (enacted in a conceived hospitality through international juridical agreements and regularization campaigns) is also combined with forgetting, on the part of their hosts, of the important economic interests and of the impact of Brazil's hegemonic regional presence in modeling the flow of migration, but also in condemning them to a similar marginal social positions, simply replicating even in more constraining ways a reality that led to their plight in the first place. It is this combination of forgiving and forgetting that places Bolivians in a double bind, in which they are forced to choose between freedom (of mobility, of work, of identity performance) or protection (of rights to residence, to education, to health assistance, to participate in the community) (Rosello 2001, 164). And the impossibility of choosing between two fundamental values is what constitutes, in important respects, the essence of the border politics evinced by these groups. As such, the gap between legal improvement and *de facto* integration remains a challenge for Bolivian migrants in these new peripheral zones of the Global South.

Bibliography

Albert, M., Jacobson, D. and Lapid, Y. 2001. *Identities, Borders, Orders: Rethinking International Relations Theory*. Minneapolis, MN: University of Minnesota Press.

Bosniak, L. 2006. *The Citizen and the Alien: Dilemmas of Contemporary Membership*. Princeton, NJ: Princeton University Press.

Comissão Parlamentar de Inquerito (CPI). 2005. Legislative Assembly of the State of São Paulo, *Final Report on Slave Working Conditions in São Paulo*. Available at: http://www.soninha.com.br/v2/mand_cpiescravo.php [accessed 25 November 2008].

Dean, K. 2007. The Sites of the Sino–Burmese and Thai–Burmese Boundaries: Transpositions Between the Conceptual and Life Worlds, in *Borderscapes: Hidden Geographies and Politics at Territory's Edge*, edited by P.K. Rajaram and C. Grundy-Warr. Minneapolis: University of Minnesota Press, 183–200.

Domingues, J.M. 2008. A Bolivia as vesperas do futuro [Bolivia at the edge of the future], *Analise de Conjuntura*, no. 9, 2–14. Available at: http://observatorio. iuperj.br/pdfs/ 51_analises_AC_n_09_set_2008.pdf [accessed 30 January 2009].

Doty, R. 2006. Fronteras Compasivas and the Ethics of Unconditional Hospitality, *Millennium*, 35(1), 53–74.

Enloe, C.H. 2004. *The Curious Feminist: Searching for Women in a New Age of Empire*. Berkeley: University of California Press.

Goes Filho, S. 2001. *Navegantes, Bandeirantes, Diplomatas: Um ensaio sobre a formação das fronteiras do Brasil* [*Sailors, Bandeirantes and Diplomats: An essay on the formation of Brazilian borders*]. São Paulo: Martins Fontes.

Hansen, T.B. and Stepputat, F. 2005. *Sovereign Bodies: Citizens, Migrants, and States in the Postcolonial World*. Princeton: Princeton University Press.

Honig, B. 2001. *Democracy and the Foreigner*. Princeton: Princeton University Press.

Hozic, A. 2002. Zoning, or, How to Govern (Cultural) Violence, *Cultural Values*, 6(1–2), 183–95.

International Organization for Migration (IOM). 2007. *Executive Report for the description and analysis of migration and human trafficking in the border area between Brazil and Colombia*. Available at: http://www.oim.org.co/modulos/contenido/default.asp?idmodulo=7&idlibro=205 [accessed 6 May 2008].

Isin, E. and Rygiel, K. 2007. Abject Spaces: Zones, Frontiers, Camps, in *The Logics of Biopower and the War on Terror*, edited by E. Dauphinee and C. Masters. New York, Hampshire: Palgrave, 181–204.

Lefebvre, H. 1974, 1999. *The Production of Space*. Oxford and Cambridge: Blackwell.

Machado, L. 2000. Limites e Fronteiras: da alta diplomacia aos circuitos da ilegalidade [Limits and Borders: from high diplomacy to illegal circuits], *Territorio*, 9, 9–29.

Molloy, P. 2002. Moral Spaces and Moral Panics: High Schools, War Zones and Other Dangerous Places, *Culture Machine*, v. 4. Available at: http://www.culturemachine.net/index.php/cm/article/view/274/259 [accessed 25 August 2008].

Ong, A. *Neoliberalism as Exception: Mutations in Citizenship and Sovereignty*. Durham: Duke University Press, 2006.

Rajaram, P.K. and Grundy-Warr, C. 2007. *Borderscapes: Hidden Geographies and Politics at Territory's Edge*. Minneapolis: University of Minnesota Press.

Ricupero, R. 2007. Os ianques somos nós [The Yankees are us]. *Folha de São Paulo*, 16 September. Available at: http://www1.folha.uol.com.br/fsp/dinheiro/fi1609200704.htm [accessed 22 October 2007].

Rodriguez, N. 1996. The Battle for the Border: Notes on Autonomous Migration, Transnational Communities, and the State, *Social Justice*, 23(3), 21.

Rosello, M. 2001. *Postcolonial Hospitality: The Immigrant as Guest*. Stanford, CA: Stanford University Press.

Schendel, W. and Abraham, I. (eds) 2005. *Illicit Flows and Criminal Things: States, Borders, and the Other Side of Globalization*. Bloomington: Indiana University Press.

Silva, S. 2003. *Virgem/Mãe/Terra: Festas e tradições bolivianas na metrópole* [*Virgin/ Mother/ Earth: Bolivian celebrations and traditions in the metropolis*]. São Paulo: Hucitec/FAPESP.

Silva, S. 2006. Bolivianos em São Paulo: entre o sonho e a realidade [Bolivians in Sao Paulo: Between dream and reality], *Estudos Avançados*, 57, 57–170.

Solimano, A. 2003. Globalization and International Migration: The Latin American Experience, *CEPAL Review*, United Nations, CEPAL–ECLAC, 80, 53–69.

Souchaud, S. and Baeninger, R. 2007. *Vínculos entre a Migração Internacional e a Migração Interna: o caso dos bolivianos no Brasil* [*Linkages between International and Internal Migration: the case of Bolivians in Brazil*]. Paper presented at CEPAL's 'International Migration and Development in Brazil' panel, Brasilia, Brazil, 30 April 2007. Available at: http://www.cepal.org/ celade/noticias/paginas/4/28454/RBaeninger.pdf [accessed 25 October 2008].

Souchaud, S. and Baeninger, R. 2008. Collas and cambas from the other side of the border: factors of the unusual distribution of Bolivian immigration in Corumbá, State of Mato Grosso do Sul, Brazil, *Revista Brasileira de Estudos Populacionais*, 25(2), 271–86.

Urry, J. 2008. *Mobilities*. Cambridge: Polity Press.

Chapter 3

Labour Migration Regulation in Malaysia: A Policy of High Numbers and Low Rights

Blanca Garcés-Mascareñas

Summary

Several authors have argued that there is a relationship between the number of migrants employed in low-skilled jobs and the rights accorded to them. For instance, Martin and Ruhs (2006) have signalled that low-skilled migration in high-income countries represents an inevitable trade-off between numbers and rights. Their argument is that the more rights low-skilled migrants have, the less advantageous (or desirable) they are. Similarly, Arango (2003) distinguishes between democratic and non-democratic or autocratic societies. While the former would recognize moral and political obligations *vis-à-vis* the immigrants while attempting to keep the numbers being admitted as low as possible, the latter would tend to have no problems letting large numbers of people in but only on condition that they are temporary labourers with limited rights. The case of Malaysia is a perfect illustration of the latter: since the early 1990s the Malaysian state did not restrict the entry of migrant workers but placed limits on time of residence, position in the labour market and social and labour rights. This chapter considers how the Malaysian state has tried to control and regulate migration flows and how this policy worked in practice.

1: Introduction

After the guestworker experiences in Europe and the United States during the 1950s and 1960s, there was general consensus that guestworker programmes had failed 'wherever and whenever they had been tried' (Martin 2000). In particular, the conclusion was that they were inherently flawed because, as the saying goes, there is nothing more permanent than temporary foreign workers. One of the main reasons given by way of explaining the propensity of temporary workers to settle was that foreigners in liberal democracies are entitled to rights under the aegis of liberal constitutions (Hollifield 1992). In a similar vein, Freeman (1995) concluded that immigration politics in liberal democracies are 'expansionist and inclusive' because the benefits related with immigration are concentrated whereas the costs tend to be diffuse.

More recently, along similar lines, Martin and Ruhs (2006) have argued that there is a trade-off, which is to say an inverse relationship, between the number of migrants employed in low-skilled jobs and the rights accorded them: the more immigrants, the fewer the rights. Taking their argument a little further, it would seem as if, in a context of foreign labour demands, low-skilled migrants are 'desirable' as long as their presence is restricted. If liberal states are self-constrained by rights and therefore cannot limit migrants' membership, this would imply that these states are *de facto* compelled to a policy of low numbers and high rights. As posed similarly by Joppke (2005: 47), 'tight numerical restrictions may well have been the price for internally including the guestworker-turned-immigrants'. With the same logic, countries with few rights' constraints would be more inclined to admit important labour migration flows as they seem to have more means to exclude migrants from within.

In fact, this same argument is implicit in the typology of different models of immigration suggested by Arango (2003: 3). Leaving aside what we might call the traditional countries of immigration (United States, Canada, Australia and New Zealand), Arango distinguishes between democratic and non-democratic or autocratic societies. While the former would recognize moral and political obligations *vis-à-vis* the immigrants while attempting to keep the numbers being admitted as low as possible, the latter would tend to have no problems letting large numbers of people in but only on condition that they are temporary labourers with limited rights. In brief, to recall the words of Martin and Ruhs, liberal democracies would restrict numbers while non-democratic or autocratic countries would restrict rights.

The case of Malaysia is a perfect illustration of the latter (see Garcés-Mascareñas and Penninx 2008). A quick review of entry policies over the past 20 years in Malaysia leads one to the conclusion that the state has indeed chosen for a policy of high numbers and low rights. Migration policies have not restricted the entry of migrant workers but have placed limits on time of residence, position in the labour market and social and labour rights. In this regard, we can conclude that, unlike in liberal states, immigration policies in Malaysia can immobilize workers, make them dependent on their employers and ensure that their stay is purely temporary. Yet, by paying attention to how these policies worked in practice, this study makes clear that state control has also its limits in Malaysia. These limitations are not imposed by legal or political means but rather by the immigrants themselves in escaping from state control by means of resorting to illegality. If we take into account that the number of irregular migrants was estimated in more than 1 million in 2006 (Syed Shahir 2006), which roughly represents 10% of the labour force and 4% of the total population, these limitations demand not only to be acknowledged but also explained.

High Numbers

Defining Numbers

The number of migrants allowed to enter and work in Malaysia has been determined by two contradictory demands. On the one hand, migrant workers were perceived as necessary in order to ease labour shortages in critical sectors such as plantations, construction, manufacturing and services. Since economic growth has depended on foreign investments that were attracted by emphasizing low labour costs, the availability of cheap foreign labour was seen as essential. On the other hand, migrant workers were also perceived as a threat to what was deemed to be the proper redistribution of wealth and employment among the different ethnic groups (Malay, Chinese and Indian). In consequence, trade unions have systematically opposed the entry of migrant workers. This dilemma between contradictory demands has been solved by letting in only those migrant workers perceived as 'needed' for economic growth and only in those economic sectors or occupations were nationals did not work. While this policy is common to most nation-states, what remains to be considered is how the Malaysian state defined this 'necessity' for migrant workers.

Although this process is not defined in any published document, it is general knowledge that employers are required to advertise their vacancies in local newspapers and through the Electronic Human Exchange System of the Human Resources Department. If no national workers are available, employers should submit an application for the recruitment of migrant workers to the Ministry of Home Affairs. These applications, according to an official of the Immigration Department, are sent to a specific technical committee that defines whether the application is 'genuine' or not (interview 6 October 2006, Kuala Lumpur). This means considering whether there are national workers available; whether the request complies with the quota established for each economic sector (for instance, in 2006, this quota was one migrant worker for every three local workers in manufacturing; but three for every one in construction); or whether applicants are direct employers or recruitment agencies, in which case applications would be rejected. Other factors that may be taken into account are the volume and duration of the project, whether the employer is a subcontractor or the main contractor and the jobs for which migrant workers are required. Despite these limitations, between 400,000 and 700,000 migrant workers enter Malaysia every year. These numbers seem to suggest that the 'necessity' of migrant workers is defined in broad terms.

Apart from this case-by-case evaluation of foreign labour demands, the Ministry of Home Affairs has regularly enforced a series of bans (in 1993–1994, 1997, 2001, 2002, 2005) on different categories of migrant workers. In 1997 this was justified by the Prime Minister Dr Mahathir Mohamed who argued that, 'The country cannot go on depending on foreign workers. We have 20 million people and 1.7 million foreign workers. If we allow this to go on we would risk losing control of our country' (*Bulletin Imigresen*, 1997; quoted in Wong and Anwar 2003: 181). While, here, the Prime Minister referred to security reasons, on other occasions the freeze on employment of migrant workers was justified by the need to protect national workers, to prevent social problems or to reduce the amount of remittances sent by migrants to their countries of origin. Despite all these arguments, employers' complaints about the persistence of labour shortages and their negative consequences on economic growth led on each occasion to an immediate lifting of the ban. For instance, in 1997 the prohibition on fresh labour recruitment meant that out of the employers' requests for 225,275 work permits in 1998, only 2,876 were granted (Wong and Anwar 2003: 181). However, as it was revealed that RM 2 billion had been lost in 1997–1998 because of labour shortages, by mid-1998 the government had announced that permission would be given to foreign exchange sectors (such as plantations) to employ 'fresh' migrant workers as well as to redeploy migrant workers from other economic sectors. In early 1999 the freeze on the importation of foreign labour was lifted in the construction, manufacturing and service sectors.

These constant shifts in terms of allowing, restricting and banning migrant entry have been interpreted by most Malaysian scholars as outstanding examples of the *ad hoc*, stop-go character of Malaysian migration policies. In fact, these shifts resulted from the dilemmas and contradictions underlying the state's decisions in the field of migration. As the Human Resources Ministry once said, 'The government was seeking to strike a balance between ensuring there is no labour shortage and employers not taking advantage of the situation at the expense of local workers' (*New Straits Times*, 28 November 1991). This balance, however, was sometimes difficult to attain. Despite the recurrent introduction of temporary bans on the employment of migrant workers, the Malaysian state did always re-open the 'gates' in the end. We can thus conclude that employers' demands were systematically attended to. This was the case not only because employers succeeded in imposing their interests but also because economic growth and development was one of the main concerns of the Malaysian state itself.

Regulating Migrants' Origin

State regulation of migration flows has sought to determine not only the number of migrant workers allowed to enter in the country but also their origins. As in the colonial past, the state aimed to create a docile and malleable labour force by diversifying migrants' origins. This has meant, in particular, countering the power of a specific sending state or the dominance of a specific national group within Malaysian national territory. The best illustration of the former is the case of the Philippines. When, in 1997, the Filipino state asked for an increase in the wages of Filipino domestic workers in Malaysia (from RM 500 to RM 750[1]),

---

1   The present exchange rate for the Malaysian Ringgit (RM) (December 2009) is US$ 1 = RM 3.39850 and has ranged from approximately RM 3.8 to RM 3.5 in the last

the Malaysian state reacted by banning their employment. An illustration of the latter is the case of Indonesian migrants. In 2002, following several riots in work places and detention camps, the government announced a 'Hire Indonesians Last' policy, that is, effectively putting a stop to the recruitment of Indonesian migrants. The official argument, as expressed by Prime Minister Mahathir, was that it was time for Indonesian workers in Malaysia to be 'replaced' by workers of other nationalities. As in the past when Indian labour was promoted by the colonial authorities to counterbalance Chinese presence in Malaysia, labour migration from countries such as Vietnam or Myanmar started to be encouraged after 2000 in order to reduce Malaysian reliance on Indonesian labour.

But to what extent could the Malaysian state determine the origin of the Malaysian migrant labour force? In fact, here too, the markets countered any policy that did not fit their demands. For instance, the ban on Filipino domestic workers was followed by an immediate reaction from employers. 'Consumers' of this specific kind of labour, which is to say families that were set on having Filipino domestic workers, protested by arguing that they should have the right and the freedom to choose the characteristics of their own domestic workers. Interestingly, their arguments were exclusively in terms of market demand. For instance, an employer protested in a local newspaper, 'Since Indonesian maids are Muslims, it is not proper to ask them to cook certain food. To hire an Indonesian maid would only cause inconvenience to us and the maid. [...] We are comfortable with Filipino maids because they can speak English and are hardworking. [...] If we can afford to pay, why not let us hire them since it is our money?' (*New Straits Times,* 8 September 1997). Similarly, a group of employers protested in an open letter to another newspaper, 'Please do not tell us that we can settle for other nationalities. We have our preference. Isn't Malaysia a democratic society?' (*Business Times*, 11 September 1998). Once again, following such protests, the ban was immediately lifted.

Partly thanks to employers' demands, the Filipino state succeeded in imposing its own conditions beyond its national borders. This state transnationalism, or transnationalism from above, resulted in fact from the commodification of Filipino domestic workers (see Ezquerra and Garcés-Mascareñas 2008). Indeed, only by envisaging them as luxury goods or consumption goods with added value, or as the 'Mercedez Benz of domestic workers', could the Filipino state impose higher wages for its domestic workers in Malaysia. In fact, in 1995 the Indonesian government had tried to do the same thing but without success. In this case, employers' protests were substantially different. For instance, one employer argued, 'With RM 1,000 a month [the wage demanded by the Indonesian state], it is better for me to hire two Filipino maids who are better trained and

---

10 years. The family average income is RM 3,000 per month. Although Malaysia has no comprehensive law on minimum wage, in 2009 some 30,000 plantation workers nationwide received a minimum wage of RM 500–600 per month (*The Malaysian Insider*, 6 June 2009).

understand English since my current Indonesian maid does not even know what a refrigerator is' (*New Straits Times*, 28 February 1995). Independently of 'the market value' of its domestic workers, Indonesia's demands were rejected on the basis of two main arguments. Firstly, Malaysia is the main destination country for Indonesian migrants. In this regard, in contrast with the Philippines, the argument was that 'they had no other alternative but to accept our conditions'. Secondly, Indonesian domestic workers are mainly employed by the Malaysian middle-class who cannot afford to pay more.

While the Indonesian government could not impose its wage conditions within Malaysian national territory, neither could the Malaysian government impose a ban on the recruitment of Indonesian migrant workers. The 'Hire Indonesians Last' policy, which was meant to stop Indonesian labour migration to Malaysia, clashed with the structural significance of Indonesian workers in the Malaysian economy. For instance, as 70% of all construction workers were Indonesians, this halt was followed by the overnight reduction of construction output by some 40%. It was also estimated that because the 'disappearance' of Indonesian harvest workers, vegetable prices would rise as much as 30% (Liow 2004: 22). In consequence, the policy was quickly recognized as unviable and abruptly rescinded after two weeks. The executive director of the Malaysian Employers Federation argued the impossibility of renouncing Indonesian workers in the following terms,

> Based on employers' experience, the Indonesian workers are more suitable to work in this country due to several reasons. Firstly, the Indonesians have no problems in adjusting to the Malaysian culture in terms of language, social, food and religion. Secondly, the working environment in Indonesia is similar to Malaysia and they have the necessary skills required in Malaysia. Language is also an important factor to be considered as the Indonesians have similar mother tongue as Malaysians and thus facilitate communication and training [sic]. Thirdly, employers have positive views on the work culture and attitude of Indonesian foreign workers who are willing to work extra hours to increase their productivity (*New Straits Times*, 14 February 2002).

While in the cases of the Philippines and Indonesia the state regulation of migrants' origins was opposed by employers' demands, in other cases it has been implemented without much conflict and protest. In 1997, for instance, a freeze on the recruitment of Bangladeshi workers was imposed arguing, first, that Bangladeshi migrants caused social unrest, particularly as a consequence of the alleged popularity of Bangladeshi men among Malaysian women. Secondly, the Malaysian government justified the halt by referring to the abuses committed by Bangladeshi recruitment agencies. As described by an Immigration Officer, 'Bangladeshi agencies charged at that time around RM 10,000 to RM 15,000 per worker. The workers themselves had to pay it. This was a lot and led to exploitation. So in 1996 we said: before recruiting more Bangladeshi workers, solve first your problem at home!' (interview 6 October 2006, Putrajaya). As a result of this halt, the presence of Bangladeshi workers decreased from representing 39.9% of all migrant workers in Malaysia in 1997 to just 3.2% in 2006. While reducing the number of Bangladeshi migrants in Malaysia, this same policy led to rising numbers of workers from new emigration countries such as Myanmar (from 2.2% in 1997 to 5.1% in 2006), Nepal (from 0 to 11.1%) and Vietnam (from 0 to 4%).

Privatization of Recruitment

In contrast to European guestworker programmes, in Malaysia the recruitment of migrant workers has always been managed by private agencies. Dubbed manpower suppliers or more recently labour outsourcing companies, these private agencies organize the whole migration process from the small village in Indonesia, Bangladesh or Nepal to the factory, plantation, construction site or household in Malaysia. Following employers' requests, recruitment agencies in Malaysia contact their counterparts in the country of origin. These counterparts recruit migrants in the villages (often through other agents) and send the required information to the Malaysian agency. Once employers agree on the characteristics of the migrant workers proposed, both the agency in the country of origin and the one in Malaysia initiate the legal procedures to send and receive them in Malaysia. Recruitment agencies in Malaysia organize not only the whole registration process but also the renewal of the work permit and the annual payment of medical check-ups, insurance and levy.

Employers have often defended the presence of recruitment agencies by stressing their role as coordinators of the recruitment process as well as their role in the deployment of migrant labour from completed jobs to new ones. From this perspective, recruitment agencies have often been presented as necessary 'managers' or 'guardians' of a migrant labour system that does not work alone or, in other words, that needs 'someone in the middle' to cope with the distance between labour supply and demand, deal with legal procedures, re-distribute migrant labour and return immigrants to their countries of origin after the prescribed period of time. This is how recruitment agencies present themselves as well. The president of the Malaysian Association of Foreign Maid Agencies went still further, stating on several occasions that recruitment agencies are the only entities that can control employers and mediate between them and migrant workers: 'If you come without an agency, who controls the employer? I told the government that foreign workers should always come through an agency. The agency makes sure that employers pay. The agency also makes sure that employers send their workers back to their countries of origin after the termination of their contracts' (interview 26 September 2006, Kuala Lumpur).

At the same time, recruitment agencies have often been portrayed as 'unscrupulous people' who overcharge migrant workers and 'cheat' them. The Malaysian newspapers are full of such cases. For instance, cases of migrant workers who have been given false promises in terms of salary and work conditions are reported almost every week. There are also cases of migrant workers who are abandoned on arrival in Malaysia after having paid huge amounts of money to their recruitment agencies. Without proper documentation or without a real employer behind their work passes, they immediately become 'illegal' and therefore may be deported to their countries of origin just after arriving in Malaysia. In fact, this is not so unlike the abuses committed by Indian recruiters (*kanganies*) in the late 19th century. Then, as now, it was regularly denounced that recruiters used bribery to encourage workers to migrate, promised young people a guaranteed good future, exploited family quarrels to induce people to migrate and gave false information about wages and living conditions in Malaya (Sandhu 1969: 100; Parmer 1960: 58; Ramachandran 1994: 60–61).

Employers, trade unions, NGOs and the government itself have coincided in denouncing recruitment agencies, accusing them of charging exorbitant fees and practising a great number of irregularities. On the one hand, employers and government officials have underlined how these irregularities make the whole recruitment process more problematic and inefficient. For instance, companies often complain that agencies are providing them with '[…] the wrong types of foreign workers and this mismatch costs them time and resources' (*Business Times*, 26 September 1992). As a representative of the Malaysian Agricultural Producers' Association stated, 'We don't take workers from the agency here, because we would receive rubbish' (interview 14 September 2006, Kuala Lumpur). Employers and the Malaysian government have also complained that exorbitant fees increase the numbers of cases of absconding or running away. As the Rural Development Minister Senator put it in 1994, '[I]f the foreign workers are required to make high repayment because of the high costs, the Government fears that they will abscond to seek other jobs' (*New Straits Times*, 7 July 1994). On the other hand, NGOs and trade unions have been more concerned with migrant workers' welfare. Their main argument has been that the presence of recruitment agencies, along with their regular and irregular practices, have increased the vulnerability of migrant workers in Malaysia.

The ongoing tension between the demand for private agents to manage the recruitment and employment of migrant workers, on the one hand, and rejection of their abusive practices, on the other, is manifest in the formulation of migration policies. In 1992 the Human Resources Ministry amended the Private Employment Agencies Act 1981 in order to require the use of private agents in the recruitment of foreign labour. This change arose from the perceived need for a more 'orderly process.' Since these agencies were familiar with the required procedures, it was thought that their involvement would help to expedite the intake of workers (*Business Times*, 26 September 1992). Three years later, however, the recruitment of migrant workers (all but domestic workers) became the exclusive responsibility of the Home Ministry's Foreign Workers Task Force. This shift was then explained by the need to circumvent this middleman's course and establish a centralized apparatus that would ensure quicker and tidier processing of workers' recruitment (*New Sunday Times*, 20 August 1995). Nevertheless, this attempt to centralize recruitment was doomed to fail. Although recruitment agencies were formally proscribed, employers never stopped using their services.

As the representative of one recruitment agency declared, 'We have always helped them. But then we were not recognized. We did all the procedures, all the papers, but under their name' (interview 20 September 2006, Kuala Lumpur). In fact, this was known and tolerated by the government. The Immigration Department repeatedly requested to deal directly with the employers but did not intervene in what employers did before and after getting the work permit (interview with an officer of the Immigration Department, 6 October 2006, Putrajaya). At the same time, this lack of recognition left recruitment agencies in a kind of legal limbo that made it even more difficult for the government to control them. This is one of the reasons why the government decided to re-legalize recruitment agencies in January 2006. Since 2006, they have been called 'outsourcing companies' and have been recognized as the legal employers of migrant workers. As 'legal' employers, they are responsible for the recruitment and stay of migrant workers in Malaysia. As recruiters, they supply or 'outsource' their foreign labour to 'real' employers. Again, this does not differ very much from the past. In the late 19th and early 20th centuries, the *kangany* not only recruited but also supervised and organized the migrant labour force within the estates. For this service, as presently occurs with the outsourcing companies, the *kangany* was paid 'head money', usually two cents a day for every worker who appeared for work (Parmer 1960: 68).

In terms of migration flows, the privatization and commercialization of recruitment but also employment of migrant workers in Malaysia has had a twofold effect. Firstly, it has increased the costs of legal migration. A comparison of the cost involved is very instructive. While in 2005 recruitment fees via regular agencies rose from RM 2,000 to RM 3,000, transport to Malaysia via the *jalur belakang* or back door (mostly by boat) costed from RM 100 to 2,200 (Kejser 2006: 10). Other studies have documented the same. In 2002, for instance, the recruitment fee from Aceh and Lombok (Indonesia) rose to RM 1,000 and RM 1,200 respectively compared with RM 500 and RM 450 for a boat passage to Malaysia (Wong and Anwar 2003: 198). In 2007, the fee paid to recruiters of Indonesian domestic workers could range between RM 1,000 to RM 2,000 (ISIS 2007). If we add to this other expenses such as the passport, induction courses, medical checks and levies, it is not difficult to understand why one of the main reasons given by migrants (particularly from Indonesia) for not coming through the official channel of contract work is the cost of legal entry (Wong and Anwar 2003: 198). In other words, given geographic contiguity, the existence of alternative social networks and, in recent years, the possibility for ASEAN citizens to enter the country with a visa being issued on arrival (since January 2007), the legal channel with its extra costs often becomes dispensable if not downright undesirable.

Secondly, the presence of recruitment agencies explains, too, why many legal migrants fall into illegality once in Malaysia. In some cases, migrants were recruited without having a real employer behind their work permits. This means that either they were abandoned once in Malaysia or they were asked to work with a different employer, which meant they were working illegally. In other cases, migrants were brought into Malaysia under forged permits. This is often done in order to speed up the procedures and lower the costs. In practice, it meant that migrants entered and stayed illegally, often without being aware of it. Finally, in other cases, the mismatch between the debts incurred in order to get to Malaysia and the salaries obtained once there led migrant workers to the almost intolerable situation of having to work for years just to pay back the initial debt. This situation, which is not very different from that of the nineteenth-century indentured workers, has induced many migrants to run away from their employers. By absconding from employers, migrants escaped from debts and bondages. However, since work permits are tied to a particular employer, this meant immediately falling into illegality.

The story of Shahjahan Babu, a Bangladeshi migrant who arrived in Malaysia in 1993, is very illustrative in this regard. Babu was recruited by the Bangladeshi recruitment agency Paradise International. He was told, 'If you work abroad, you will be able to bring back money. The more you pay, the more you will earn'. However, the situation in Malaysia turned to be very different. When he landed in Malaysia, the hotel work he had been promised turned out to be labour on a construction site. The next revelation was that his passport was forged, so that, to add insult to injury, he was illegal too. His own words, recorded in a tape he sent back home, say it all

> I spent so much to come here as a legal worker. And now to serve their interest [recruiters], they've made us illegal. What are their intentions? Of us five Bangalees, they've separated us all … and put us at different sites, one here, another there. Promising us hotel-work, they put us in construction, heavy loads to lift, such hard work … yet I didn't tell you, from 7 in the morning till 12 midnight, no wages, nothing. Finally, after a lot of pleading, they fixed our wages at RM 300. Do we feed ourselves or send money home? Yet, to survive, we'd have stayed […] We called our agency. They said 'get out'! We've nothing to do with you […] Who will be held accountable for this? Who? (from the documentary *My Migrant Soul*, directed by Yasmin Kabir).

Low Rights

Immobilization of Migrant Labour

Migrant labour in Malaysia has always been restricted to particular economic sectors. While in the late 1980s it was exclusively permitted in plantations and domestic services, during the 1990s permission was extended to the construction, manufacturing and service sectors. The idea behind these limitations has been to restrict the employment of migrant labour to those jobs rejected by local workers. While both employers and trade unions have agreed about the fact that local workers should be given priority in the labour market, they have disagreed when identifying the demand for migrant workers. On the one hand, employers have always insisted that locals were 'too choosy' to work in plantations, construction, manufacturing and particular services, and, hence, foreign labour was required to cover labour shortages in these sectors. On the other hand, trade unions have denounced the fact that these labour shortages were not the result of a 'genuine' lack of manpower but of poor wages and work conditions. The result has been a changing migration policy that has opened up these sectors to migrant workers in periods of economic growth while closing them during economic slowdowns such as in 1997–1998 and 2002.

In order to restrict the presence of migrant workers to specific economic sectors, their inflow has been regulated by work permits (instead of residential status) that are issued for a specific economic sector and tied to a particular employer. This policy has had the backing of the main interest groups. First of all, for employers, the immobilization of migrant workers has meant the reduction of migrant-labour turnover, particularly in those sectors with lower wages and poorer working conditions. In other words, it prevented migrant workers from leaving their initial employment to seek better job opportunities. Their immobilization is, moreover, the only legal guarantee whereby employers can recover their initial investments in terms of recruitment fees, medical check ups and annual levies. Secondly, trade unions have also been in favour of this policy since it prevents migrants from displacing local workers in the labour market. Thirdly, with this policy the Malaysian state has sought to hold employers responsible for the presence of migrant workers in Malaysia as well as for their return to their countries of origin. This responsibility was reinforced by the introduction in 1992 of a mandatory security bond (between RM 250 and RM 5,000 according to nationality and economic sector) that is only refunded to the employer once the migrant worker has left the country.

The immobilization of migrant workers has been denounced by most Malaysian and international NGOs. Although migrant workers (except domestic workers) are protected under the Employment Act, their reliance on a particular employer effectively prevents them from seeking redress in the labour or industrial court. Since the Immigration Act clearly states that a migrant worker is only allowed to be employed and to stay in the country within the premises of the enterprise stated in the work permit, if the migrant worker wants to discontinue his or her employment due to abuse or exploitative work conditions, or the work permit is cancelled by the employer after having being brought to court, the migrant worker has to return home. Sometimes a special pass visa is issued in the latter circumstance but it has to be renewed monthly and does not give permission to work. Since court cases can take months or even years, this means that, in practice, most migrant workers are forced to return home before the end of the trial (Tenaganita 2005: 26–34).

In practice the immobilization of legal migrant workers seems to lead in many cases to a situation of 'sanctioned bondage' (see Kassim 1995). As their mobility is restricted by the work permit, legal migrants have to accept the terms and conditions of their contracts, they do not have the freedom to move from job to job and, their labour rights are restricted since their legal presence in the country depends on their employers. In this regard, Kassim concludes that having legal status accentuates rather than diminishes exploitation of migrant workers by their employers or, in other words, legal employment can be counterproductive for the workers (Kassim 1995: 1). In contrast, illegal migrants are not tied to their employer as there is no agreement signed and they can leave if and when they want. This is evidenced by the high rate of job mobility among illegal migrants (Wong and Anwar 2003: 220). In this particular aspect, illegality would seem thus to be an advantage to the migrant worker rather than a disadvantage.

Given these differences and the impossibility of improving their working conditions by legal means, many legal migrant workers leave their employers and therefore become illegal. This is what is daily described in the Malaysian newspapers as cases of 'absconding' or 'running away'. Although there are no data on the total number of absconders, there is a general perception that this is a common phenomenon. For instance, in 1997 an immigration official declared to a Malaysian newspaper that most illegal migrant workers working at the new international airport had run away from plantations in search of better wages (*The Malay Mail,* 12 June 1997). A member of the Malaysian Palm Oil Plantation observed along similar lines that plantation workers run away as soon as they have a friend working in the construction sector (interview 21 September 2006, Kuala Lumpur). Rudnick (2009: 181) estimates that 20% of the Bangladeshi women employed in factories and an undetermined higher percentage of Bangladeshi men absconded from their initial jobs. When official data about cases of 'running away' are given, they refer exclusively to domestic workers. In 2005, 19,406 cases of running away were denounced to the Immigration Department compared to 18,358 in 2004 and 17,131 in 2003 (*New Sunday Times*, 2 July 2006). According to a representative of the NGO Migrant Care, there were 30,000 cases of running away in 2007, which represented approximately 10% of all legal migrant domestic workers in Malaysia (interview 11 January 2008, Kuala Lumpur).

On the basis of these data, many recruitment agents and even government officials suggest that employers should not give migrant domestic workers a day off each week. Agents and politicians commonly argue that domestic workers 'easily fall in love' or they are 'easily manipulated'. However, if we take into account that their situation is even more fragile than that of the other legal migrants, we might well conclude that 'absconding' is the only real alternative they have if they are to improve their situation. Domestic workers are not included in the Employment Act and neither are minimum wages or minimum working conditions specified for them. As alleged 'family members' and 'non workers', their bargaining capacity is even more limited. What can they do if they are not paid? Or if they have to work 20 hours a day or cannot have any day off? Or if they are paid much less than promised? In many cases, they run away. As Beeman argued (1985: 173), regarding Indian workers in colonial Malaya in the late 19th and early 20th centuries, since they do not have any means of bargaining, 'running away' or 'absconding' may have become an individualistic way of trying to improve their situation.

Taxation of Migrant Labour

Together with the immobilization of migrant workers, taxation seeks to control immigrant presence in Malaysia. Following the example of Singapore, a levy was imposed in 1992 to reduce the employers' reliance on migrant workers. As stated by the Human Resource Minister in 1991, the levy aimed to '[…] control the influx of cheap and unskilled labour into the country' and to '[…] keep a close check on the workers' (*New Straits Times*, 16 May 1991). This was done by imposing an annual tax per migrant worker according to the economic sector and skills. The logic behind this variation was to impose a higher levy in those sectors where local workers could still be found and a lower one in those sectors where foreign workers were really in demand.

As with all migration policies in Malaysia, the levy on foreign workers has been adapted to the different and changing requirements of the labour market: in periods of higher unemployment the levy has been raised in order to protect national workers while in periods of lower unemployment it has been reduced. This flexibility, however, is not exempt of contradictions. In particular, protection of the national labour market has not always coincided with economic requirements. For instance, in January 1998 the levy was increased to '[…] discourage the influx of foreign workers in the country and to reduce foreign labour dependence' during the economic downturn that followed the Southeast Asian financial crisis of 1997 (*New Straits Times*, 2 January 1998). However, in December of the same year and once again in tune with Singaporean migration policies, the levy was reduced in some sectors (particularly in the export industries) to '[…] ease the burden on employers' and promote economic recovery (*New Straits Times*, 28 December 1998). This contradiction is also manifested within the government itself. While, in 1992, the Labour Department was in favour of the levy in order to protect local workers, the Primary Industries Minister expressed his doubts:

> The plantation sector must ultimately be able to make use of foreign labour to its advantage. While remuneration of foreign labour should not be such that it would displace the use of local labour, it would certainly not be in Malaysia's advantage if foreign labour turned out to be more expensive than local labour (*New Straits Times*, 27 May 1992).

The same conflict of interests regarding the introduction of the levy also arose between the employers' organizations and trade unions. On the one hand, employers' organizations complained that the levy was too high and would cut profits and, therefore, reduce general economic growth. As stated by the president of the United Planting Association of Malaysia:

> The plantation sector is plagued by numerous problems, threatening its very existence. The labour shortage and escalating production costs against a backdrop of poor commodity prices are only some of the problems the plantation sector

cannot hope to resolve on its own. This is why we continue to appeal to the government to be more sympathetic and sensitive to the plight of the agricultural sector as and when it reviews the various policies affecting plantation companies so that their continued growth can be ensured. For instance, the proposed levy on foreign workers will further aggravate the problems facing the sector (*Business Times*, 23 May 1991).

On the other hand, trade unions welcomed the introduction of the levy as a first step towards the protection of national workers. However, from 1992 onwards, in its efforts to overcome for once and for all the displacement of national workers in the labour market, the Malaysian Trade Union Congress (MTUC) has put pressure on the government to raise the levy and impose a minimum national wage. The official response has always been the same: both options would be detrimental to economic growth.

But this compromise was in fact very difficult to maintain. As with other policy measures, the device of the levy ended up giving priority to the demands of employers. This came about as a consequence of a double (interconnected) change. First of all, employers started to deduce the levy from workers' monthly wages. In 1993, just one year after the introduction of the levy, the government officially recognized the employers' right to transfer the burden of the levy to migrant workers. Secondly, and partly as a consequence of this, the levy shifted from being a tax imposed on those employers that relied on foreign labour to being an income tax paid by migrant workers. The very day that the Immigration Department started to consider the possibility of allowing the deduction of the levy from migrant workers' wages, its objective was re-defined. As an officer from the Immigration Department stated, '[T]he levy is to ensure that foreign workers make financial contributions, just like local workers, for the development of public facilities and social amenities that they enjoy or use while working in Malaysia' (*New Straits Times*, 2 January 1993).

In practice, the introduction of the levy has had a twofold effect on migrant workers' lives. The first is that it has increased their dependence on employers since now their bondage is not only defined by the conditions of the work permit (as described above) but also established in practice through the debt that re-starts every year when the employer advances the payment of the levy and then deducts it monthly from the migrant workers' wages. To be more precise, if migrant workers leave their jobs, the employer loses the amount of levy that remains to be deducted from their monthly wages. This has led employers to retain foreign workers' papers in order to prevent them from running away. Although this practice is clearly not permitted by the Immigration Act, once again it has been accepted by the Immigration Department. In the words of the president of one trade union (National Union of Plantation Workers), 'Foreign workers are tied to their employers. Why? Because employers pay in advance for the costs (levy, insurance, etc.), so they consider that they have the right of ownership' (interview 9 October 2006, Kuala Lumpur).

The second effect is that, once again, the levy pushes up the price of legality. In short, it is more expensive to be a legal than an illegal migrant. Most Malaysian scholars have pointed out this difference as one of the main reasons why migrants prefer to remain or become illegal (Battistella 2002: 363; Pillai 2000: 142; Hugo 1995: 277; Ruppert 1999: 33; Kassim 1993a: 5–6; 1993b: 6; 1994b: 3–4; 1995: 7; 1996: 2; 1997: 5; Bagoes Mantra 1999: 63; Wong and Anwar 2003: 192–8). This was also one of the main reasons given by the illegal migrants themselves in a survey done on the basis of 100 respondents in Peninsular Malaysia (see Wong and Anwar 2003). In short, although to run away from their employers makes them 'illegal' and may imply having to leave their passport behind, this can sometimes become a real alternative when legality imposes an extra burden in an already very limited economic situation.

Temporality of Foreign Labour

There is general consensus that migrant workers should remain only temporarily in Malaysia. As stated many times by employers, trade unionists and government officials, they are 'temporary workers but not migrants' or 'they came here to work, not to get the permanent residence permit' (interviews 13 September 2006 and 20 October 2006, Kuala Lumpur). As in the past, they are still considered 'birds of passage'. Their temporality is, however, of a different nature. While, in the late 19th and early 20th centuries, migrants were only deported in case of unemployment or health problems, since the late 1980s migrant workers have come to Malaysia with short-term contracts that may be extended for a maximum period of five to seven years. The temporality of contemporary migrants seeks not only to reduce social security costs but also to prevent their incorporation into Malaysian society (see Garcés Mascareñas 2008). We might say, then, that the presence of migrant workers in Malaysia has been governed by different types of temporality.

The first type is defined, as in the past, according to labour demands. While in periods of economic growth new migrant workers are recruited and those already in Malaysia are allowed to stay, in times of economic downturn new recruitments are frozen and migrant workers in the hardest-hit sectors have to leave. By repatriating them, the Malaysian government seeks to reduce the costs of unemployment and, at the same time, give priority to employing local workers. Perfectly illustrating this logic are the mass repatriation programmes that followed the financial crisis of 1997. While, in the early 1990s, the number of migrant workers increased in keeping with labour demands, in 1998 the Malaysian government immediately halted the issuance of renewals. In particular, it was announced that 200,000 migrants, mostly working in construction, would probably be laid-off (*New Straits Times*, 6 December 1997) and that work permits for 700,000 migrants in the construction and service sectors (except domestic workers) would not be renewed on expiry (*New Straits Times*, 9 January 1998). Apart from exceptions made for some categories, work permits which expired in August 1998 were not renewed, which meant that 159,135 migrant workers had to leave the country (Wong and Anwar 2003: 181). As it happened with the bans on entry, this freeze was lifted a few months later. Once again, the measure was justified by the need to safeguard economic growth.

The on-going tension between, on the one hand, protecting local workers and, on the other, promoting economic growth through the importation of migrant labour has never been resolved. The strains on the system appeared yet again when local unemployment rose from 3.1% in 2000 to 3.7% in 2001 (Kanapathy 2004: 395). In response to this increase and following pressure from trade unions, the Malaysian Parliament passed legislation setting a maximum of three years for the period in which a migrant might hold a work permit. This changed the status of many migrant workers from 'legal' to 'illegal' practically overnight. With the implementation of this policy, those workers who had been covered by work permits for more than three years were immediately deemed 'illegal' and repatriated at three months' notice. However, even while thousands of migrant workers were being repatriated to their countries of origin, the government continued to allow new recruitments in the agriculture sector (*New Straits Times*, 5 November 2001). The old argument was trotted out once more: labour shortages in these sectors could not be covered by local workers and production could not be stopped without affecting the whole national economy.

A second type of temporality is linked to migrant workers' health. In contrast with that defined by labour demands, this second type is applied at the individual level by repatriating any migrant workers who are deemed 'medically unfit'. Being 'medically unfit' means having such diseases as Hepatitis B, Tuberculosis, Syphilis or HIV/AIDS and, for female migrant workers, being pregnant. As in the past, this policy seeks to reduce social costs (both in terms of the social security system as well as regarding the spread of particular diseases) while maximizing the foreign labour force by keeping in the country only the fittest workers who are deemed best able to work. In the case of pregnant women, the policy aims to avoid reproduction costs as well as the settlement of migrant workers in the country. In contrast with other kinds of data, there is a great deal of information available about the number and characteristics of 'unfit' migrant workers. This may be related with social perceptions and the political will to associate migrant workers with diseases and other 'social problems'. To be more specific, 18,154 cases of 'medically unfit' migrants (or 3.6% of the total foreign labour force) were reported in 1998, 7,276 in 1999, 6,914 in 2000, 9,284 in 2001 and 8,827 in 2002 (Kanapathy 2004: 399). In 2004, the highest number was found in the agriculture sector, with 6,500 cases or 35.2% of all migrant workers employed in this sector *(The Malay Mail,* 9 December 2004).

Finally, migrant workers are not allowed to stay in Malaysia for more than five to seven years. This third type of temporality is also implemented at the individual level and again aims to prevent migrant workers' settlement in the country. The logic is to ensure that migrant workers come only to work or that they remain as 'pure labour' without becoming settled migrants. This results in a migrant labour system that is constantly renewing its labour force. As described by the president of the Malaysian Employers Federation, 'Foreign workers are only allowed to work. They come to work and, once they finish, they have to go back. They come and go, they come and go, all the time' (interview 13 September 2006, Kuala Lumpur). While assuring a flexible, external labour supply, this constant influx and outflow of migrant workers seems to militate against productivity. As this interviewee went on to explain, every year about 400,000 or 500,000 'fresh' migrant workers enter Malaysia. Employers then have to train them over and over again without being able to retain their skills for the company's benefit. Following employers' complaints, 'certified skilled workers' are exceptionally allowed to stay for ten years. However, in the end, the result is the same: they always have to leave. Despite its impact on productivity, this is accepted by all parties. As the president of the Malaysian Employers Federation puts it, 'We are not supposed to have these people here for ever, are we?' (interview 13 September 2006, Kuala Lumpur).

The only migrant workers who are not required to leave Malaysia after five, seven or ten years are domestic workers. According to the government guidelines for foreign domestic workers, they can keep renewing their work permits until they are 45 years old. However, as many interviewees informed me, they can stay in Malaysia as long as they want since their birth certificates can easily be falsified at will. Domestic workers are thus the only migrant workers who can stay in Malaysia (almost) permanently. This does not mean, however, that they can officially settle in the country and get a permanent residence permit. As an interviewee from an agency specializing in domestic workers states, 'The government is not obliged to give you permanent residence. It depends on what you have done. What is your contribution to the nation as a maid? I don't see any reason for giving them permanent residence. This is for engineers' (interview 16 September 2006, Kuala Lumpur). Hence, domestic workers, unlike other migrant workers, can be eternal temporary migrants in Malaysia.

In practical terms, these three forms of temporality have had a triple effect. First of all, as I have noted above, they have brought about a continuous labour turnover that may disrupt productivity. Some employers, however, did not see this as a problem since most migrant workers have low-skilled jobs. Moreover, as one recruitment agent remarked, new labour is cheap labour. 'We don't like to depend on them. If they become skilled workers, they can ask for more money. Unskilled new workers are much cheaper' (interview 29 September 2006, Kuala Lumpur). Secondly, it has increased the costs of the whole labour migrant system since old migrant workers have to be sent back to their countries of origin while new ones have to be recruited and brought in. Thirdly, this temporality introduces a factor of unpredictability into the supply of migrant labour. Employers can hardly plan the number of migrant workers they will be allowed to have in the future when their presence in Malaysia depends on the general economic performance.

Naturally, this unpredictability affects migrant workers, too, as they can be required to leave at any moment. This is particularly hard on the migrant if we take into account the fact that many have paid considerable sums of money to get to Malaysia. What happens to those migrant workers who have sold their properties back home or incurred debts in order to migrate to Malaysia when they are suddenly ordered to go back because they are no longer required, or because they are ill or pregnant? Among my interviewees there was general agreement that, in many cases, they decide to stay in Malaysia even if this entails becoming 'illegal' (see as well Rudnick 2009: 177). This is also shown in the cases of many interviewees in Wong's and Anwar's survey of illegal migrants, for example a 24-year-old, unmarried woman from a rural district in Aceh. After she had worked three years in a factory, her work contract was not renewed and she was supposed to go back home, but she ran away and sought refuge in her sister's home in a suburb of Kuala Lumpur (Wong and Anwar 2003: 192). Unfortunately, although this response is frequently observed, there are little or no data to illustrate it, possible owing to the political will to underscore certain aspects of the situation (such as the incidence of particular diseases among migrant workers) while obscuring others (such as the number of legal migrants that move into illegality).

Conclusions

Malaysia has clearly opted for a policy of high numbers and low rights. Similar to other guestworker programme, the Malaysian state did not restrict the entry of migrant workers but placed limits on their stay. This has been done in three fundamental ways. Firstly, their work permit is issued for a specific economic sector and tied to a particular employer. As denounced by most Malaysian and international NGOs, this has resulted in a situation of 'sanctioned bondage' as migrants do not have the freedom to move from job to job and their labour rights are in practice restricted since their legal presence in the country depends on their employers. Secondly, the shift whereby the levy changed from being a tax imposed on employers to being an income tax on foreign workers has raised the price of being legal and, indirectly, the immigrants' dependence on their employers. Thirdly, the immigrant workers' stay in Malaysia is temporary in three different ways: they are 'returned' or 'repatriated' in case of economic downturn, illness or pregnancy, and after five or seven years of working in the country. The final aim of these different time frames has been to get 'workers' instead of 'migrants', to talk about a policy of high numbers means that employers obtained as many workers as demanded. When in times of crisis (for example 1997 and 2001) the Malaysian state closed down or restricted entry, the employers' reaction was swift. Even in times of crisis and growing unemployment, the market still depended on foreign labour. Hence, so the employers argued, if the state wanted to continue promoting economic growth, it would have to open up entry again. Given that the state's legitimacy also depended on its ability to guarantee economic growth, the government complied on each occasion. Although Malaysian scholars have interpreted these swings in immigration policy as a demonstration of its *ad hoc* nature and lack of coherence, they were really part of a continuum. The present study reveals how the entry of migrant workers was in fact never a matter for negotiation: entry policies simply responded to the market demand. In short, the market has always ruled.

While labour demands have always been given response, the demand for closure has been satisfied by restricting migrants' presence in the country (see Garcés-Mascareñas 2010a). This low-rights policy resulted from the fact that neither the legal, nor the political systems have constrained the state in its capacity to control migration and exclude migrants from within. In this regard, it is true, as assumed by many Western scholars, that the government of Malaysia could get around rights-based impediments 'because there are fewer legal or institutional constraints on the behaviour of states *vis-à-vis* foreign nationals' (Hollifield 2002: 11). However, no legal and political constraints does not mean no constraints. In practice restrictions in migrants' rights have also had their limits in Malaysia. These restrictions were not so much called into question by the legal or political system but directly challenged by the practices of the immigrants themselves. The resort to illegality, both by those who entered the country illegally and those who became illegal immigrants on leaving their employers, has made it possible for people to 'escape' the restraints imposed by the state-regulated migrant labour system. Illegal migrants, unlike 'legal' immigrants, can change jobs, can to some extent negotiate their salary and working conditions, do not have to pay extra to enter or remain in the country and can prolong their stay independently of the economic situation or their state of health, or beyond the years stipulated by law (see Garcés-Mascareñas 2010b).

This resort to illegality as a way to escape from state control means that in Malaysia the attempt to turn foreign workers into mere merchandise to be imported and exported as and when demanded has not been completely successful either. Here, too, the deluded notion that immigration is a purely economic matter to be managed by the state has been challenged by the fact that 'human beings came'. While in the European guestworker examples this humanity of migrant workers translated, in the medium and long term, into permanent residence, in Malaysia it has been translated into migrants' illegality. One might well ask to what point these two outcomes might be explained by the political context and the role of rights. To be more precise, to what point has the illusion of migration 'management' as an economic matter been translated over time into permanent migration in the liberal democracies and illegal migration in the non-liberal democracies?

Bibliography

Arango, J. 2003. Dificultades y dilemas de las políticas de inmigración. *Circunstancia. Revista de Ciencias Sociales del IUIOG*, 1(2), Septiembre.

Bagoes Mantra, I. 1999. Illegal Indonesian Labour Movement from Lombok to Malaysia, *Asia Pacific Viewpoint*, 40(1).

Battistella, G. 2002a. Unauthorized Migrants as Global Workers in the ASEAN Region, *Southeast Asian Studies*, 40(3).

Beeman, M.A. 1985. *The Migrant Labor System: The Case of Malaysian Rubber Workers*. PhD Thesis, University of Illinois.

Ezquerra, S. and Garcés-Mascareñas, B. 2008. *Towards Transnationalism from Above: The Case of the Philippine state in Malaysia*. Paper presented at the International Sociological Association Conference, 7–8 September, Barcelona.

Freeman, G.P. 1995. Modes of Immigration Politics in Liberal Democratic States, *International Migration Review*, 29(4), 881–902.

Garcés-Mascareñas, B. 2008. Continuities and Discontinuities of Labour Migration Regulations in Malaysia: From Colonial Times to the Present, in *Gender and Illegal Migration in a Global and Historical Perspective*, edited by M. Schrover et al. Amsterdam: Amsterdam University Press.

Garcés-Mascareñas, B. and Penninx, R. 2008. Managing Labour Migration to Spain and Malaysia: A Question of Numbers versus Rights? in *Migratierecht en Rechtssociologie: gebundeld in Kees'studies [Migration Law and Sociology of Law: collected essays in honour of Kees Groenendijk* (Liber Amicorum Prof. Mr. C.A. Groenendijk)], edited by A. Böcker, T. Havinga, P. Minderhoud, H. van de Put et al. Nijmegen: Wolf Legal Publishers, 79–87.

Garcés-Mascareñas, B. 2010a. Fronteras y confines de un estado postcolonial. El caso de Malasia, in *Migraciones y fronteras: Estudios de caso y aproximaciones metodológicas*, edited by M.E. Anguiano and A. López Sala. Barcelona: Icaria/CIDOB.

Garcés-Mascareñas, B. 2010b. Legal Production of Illegality from a Comparative Perspective: The Cases of Malaysia and Spain, *Asia Europe Journal*, 8(1).

Hollifield, J.F. 1992. *Immigrants, Markets and States: The Political Economy of Postwar Europe*. Cambridge: Harvard University Press.

Hollifield, J.F. 2002. *Migration and International Relations: The Liberal Paradox*. Working Paper.

Hugo, G. 1995. Labour Export from Indonesia: An Overview, *ASEAN Economic Bulletin*, 12(2), 275–98.

Joppke, C. 2005. Exclusion in the Liberal State. The Case of Immigration and Citizenship Policy, *European Journal of Social Theory*, 8(1), 43–61.

Kanapathy, V. 2004. *International Migration and Labour Market Developments in Asia: Economic Recovery, The Labour Market and Migrant Workers in Malaysia*. Paper prepared for the Workshop on International Migration and Labour Markets in Asia.

Kassim, A. 1993a. Immigrant Workers in Malaysia: Issues, Problems and Prospects, in *Malaysia and Singapore: Experiences in Industrialisation and Urban Development*, edited by B.H. Lee and S. Oorjitham. Kuala Lumpur: Faculty of Arts and Social Sciences, University of Malaya.

Kassim, A. 1993b. *The Registered and The Illegals: Indonesian Immigrants in Malaysia*. Paper presented at the Seminar on Movement of Peoples in Southeast Asia organised by PMB-LIPI, Jakarta, Indonesia, 17–19 February.

Kassim, A. 1994. Foreign Labour in Malaysia, in *Regional Development Impacts of Labour Migration in Asia*, edited by W. Gooneratne, P.L. Martín and H. Sazanami. Nagoya: UNCRD.

Kassim, A. 1995. *Foreign Workers in Malaysia: An Analysis of Sanctioned Bondage*. Paper presented at the Regional Conference of the International Council of Psychologists on 'Psychological Issues in a Growing Global Community', 10–12 August, Manila.

Kassim, A. 1996. *Labour Migration in ASEAN: Issues and Problems from the Malaysian Perspective*. Paper presented at the 7th Southeast Asia Forum, 3–6 March, organised by ASEAN-ISIS, Kuala Lumpur.

Kassim, A. 1997. *Management of Foreign Labour: A Malaysian Experiment*. Paper presented at the 2nd Asia Pacific Conference of Sociology, 18–20 September, University of Malaya.

Kejser, L. 2006. *Illicit Transnational Movements: Impact and Responses in South East Asia*. Paper presented at the Conference on the Challenges of Global Migration and Forced Displacement, 1–2 August, Kuala Lumpur.

Liow, J.C. 2004. *Malaysia's Approach to its Illegal Indonesian Migrant Labour Problem: Securitization, Politics or Catharsis?* Paper presented in IDSS-Ford Workshop on non-traditional security in Asia, Singapore, 3–4 September.

Martin, P. 2000. Guest Worker Programmes for the 21st Century, *Backgrounder*, Center for Immigration Studies, Washington.

Martin, P. and Ruhs, M.P. 2006. *Numbers vs Rights: Trade-offs and Guest Worker Programmes*. Working Paper no. 40, Oxford: University of Oxford.

Parmer, J.N. 1960. *Colonial Labour Policy and Administration: A History of Labour in the Rubber Plantation Industry in Malaya, c. 1910–1941*. New York: J.J. Austin.

Pillai, P. 2000. Labour Market Developments and International Migration in Malaysia, in *Migration and the Labour Market in Asia*, edited by Organisation for Economic Co-operation and Development. Paris: OECD.

Ramachandran, S. 1994. *Indian Plantation Labour in Malaysia*. Kuala Lumpur: S. Abdul Majeed for INSAN.

Rudnick, A. 2009. *Temporary Migration Experiences of Bangladeshi Women in the Malaysian Export Industry from a Multi-Sited Perspective*. Amsterdam: Amsterdam University Press.

Ruppert, E. 1999. *Managing Foreign Labour in Singapore and Malaysia*. World Bank papers.

Sandhu, K.S. 1969. *Indians in Malaya: Some Aspects of their Immigration and Settlement*. Cambridge: Cambridge University Press.

Scott, J.C. 1985. *Weapons of the Weak: Everyday Forms of Peasant Resistance*. New Haven: Yale University Press.

Shahir, S. 2006. *Protection of Migrant and Refugee Rights in Malaysia*. Paper presented at the Conference on the Challenges of Global Migration and Forced Displacement, 1–2 August, Kuala Lumpur.

Tenaganita. 2005. *Migrant Workers: Access Denied*. Kuala Lumpur: Tenaganita Sdn. BhD.

Wong, D.T and Afrizal Teuku Anwar, T. 2003 *Migran Gelap:* Indonesian Migrants in Malaysia's Irregular Labour Economy, in *Unauthorised Migration in Southeast Asia*, edited by G. Battistella and M.B. Asis. Manila: Scalabrini Migration Centre.

Chapter 4

Examining Labour Migration Regimes in East Asia: Appearance and Technique of Control in Taiwan*

Melody Chia-Wen Lu

Introduction

Much has been theorized on the economic and development models of the developmental states in East and Southeast Asia;[1] however, so far the political theories have not emphasized that the economies benefit from migrant labour forces, and that the recruitment and control of migrant labour is an integral and crucial part of the states' developmental strategies, willingly or not. All these developmental states import a large number of migrant workers primarily from neighbouring countries in Asia, while developing policies to prevent particularly low-skilled migrants to become citizens or long-term residents. The People's Republic of China (PRC) is an exception to this; nevertheless the PRC also applies a strict migration regime to its domestic 'rural workers' that shares similar characteristics with the guest worker policies in some Asian states.

Since the early 1990s, migrant labour regimes in East-Asian states have attracted attention from migration scholars and several case studies have been included in the volume on the international migration.[2] Most of this literature focuses on how migration is controlled on a national basis and describes policies of particular states. This chapter is a case study of a receiving country, Taiwan, which has moved from fairly loose labour controls to a highly regulative and efficient migration labour regime within a short period. I analyse the process of this shift within the context of migrant labour regimes in East Asia and compare Taiwan's experiences with Singapore, Japan and South Korea. By doing so I will

* This chapter is a result of my on-going research project 'Technologies of Governmentality and Migration Policies in South Korea and Taiwan', made possible by Fieldwork Research Grant (2008) of the Modern East Asia Research Centre at Leiden University, the Netherlands, and Fieldwork Fellowship (2009) of the Korea Foundation. I am very grateful for their support.

1   See for instance, Woo-Cumings 1999; Boyd and Ngo 2005.

2   See for instance, Cornelius, Tsuda, Martin and Hollifield 1994; Athukorala and Manning 1999.

demonstrate that the designs of labour migration regimes in these countries are inspired by their neighbours as well as shaped by labour-sending countries in Asia rather than experiences in the West. These policy interrelations are developed in the absence of a regional framework and policy-making mechanisms. Each state takes a unique path in adopting its own technique of control as a result of domestic politics and the degree of complying with international norms.

The first part of this chapter provides an overview of the development of migrant labour regimes in four countries in East Asia: Japan, Singapore, South Korea and Taiwan. I will highlight the characteristics of migrant labour regimes in these receiving countries with reference to each other, and identify the international and domestic factors influencing migrant labour policies at the time when these policies were designed and when the paradigms of control were shifted. In other words, I focus on the process of the appearance of control, the problems of the control experienced, and the remedies these states adopt to solve the control problems.

The second part of this chapter documents the techniques of control Taiwan. I draw from the migration scholarship inspired by Foucault's concepts of governmentality and biopower to analyse these techniques. This scholarship argues that migration and migrants are perceived as a security problem by the host society, and 'art of governing' is applied to control this group of population.[3] Central to these concepts is the exercise of power via social actors beyond the state machinery, through which the state violence toward migrants is justified or naturalized. In this chapter I discuss two techniques of control: governance at a distance and discipline of body and sexuality. Governance at a distance[4] refers to the technique of control and surveillance that the state delegates to labour recruitment agencies and employers. The discipline of body and sexuality is justified by the health professionals and some academicians who produce scientific information that construct migrants as threats to public health and 'population quality', thus allowing the state to exercise biopower on them.

Due to the limited scope of this chapter, I am not be able to discuss the role of civil society, particularly migrant workers' organizations and local human rights organizations, in challenging the practice and rationality of control by protests and by proposing alternative discourse. Neither will I discuss how migrants themselves develop coping mechanisms to these controls.[5] As I will demonstrate in this chapter, even under the same model of the developmental state, the civil societies in East Asian states have different degrees of influences in policy-making and in shaping the public perceptions towards migrant populations. The analysis of the effectiveness of migration control should also take into account the relatively weak influence of these groups despite a vibrant civil society in the democratization process in Taiwan.[6] This, however, is beyond the scope of this chapter.

---

3   Bigo 2002; Morris 1998.

4   This term is used by Rose and Miller 1992, quoted by Morris 1998, 945.

5   For these strategies and performances, see Lan 2006.

6   For instance, women's organizations and anti-trafficking NGOs are actively involved in the governance of marriage immigrants and cross-border marriages in Taiwan.

Overview of Labour Migration Regimes in East Asia

Nevertheless a few contexts can be discerned as the regional trend. First, one of the features of the developmental states is efficient and capable government bureaucracies which are shielded from and less challenged by the political and social pressures in the policy-making and implementation process, thus allowing the states to engineer economic and social policies devoted to economic growth; this is particularly the case during the 1980s and early 1990s when most of the migrant labour regimes in East Asia were designed or institutionalized. Second, prior to the design and institutionalization of these migration labour regimes, there existed a well developed labour-exporting system and labour brokering industry in some Southeast Asian countries, such as the Philippines, Thailand and Indonesia, which was developed earlier from labour-exporting to the Middle East and the West. Labour export was embedded in these nations' economic strategies, to the extent that the state and corporate actors actively engaged in exporting labour in the diplomatic and trade negotiations.[7] Third, although some sending states set up mechanisms to protect migrants' rights and protested in several cases of their citizens experiencing abuse, there existed no regional framework in monitoring violations of migrants' rights; only very recently the issue of security (human trafficking) and migrants' human rights start to surface on the agenda of ASEAN meetings, and the transnational networks of migrant activist groups start to gain visibility.

Singapore: High Dependency on Foreign Labour

Singapore and Hong Kong are city states that have been very integrated into the global economy since their formation as entrepôts of the British Empire, with the majority of their populations being immigrants. Both states adopt clear strategies to welcome foreign high-skilled professionals and to recruit low-skilled labourers on a temporary basis. Singapore is the first Asian state which developed a labour migration regime, which is also by far the most regulative and sophisticated. Right after independence in 1965, the Singaporean government implemented the Regulation of Employment Act (1965) to regulate the commuting unskilled workers from neighbouring Malaysia, issuing one-year work permits. In 1978, the scheme was broadened to other Asian 'non-traditional' countries in South and Southeast Asia, as Malaysia's economy kicked off and started to experience labour shortages. Kaur notes that although termed 'non-traditional', the flows from these countries reflect continuity with the colonial period.[8]

See Wang and Bélanger 2008.

 7   Hugo and Stahl 2004.

 8   Kaur 2006. For a summary of the development of Singaporean policy, see also Wong 1997.

Singapore's guest worker policy and border control measures were institutionalized in the late 1980s and early 1990s, with the implementation of the Immigration Act (1988) and the Employment of Foreign Workers Act (1990). To summarize, the Singaporean state deploys four main measures to regulate the entry of migrant labour and to ensure that they remain transient. These are: 1) work permit systems; 2) quota system in certain sectors; 3) foreign levy scheme; and 4) internal enforcement. The first two measures, the work permit and quota system, allow the state to adjust the labour supply in each sector and repatriate workers at times of recession, and control the gender and ethnic compositions of its overall migrant labour force and of respective sectors according to Singapore's economic development goals and its relations with the sending countries.[9] The levy scheme aims at discouraging low-skilled labour and gives incentives to semi- and high-skilled labour, as the monthly levy the state charges to employers of low-skilled migrant workers is substantively higher than those of skilled workers, which also constitutes a substantive revenue for the government.[10] The internal enforcement aims at reducing irregular migration, with measures such as regular physical check-ups, heavy financial and psychical penalties to migrants, as well as retraction of welfare benefits of employers or citizens who harbour illegal migrants. By applying these measures, the Singaporean state manages to create an 'internal border' and extends its surveillance throughout its territory. These measures were adopted later by Taiwan and Malaysia with certain variations, on which I will elaborate when I discuss Taiwan's case (see also Garcés-Mascareñas in this volume).

A key element in Singaporean policy that has not been adopted or achieved by other Asian states is a highly sophisticated and stratified permit system that categorizes migrants according to their skill level and income, thus creating a hierarchy of migrants. The residential duration and the political and social rights that a foreigner is entitled to also follow this hierarchy. For instance, Employment Pass holders (professional and high income) are allowed to stay for five years (renewably) and no levy is charged to their employers. The semi-skilled workers (S-pass) are allowed to stay for three years (renewably up to 10 years), and unskilled workers (R-pass) can stay for two years and have to have their pass reviewed annually. Restrictions with respect to certain nationalities are applied to semi-skilled and unskilled workers but not to professionals. In addition, the semi-skilled and high-skilled workers are eligible to apply for a long-term residence permit, while unskilled workers are prohibited to bring their family members, to get pregnant and to marry Singaporean citizens.[11]

---

9   For instance, after the Asian financial crisis in 1997, the number of work permits cancelled rose (Huang and Yeoh 2003).

10   The levy varies according to sectors. The 2001 figure shows that the monthly levy for a skilled worker is S$30 and for an unskilled one S$240–470 (Huang and Yeoh 2003, 81).

11   For a detailed description on the categories of permits and respective restrictions, see Ruppert 1999 (http://ideas.repec.org/p/wbk/wbrwps/2053.html#provider); see also Wong 1997.

Japan: Unwilling Host Resulted in Irregular Migration

Japan's attitude toward immigration and labour migration can be characterized as reluctant and resistant. Before the early 1970s Japan was able to cope with its labour shortage mainly by increasing productivity and by pooling rural and female labour. Due to its demographic transition Japan started to experience chronic labour shortage in the 3D sectors since the early 1970s, yet despite this the government and the corporations chose not to depend on formalized unskilled labour migration except for entertainers from other East- and Southeast-Asian countries, who are categorized as 'skilled labour'. After the 1990 revision of the Immigration Control and Refugee Recognition Act, the Immigration Law allows three channels for the *de facto* entry of unskilled workers, while continuing to receive professionals and skilled labour. The first is the return migration of overseas Japanese and their descendants, the *Nikkeijin*. The second concerns the 'Technical Internship Trainee Program' launched in 1993, which catered for Japanese multinational companies who can recruit trainees for their overseas operations. The third channel is for foreign students who are eligible to work limited hours.[12] These three categories of migrants enjoy different rights and are subjected to different control measures. *Nikkeijin* are given access to residential status with no restriction on employment and economic activities, while the trainees are tied to employers and limited residential periods. This results in a large number of overstaying trainees and students, which constitutes the majority of the migrant labour force. The number of overstayers reached its peak in the early 1990s, amounting to 300,000 in 1993. Since then the government has tightened control, which has reduced the number of irregular migrants to 250,000 in the mid-2000s. The measures of control include, amongst others, stricter examination of the residential status upon entry, strengthening detection and deportation, and investment in detention facilities.[13]

South Korea: From Unwilling Host to Regulatory yet Pro-migrants' Rights Regime

Among the East-Asian states, South Korea undergoes the most dramatic shift in its immigration policies and labour recruitment and management strategies. Compared to Japan and Singapore, South Korea and Taiwan experience labour shortages relatively late in the 1980s. South Korea opted for adopting Japan's trainee program in passively bringing in unskilled workers. The major differences between South Korea's 1991 Industrial Technical Training Program (ITTP) and the Japanese trainee program lie in the sectors and employers. Initially the ITTP was designed for transnational Korean companies for their overseas posts, but

---

12 Athukorala and Manning 1999; Takeyuki and Wayne 2004.

13 For statistics and detailed description of recent control measures, see Kashiwazaki and Akaha 2006 (source: http://www.migrationininformation.org/Feature/print.cfm?ID=487).

later upon the lobby of the Korean Federation of Small Business (KFSB) it was extended to small and medium enterprises.[14] The enterprises who employed trainees were relatively weak economic and political actors in South Korea, as the majority of the Korean economy is supported by large conglomerates (*chaebol*), whose employees are normally unionized native workers, who resisted the hiring of foreign labourers. As a result of the strong native labour movement, the trainee system only applies to small and medium enterprises. The implementation body of the ITTP is the Korea International Training Cooperation Corps (KITCO), composed of KFSB members as well as foreign diplomats. The relatively weak position of the employers versus the labour movement and civil society groups provides a key context of Korea's unique experience in developing a pro-human rights policy at the later stage. The heavy involvement of the government in the labour recruiting process also contributes to a unique model which is different from other East-Asian regimes that rely on private recruitment agencies.

By the mid-1990s, the exploitation of trainees and low-wage workers had contributed to high overstaying or runaway rates and resulted in high numbers of undocumented workers. There were also several high profile protests organized by migrants that won overwhelming support from NGOs, social movements, and the general public. As a response, in 1996 the Foreign Workers' Employment and Human Rights Protection Law was proposed by the Ministry of Labour. However, before the legislative procedure of this law could be completed, South Korea was hit by the Asian financial crisis and the law was not passed. Since then up to 2002, civil society and migrant groups have been pushing for legislation.[15]

The 1997 crisis saw the drastic drop in labour shortage (to a half) and the number of migrant workers. The latter was due to deportation and voluntary repatriation organized by the Korean government. However, in two years' time the number of migrants, both legal and illegal, increased again. The financial crisis also induced a shift in preference towards co-ethnic Koreans, i.e. ethnic Koreans in the PRC and Russia. Before the financial crisis, there were a large number of ethnic Korean Chinese, *Joseonjok*, working in South Korea. However, unlike Japan, Korea did not give privileged residential and working status to ethnic Koreans, though they were favoured in various sectors due to shared language and cultural knowledge. After 1997, the 'Act on Immigration and Legal Status of Overseas Koreans' (the Overseas Korean Act) was proposed (and passed in 1999), which aims at promoting investment of overseas Koreans in their homeland and at encouraging their participation in the economic recovery of Korea. The Act technically excludes ethnic Koreans from China and the former Soviet Union (*Koryoin*) because most of the Koreans there left before the founding of the Republic of Korea in 1948. This exclusion was contested by protests organized by the *Joseonjok* community

---

14   Athukorala and Manning 1999.

15   For detailed description of these protests and support from civil society, see Lim 2003; for analysis of the immigration policies since 1987, see H.-K. Lee 2008.

and civil society groups. Eventually, the article excluding *Joseonjok* and *Koryoin* was ruled unconstitutional by the Constitutional Council in 2001.[16]

Migrants' protests in the mid- and late 1990s as well as the failed legislative process of the 1996 Foreign Workers' Employment and Human Rights Protection Law had a profound impact on how issues of migrant workers are framed in South Korean society. In view of the scale of irregular migration and the exploitative nature of the trainee system, the South Korean government launched a new labour policy: the Employment Permit System (EPS) in 2003. There were several minor policies catering for *Joseonjok* and *Koryoin* between 2002 and 2004 that assigned sectors reserved only for ethnic Koreans. These policies were integrated as one EPS system in 2007. On the surface, the 2007 EPS is a combination of the Singaporean work permit system and the Japanese *Nikkeijin* policy; however, if we take a closer look we discover some fundamental differences. The EPS system, in its design, allows foreign (non-ethnic Korean) workers to work in Korea for a fixed period of time; however, during their stay in Korea they enjoy same wage standard, benefits, protection, and freedom to change employers as native workers.[17] It also aims at reducing exploitation in the recruitment process in that the government agency and counterpart government agency in the sending countries recruit migrants directly. The regulation on ethnic Koreans is much more sophisticated than the Japanese *Nikkeijin* policy, in that different types of visas and permits are issued to ethnic Koreans of different educational and skill levels and with different degrees of kinship ties with Korean citizens.

Appearance of Control in Taiwan

Due to Taiwan's isolation from the international community, its immigration policies are relatively independent from the international human rights and labour conventions. Taiwan applies rules of border control mainly following the state's logics of safeguarding national security and 'population quality'. Currently there are three ways for a foreigner to legally enter and reside in Taiwan more than three months: via a labour contract, marriage or study, where the labour migrants constitute the largest number. Except for student visas, the criteria of labour and marriage migration are ethnic, class and gender specific. Overseas Chinese businessmen enjoy special privileges and can easily get Taiwanese citizenship. Citizens from developed countries (Europe, North America, Australia and Japan) are able to apply for a work permit easily and the marriage immigrants from these

---

16   For a discussion on how the Overseas Korean Act technically excludes the *Joseonjok,* see C. Lee 2003.

17   The clauses that protect migrant workers' equal rights with native workers were retracted and migrants' rights were compromised under the President Lee Myung-bak regime since 2008. See Liem 2010 (http://www.amrc.org.hk/alu_article/all_out_attack_on_migrant_workers_a_look_at_recent_trends_in_south_koreas_policy_on_fore).

regions are not subjected to any restrictive measure.[18] Except for political rights (e.g. voting), at times they enjoy better social welfare provisions than Taiwanese nationals. As a result, they (overseas Chinese and citizens of developed countries) are not subjected to labour migration control.[19] In contrast, citizens of the People's Republic of China (henceforth 'Mainland Chinese') were barred from labour migration until very recently,[20] and Mainland marriage immigrants are subjected to harsher screening and controlling measures than other nationals.

In the mid-1980s Taiwan started to experience a structural labour shortage, which became acute with the implementation of the '14 major State Development Projects' in 1984.[21] Initially the Taiwanese government, like Japan and South Korea, hesitated to recruit foreign workers formally and opted for enlarging the labour pool from the rural areas and the older and younger labour force, and prepared to convene military force to support major state development projects. This resulted in substantive numbers of illegal migrants from Southeast Asia who entered Taiwan with tourist visas and worked in the construction and manufacturing sectors.[22] Under the pressure from the business elite, the Taiwanese government compromised and decided to recruit foreign workers as a 'special project' which aimed at solving temporary labour shortage rather than structural change. In 1989, the quota for migrant workers was opened for application; however, it was not until 1992, with the enactment of the Employment Service Act, that the guest worker policy was officially implemented. The basic principles and procedures are as follows:[23]

- Guest workers are recruited only to supplement and not to replace the native workers. Quotas of migrant workers are industry and sector specific, and are adjusted every year. Table 4.1 shows the change of the quotas by sector. The adjustment of quotas is made according to the deemed demands of the sectors that are supposed to be temporary. The rationale is to help or protect a specific industry for a particular period; however, eventually the industry should be able to stand on its own without employing migrant workers,

---

18   Tseng 2006.

19   Lucy Cheng argues that the definition of 'overseas Chinese' is also class selective in that only the businessmen and tertiary students are welcomed. The lowly educated ethnic Chinese in Southeast Asia, however, fall under the categories of the guest worker and marriage migration schemes and are not considered 'Chinese' in the policy. Cheng 2002.

20   Mainland Chinese in academic, scientific and other high-tech professions can enter Taiwan and 'conduct professional activities' for a certain period time. (Tseng 2006, 96–7). The low-skilled mainland Chinese workers are excluded from the guest worker policy. For the politics and rationale of such exclusion, see Lu 2008, 111–58.

21   For the political and economic contexts of the labour shortage, see Pan 2003, 23–30.

22   It is estimated that by 1988 there were 13,470 overstayed visitors from Southeast Asia, with the majority from Thailand and the Philippines (Pan 2003, 23).

23   J. Lee 2002.

therefore the demand for migrant workers will eventually diminish, so it is assumed. The government first decides on an 'acceptable' total number of migrant workers that Taiwanese society can absorb in a given year and consults the industry representatives, scholars and the labour union (of native workers) to decide on the quotas for each sector/industry. Other than care and domestic workers who are employed by individual families, small companies with less than 10 employees in other sectors are prohibited to employ migrant workers. It is pretty much the game of state enterprises, multi-national companies and major consortium groups.

- Guest workers are recruited on a temporary basis and cannot become permanent immigrants or citizens. They are only allowed to stay for two years and their contracts and residential permits are tied with a specific employer or a recruitment agency. I will elaborate on the mechanisms applied in order to prevent them becoming long-term or permanent immigrants. There is no limitation to staying periods for the white-collar workers and they can change their employers.
- The social cost of guest workers should be minimal. They are not allowed to bring family members, to marry or to get pregnant. Once pregnant the female workers will be deported. Those who are found guilty of committing even a very minor crime will also be immediately deported.
- The numbers of workers from each country are determined by market demand as well as the profit margins of the recruitment agency.[24] Table 4.2 shows the number of workers by the countries of origin over the years.

From these principles it is clear that Taiwan's foreign labour policy is very similar to the Singaporean model. As the policy-making process was not transparent, it remained a puzzle why Taiwan opted for the Singaporean model instead of Japan's and Korea's trainee systems, in view that otherwise Taiwan has been much influenced by Japan due to its colonial past and geo-politics in East Asia. What can be established from the official record is that prior to the 1992 Employment Service Act, the government had commissioned scholars to investigate the guest worker policies in the West, Asia and Middle East. The Chairman of the Council of Labour Affairs (CLA) and legislators embarked on several trips to Southeast Asia to 'learn the experiences from Southeast Asian neighbours'. The report of the study trip to Singapore in 1989 states that Singapore has the most comprehensive

---

24   The migrant workers who are recruited by the agency have to pay a referral fee to the agency, which is different according to the nationality of the workers and the jobs. It is estimated that 67% of foreign workers were recruited by a brokering agency in 1999. The average charge is US$2,241 for each job placement. Thai and Filipino workers pay much more than Indonesians and Malaysians (data from Council of Labour Affairs, quoted by Lee 2002, 57). Those who are recruited by the employers directly (large enterprises) do not have to pay a referral fee. The employers and the brokering agencies have to pay a settlement fee per migrant worker to the government.

Table 4.1   Quota of guest workers by sector in Taiwan, 1991–2007*

Sector/year	1991	1993	1995	1997	1999	2001	2003	2005	2007
Governmental infrastructure	2,999	17,287	35,117	40,138	41,588	29,619	12,747	6,193	5,992
6 industries	--	7,506	6,433	5,875	2,259	208	71	55	50
Care workers	--	1,320	8,902	26,233	67,063	103,780	115,724	141,752	159,702
Domestic work	--	6,205	8,505	12,879	7,730	9,154	4,874	2,263	2,526
Sailor	--	426	1,454	1,144	993	1,249	3,396	3,147	3,786
68 occupations	--	23,837	18,157	17,636	12,785	2,292	387	178	143
73 occupations	--	28,198	20,423	16,107	892	207	158	147	138
Pottery etc.	--	10,409	16,597	19,534	1,438	192	135	117	106
Setting up new plants	--	22,377	34,654	37,018	7,251	459	193	168	153
EPZ Special Projects	--	--	4,813	4,607	467	212	18	6	6
3K Special Projects	--	--	20,537	3,428	146	51	50	45	11,541
Major investment manufacture	--	--	11,089	36,160	67,128	50,520	47,226	40,379	34,705
Major investment construction	--	--	1,095	1,405	2,929	2,502	301	6,087	1,677
7 industries Special Projects	--	--	1,275	3,304	142	17	14	12	9
Manufacture 2-year restructuring	--	--	--	22,928	81,915	93,405	91,728	87,657	83,084
Non high-tech manufacture	--	--	--	--	241	10,361	22,206	36,163	48,236
High-tech manufacture	--	--	--	--	--	377	922	3,027	3,641
Total	2,999	97,565	189,051	248,396	294,967	304,605	300,150	327,396	357,937

* Figures from 1991–2003 are quoted by Lo 2007, 101. Figures in 2005 and 2007 are from EVTA 2005.

Table 4.2   Number of migrant workers by nationality in Taiwan, 1994–2008

	Indonesia	Malaysia	Philippines	Thailand	Vietnam	Mongolia	Total
1994	6,020	2,344	38,473	105,152	--	--	151,989
1995	5,430	2,071	54,657	126,903	--	--	189,051
1996	10,206	1,489	83,630	141,230	--	--	236,555
1997	14,648	736	100,295	132,717	--	--	248,396
1998	22,058	940	114,255	133,367	--	--	270,620
1999	41,224	158	113,928	139,526	--	--	294,967
2000	77,830	113	98,161	142,665	7,746	--	326,515
2001	91,132	46	72,779	127,732	12,916	--	304,605
2002	93,212	35	69,426	111,538	29,473	--	303,684
2003	56,437	27	81,355	104,728	57,603	--	300,150
2004	27,281	22	91,150	105,281	90,241	59	314,034
2005	49,094	13	95,703	98,322	84,185	79	327,396
2006	85,223	12	90,054	92,894	70,536	36	338,755
2007	115,490	11	86,423	86,948	69,043	22	357,937
2008	127,764	11	80,636	75,584	81,060	5	365,060

Source: Employment and Vocational Training Administration, Council of Labour Affairs, Executive Yuan, Taiwan, ROC (2009).

foreign labour policy and recommends Taiwan to follow Singapore's experience. More specifically, it mentions that the control measures of regular medical check-ups, limited durations of permit to stay, security bonds, levies, as well as sector-specific quotas are to be copied. The report also says that Singapore's categories of permits are overcomplicated, and recommends issuing only one type of work permit to low-skilled labour, as 'the professionals need not to be regulated so as to enhance Taiwan's scientific development and international cultural exchange'.[25]

Another factor influencing the policy choice, particularly in identifying the sources (sending countries) and recruitment methods is the lobbying efforts of the sending countries as part of their labour export strategies. The Chairman of the CLA openly acknowledged that government officials together with representatives of recruitment agencies in several sending countries in Southeast Asia had approached him in the mid-1980s. In the preparatory period prior to the 1992 Employment Service Act, he also visited these countries. This was the period when Taiwan was seeking support from neighbouring countries to apply for the GATT membership, and the Foreign Minister had publicly recommended recruiting migrants from Thailand, Indonesia and the Philippines in exchange of the support of these governments for Taiwan's application. Although the actual process of trade negotiation between Taiwan and these states was not made public, and the Chairman of CLA denied that there was diplomatic pressure, he nevertheless acknowledged that the diplomatic relation is one of the considerations in choosing

---

25   Council of Labour Affairs 1989.

sending countries. Eventually, it was decided to recruit migrant workers from four countries, the Philippines, Thailand, Malaysia and Indonesia.[26] The imported quota often becomes the bargaining chip of the diplomatic relations and bilateral trade negotiations between Taiwan and these sending countries in the following years.

As mentioned earlier, these sending countries had developed migrants export regimes and labour-brokering industries. The recruitment procedure in the initial policy design was driven by the existing systems and dominated by the labour recruitment agencies of the sending countries. In the mid-1990s Taiwanese also developed its own (and transnational) labour-brokering industry. Compared with Singapore, Taiwanese government now adopts a liberal attitude in regulating labour brokering agencies, and gives these agencies more power not only to recruit but also to manage migrant workers after they enter the border. As a result, Taiwan develops a unique controlling technique of migrants via recruitment agencies, which I will elaborate in the following sections. The labour recruitment and management agencies become the most exploitative element in the labour regime, which the South Korean regime tries to eliminate while the Taiwanese regime actively embraces it.

Another major difference between guest worker policies in Taiwan, Singapore and South Korea lies in sectors open to migrant labours. Although Taiwan, Singapore and South Korea's Employment Permit System adopt sector-specific quota systems, Singapore's attitude is proactive in supplying labour to more sectors, and it mainly uses the levy system to reduce the dependency. In comparison, Taiwan and South Korea's attitudes are preventive, and their permit and quota systems directly aim at protecting native workers and only recruit migrants in sectors that experiencing extreme labour shortage. Taiwan chooses to recruit migrant labourers in major state and multinational projects as well as in domestic work. Regarding domestic and care work, the chairman of the CLA explains that Taiwan's policy privileges the care work sector in that it does not set a quota in its initial design. Compared with the preventive and passive attitude in setting quotas in all other sectors for a limited period, he states that 'Care work, I remember we are active [in including it], because we discover this [care labour] is a serious problem.'[27] In comparison, South Korea mainly assigns migrant worker quotas to small and medium enterprises, and resisted in recruiting domestic worker and care workers until very recently.

By the end of 2005, there are over 320,000 guest workers working legally in Taiwan, constituting about 3.1% of the total labour force and 9.5% of the low-skilled labour pool in Taiwan.[28] Learning from the experiences of the 'failed' guest worker policies in Europe, the newly industrialized states in Asia are determined to develop schemes that keep foreign workers temporary and to make it difficult

---

26   For detailed description of the policy making process and the positions of different ministries, see Pan 2003, 41–4.

27   Quoted by Pan 2003, 49.

28   EVTA 2005.

for them to overstay.[29] The methods the Taiwanese government employs can be summarized in two aspects: governance at a distance; and disciplines of body and sexuality.

Techniques of Control in Taiwan

Control Mechanism: Governance at a Distance

To ensure that migrant workers stay as temporary migrants, the initial design of the guest worker policy is to implement a very strict two-year contract only for all migrants. Their contracts and residential permits are tied to a specific employer or a recruitment agency. This puts employers in a power position to fire or exploit a worker, leaving the worker with little bargaining power. Many employers prefer to hire workers from the recruitment agencies in order to reduce the cost of management and replacement of workers. In principle it is also more advantageous for a worker to have their contract tied with an agency rather than with a specific employer, in that in case of abuse or unsatisfying working conditions, particularly in the domestic work sector, the worker can go back to the agency and demand changing the employer without having to infringe the contract and return home. However, in reality this seldom happens, for the reasons that the agency virtually always sides with the employers and ignores the complaints of workers, or that workers have to pay a substantial amount of referral fee (see footnote 18) for every job placement. Therefore, when a worker cannot bear the working conditions, they have in practice only two options: 1) to organize a collective protest; or 2) to run away and become illegal. The domestic workers who live in isolated environments and who have minimal bargaining power often opt for the latter.

The two-year contract restriction proved to be too strict and upon the protest of the employers it became possible to extend for another year. After the Taiwanese regime change in 2000, it was further relaxed that upon the request of the employers it became possible for 'the migrant workers of good character' first of all to return home after completing the three-year term and then reapply to come back to the same employer for another three-year term. But after the total six-year term it is not possible to reapply again.[30] This relaxed system is coupled with a tighter and coordinated control, implemented in such a way that the authorities[31] coordinate the employment record and immigration information (entry into and exit out of

---

29   Cf. Yaw 2002; Tseng and Wang (forthcoming).

30   Cf. J. Lee 2002, 59–60.

31   Various governmental authorities are involved and coordinating in such operations: Council of Labour Affairs; Immigration office in the airport; police offices in local governments with the cooperation of recruitment agencies; and even the employers' representative group, Chinese National Federation of Industries (Tseng and Wang, forthcoming).

Taiwan) so that the workers, upon completing the six-year term, will not be able to enter Taiwan (not even with a tourist visa).

The adjustment of the quota, its categorization and six-year contract are not designed to take into consideration the needs of the individual employers or industries. Oftentimes it is more advantageous for employers to retain the workers. However, if an employer wishes to retain a worker, he or she will have to pay a higher price to reapply for the same worker, and after six years it will not be possible at all. When employers desire to hire the same workers and retention is not an option, the only possible way is for migrants to use a fake passport to enter Taiwan. Despite the preference of retaining the domestic worker, those who are cared for, either children or the elderly, have no decision making power. In addition, the employers of domestic workers, though in large number, are not an organized influential political force to challenge the limited quota and six-year-contract regulations.

According to at least one labour recruitment agency, using fake passports is not uncommon among Indonesians and Vietnamese but rare for Filipinos, Thai and Malaysians.[32] The fact that the agency can talk about it openly reveals that it is an open secret that the authorities are probably aware of yet turn a blind eye on. There are no statistical data on how widespread the practice of entry with fake passports is, and the government does not make any effort to prevent it or to penalize the offenders (both migrants and agencies). As a consequence, the figure of entry with fake passports is not reflected in the statistics of illegal or irregular migration. As far as the Taiwanese government is concerned, the workers holding a passport, real or fake, are considered regulated legal migrants. The main concern of the Taiwanese government is migrant workers' overstaying or 'running away' (from the employers or agencies that the contracts specify) before their terms of employment expire. In the late 1990s, the rate of runaway workers was very high, and it is estimated that 30% of the employing companies had runaway workers.[33] To solve this problem, the government initially adopted a reward system that gave bonuses to policemen who caught runaway workers. This system did not work effectively. Eventually the government developed a system that delegates the responsibility of ensuring that migrant workers actually leave the country to employers and agencies, which Tseng and Wang term the 'governance at a distance' system. If a worker runs away or overstays, his or her employer will be penalized by not being able to replace the quota. The employer will therefore lose one unit of productive labour force. All the recruitment agencies are evaluated annually and classified into A, B, and C categories, and among the evaluation criteria, the 'escape rate' is the most important one. The more workers recruited by a particular agency overstay or run away, the higher risk this agency runs of losing its license. This is why retaining, despite its economic advantages for both employers and

---

32 Participant observation in July 2002 in Taichung, Taiwan, where I worked as an intern in a recruitment agency.

33 According to CLA report 2000, quoted by J. Lee 2002, 58.

migrants, is not an option. This kind of 'governance at a distance' proves to be more effective than rewarding policemen or charging fines to employers.

Employers and agencies developed various surveillance mechanisms to ensure that a worker does not overstay or run away. These mechanisms are employed by the agencies themselves, so on the surface the government can wash its hands clean. However, taking a close look at the operations, we discover that they are encouraged and supported by the government. One of the most effective mechanisms is the 'deposit' policy introduced in 1998, which gives the employers the rights to deduct up to 30% of the monthly salary of workers and deposit it into a saving account. Workers are not allowed to withdraw the money until their term of employment terminates and they have to leave the country. This arrangement is formalized in the labour contract. By 1999, an estimated 83.26% of employers in the manufacturing industries and 70.3% in the construction industries had utilized such a system.[34] This measure further increases the power of the employers and opportunities of exploiting workers, as in some cases the employers simply refused to return the money to workers, or the money 'disappeared' in between administrative and accounting procedures. Many individual employers of domestic workers consider this system beneficial to workers because 'we help them to save money so they don't spend it on useless things [pretty dresses]. They come all the way to work and save money to send home, isn't it?'[35]

Other surveillance mechanisms include keeping a worker's passport; and picking up workers from the working place and escorting them directly to the airport. In short, from the moment the workers get their deposit money, they are under strict surveillance until they step into the plane. Under such strict surveillance, the airport became the last place for escape. It is estimated that an average of 20–30 workers ran off and disappeared from the airport every month in 2004–5.[36] In 2006 a new measure was introduced to eliminate the opportunity of workers' escape in the airport. Service counters were set up in the arrival and departure halls of international airports by the Chinese National Federation of Industries, which is an employers' association. This project is sponsored by the Council of Labour Affairs. Although the CLA promotes this project as protection of migrant workers' human rights as the last opportunity for workers to file complaints to their employers, in the official news release of the opening of this project it is stated that the main purpose of these counters is to prevent migrant workers from running away upon arrival or departure.[37] Special personnel are assigned to accompany and guide workers in groups to pass the passport control and see to it that they board on the flight; or vice versa, see to it that they are at the hand of their recruitment agency upon arrival. In the whole process the workers are requested to carry a Foreign

---

34   Source: CLA report 2000, 8, quoted by Lee 2002, 58.

35   My fieldwork observation in Baihe, Southern Taiwan in November, 2003. Lan records the same reaction from employers (Lan 2006).

36   Source: Airport patrol office, quoted by Tseng and Wang (forthcoming).

37   Cf. Tseng and Wang (forthcoming).

Worker's ID and wear special clothing which looks like prisoner garment. Such an operation can be compared with a high-security guarded operation of transporting criminals or repatriation. Though the workers have done nothing wrong and did not commit any crime, they are treated as suspects or criminals the moment they arrive in Taiwan.

In the case of workers who give up the deposit money and run away, the recruitment agencies often attempt to 'catch them' and send them back to their home country, so that they will be counted as persons who voluntarily terminated their contract rather than 'escapees'. In such cases the workers lose all the deposit money.

Control Mechanisms: Disciplines of Body and Sexuality

The process of disciplines of body and sexuality starts before migrants arrive in Taiwan. As part of the recruitment procedure migrants receive physical and psychological evaluations, which is standardized by the sending states. Lan also documents the disciplining practice in the training centres in the sending countries that de-sexualize rural women and turn them into ideal maids, what Rudnyckyj calls 'technologies of servitude'.[38] After arrival, Taiwanese agencies also facilitate the periodical health check-ups of migrants. The physical check-up is mandatory prior to entry as part of the application procedure. Upon arrival, the migrants will be checked again by Taiwanese doctors and then periodically re-examined in Taiwanese hospitals. Ensuring all workers receive periodical check-ups is part of the evaluation of the recruitment agency; a task that the agency takes seriously lest they might lose their business license.

The rationale of frequent physical check-ups originates from the fear of sexually transmitted diseases (STD), HIV and other epidemic diseases. However, tourists, expatriates and foreign businessmen are not subjected to frequent check-ups and only migrant workers are singled out as high-risk groups. As Tseng points out, this selective criterion is not empirically grounded, and Lee argues that migrant workers are among the low-risk group of diseases.[39] Nevertheless, the governmental reports issued by the public health authorities constantly point their finger at migrant workers and marriage migrants from Southeast Asia and China whenever there is a potential outbreak of epidemics, and publish statistics or reports of individual cases of infected migrants. Despite the fact that these statistics fail to establish a real public threat caused by migrants, such reporting creates public alarm and reinforces negative images toward them, and thus justifies the need to exercise control over migrants' bodies.[40]

Using Foucault's concept of 'bio-power', Tseng and Wang identify four types of treatments of foreigners' bodies with which the Taiwanese government

---

38 Lan, 2006; Rudnyckyj 2004.
39 Tseng 2006; J. Lee 2002.
40 Cf. Tseng and Wang (forthcoming).

exercises different degrees of bio-power. Firstly, international businessmen, professionals and expatriates in multi-national companies are exempted from any health check-ups even prior to entry. The second category applies to employers from developed countries, who are required to submit the physical check-up reports while applying for a work permit and are to be re-examined when they renew the permit. Thirdly, migrant workers in general, as I have described above, are subjected to periodical check-ups. They are deported if they fail to comply with this regulation or when they are found to be the carrier of above-mentioned bacteria or viruses. The fourth type of bio-power is exercised specifically with respect to female migrant workers in order to prevent them from getting pregnant. It is compulsory for all female workers to do pregnancy tests prior to entry as part of the check-ups. After arrival they are immediately re-examined in suspicion of previous records being falsified. In women's labour contracts it is specified that they cannot become pregnant. In the earlier regulation, they were to be deported immediately once they were found pregnant, regardless of whether or not the father was a Taiwanese citizen. Upon the protest of human rights and migrant groups, in the revised regulation, immediate deportation is no longer mandated;[41] however, pregnant female workers are considered to have infringed their contract. They are likely to be kept in a detention centre until the baby is born. Both mother and child would then be deported unless the father (Taiwanese citizen) claims the custody of the child. The mother will still be deported. As mentioned earlier, the mechanisms of discipline of the female body through medical surveillance and prevention of pregnancy are copied from the Singapore regime. Today Singapore still applies these harsh mechanisms to female migrants, to the extent that in the work contract it states that low-skilled female migrants are not allowed to marry Singaporean citizens. Procreating bodies are treated as diseased bodies and considered illegal, illegitimate and subject to immediate deportation.[42]

Taiwan exercises the *jus sanguinis* principle in its Nationality Law, that is, the nationality of the Republic of China is inherited from the parents, particularly the father.[43] The purpose of preventing female workers from becoming pregnant is not excluding them or the child from obtaining citizenship, as a foreigner can only become a Taiwanese citizen by marriage. The purpose of pregnancy prevention is to reduce the social cost of health care and welfare provisions even during the short period of pregnancy, to prevent them from developing strong ties with Taiwanese citizens, and to discourage them to become the wife or mother of Taiwanese.

---

41   Guideline of Employment of Foreigners, Article 16, CLA, revised in September 2001.

42   Huang and Yeoh 2003.

43   Cf. L. Chen 2005.

4.3: Number of Illegal Migrant Workers: A Success Story?

As a result of the above-mentioned controlling mechanisms, the number of illegal migrant workers, defined as overstaying or runaway, is actually very low, as compared to neighbouring countries in East Asia. In 1995, the percentage of illegal migrants against the total number of guest workers of the year was 6.7% in Taiwan. By 1998, as Table 4.3 shows, it had dropped to 1.8% and stayed below 2% until 2001. In both absolute and relative numbers, illegal migrant workers in Taiwan are far less numerous than in Japan and South Korea.

Taiwan can be considered to be a success story in managing guest workers and in preventing them from becoming irregular migrants, from the perspective of the state. The techniques of 'governance at a distance' adopted by the Taiwanese government proves to be effective. These mechanisms are implemented at the cost of the harsh working conditions and living experiences of the migrant workers, whose basic human rights are ignored and who are subjected to multiple surveillance mechanisms. Despite the lack of evidence that migrant workers pose health and security threats to Taiwanese society, various governmental authorities continue to conduct surveys and release reports regularly to alarm the general public. For instance, a government commissioned report states that the rate of crime committed by migrant workers is very low; however, it concludes that this is the result of their long-working hours, implying that migrants do not have time to commit crimes, not because they do not want to.[44] Such essentialized opinions

Table 4.3   Number and percentage of 'disappeared' migrant workers by country of origin in Taiwan

	Indonesia		Philippines		Thailand		Vietnam		Total of the year		Total number 'on the run'
	No.	%	No.	%	No.	%	No.	%	No.	%	
1998	493	2.8	2,450	2.3	1,728	1.3	--	--	4,689	1.8	6,646
1999	760	2.5	1,882	1.6	1,403	1.0	--	--	4.057	1.4	5,504
2000	1,680	2.9	1,303	1.2	1,234	0.9	35	0.7	4,288	1.4	5,514
2001	2,804	3.2	1,048	1.2	942	0.7	293	2.8	5,089	1.6	6,220
2002	3,809	4.0	643	0.9	1,042	0.9	1,584	7.8	7,079	2.3	8,143
2003	3,411	4.6	873	1.2	1,171	1.1	4,233	9.6	9,688	3.2	11,125
2004	1,978	4.9	1,177	1.4	1,369	1.3	7,536	10.2	12,060	4.0	16,593

Source: Council of Labour Affairs, 2003*
* As quoted by Lo 2007, 39. The terms 'disappeared migrant workers' and 'total number on the run' are used by the original reports. Percentage = 100% × disappeared number (of workers from a given country)/total number (of migrant labourers from this country). Total number 'on the run' = accumulated number deducting the ones being caught and deported.

---

44   See CRD 1999, 23–4.

and interpretations are visible in popular discourses and policies, which serve as justifications for governmentality. As a result all migrants are treated as would-be criminals. The presence of guest workers itself is an irregularity that the authorities cannot live without, but would try their best to contain while they are here, and to make sure they go away.

Concluding Remarks

In the overview of migrant labour regimes in East Asia, it can be established that the design of labour migration regimes is inspired by neighbouring countries in Asia rather than experiences in the West. The initiatives were taken by individual states rather than imposed by the international norms; however, the existing labour-exporting regimes play an important role in lobbying for their migrants. This is clearly demonstrated in the cases of Singapore, Malaysia, Taiwan and later South Korea. Other than the lobby of sending countries, the criteria of migrant labour recruited for specific sectors are ethnic and gender selective, with Japan and Korea favouring their co-ethnics, while Taiwan discouraging it; with Singapore and Taiwan actively recruiting domestic workers and care workers, while Japan and Korea passively allowing their co-ethnics to work in these sectors.

From this overview I hope to raise the question and partially answer it why these states that share similar macro-structural factors such as an export-oriented economy, demographic transitions, and strong and efficient state machinery, adopt very different strategies in coping with labour shortage and controlling migrant workers. Each state develops its own control mechanism as a result of domestic politics and the degree of complying with international norms. The state's attitude towards migrant labour determines how the issue and problem of control is framed; however, they can also be contested by the migrants' resistance and reactions from the civil society, which have international human rights mechanisms at their disposal. South Korea's EPS is an example of migrants and supporting civil society groups' successfully influencing policy directions. This leads to another question why the migrant group and civil society in Taiwan and other East Asian countries are not able to achieve the same level of influence.

Taiwan has shifted from fairly loose labour controls to a highly regulative and efficient migration labour regime within a short period. It can be considered a success story in managing guest workers and in preventing them from becoming irregular migrants, from the perspective of the state. It adopts the Singaporean model of guest worker policy, in categorizing high-skilled and low-skilled workers and in applying techniques of disciplining the body and sexuality of low-skilled ones. However, due to the combination of factors such as sectors (state-owned and large enterprises) and privatization of recruitment and management, it develops a distinct technique of control: governance at a distance via recruitment agencies and employers. This strict regulative regime was not uncontested, as it contradicts the interests of individual employers and violates migrants' human rights. However, individual employers and migrants are not able to influence the policy and public discourse on migration control as compared to industrial employers and other political actors.

Bibliography

Athukorala, P.-C. and Manning, C. 1999. *Structural Change and International Migration in East Asia: Adjusting to Labour Scarcity*. Oxford and New York: Oxford University Press.

Bigo, D. 2002. Security and Immigration: Toward a Critique of the Governmentality of Unease, *Alternatives/Cultures & Conflicts*, 27, 63–92.

Boyd, R. and Ngo, T.-W. (eds) 2005. *Asian States: Beyond the Developmental Perspective*. London: Routledge.

Castles, S. and Alastair, D. 2002. *Citizenship and Migration: Globalization and the Politics of Belonging*. New York: Palgrave.

CDV (Commission of Research and Development, Executive Yuan). 1999. *Research Report on Problems of Management of Foreign Workers*. Taipei: CDV.

Cheng, L. 2002. Guest Workers, Citizenship and Nation-building Ideology, *Taiwan: A Radical Quarterly in Social Studies*, 48, 14–46.

Cornelius, W., Tsuda, T., Martin, P. and Hollifield, J. (eds) 1994. *Controlling Immigration: A Global Perspective*. Stanford: Stanford University.

Council of Labour Affairs, ROC. 1989. *Study Trip Report of Singapore's Foreign Labour Management*. Taipei: ROC, August.

EVTA (Employment and Vocational Training Bureau, Council of Labour Affairs, ROC). 2005. *Employers' Survey on the Use of Foreign Workers*. Taipei: EVTA.

Huang, S. and Yeoh, B.S.A. 2003. The Difference Gender Makes: State Policy and Contract Migrant Workers in Singapore, *Asian and Pacific Migration Journal* 12(1–2), 75–97.

Hugo, G. and Stahl, C. 2004. Labour Export Strategies in Asia, in *International Migration: Prospects and Policies in a Global Market*, edited by D. Massey and J.E. Taylor. Oxford: Oxford University Press, 174–200.

Kashiwazaki, C. and Akaha, T. 2006. *Japanese Immigration Policy: Responding to Conflicting Pressures*. http://www.migrationinformation.org/Feature/display. cfm?id=487, dowloaded on 18 October 2010.

Kaur, A. 2006. Order (and disorder) at the Border: Mobility, International Labour Migration and Border Controls in Southeast Asia', in *Mobility, Labour Migration and Border Controls in Asia*, edited by A. Kaur and I. Metcalfe. New York: Palgrave Macmillan, 23–51.

Lan, P.-c. 2006. *Global Cinderellas: Migrant Domestics and Newly Rich Employers in Taiwan*. Durham and London: Duke University Press.

Lee, C. 2003. 'Us' and 'Them' in Korean Law: The Creation, Accommodation and Exclusion of Outsiders in South Korea, in *East Asian Law: Universal Norms and Local Cultures*, edited by A. Rosett, L. Cheng and M.Y.K. Woo. Curzon: Routledge, 106–36.

Lee, H.-K. 2008. The Shift in Immigration Policy Towards Expansion and Inclusion in South Korea, *Korean Journal of Sociology*, 42(2), 104–37.

Lee, J. 2002. The Role of Low-skilled Foreign Workers in the Process of Taiwan's Economic Development, in *Migrant Workers in Pacific Asia*, edited by A. Yaw and I. Debrah. Portland: Frank Cass & Co., 41–66.

Liem, W.-s. 2010. *All-out Attack on Migrant Workers: A Look at Recent Trends in South Korea's Policy on Foreign Labour*. Asian Monitor Resource Centre website, 1 March (http://www.amrc.org.hk/alu_article/all_out_attack_on_migrant_workers_a_look_at_recent_trends_in_south_koreas_policy_on_fore).

Lim, T.C. 2003. Racing From the Bottom in South Korea? The Nexus between Civil Society and Transnational Migrants, *Asian Survey*, 43(3), 423–42.

Lo, C.-C. 2007. *Taiwan Waiji Laogong Yenjiou* (*Studies on Foreign Workers in Taiwan*). Taipei: Institute of Economics, Academia Sinica.

Lu, M.C.-W. 2008. *Gender, Marriage and Migration: Contemporary Marriages between Mainland China and Taiwan*. PhD dissertation, Leiden University, the Netherlands.

Massey, D. 1994. *Space, Place and Gender*. Minneapolis: University of Minnesota Press.

Morris, L. 1998. Governing at a Distance: The Elaboration of Controls in British Immigration, *International Migration Review*, 32(4), 949–73.

Pan, S.-w. 2003. *The Making of the Foreign Labour Policy – Analysis of Policy Network*. MA Thesis, Graduate School of Labour Studies, National Chung-Cheng University, Taiwan.

Rudnyckyj, D. 2004. Technologies of Servitude: Governmentality and Indonesian Transnational Labour Migration, *Anthropological Quarterly*, 77(3), 407–34.

Ruppert, E. 1999. *Managing Foreign Labour in Singapore and Malaysia: Are there Lessons for GCC Countries?* The World Bank Policy Research Working Paper Series no. 2053 (http://ideas.repec.org/p/wbk/wbrwps/2053.html#provider).

Skeldon, R. 2000. *Myths and Realities of Chinese Irregular Migration*. Consultant Report for International Organization for Migration. Geneva: IOM.

Tsay, C.-l. 1992. Clandestine Labour Migration to Taiwan, *Asian and Pacific Migration Journal*, 637–56.

Tseng, Y.-f. 2006. Who Can Be Us? Class Selection in Immigration Policy, *Taiwan: A Radical Quarterly in Social Studies*, 61, 73–105.

Tseng, Y,-f. and Wang, H.-z. Forthcoming. Governing Migrant Workers at a Distance: Effective Governmentality to Keep Guestworkers Status Temporary in Taiwan, *International Migration Review*.

Tsuda, T. and Cornelius, W. 2004. Controlling Immigration: The Limits of Government Intervention, in *Controlling Immigration: A Global Perspective*

(Second Edition), edited by W.A. Cornelius, T. Tsuda, P.L. Martin and J.F. Hollifield. Stanford: Stanford University Press, 3–48.

Wang, H.-z. and Bélanger, D. 2008. Taiwanizing Female Immigrant Spouses and Materializing Differential Citizenship, *Citizenship Studies*, 12(1), 91–106.

Wong, D. 1997. Transience and Settlement: Singapore's Foreign Labour Policy, *Asian and Pacific Migration Journal*, 6(2), 135–67.

Woo-Cumings, M. 1999. *The Developmental State*. Ithaka, NY: Cornell University Press.

Wu, H.-l. and Wang, S.-w. 2002. The Trend in Foreign Workers, Economic Linkage and Policy in Taiwan, *Journal of Population Studies*, 22, 49–70.

Yaw, A. Debrah. 2002. Introduction: Migrant Workers in Asia Pacific, in *Migrant Workers in Pacific Asia*, edited by A. Debrah Yaw. Portland: Frank Cass & Co., 1–18.

Yoon, In Jin. 2008. *Multicultural Policies and Programs of South Korea: The Role of the State and Civil Society*. Paper presented at the 2008 Sociology faculty seminar at Korea University, Seoul, July 18.

Chapter 5

Implications for Policy Discourse: The Influx of Zimbabwean Migrants into South Africa

Mark Nyandoro

Summary

South Africa has been a major destination for forced immigrants from across Africa, but more so from Zimbabwe. The major 'push factors' for these migrants range from wars, political persecution to serious poverty, hyper-inflationary trends and unemployment whilst the 'pull factors' to which members of poor households are responding include, *inter alia*, the relatively higher standard of living and the 'promise' of better job opportunities in South Africa. This chapter's main hypothesis is that the influx of big numbers of irregular economic migrants or refugees from Zimbabwe into South Africa since independence in 1994 has revealed major immigration policy limitations on the part of the state, regional actors and intergovernmental agencies. Clearly, the imperativeness of a more coordinated and coherent response across states, agencies and policy fields cannot be over-emphasized.

This chapter will examine whether the policy boundaries in the recipient country need to be configured or re-configured to regularly manage the huge influx and the attendant levels of social protection required for both lawful and illicit labour migrants. In the process, the reaction of the South African government, which wavers between 'soft' and draconian, can be used as an important benchmark in analysing the state's capacity to promote policies that help maximize the benefits and minimize the risks and cost of migration to itself as well as for the poor and vulnerable people and other migrants. The chapter will draw from various methodological approaches in enhancing the discussion on transforming the boundaries of policy areas in order to either build stronger border controls and 'fortresses' or promote the free-movement for all.

Introduction

Labour migration control claims and the debate around population movement in Southern Africa are not peculiar phenomena to Zimbabwe and South Africa.

Issues of labour migration can be explored from an interdisciplinary and multi-facetted perspective involving the world's five or six major continents. However, this chapter pays particular attention to the frictions which arise inside South Africa as a result of the political capital invested in very light border controls at the South Africa–Zimbabwe border in Beitbridge. A major point of departure in this chapter is the analysis of the traditional pattern of migration in Southern Africa as circular depending on the migrant worker accumulating sufficient income to move home. It also belies some of the American approaches around 'push-pull factors' which result in claims that all migration is permanent.[1] Literature on Southern Africa by Mlambo,[2] Kok, Gelderbom, Oucho and Van Zyl[3] reveal that in the region the 'mobility transition' patterns as postulated by Zelinsky[4] were never quite interrupted. Kok and other scholars offer insights into contemporary issues pertaining to migration in South and Southern Africa, focusing on the changes in patterns of migration. While scholars such as Cross, Mngadi and Themba[5] believe that circular migration is in decline, Ndegwa, Horner and Esau[6] as well as Gaidzanwa[7] believe that it is highly ubiquitous. The movement of Zimbabwean regular or irregular migrants to South Africa which became more commonplace in the 1990s than in earlier decades demonstrates that circular migration is animate. However much of the research on Southern African labour migration control shows that there has been little serious engagement on circular migration and its implications for policy discourse. The author has, therefore, identified this as a gap that needs to be filled.

It can be noted that since its independence in 1994 South Africa has been made to contend with the huge and phenomenal influx of both regular and unlawful migrants from Zimbabwe. Not only did it have to deal with immigrants from its Southern African neighbour but also from other countries across the entire spectrum of the African continent. However, a significant proportion of either economic migrants or refugees come from Zimbabwe – a situation that seems to have been compounded by the recent South African government decision in May 2009 to scrap off visa requirements for Zimbabwean visitors to the country. A major loophole in policy discourse has been the apparent failure by the government of South Africa to balance its earlier controversial policy of quiet diplomacy or constructive engagement towards Zimbabwe during President Thabo Mbeki's administration with the imperative to plug the glaringly loose border controls at the Beitbridge entrepot. Border controls which had been kept relatively intact for security reasons

---

1   For detail on this see Durand, Malone and Douglas 2003; Borjas 2007; and Borjas 1995.
2   Mlambo 2008.
3   Kok, Gelderbom, Oucho and Van Zyl 2007.
4   Zelinsky 1971.
5   Cross, Mngadi and Themba 1998.
6   Ndegwa, Horner and Esau 2004.
7   Gaidzanwa 1999.

during Apartheid have been flaccid since the coming of independence to the Republic.[8] The former President's lacklustre response to the Zimbabwean crisis transcending a decade, coupled with the rather inept management of the border is primarily responsible for unleashing numerous documented and undocumented aliens into South Africa.

This chapter project on migration and mobility in Southern Africa has been prompted by, among other things, the state of affairs in Zimbabwe and the xenophobic violence that hit South Africa in May 2008 whose reincarnation has been witnessed during the service-delivery remonstrations that rocked Balfour in Mpumalanga Province and other isolated centres of the Republic in late July 2009.[9] It is also tied in to larger issues of the way water, housing and other service delivery issues impact borders and thus regional politics. The chapter discusses the circumstances informing the process of migration between Zimbabwe and South Africa from 1994 to 2009. Furthermore, it locates migratory patterns in the Southern African region in historical perspective by emphasizing why South Africa has virtually maintained an 'open-door' policy regarding migrant labour, inflows of refugees and other people intending to come into the country since time immemorial.

All types of migration seem to have implications on cheap labour supply for the Republic's relatively more advanced industrial sector on the continent. In fact, South Africa's desire to have tighter border controls in the face of economic turmoil in particular in her northern neighbour (Zimbabwe) is often overshadowed by the labour imperative and concerns which are not exclusively confined to the need to maintain cordial relationships pre-dating the two countries' liberation struggles. The inflow of people either as labourers, shoppers or traders has therefore been quite a regular and accepted phenomenon. Nevertheless, from a resource point of view the government of South Africa seems to be over-stretched and seriously lacking capacity to deal with this situation. The magnitude of the challenge especially in a world in recession mode calls not only for a mere understanding of the shifting paradigms of migration control but also for a synchronized and coherent response across states, agencies and policy fields.

The chapter argues that the policy boundaries in South Africa as the recipient country need to be re-configured in an attempt to manage an influx of people which continues to escalate due to socio-economic and political instability in Zimbabwe. Zimbabwe which is arguably the largest sending country has experienced a decade-long crisis of major proportions. Besides, the installation on 15 September 2008 of the nascent Global Political Agreement (GPA)-brokered Government of National

---

8   In this chapter, unless otherwise stated, the word 'Republic' will be used to refer to the Republic of South Africa.

9   Xenophobia or Negrophobia as it is known in certain circles, is an extreme form of discrimination and a serious threat to democratic principles and values. South Africa can only hope that xenophobia is not a reincarnation of the country's divided and fractured past. For detail on this see Nyandoro 2008a, 24.

Unity (GNU) comprising the former ruling party, the Zimbabwe African National Union-Patriotic Front (ZANU-PF) and the two separate MDC formations led by Morgan Tsvangirai and Arthur Mutambara, has not positively and significantly impacted on the economy to ameliorate the plight of disadvantaged communities in the country. This less privileged category of people has always perceived South Africa as a paradise and their entry into the country has persisted unabated over a long historical period. For a number of undocumented people among this group it has never been very difficult to slip into the Republic due to fluid border controls or the sheer absence of 'fortresses'. Even proponents of 'Fortress South Africa' have been sceptical about the costs and South Africa's effectiveness in sealing the borders.[10]

The lack of 'fortresses' was probably intended to facilitate the free-movement of all peoples as enshrined in the United Nations (UN) Charter. For example, the Universal Declaration of Human Rights which was adopted and proclaimed by the United Nations General Assembly resolution 217 A (III) of 10 December 1948, in particular, recognizes in its preamble that the inherent dignity and of the equal and inalienable rights of all members of the human family is the foundation of freedom, justice and peace in the world.[11] This also entitled all people to the right to migration and mobility. The two Southern African Development Community (SADC) neighbours, Zimbabwe and South Africa, according to the latter's Labour Minister, Membathisi Mdladlana, actually subscribe to the 'free movement of labour in the region'.[12] This resolution among other things offers international protection to the migrant who is endeavouring to eke out a living in otherwise very adverse foreign labour conditions.

Writings on migrant labour in Southern Africa suggest that labour migrants and their families regard labour migration as a stage in a man's life through which he hopes to accumulate wealth to invest in agriculture. In his influential work on migrant labour in Lesotho, Colin Murray has argued that 'the paradigm of the successful migrant career for a man is to establish his own household and to build up a capital base, through the acquisition of land, livestock and equipment, to enable him to retire from migrant labour and to maintain an independent livelihood at home'.[13] Several scholars, including the author of this chapter contend that the process of labour migration is responsible for ploughing cash back into the sending communities.[14] Furthermore for M.S. Das, with specific reference to African students migrating to the United States of America (USA), people tend to migrate

---

10   Bernstein, Schlemmer and Simkins 1997, at http://www.cde.org.za/article.php?a_ id=152, accessed on 15 September 2009.

11   UN 2006.

12   Membathisi Mdladlana, South African Labour Minister cited in Muleya 2009 at http://www1.herald.co.zw/inside.aspx?sectid=9272&cat=1, accessed on 28 August 2009.

13   Murray 1981, 41.

14   Mark Nyandoro 2008b.

from one area to another to improve their socio-economic status.[15] However, there seems to be a dynamic and on-going process of status determination because once one crosses a state border the individual is no longer a citizen but a migrant. Consequently, one region's citizens may be another region's labour migrants.

In the main, the movement of people from one place to another can be divided into forced and voluntary migration, but whether it is forced or intended migration the process has had its positive and adverse effects. The positive contribution of foreign labour to the growth and development of the South African state's farming and mining industries is well documented. To address the deleterious consequences of immigration to South Africa, it is argued, the government of the Republic needs to put up social security measures to help alleviate the impact. On a broader scale, SADC countries should adopt policies on managing migration and social integration processes in the region. This is so because Zimbabwean migrants are not only settling in South Africa. They end up in other regional and continental destinations. In light of the fact that the whole of Africa could face more social instability and increased incidences of migration especially to South Africa due to rising poverty, bilateral and other collaborative mechanisms are necessary in controlling the movement of people. This is particularly so because more than any other country in the region, South Africa's comparatively higher industrial development and better standard of living has enhanced and maintained historically existing migration trends. In view of this, the chapter ends with an evaluation of the implications for policy discourse of the influx of migrants into South Africa especially from Zimbabwe.

The Influx of Migrants into South Africa: Past and Present

Accounting for the influx of Zimbabwean and other migrants into South Africa has been one of the major preoccupations of migration scholars in recent years. There are a multiplex of factors which can be used to explain migration. These include but they are not restricted to reasons such as running away from religious or political persecution, famine, war and unemployment. M.S. Das, for example, divides the factors that motivate people to emigrate into 'push and pull factors'. He is in favour of a 'theory that suggests that circumstances at the place of origin (such as political crises, persecutions, poverty and unemployment) repel or push people out of [their home country] to other places that exert a positive attraction or pull (such as a high standard of living, better job opportunities and/or greater income)'.[16] The latter induce and reinforce trends towards settling permanently in the receiving country.

---

15 Das 1974, 74.

16 Most migrants have been lured by relatively higher standards of living in the recipient countries. For detail on this see Das 1974, 74–83.

Historically labour migration was propelled, among other things, by the South African gold and diamond discoveries of the late 19th century on the Witwatersrand and Kimberly mines respectively. The dire need for cheap labour led to massive recruitment of workers by an agency called the Witwatersrand Native Labour Association (WNLA or WENELA) in South Africa.[17] Since 1894 the need to raise money for various forms of tax, ranging from hut, dog, cattle and poll taxes, which were primarily instituted to procure African labour for European-owned enterprises, had forced many Southern Rhodesian[18] men including migrants from Northern Rhodesia (now Zambia), Nyasaland (Malawi) and Portuguese East Africa (Mozambique) to search for work on the white farms and mines in the Republic. Voluntary and forced migration which dates back to the rush for gold and diamond was the precursor to the rapid movement of people since the end of Apartheid. For Zimbabwe, economic collapse reflected through massive retrenchments, joblessness, the flight of medical professionals and exorbitant hikes in school fees following the implementation of the Economic Structural Adjustment Programme (ESAP) in 1991[19] and subsequently the grave socio-economic and political conundrum dating back to the late 1990s combined to lead to an escalation of both licit and illicit migrants into South Africa and to a lesser extent into Botswana. The adoption of controversial agrarian reforms in 2000[20] exacerbated Zimbabwe's economic meltdown. The country's once revered agrarian, manufacturing and industrial sectors collapsed. With it, education, health and other social services including the aquatic infrastructure also capitulated culminating in unprecedented outbreaks of water-borne diseases such as diarrhoea and cholera.[21] The most recent outbreaks of cholera in the period from August 2008 to the first quarter of 2009 bear testimony to a faltering health situation. As already indicated the cholera dimension was not the only dynamic that influenced migration to South Africa. Comparatively, incomes in Zimbabwe as the home country of most of the immigrants are relatively much lower than in South Africa and this makes a

---

17   Van Onselen 1976. See also Webster 1978; and *The Rhodesia Herald*, 4 August 1900. WENELA's counterpart in colonial Zimbabwe was a specially created labour recruitment agency, the Rhodesia Native Labour Bureau (RNLB). According to Van Onselen in his book entitled: *Chibaro*, this agency was responsible for recruiting 'chibaro' or forced labour for the white mines and farms.

18   Southern Rhodesia was the colonial name of the independent state of Zimbabwe.

19   For detail on the deleterious impact of ESAP on Zimbabwe see Mlambo 1997, xi; Mlambo and Pangeti 2001, 163; Nyambara 1999 and Gaidzanwa 1999.

20   Sachikonye 2003.

21   Nyandoro 2009, unpublished; Australian Government, Department of Health and Ageing 2008, at http://www.health.gov.au/internet/main/publishing.nsf/Content/ohp-surv-isr-2508.htm, accessed on 18 February 2009; Fleming, IFRC 2008 at http://www.ifrc.org/Docs/News/pr08/7608.asp, accessed on 19 Feburary 2009; WHO 2009 at http://www.un.org/apps/news/story.asp?NewsID=29972&Cr=zimbabwe&Cr1=cholera, accessed on 5 March 2009; Anon 2008 at http://www.thezimbabwetimes.com/?p=8701, accessed 2009; and Musemwa 2009, unpublished.

return to the sending country less appealing as conditions there are less attractive. Towards the end of 2008 the cholera pandemic, though, compelled many infected and affected Zimbabweans to migrate to South Africa which possessed superior medical facilities.

South Africa which has also been inundated by immigrants from across Africa has therefore become a major destination for Zimbabwean immigrants fleeing the country in the wake of the crippling economic crisis and indeed the world's worst cholera outbreak in recorded history.[22] According to a report in January 2009 by Eric Laroche, the Assistant Director for the World Health Organization's (WHO) Health Action in Crises Cluster, 'Unless drastic action is taken by all players in this crisis, more [than the 3,000 fatalities already recorded] Zimbabweans will succumb to the outbreak, and other countries in the Southern African region will face the continued threat of spill over epidemics.'[23] This was more so due to the absence of cross-border health policies between Zimbabwe and South Africa.[24] It was no secret that health services were overstretched and literally failing to cope with increased demand for services. Potentially, in the opinion of J.G. Todd this had the effect of damaging future relations between the cold-hearted region and a resurrected Zimbabwe.[25] Indeed, South Africa suffered from some imported cases from Zimbabwe, including some local strains of *vibrio cholerae* – the bacterium which causes cholera.[26] The outbreak of the water-borne epidemic in Zimbabwe stimulated further waves of migration into South Africa where disease victims hoped to access better medicinal supplies.

In fact, besides cholera, the prevailing lack of sanity in Zimbabwe since the late 1990s coupled by the fact that democracy and governance issues have not been prioritized in this vulnerable, weak and fragile African state, has perennially unleashed waves of migration not only to South Africa but also to Botswana, Namibia, Swaziland and Lesotho in the SADC region, the United Kingdom (UK), the United States of America and other parts of the globe. This marked the globalization of the Zimbabwean crisis. Primarily, the crisis in Zimbabwe in the previous decade has been the major push factor for unprecedented waves of migration to the Republic. The emergence of the latter as an economic power house in the SADC region has also significantly acted as a pull factor. Traditionally, South Africa has always had a 'soft' spot for Zimbabwean immigrant labour. Nevertheless, despite the huge migration flows into the Republic not much attention has been paid

---

22   WHO cited in Anon 2009, 7.

23   Eric Laroche cited in Anon 2009, 7.

24   This situation is similar to what one finds elsewhere in the SADC region where there are also no cross-border health policies among nations, for instance, between Lesotho and South Africa – a situation that is making it very difficult to contain pandemics like HIV/AIDS. For detail on Lesotho and South Africa see Palitza 2009 at http://allafrica.com/stories/200903310403.html, accessed on 11 September 2009.

25   Todd 2007, 445 cited in Mlambo 1997, 10.

26   Faruque 2008.

to the implementation of social protection systems to mitigate the effects of sudden and sometimes unplanned relocation of people. In the circumstances the migrants have been compelled to come up with their own social protection measures.

Survival and Coping Strategies: Zimbabwean Migrants and Social Protection

Migrating to South Africa and working as migrant labour, though cumbersome, is a flourishing business for many regional workers beset by crises in their home countries. Migration can provide households with an important source of income and livelihoods, and potentially a path out of poverty. However, migrant workers also face a number of risks associated with working in a foreign country and with their specific employment status as migrant labour. Vulnerability and the enormity of the risks are determined by factors such as the gender of the migrant worker, their household profile, whether they have migrated with or without dependent household members, their coping capacity and the availability of protection mechanisms. Social protection strategies drawing on a combination of access to social assistance and insurance, corporate social responsibility and reciprocity regimes between migrants and their host communities help to promote the livelihoods of migrant workers and their households. An examination of the coping mechanisms that Zimbabwean immigrants to South Africa have devised to cushion themselves and their families back home from endemic hunger and poverty as the social and economic situation in their country reached almost irretrievable proportions is necessary. Social protection is an emerging field of interest in development policy as a core element of the objective to halve world poverty by 2015 – one of the most daring of all Millennium Development Goals.[27] It is conceived quite broadly to refer to all measures that assist individuals, households and communities to better manage the income and other risks that create and perpetuate vulnerability. It is primarily a movement away from social assistance and welfare programmes of the late 1980s and early 1990s to include preventive and promotive initiatives that constitute 'springboards' out of poverty and into productive livelihoods.[28] Social protection can include risk management actions taken by migrants and migrants' families themselves and services and measures provided by the state, Non-Governmental Organisations (NGOs) and other organizations. In many ways, state policy impacts variously on migrants' livelihoods, rights and levels of social protection. Migration has also disproportionately affected both lawful and illicit Zimbabwean migrants. Nonetheless, Zimbabwean migrants and their families have largely been responsible for their own social protection or risk management

---

27   Yunus 2003 at http://www.da-academy.org/Halvepoverty.html, accessed on 8 September 2009.

28   In the USA, for example, there was an increasing trend in the amount of welfare immigrants received in comparison to what the indigenous population collected.

actions in the general absence of a number of potential services and measures that could have been provided by the state, NGOs and human rights organizations in the host country. Primarily, different actors (government, donor agencies, civil society and migrant networks) can play important roles in supporting and developing a more integrated social protection strategy for migrant labour. There is a definitive link between migration and social protection which is twofold. First, migration is often in itself a social protection measure in which members of poor households may migrate in response to low incomes, food insecurity or external shocks in order to protect the household. In addition, migration may also create new social protection needs for those who migrate and for those who are left behind. Some traces of the social protection mechanisms developed by Zimbabwean migrants working in South Africa are analysed in this chapter.

However, according to migration experts social protection strategies vary according to whether workers migrate with dependent household members or dependents remain in the source location. In each of these cases, therefore, how do immigrants self-insure? There is no easy answer to this rather complex question. The absence or the inadequacy of food (for a country that used to be the grain basket of the region), well-developed capital markets and other insurance schemes compared to industrialized nations has exposed Zimbabwean families to excessive socio-economic risk. In these circumstances the affected families needed to self-insure against such sudden declines in economic fortune by embarking on migration to South Africa, among other countries, in search of employment. Foreign migrants usually secure employment in diverse sectors of the economy on the basis of their own qualifications, their willingness to engage in extraordinarily tough tasks and sometimes through continued affiliation to their kinship groups that departed for South Africa decades earlier. In many instances, kinship networks mean it is not very difficult to find a job or sanctuary in the receiving country.[29] Zimbabwean migrants working in South Africa's agricultural, industrial, mining, construction and domestic service sectors have devised an array of survival and coping strategies. The undocumented people especially have at most times found ways of obtaining phoney work permits and temporary residence permits in a bid to ensure the survival of their kinsfolk who stay behind. Once they secure a job they support their families at home through money transfers. The remitting patterns of immigrants can be used to illustrate how both documented and undocumented Zimbabweans self-insure.

Remittances have played a part in upholding families in Zimbabwe over the last decade. The huge influx of irregular economic migrants from Zimbabwe into South Africa, notwithstanding the xenophobic backlash in May 2008 in parts of Gauteng, KwaZulu Natal (KZN) and the Western Cape Provinces and later

---

29 It can be ascertained that when Zimbabwean migrants enter South Africa instead of awaiting the erection of a government or United Nations (UN) refugee camp they quickly dissipate as they join their relatives already living in several towns and farming settlements of the Republic.

in July 2009 in Balfour (Mpumalanga) on the one hand and the risk of massive
deportations on the other, has rescued millions of people from imminent death
from hunger and starvation through wage remittances. Migrants have repatriated
money to their families through informal channels such as asking people they
know who might be travelling home to deliver money or ferry goods or groceries
to their families. This became a very lucrative business for the many bus drivers
plying the Johannesburg to Harare as well as the Johannesburg to Bulawayo
routes as they demanded a fee for their services. As the need to remit money and
groceries grew with the escalation of the Zimbabwean crisis the opportunities
available for certain people to make a fortune led to the emergence of the so-called
'malichas' who did not only act as transporters of money, goods or groceries to
migrants' families in Zimbabwe but became involved in the smuggling of people
into South Africa through the Beitbridge border post.[30] The trafficking of human
beings for purposes of prostitution and indeed the ferrying of all sorts of other
contraband such as mandrax, cannabis ('dagga') and cocaine for sale across the
border became a common occurrence.[31] As more and more players entered the fray
the transportation of goods became a booming business. Remittances which gave
rise to increased parallel or black market activities created a lucrative secondary
economy in Zimbabwe. In the process, banks have come to recognize the untapped
potential for business in this burgeoning remittance market. Economists have
begun to note that pecuniary remittance inflows into developing nations such as
Zimbabwe are, in many cases, catching up to and exceeding traditional sources of
foreign currency earnings, and the research community is exploring the potential
impact of immigrants' money flows on the economic development of states
receiving remittances.[32] Likewise, government officials have intensified efforts to
control money laundering and other illicit transactions and to bring immigrants'
transactions into the formal transfer market.[33] Such tasks would minimize the
opportunities for criminals to camouflage their transactions by sharing informal

30   The 'malichas' are indigenous transport or lorry owners who are often paid to
ferry people or irregular migrants, money and goods or groceries across the South African
border.
31   In their effort to deter irregular activities at ports of entry and exit which include
Beitbridge, OR Tambo International Airport and Durban Harbour Border police have seized
dangerous drugs such as cannabis derived from the hemp plant, mandrax and cocaine. From
1 April 2007 to 31 March 2008 at Beitbridge – a designated land port – the police recovered
86 stolen vehicles and seized goods and drugs worth an estimated R4,778,775 and R163,360
respectively. This information can be gleaned from the *South African Police Service (SAPS)
Annual Report 2007-2008*, at http://www.saps.gov.za/saps_profile/strategic_framework/
annual_report/2007_2008/8_prg5_prot_and_sec_services.pdf, accessed on 21 September
2009, 137–45.
32   For a comparative and in-depth historical policy study of Italy as a classic sending
state bent on encouraging and benefiting from remittances generated by its emigrants abroad
('Italians abroad') see Choate 2007; and Marcelli and Lowell 2005.
33   Goredema 2004.

channels traditionally used by immigrants to transfer funds abroad. Quite evidently, remittances have propped up the Zimbabwean economy during the ongoing crisis.

In developed countries, the existence of well-developed capital markets and other insurance schemes helps to protect families against excessive risk. Although risk insurance exists in America, some families are still dramatically beset by economic risks.[34] Nevertheless, unlike in America and some European countries insurance mechanisms of any kind are either absent or not sufficiently reliable in poorer countries where families need to self-insure against sudden declines in economic fortune. One way that families do this is by sending earners to other countries. This has been a common practice in Zimbabwe where at the height of the economic crisis some parents literally terminated school for their children in a veritable attempt to get them over to South Africa to work and repatriate money to sustain the family they left behind. Moreover, a number of schools had closed almost indefinitely due to lack of teachers in a massive and crippling brain-drain which also adversely affected the health delivery system.[35] Broadly analysed, this means that in developing countries the lack of well-developed capital markets and other insurance schemes to help protect families against excessive risk exacerbates their plight. Families in poorer countries therefore need to self-insure against sudden declines in economic fortune. As in the Zimbabwean situation, one way that families do this is by sending earners to countries like South Africa, Botswana and Namibia. Nonetheless, whilst regular migration is bound to get out of control with the removal of the hitherto existing visa procedures and the potential of getting construction jobs as preparations for the 2010 World Cup soccer extravaganza hot up it is worrying that there seems to be no clear policy on curbing irregular entry into South Africa as Zimbabwe's economic woes persist. The reaction of the South African government, which wavers between 'soft' and draconian, can thus be used as an important benchmark in analysing the state's capacity to control and regulate as well as promote policies that help maximize the benefits and minimize the risks and cost of migration for poor and vulnerable people.

Attempts at Control and Regulation

In Southern Africa if not on the whole African continent, South Africa is a good example to demonstrate the problems caused by population movement and the construction of controls around borders or the lack of it. Incidentally, most literature on Southern Africa details national migration trends, but glosses over

---

34 Hacker 2007, at http://www.tobinproject.org/welcome/downloads/RP_Universal_ Risk_Insurance.pdf, accessed on 21 September 2009, 1–10.

35 Schools only re-opened in March 2009 following the formation of the Government of National Unity. For a parallel analysis of the brain drain debate see Grubel and Scott 1966.

how migration is controlled and how risk can be minimized on a bilateral or on a broader base. Notwithstanding the earlier WENELA agreement and some such arrangements it is only in August 2009 that serious overtures were made to control and in essence regularize the untenably high labour inflows from Zimbabwe into South Africa and ensure safe labour migration. The implementation of the government's draft green paper on international migration which sought, *inter alia*, an elaborate categorization of skills required in the labour market, regulate migrant worker quotas and sanction employers who engaged unregistered cross-border workers has been kept in abeyance for some time.[36]

In a plausible move, on 27 August 2009 Zimbabwe and South Africa signed a four-year agreement at the International Organisation for Migration (IOM) reception centre in the border town of Beitbridge.[37] The accord was intended to promote 'safe labour migration' between the two SADC members.[38] The agreement which seeks to strengthen cooperation and support in the fields of labour and employment would specifically facilitate the safe and temporary migration of Zimbabweans to work in the commercial agricultural sector of the Limpopo Province.[39] The agreement which initially focuses on Limpopo Province farm workers[40] and is ultimately expected to be applied throughout South Africa was reached in an effort to prevent the rampant exploitation of irregular immigrants who lacked proper documentation. Most Zimbabwean migrant labourers without proper documents were grossly underpaid or were invariably paid an exploitation wage.[41] These farm workers find it difficult to recover their money in unpaid or reduced wages because they hardly have recourse to legal representation against some unscrupulous farm employers.

South African labour regulations have stipulated an average minimum wage for farm workers of R1,600 per month,[42] but some farm owners pay a lower migrant wage than this. In fact, the influx of migrants is responsible for undercutting local labourers' wages.[43] For Zimbabwe's Labour and Social Welfare Minister, Paurina

---

36   Bernstein, Schlemmer and Simkins 1997 at http://www.cde.org.za/article.php?a_id=151, accessed on 15 September 2009.

37   Muleya 2009 at   http://www1.herald.co.zw/inside.aspx?sectid=9272&cat=1, accessed on 28 August 2009.

38   Ibid.

39   Paurina Mpariwa, Zimbabwe's Labour and Social Welfare Minister cited in Muleya 2009 at http://www.irinnews.org/Report.aspx?ReportId=85891, accessed on 28 August 2009.

40   Zimbabweans have been the mainstay of the commercial farming labour force in Limpopo Province for several decades.

41   Nyandoro 2008b.

42   Muleya 2009 at   http://www1.herald.co.zw/inside.aspx?sectid=9272&cat=1, accessed on 28 August 2009.

43   For a comparative analysis of how waves of immigrants have come, particularly from Europe, Asia, and the Americas (especially Mexico) to enjoy the high wages available in the USA and escape the relative penury of their home countries and lowering the wages

Mpariwa, 'the facility [which was set up in Beitbridge] came into effect after the joint ministerial mission to Limpopo Province realized that scores of irregular Zimbabwean farm workers were employed there and decided to regularize and regulate the long-standing practice'.[44] The pilot phase of the project requires that South African farmers seeking Zimbabwean labour furnish the new labour migration centre in Beitbridge[45] with their requirements. This initiative though seems to be a belated attempt to control irregular labour migration as much as it is reflective of the failure by the two governments to build on and improve on the earlier labour recruitment mechanisms started during the WENELA process of the early 20th century. A sizeable number of farmers, though, are worried about immigration legislation as they prefer the perpetuation of the existing fluid situation which 'entitles' them to exploit labour away from the full glare of the law or statutory controls.

It can be asserted that the signing ceremony at the IOM-run Beitbridge Labour Centre was the culmination of several meetings dating back to January 2006 held between the two countries' labour ministries. The agreement which was presided over by Zimbabwe's Labour and Social Welfare Minister, Mpariwa, and the South African Labour Minister, Mdladlana, covers labour dispute resolution and social dialogue; labour law reform; social security; employment services; Beitbridge migration centre; joint technical taskforce on occupational health, safety and asbestos; as well as facilitation of the interface between ex-Zimbabwean migrant workers in gold mines of the Republic of South Africa and previous employers or the ex-employing agencies.[46] The other stakeholders to the cooperation agreement and Memorandum of Understanding (MoU) are Home Affairs, Foreign Affairs, the IOM, the International Labour Organisation (ILO) and the Limpopo Province Farmers' Union.[47]

These will work in cooperation with the South African Labour Minister who has denounced the ill-treatment of Zimbabwean irregular immigrants by some farmers and emphasized the importance of inter-governmental or inter-state collaborative frameworks that prioritized the issuance of authentic identification and employment documentation.[48] As an essential measure the two governments are working on modalities to ensure that immigrant farm workers get full labour and social security benefits.[49] Erin Foster, the IOM information and communication

---

and working conditions of undocumented migrants, regular immigrants and American citizens alike see Davis and Weinstein 2005 at http://www.cis.org/articles/2005/back205. pdf, accessed on 1 September 2009, and Durand, Malone and Massey 2003.

44   Mpariwa, Zimbabwe's Labour and Social Welfare Minister cited in Muleya 2009.

45   A database of jobs and all requirements will be maintained at the Beitbridge Labour Centre situated in the border town.

46   Muleya 2009.

47   Ibid.

48   Membathisi Mdladlana, South African Labour Minister cited in Muleya 2009.

49   Ibid.

officer based in the Zimbabwean capital, Harare, testified to the fact that the pilot scheme would facilitate the temporary migration of seasonal workers primarily from Zimbabwe's three southern districts of Chiredzi, Masvingo and Beitbridge to South Africa's northern Limpopo Province.[50] For Erin Foster, the goal of the project was 'to reduce the dangers for migrants … [and] limit the risks that exist for individuals'.[51] This could be achieved by the issuing of passports and work permits to the migrants for the duration of their contracts in line with South Africa's recent announcement of a Special Dispensation Permit for Zimbabweans wanting to live and work in South Africa.[52] The agreement to reduce irregular migration and promote safe, regular migration options[53] is therefore a noble attempt to facilitate the easier flow of labour traffic between Zimbabwe and South Africa in an atmosphere free of major risks to the migrant. The accord nonetheless seems silent on the potential risks to the local South African citizenry.

In this respect, South Africa and Zimbabwe could draw some vital and useful lessons from the European Union (EU) project. The EU, with its emerging common migration policy, offers prospects for the development of a generic framework that embodies trans-national migration experiences – an aspect that seems to be missing in most migration discourses in Southern Africa in particular. Geddes has made a veritable attempt to focus on the 'global politics of labour migration.'[54] The following section on whose responsibility it is to curb irregular migration, where necessary, tries to situate the Zimbabwe-to-South Africa migration narrative within a broader Southern African context. The examples of Zimbabwe and South Africa reveal that the extent and purpose of state control and how it is carried out differ substantially from state to state. The section and indeed the entire chapter, therefore, deals with a multifaceted approach to migration which is its main advantage over other works on migration as it does not generally focus on a limited geographical area, but embraces some regional, continental and internationalist perspectives for further scholarly exploration.

Is it South Africa's or Zimbabwe's Responsibility to Curb Unlawful Migration?

As South Africa is primarily an obvious destination for irregular immigrants from Zimbabwe it can be asserted that the country has a duty, first and foremost,

---

50   IRIN 2009 at http://www.zimbabwesituation.com/aug28_2009.html#Z18, accessed on 28 August 2009. See also IRIN, 2009 at http://www.irinnews.org/Report.aspx?ReportId= 85891, accessed on 28 August 2009.

51   Ibid.

52   The IOM cited in IRIN 2009 at http://www.zimbabwesituation.com/aug28_2009. html#Z18, accessed on 28 August 2009.

53   IRIN 2009.

54   Geddes, 2007, 63. See also Geddes 2003.

to find ways of either preventing or regulating the stream of people crossing its borders almost willy nilly. For her part, Zimbabwe which is the main source of these emigrants, the temptation by its people and others beyond its borders to prefer South Africa of all the potential regional destinations is stimulated by the latter's gigantic economic status compared to other Southern African countries. In particular Zimbabweans despite the risks they are exposed to are still perpetually inclined to enter South Africa irregularly because of the relatively higher wages there. Steady remuneration makes it possible for them to send a percentage of their earnings on a regular and sometimes irregular basis back to their families in the sending country. Besides, the process of obtaining legal entry has been made cumbersome by the exorbitant visa fees charged previously and by the fact that it could take several years to acquire the requisite documentation.

In a generally welcome move on 5 May 2009, notwithstanding some bureau-cratic hurdles, the South African government waived visa requirements and stringent labour regulations for Zimbabweans wishing to travel or work in that country.[55] The regulation came into effect on 1 May 2009. This though was a delay in the enforcement of the SADC Protocol on the Facilitation of Movement of Persons (FMPP) signed by the regional body's nine members, including South Africa and Zimbabwe.[56] It can be noted that prior to the implementation of the visa-free regime Zimbabwean immigrants were required to seek a visa of R2,000 (whose processing took rather too long) in order for them to travel to South Africa and the South African police would raid the *émigrés* including farm workers and deport them for breaching the country's immigration laws.[57] For example, statistics released by the IOM show that South Africa deported an estimated 80,000 irregular Zimbabwean immigrants in the period from May to December 2006, 950 of whom were unaccompanied minors.[58] Nevertheless, the abolition of visas was not without its own problems. The impact of the scrapping of visa requirements between Zimbabwe and South Africa was evident in the flood of undocumented Zimbabweans who crossed into the Republic through dubious channels. The massive inflows of people have been exacerbated by flourishing corruption at Beitbridge – arguably the biggest point of entry by foreign nationals into South Africa. As will be illustrated in this chapter, the proclivity to accept bribes by state officials tasked with the duty to man the borders was very high. Therefore, given such loopholes, the strictures imposed by unaffordable visa fees demanded earlier and the long waiting time for a visa to be granted, even if a person has applied he/she may choose to migrate irregularly anyway. For this reason, what

55 Muleya 2009 at http://www1.herald.co.zw/inside.aspx?sectid=9272&cat=1, accessed on 28 August 2009. See also Herald reporters 2009 at http://www.herald. co.zw/inside.aspx?sectid=4058&cat=1, accessed on 6 May 2009.

56 Leslie 2008, 29.

57 Muleya 2009.

58 Anon 2007a at http://ww.irinnews.org/Report.aspx?ReportId=64340, accessed on 10 September 2009.

type of control paradigms does the migration situation in the region demand from the South African authorities, for instance, the Departments of Home Affairs and Foreign Affairs? Arguably, there is need for interaction between connected yet asymmetrical control systems. This interaction should take into cognizance the position of the individual migrant in the various migration-control scenarios that states develop or have not yet developed.

Clearly because it was not going to be easy on the basis of quiet diplomacy or any draconian measures to stop Zimbabweans aspiring for greener pastures from entering South Africa, the receiving state from the onset should have advocated regulation as an alternative. In other words, the South African government should have promoted policies that helped maximize the benefits and minimize the risks and cost of migration to itself as well as for the poor and vulnerable people and other migrants be it from Zimbabwe, Zambia, Malawi, the Democratic Republic of the Congo (DRC), Nigeria, Somalia, Ethiopia, Liberia, Sudan or any part of the continent.[59] As a rule and in line with its strong regional position South Africa needed to be decisive in its intervention to resolve the crisis ravaging Zimbabwe in order to forestall problems that were spilling into its territory as the economic catastrophe in its northern neighbour deteriorated. It can be argued that the problem of the influx of irregular Zimbabwean migrants was thrown to the fore by incidents of xenophobic violence in May 2008 which revealed the adverse impact of the Zimbabwean conundrum on South African society.[60] Xenophobia or anti-alienism occurred against the backdrop of the huge influx of Zimbabweans who were blamed by South Africans (as in the American and Mexican situation) for crime and 'stealing jobs' from locals but there is no official data to support these claims.[61] Xenophobic violence is not only responsible for displacing people but it is a blatant contravention of the twin International Conventions against torture and other cruel, inhuman or degrading treatment or punishment of those perceived to be foreigners. In addition, it is an infringement of the convention on the protection of the rights of all migrant workers and members of their families.[62]

Perhaps, xenophobia could have been pre-empted among other things through attempts at linguistic integration. Nevertheless, linguistic issues as an important terrain in understanding how immigrants become integrated into their new environments require further research especially as language seems to be one yardstick that can be used to measure an immigrant's acceptability or otherwise when he/she arrives in a foreign country. Whilst xenophobia cannot be condoned, it cannot be denied that the huge numbers of people seeking social, economic and

---

59   South Africa has large immigrant populations from Germany, Belgium, the Netherlands/Holland, France, the United Kingdom, America, India, Spain, Italy and many parts of the African continent.

60   *The Star*, 20 March 2008.

61   Anon 2007a at http://ww.irinnews.org/Report.aspx?ReportId=64340, accessed on 10 September 2009.

62   Nyandoro 2008a, 24. See also UN 2006.

political refuge in South Africa impacted on service delivery issues in a big way – a situation that had not been anticipated.[63] It is important to note that a reaction to the acute shortage of food, fuel, electricity, water and sanitation facilities in Zimbabwe has seen many people risking their lives by crossing the Limpopo River in search of survival. Hence, economic, political and other migrants placed considerable stress on South Africa's infrastructure in several ways as they searched for jobs, food and descent livelihoods. The impact of receiving huge numbers of immigrants not only from Zimbabwe but also from other parts of the world through a rather porous Beitbridge border post and other ports of entry and exit like OR Tambo International Airport and Durban Harbour has been enormous. The arrival of many migrants had deleterious consequences on South Africa with regard to social services and employment. In policy circles, migration has also highlighted some key elements in the politics of water, including its usage, availability and public health concerns. There has been a lot of apprehension regarding hydrological-related issues such as: where are irregular migrants going to get their water (i.e. concerns around the source of water provision and sustainability); who is going to pay for that water consumed by the irregular migrants; and could local municipalities sustain the increased demand for water and sanitary facilities exerted by undocumented people who were not planned for in the budget? Indeed, irregular migration is negatively impinging on housing provision, water supplies, sanitation and other social amenities. The millions of Zimbabwean refugees in South Africa are, thus, placing a considerable burden on the South African fiscus.[64]

Xenophobic attacks on foreigners or those deemed to be foreigners though would not address the niggling service delivery issues in South Africa. A state or civil society-initiated approach was necessary to address a potentially explosive situation. For example, the greater the number that arrived the more the government in collaboration with non-state actors needed to come on board and alleviate the problem of housing and water infrastructure which was clearly brought under enormous strain.

Estimates reveal that as many as three million regular and irregular Zimbabwean migrants had by January 2007 entered the Republic which has a total population of about 48 million.[65] A significant number were living in overcrowded make-shift refugee camps or informal settlements without clean safe water or proper sanitation. At this juncture the host government should have intervened or at least appealed to the UN and its humanitarian agencies to create temporary settlement

---

63 One South African Home Affairs Officer recounting how Zimbabweans were coming over on a very wide band across the Limpopo River said it was impossible to calculate numbers and because it was an unusually large number of people moving in a giant wave across the river, he felt the movement could only be described in terms of a 'tsunami'. For detail on this see Anon 2007b at http://www.zimonline.co.za/Article.aspx?ArticleId=1716, accessed on 2 September 2009.

64 Mlambo 2008, 20.

65 Anon 2007a.

facilities that promoted good hygienic standards. This could have prevented some cases of cholera which sporadically afflicted a number of South African provinces such as Limpopo, Mpumalnga, Gauteng and KwaZulu Natal to name a few. In fact, imported cholera cases from Zimbabwe coupled with some local strains of the highly contagious and lethal disease gave rise to new forms of xenophobia in 2009 based on human health concerns – forms that are diametrically opposed to the reasons advanced for the xenophobic attacks experienced in May 2008.

It was, thus, imperative for South Africa to take action not only against the unlawful exodus of people but also against Zimbabwe which did not seem to make serious effort to end the unprecedented socio-economic and political crisis wrecking the country. Such timely action was necessary because it would substantially lessen South Africa's burden. It would also have drastically diminished the costs incurred by South Africa through, *inter alia, ad infinitum* deportations of large numbers of people, the erection of security fences as well as the construction and maintenance of detention or custodial centres such as the notorious Lindela Holding Facility. This detention infrastructure established in 1996 also known as the Lindela Repatriation Centre is situated 30 km from Johannesburg and it is the country's largest detention facility for undocumented or unauthorized immigrants. It is run by South Africa's Department of Correctional Services.[66] In any case, arresting and subsequently deporting irregular migrants was not an effective strategy for South Africa to determine the number of inflows of people because these people often found their way back. They usually devised ways of avoiding detection and deportation by immigration authorities. This resulted in some migrants being apprehended several times and each time declared as new arrivals. What this, therefore, meant was that it was difficult to use apprehensions to compile a correct and comprehensive statistical representation of new immigrants in a given reporting period.

Furthermore, the immigration department and crime prevention units were strained and overwhelmed as corruption reined supreme at the Beitbridge border post. To avoid imminent arrest and deportation some irregular immigrants masqueraded as South African nationals. This was made possible by obtaining false identity documents through bribing Home Affairs officials.[67] It is regrettable that some of the illicit entries by labour migrants from Zimbabwe into South Africa are still occurring not through clandestine but official entry points after prevailing on

---

66   According to the Lawyers for Human Rights (LHR), it is not easy for human rights organizations to monitor the various locations where foreigners are detained, including prisons, airports, police stations, an old dilapidated sports hall on a military base and the infamous Lindela Holding Facility. For more detail see Anon 2009 at http://www. globaldetentionproject.org/countries/africa/south-africa/introduction.html, accessed on 10 September 2009.

67   Former President, Thabo Mbeki, admitted that there was 'widespread corruption' in the Home Affairs Department after more than 200 Zimbabweans were found in possession of South African passports in early 2007. For detail on this see Anon 2007a.

the officials to take a bribe of a couple of rands or United States dollars. Frequent travellers through the Beitbridge entry point have testified to a complex network of shady and illicit deals going on with respect to the clearing of visitors from other countries to South Africa by the immigration and customs departments. Some corrupt immigration and customs officers including other underhand border control security officers are playing a major part in helping irregular migrants circumvent immigration laws regarding entry into the Republic especially through Beitbridge. More full proof measures should have been employed by the South African government to stop irregular immigration. Since Zimbabweans comprise the majority of recent irregular immigrants residing in South Africa there has been a consistent increase in attention paid to the Beitbridge border over the years. Nevertheless, a significant proportion of the people deceitfully entering the Republic is smuggled in with the connivance of officers who receive kickbacks in return. Undoubtedly, corruption is rampant and it is disconcerting to note that irregular immigrants are actually infiltrating into the country through official and not surreptitious points as suspected earlier. Such a practice has wide-ranging ramifications for immigration policy in a country that is struggling to redefine its immigration procedures or rules since the termination of Apartheid largely due to limited institutional capacity.[68]

However, it is plausible that the South African government has realized, though belatedly, the vital benefit of regularizing Zimbabwean immigrants' tenure in the country. In many ways, it should allay xenophobic attitudes since unregulated immigration has partly been at the centre of tensions[69] not only between Zimbabwean and South African citizens employed on the farms but even beyond this sector. Indeed, working collaboratively as states and realizing that this was as much a Zimbabwean as it was a South African problem is one of the ways of addressing the issue of irregular labour migration. This should form the basis of a sound regional migration policy premised on political and economic approaches well-suited to addressing particular labour questions.[70]

Implications for Policy Discourse

The massive influx of irregular migrants from Zimbabwe into South Africa which increased with the advent of independence in 1994 and its implications call for the formulation of new policy frontiers. The state, regional actors and intergovernmental agencies have not been without their own limitations in

68   Bernstein, Schlemmer and Simkins 1997 at http://www.cde.org.za/article.php?a_id=151, accessed on 15 September 2009.

69   Membathisi Mdladlana, South African Labour Minister cited in Muleya 2009; *The Herald*, 28 August 2009 at http://www1.herald.co.zw/inside.aspx?sectid=9272&cat=1, accessed on 28 August 2009.

70   Freeman and Kessler 2008, 656.

addressing major immigration-related issues. Evidently, there is an absolute need to have a more coordinated and coherent response across states, agencies and policy fields in the SADC region in general and between Zimbabwe and South Africa in particular. Crush and Tevera in their work on migration in Zimbabwe have also identified the compelling need for Southern African countries to harmonize regional migration policies to facilitate easier and freer movement of people across the region.[71] Tevera's position endorses the fact that deliberate policy towards facilitating the immigration of foreigners with rare or exceptional skills who make a significant contribution to the development of the South African economy should be adopted.[72] There is a great deal of controversy and a clear conflict between Mpariwa's Labour and Social Services Ministry perspective and Crush and Tevera's call for free movement regimes in the Southern African region. However, flows of people should be rationally and efficiently controlled in a manner that assures the states of an orderly migration regime.

The shortcomings in dealing with migration associated problems especially in the period prior to the labour-regularization regime adopted in Beitbridge in August 2009 reveal that the policy boundaries in the recipient country need to be reformed or transformed to legally manage the huge influx and the attendant levels of social protection required for both lawful and illicit migrants. Quite plainly, the influx of people into the Republic which does not seem to be abating is exerting a lot of pressure on service delivery and the state. The state, non-state entities including civic society, local municipalities, hospitals and other institutions should devise clear lines of action.

For many observers, the Republic seemingly stands hapless in the face of huge waves of migrants encroaching onto its territory almost every day despite the fact that South Africa has always had considerable economic and to some extent political leverage over its northern neighbour. Why it has not invoked this power and pass explicitly anti-irregular migration laws, in contrast to Crush and Tevera's view on open movement, is quite astounding. Noticeably, the South African government is averse to the huge influx of refugees from Zimbabwe and the general chaos if not near state of anarchy at the border post.

As propounded by the moral hazard immigration theory the inflow of unskilled workers has a detrimental effect on South Africa because it harms the economic opportunities of particularly unskilled or semi-skilled South African workers. In addition, as the number of immigrants increases, the number of workers in the economy also increases. This creates competition in the labour market, thus wages fall (i.e. undercutting of local wages). It is not easy to gauge the exact number of undocumented aliens entering South Africa, but the figures are higher than before the onset of the crisis in Zimbabwe. In clear conflict with the UN as well as

---

71   Crush and Tevera 2000 at http://www.queensu.ca/samp/sampresources/sampublications/policyseries/policy25.htm, accessed on 11 September 2009, 1.

72   The CDE has emphasized the advantage of skilled foreign labour to the South African economy. See CDE 2008, 52.

Crush and Tevera's free movement advocacy, it has been suggested that because immigration has been perceived as detrimental to unskilled workers at home, therefore, for certain sections of South Africa immigration should be limited, or those who are irregular should be deported. This would bring back much of the job security that South African nationals deserve. On the other hand, however, opponents of this theory argue that this is not just treatment of foreigners. Perhaps, the appeal made by the Zimbabwean government's Labour and Social Services Minister to the private sector to come on board and assist migrant workers who travel with vulnerable children with donations to alleviate their plight in foreign countries should be commended.[73] For the Minister, the Beitbridge reception and support centre ably assisted by the IOM provided interim care and protection to unaccompanied children deported from South Africa pending reunion with their families or pending placement in alternative care.[74] This initiative by Zimbabwe with the support of South Africa creates ample possibilities for rapidly changing sending-state policies in the new millennium.

Such opportunities though can only succeed if they take into account the industrialists' interests. For instance, it has been suggested that illicit migration will not be very easy to stamp out because diverse South African entrepreneurs' vested economic interests seem to thrive on a steady supply of cheap Zimbabwean refugee labour moving freely into the country. This implies that South Africa's foreign policy mode with regard to labour supply matters has often been laid-back and driven by its farming community and industrial enterprises' quest for labour and for this reason it needs to be significantly modified. Clearly, the interests of certain business classes in South African society stand to benefit from the constant and unchecked flow of labour into the Republic. Nevertheless, although South Africa has benefited from both skilled and semi-skilled manpower inflows from Zimbabwe, it is obviously not benefiting in net terms. This should force it to urgently redefine its immigration policy which has remained unclear for many years.

Conclusion

This chapter on labour migration, its motivation and the policy framework within which societies operate has revealed aspects of international, regional and local migratory patterns with particular emphasis on the migration of people between Zimbabwe and South Africa. In the literature, the Republic's long-standing posture on irregular migrants especially from its northern neighbour has often been criticized. There is clearly a wide body of local and international opinion that regards South Africa's handling of the migration issue within its foreign and

---

73 Manzongo 2009 at http://www1.herald.co.zw/inside.aspx?sectid=9413&cat=1, accessed on 31 August 2009.
74 Ibid.

home affairs ministries as rather inadequate and ineffectual. Apparently, it is not easy to suggest a unitary solution to the array of challenges posed by migration. A multifaceted approach that acknowledges the important role that can be played by states, communities, individuals, local, regional, continental and international agencies could help proffer lasting solutions to a problem that is threatening to haunt South African society given the innumerable service delivery-cum xenophobic reactions that have been witnessed since May 2008 and indeed recently in July 2009. Most of these responses and attitudes cannot be divorced from the internal and external geopolitical conditions extant in both Zimbabwe and South Africa as far as the issue of labour migration is concerned. Migration has indeed exhibited both its positive and baneful effects.

Some positive and deleterious implications for policy discourse of the influx of migrants into South Africa at the height of Zimbabwe's economic anguish have been outlined. In addition, the chapter has illustrated that historically South Africa has served as a haven for Zimbabwean refugees and migrants since the mineral discoveries of the late 19th century although the trend assumed major dimensions with the advent of South Africa's independence in 1994. From the foregoing it can, therefore, be ascertained that a very robust and highly coordinated response across states, agencies and disciplinary fields should be adopted to ensure that migration's benefits are not necessarily obscured by its disadvantages. In the past, the lack of clear policy in both South Africa and Zimbabwe in dealing with the migrant 'problem' portrayed a picture of conflicting and uncoordinated solutions. It is a plausible suggestion that 'sending states must continue to renegotiate their relations with their migrants in their domestic politics and to the global system, while receiving states must begin to discuss more openly how globalization, relations with sending states, and assimilation processes will affect their own futures and the possibilities of diasporic membership'.[75] Such a dialogue process will not only ameliorate the relationship between the migrant's country of destination and his/her country of origin but it will also influence an improvement in the migrant's general situation. In the process questions pertaining to issues of ownership such as: To whom does the migrant belong and after he/she has crossed the border, is he/she no longer a citizen can be amicably addressed? Thus, at the policy level, more interventions are needed for a better understanding and handling of migratory labour arrangements.

On the whole, this chapter has highlighted the turmoil on the ground which has been caused by the contested control claims on labour migration between the two countries. For opponents of the free movement of labour theory, policy boundaries in South Africa need to be re-configured to regularly manage the influx of undocumented migrants from Zimbabwe. The chapter thus proffers significantly contrasting perspectives of labour migration control compared to some US and other international experiences.

---

75   R.C. Smith 2003, 749.

References

Anon. 2002. *Global Detention Project: South Africa Country Profile*, June, at,http://www.globaldetentionproject.org/countries/africa/south-africa/introduction.html.

Anon. 2007a. *Zimbabwe: South Africa Tries to Close the Back Door*, 11 January, at http://ww.irinnews.org/Report.aspx?ReportId=64340 [accessed: 10 September 2009].

Anon. 2007b. *Hot Seat Transcript: Human Tsunami Hits SA as Zimbabweans Flee*, 17 July, at http://www.zimonline.co.za/Article.aspx?ArticleId=1716.

Anon. 2008. UN Security Council to discuss Zimbabwe, *The Zimbabwe Times*, 10 December, at http://www.thezimbabwetimes.com/?p=8701.

Anon. 2009. Zimbabwe Cholera Crisis One of World's Worst, *The Water Wheel*, 8(2) (March/April).

Assefa, T., Rugumamu, S.M. and Ahmed, A.G.M. 2002. *Globalization, Democracy and Development in Africa: Challenges and Prospects*. Addis Ababa: Organization for Social Science Research in Eastern and Southern Africa/OSSREA.

Australian Government, Department of Health and Ageing. 2008. CHOLERA: Zimbabwe and Regional Spread, *International Surveillance Reports*, 22 November–5 December, at http://www.health.gov.au/internet/main/publishing.nsf/Content/ohp-surv-isr-2508.htm.

Bernstein, A., Schlemmer, L. and Simkins, C. 1997a. Fortress SA is Hardly a Wise Way to Discourage Aliens, *Business Day*, 11 June, at http://www.cde.org.za/article.php?a_id=152.

Bernstein A., Schlemmer, L. and Simkins, C. 1997b. Migration Controls Need to be Liberalized, *Cape Times*, 16 July, at http://www.cde.org.za/article.php?a_id=151.

Borjas, G.J. 1995. The Economic Benefits of Immigration, *Journal of Economic Perspectives*, 9(2).

Borjas, G.J. 2007. *Mexican Immigration to the United States*. Chicago: University of Chicago Press.

Center for Development and Enterprise (CDE). 2008. Immigrants in Johannesburg: Estimating Numbers and Assessing Impacts, *CDE In Depth*, 9 (August).

Choate, M.I. 2007. Sending States' Transnational Interventions in Politics, Culture, and Economics: The Historical Example of Italy, *International Migration Review (IMR)*, 41(3).

Cross, C., Mngadi, T. and Themba, M. 1998. Constructing Migration: Infrastructure, Poverty and Development in KwaZulu-Natal, *Development Southern Africa*, 15(4).

Crush, J. and Tevera, D. 2000. Zimbabweans who Move: Perspectives on Iinternational Migration in Zimbabwe, *Migration Policy Series*, 25, Southern African Migration Project, at http://www.queensu.ca/samp/sampresources/samppublications/policyseries/policy25.htm.

Das, M.S. 1974. Brain Drain Controversy and African Scholars, *Studies in Comparative International Development (SCID)*, 9(1) (March).

Davis, D.R. and Weinstein, D.E. 2005. United States Technological Superiority and the Losses from Migration, *Backgrounder: Centre for Immigration Studies Report*, February, at http://www.cis.org/articles/2005/back205.pdf.

Durand, J., Malone, N.J. and Massey, D.S. 2003. *Beyond Smoke and Mirrors: Mexican Immigration in an Era of Economic Integration*, New York: Russell Sage Foundation/RSF.

Faruque, S.M. and Nair, G.B. 2008. *Vibrio Cholerae: Genomics and Molecular Biology*. Dhaka: Caister Academic Press.

Fleming, J. 2008. *Zimbabwe: IFRC Ramps Up Assistance in Response to Escalating Cholera Crisis in the Southern African Region.* International Federation of Red Cross and Red Crescent Societies, News: Press releases, (UN and NGO Press Releases), 3 December, at http://www.ifrc.org/Docs/News/pr08/7608.asp.

Freeman, G.P. and Kessler, A.E. 2008. Political Economy and Migration Policy. *Journal of Ethnic and Migration Studies*, 34(4) (May).

Gaidzanwa, R. 1999. *Voting with their Feet: Migrant Zimbabwean Nurses and Doctors in the Era of Structural Adjustment*, Research Report No. 111. Uppsala: Nordiska Afrikainstitutet.

Geddes, A. 2003. *The Politics of Migration and Immigration in Europe*. London: Sage Publications Ltd.

Goredema, C. 2004. *Money Laundering in Southern Africa: Incidence, Magnitude and Prospects for its Control*, ISS Occasional Paper 92. Pretoria: Institute for Security Studies (ISS).

Grubel, H. and Scott, A.D. 1966. The International Flow of Human Capital, *American Economic Review*, 56, 268–74.

Hacker Jacobs, S. 2007. *Universal Risk Insurance: Stop-Loss Protection for Middle-Class Family Finances*, Discussion Paper in The Tobin Project Risk Policy Working Group, 6 May, at http://www.tobinproject.org/welcome/downloads/RP_Universal_Risk_Insurance.pdf.

Herald reporters. Visa-free regime starts, *The Herald*, 6 May 2009 at http://www.herald.co.zw/inside.aspx?sectid=4058&cat=1.

IRIN. 2009a. *Passage of Seasonal Zimbabwean Migrants Eased*, 27 August, at http://www.zimbabwesituation.com/aug28_2009.html#Z18.

IRIN, 2009b. *Passage of Seasonal Zimbabwean Migrants Eased*, 27 August, at http://www.irinnews.org/Report.aspx?ReportId=85891.

Kok, P., Gelderbom, D., Oucho, J. and Zyl, J. van. 2007. Migration in South and Southern Africa: Dynamics and Determinants, *African Security Review*, 16(2).

Leslie, R. 2008. *Migration from Zimbabwe: Numbers, Needs and Policy Options*. Johannesburg: CDE.

Manzongo, J. 2009. Help Migrant Workers: Govt, *The Herald*, 31 August, at http://www1.herald.co.zw/inside.aspx?sectid=9413&cat=1.

Marcelli, E.A. and Lowell, B.L. 2005. Transnational Twist: Pecuniary Remittances and Socioeconomic Integration among Authorized and Unauthorized Mexican Immigrants in Los Angeles County, *International Migration Review (IMR)*, 39(1).

Mlambo, A.S. 1997. *The Economic Structural Adjustment Programme: The Case of Zimbabwe, 1990–1995*. Harare: University of Zimbabwe Publications.

Mlambo, A.S. 2008. *South Africa's Reaction to the Zimbabwean Crisis*. Paper presented to the University of South Africa's (UNISA) Graduate School Seminar, Pretoria (29 May).

Muleya, T. 2009. Zim, SA Sign Labour Migration Agreement, *The Herald*, 28 August, at http://www1.herald.co.zw/inside.aspx?sectid=9272&cat=1.

Murray, C. 1981. *Families Divided: The Impact of Migrant Labour in Lesotho*. Cambridge: Cambridge University Press.

Musemwa, M. 2009. *From 'Sunshine City' to a Landscape of Disaster: The Politics of Water, Sanitation and Disease in Harare, Zimbabwe, 1980–2009*. Unpublished paper presented at the South African Historical Society (SAHS) Biennial Conference, Pretoria, 22–24 June.

Ndegwa, D., Horner, D. and Esau, F. 2004. *The Links Between Migration, Poverty and Health: Evidence from Khayelitsha and Mitchell's Plain*. Centre for Social Science Research (CSSR) Working Paper No. 73. Capetown: University of Cape Town.

Nyambara, P.S. 1999. *A History of Land Acquisition in Gokwe, Northwestern Zimbabwe, 1945–1997*. PhD dissertation. Evanston, IL: Northwestern University.

Nyandoro, M. 2008a. Strengthening the Capacity of National Institutions in South Africa, in *HURISA National Conference Report*, edited by I. Cornelissen, Willow Park: Human Rights Institute of South Africa (HURISA).

Nyandoro, M. 2008b. *Development and Differentiation: The Case of TILCOR/ ARDA Irrigation in Sanyati (Zimbabwe), 1939–2000*. Saarbrucken: VDM publishers.

Nyandoro, M. 2009. *Historical Overview of the Cholera Outbreak in Zimbabwe (2008–2009)*. Unpublished paper presented at the Southern African Historical Society (SAHS) Biennial Conference, Pretoria: UNISA, 22–24 June.

Palitza, K. 2009. *Lesotho: Migration Calls for Cross-Border Health Policies*, 31 March, at http://allafrica.com/stories/200903310403.html.

The Rhodesia Herald, Salisbury, 4 August 1900.

Sachikonye, L.M. 2003. From 'Growth with Equity' to 'Fast-Track' Reform: Zimbabwe's Land Question, *Review of African Political Economy*, 30(96), *War & the Forgotten Continent* (June).

Smith, R.C. 2003. Diasporic Memberships in Historical Perspective: Comparative Insights from the Mexican, Italian and Polish Cases. *International Migration Review (IMR)*, 37(3), *Transnational Migration: International Perspectives*.

South African Police Service (SAPS) Annual Report 2007–2008, at http://www.
   saps.gov.za/saps_profile/strategic_framework/annual_report/2007_2008/8_
   prg5_prot_and_sec_services.pdf [accessed: 21 September 2009].

The Star, 20 March 2008.

Todd, J.G. 2007. *Through the Darkness: A Life in Zimbabwe*. Cape Town: Zebra
   Press.

UN. 2006. *The Core International Human Rights Treaties*. New York and Geneva:
   Office of the United Nations High Commissioner for Human Rights/OHCHR.

Van Onselen, C. 1976. *Chibaro: African Mine Labour in Southern Rhodesia
   1900–1933*. London: Pluto Press Limited.

Webster, E. (ed.) 1978. *Essays in Southern African Labour History*. Johannesburg:
   Ravan Press.

WHO, 2009. *Zimbabwe's Cholera Crisis Worsens as Number of Dead, Infected
   Climbs*. UN News Centre, at http://www.un.org/apps/news/story.asp?NewsID
   =29972&Cr=zimbabwe&Cr1=cholera.

Yunus, M. 2003. *Halving Poverty by 2015: We Can Actually Make It Happen*. The
   sixth annual Commonwealth Lecture, London: Commonwealth Institute, 11
   March, at http://www.da-academy.org/Halvepoverty.html.

Zelinsky, W. 1971. The Hypotheses of the Mobility Transition. *Geographical
   Review*, 61.

SECTION II
The Appearance of Control: Examining Labour Migration Regimes with High Control Claims

Elspeth Guild and Sandra Mantu

The second section presents countries that invest substantially more in their labour migration policies; because of sustained investment, these countries manage to project a certain narrative of labour migration control which portrays them as being in control over their borders and of movement across them, be it for labour migration purposes or not. All states examined in this section (Canada, Australia, Japan and the Member States forming the European Union) have highly elaborate migration systems that mix external, internal, social and externalized forms of controls, which give a very strong impression of direction and power over the regulation of movement. There is an openly acknowledged preference for certain types of labour migration (highly skilled and skilled) coupled with restrictive policies regarding movement for the purposes of family reunification and asylum. The geographical diversity has been maintained, although it is worth pointing out that history also plays an important part in the development of labour migration policies. For example, Japan is trying to escape the label of 'isolationism' and make amends with its past and acquire legitimacy in the area by addressing human rights concerns in its labour migration policy and its implementation. Canada and Australia share similarities in the starting points of their policies (their preference for white, British/European labour migrants for long-term settlement) that have influenced the design of their current policies, especially the idea that migration is for long-term settlement, while the selection of migrants on the basis of their nationality, ethnic origin or race has been formally abandoned. For the Member States of the European Union, geography and history also play a part in the choices made with regard to who is allowed to enter and for what purposes. The politicization of migration control is evident in all cases, as some migrants are exempt from control or subjected to preferential treatment. The capacity of the state to allocate legal status and attach consequences to its loss, in the form of diminished economic capacity and irregularity of presence, is one of the essential elements of the control mechanisms put in place. The image of the highly skilled migrant as a sort of 'super-migrant', highly adaptable to the demands of the market and in no need of integration, dominates the labour migration narratives of these countries, although their economic realities point towards more complex demands in terms of labour migration.

Chapter 6

'Advantage Canada' and the Contradictions of (Im)migration Control

Christina Gabriel

The Federal Government of Canada has pledged to increase 2009 immigration levels to allow between 240,000 and 265,000 permanent residents. The Economic Class accounts for more than half the projected immigration goal at 156,600 (CIC 2008). This move, in the midst of a deepening global economic crisis, is in line with the Government's economic plan *Advantage Canada: Building a Strong Economy for Canadians*. It maintains that processes of globalization and the emergence of a knowledge-based economy necessitate that skills, education and adaptability of a nation's workforce are keys to global competitiveness. Within this neo-liberal rationale particular forms of labour migration become increasingly important.

> Our immigration policies should be more closely aligned with our labour market needs … Particular attention should be given to skilled temporary foreign workers with Canadian work experience and foreign graduates from Canadian colleges and universities, as these groups are well placed to adapt quickly to the Canadian economy (Department of Finance 2006, 49).

On the one hand, the state's recent immigration directions can be read as part of a dominant national imaginary that constructs Canada as a nation that is welcoming of immigrants, that offers the promise of citizenship to all and is a pioneer of a multicultural model of integration. Certainly, Canada does accept large numbers of newcomers each year. In fact, the country has admitted more immigrants and refugees for permanent settlement per capita than any other country (Elrick 2007, 1). But, on the other hand recent changes especially in terms of labour migration provide a more complex picture. Indeed *Advantage Canada's* emphasis on the ability of newcomers to adapt to the economy rather than society is telling.

This chapter addresses the broad theme of migration control by considering some recent shifts in Canadian immigration policy. Canada can be characterized as a labour migration regime with high control claims. Indeed, the points-based selection model designed to select the 'ideal immigrant' – potential Canadian citizens – can be considered as the basis for these claims. It's a model that is much touted and emulated. However the experience of recent migrants stands at odds with goals of the selection model. Despite the continual-fine tuning of the selection model in favour of 'skilled workers' the labour market experiences of recent immigrants to Canada has become an increasing source of concern to academics, think tanks, policymakers, organized labour and immigrants themselves. Coupled with this trend is the rapid expansion of the temporary foreign worker category. Here, employer driven programs import a flexible, immobile migrant workforce to respond to market needs. These new programs are also indicative of a greater attempt to manage migration.

This chapter begins by exploring how a discourse of 'home' and nation prefigure the inclusions and exclusions engendered by immigration policy and practices. These discourses are implicated in the constitution of national labour markets and have particular currencies in settler societies (cf. Stasiulis and Yuval-Davis) such as Canada. The second part of the chapter provides an overview of the range of recent reforms to Canada's labour migration regime. This regime, as will be demonstrated, is characterized by multiple modes of entry that are associated with new forms of stratification and rights. Increasing differentiations in terms of mode of entry stand at odds with many mainstream Canadians' image of their nation.

Opening and Closing Doors: The Politics of Home and Nation

This section outlines how the analytics of home and nation inform the dynamics and politics of immigration control. Forms of control whether immigration and citizenship rules, regulations and practices play an important role in settler societies insofar as they are implicated in the creation of a new nation – 'a bounded space into which only some of the people can walk some of the time' (Bhattacharjee 1997, 317). Today, the dimensions of control are framed by dual concern to secure the nation against those perceived as threat – low-skilled workers, irregular migrants, smugglers, criminals, terrorists – while facilitating the entry of desired migrants such as investors and high-skilled workers. To some extent, as Sandra Lavenex has pointed out, questions of control have largely been framed in relation to the ability of states to deter the former type of migration. But 'this debate fails to account for states' approach to desired forms of migration' (2006, 34) of which certain types of labour migration are an example.

The Politics of Home

In Canada the desire to balance the tension between perceived threats and desired forms of migration is captured in the Minister of Immigration's, Elinor Caplan, remarks during the introduction of the 'Immigration and Refugee Protection Act' in 2000.

> Immigrants and refugees are now the main source of Canada's population and
> labour force growth. Our social and economic future, the very nature of the
> country, depends on them, and on our immigration and refugee policies. We

must close the back door to illegal entrants who abuse our laws, and open the front door to those on whom our growth and prosperity depends (Speech to the Fifth International Metropolis Conference, Vancouver, November 14, 2000).

Caplan's image of front and back doors evokes the familiar and powerful metaphor of the nation as a home.

The idea of home, however, can also motivate a deeper understanding of the politics of migration. William Walters' draws on the idea of home to develop an interesting analytic domopolitics which 'aspires to govern the state as a home' and exists in tension with a liberal political economy (2004, 237). This conceptualization draws attention to particular dynamics and features that mark the governance of security in the UK (2004, 241). The rationale that informs many measures is the invocation of home:

> ... the home as hearth, a refuge or sanctuary in a heartless world; the home as *our* place, where we belong naturally, and where, by definition, others do not; international order as a space of homes – every people should have (at least) one; home as a place we must protect. We may invite guests into our home, but they come at our invitation; they do not stay indefinitely.... Hence domopolitics embodies a tactic which juxtaposes the 'warm words' of community, trust, and citizenship with the danger words of a chaotic outside – illegals, traffickers, terrorists; (2004, 241).

Domopolitics then is intimately related to the governing of a population: 'who we are, what kind of state it is that governs us, how we are to be governed' (2004, 243). Thus, domopolitics not only provides an analytic for considering recent developments in the field of conventional security but also can be used to assess broader directions *vis-à-vis* economic security which necessitates facilitating the easy entry of the right kinds of 'human capital' (2004, 255). Further, Walter's conception of 'invited guests' can be considered in relation to temporary worker programs. In the case of Canada these forms of labour migration have grown and are predicated on the assumption that 'guests' will return to their own homes at the end of their work term as opposed to staying in 'our' home past their 'welcome'.

Relatedly and in an important intervention, Nandita Sharma explores the connection between home and nation to analyze migrant labour in Canada. She writes:

> By making themselves at home in the nation, the national state relies on the complicity of those with national subjectivities to make common sense of the highly differential treatment accorded those classified as the nation's Others, particularly those placed in legal state categories, like migrant worker, that organize their foreign-ness (2006, 4–5).

Sharma uses the term 'home economics' to capture the dynamics whereby unequal state categories draw lines through the nation's population (2006, 4). Conceptions of home and homelessness position and legitimize the denial of citizenship rights, entitlement and protections to migrant workers. She writes: 'it is the process of *differential inclusion* – not simply exclusion – that works to facilitate how people are seen – and see themselves – as being at home or not in the spaces in which they find themselves' (2006, 18).

At the centre of many current migration policies and practices today is a particular de-raced, de-gendered, but nonetheless celebrated archetypical subject: the high-skilled, self maximizing individual for whom national borders and political allegiances matter little. There is the assumption that such individuals hit the ground running – a win–win situation for all. For those constructed in this manner borders may mean very little but for others – especially migrant workers or those with irregular status – borders are in every aspect of their lives (Sharma 2006, 4).

Skill has proven to be one significant determining marker within labour migration. Drawing on the European situation, Eleonore Kofman has argued that the introduction of 'managed migratory regimes' has produced increasing differences in terms of mode of entry, education and skills leading to deepening civic stratification. 'There was a widening differentiation in entitlements between denizens, defined as long-term residents, temporary permit holders and those waiting for a decision about their status and the undocumented' (Kofman 2008, 14). In Canada, very similar processes of differentiation and stratification find expression in nationally specific ways. Of particular importance in the case of labour migration is the relationship between different categories of permanent and temporary residents.[1]

Immigration and Nation-Building

Whenever I travel abroad, or receive foreign visitors here at home, I am struck by how enthusiastically the rest of the world sees our model of pluralism and immigration. That success is no accident. It is the result of our history, of the values rooted in that history. A history of accommodating differences in culture, language, and religion, rather than trying to impose a false conformity (Jason

---

1   According to CIC, Permanent Residents are those individuals who have permanent resident status in Canada. Of particular importance are economic immigrants: 'Permanent residents selected for their skills and ability to contribute to Canada's economy. The economic immigrant category includes skilled workers, business immigrants, provincial or territorial nominees and live-in-caregivers and Canadian Experience Class.' In contrast temporary residents are 'foreign nationals who are lawfully in Canada on a temporary basis under the authority of a valid document. Temporary residents include foreign workers, foreign students, the humanitarian population and other temporary residents' (CIC 2009).

Kenney, Minister of Citizenship and Immigration, Address to the Canadian Club November 2008).

This is the 'official' or dominant view of Canada's history of immigration. As such it functions as part of the story of the Canadian nation what Anderson (1983) famously termed an 'imagined community'. This is a story of a settler society largely built on the efforts of French and English settler populations. It is a story that excludes and marginalizes indigenous peoples, 'other' migrants and many newcomers (Abele and Stasiulis 1989; Stasiulis and Jhappan 1995; Thobani 2007). Thus it is a story that is 'usually the property of elites, who use them to reinforce the status quo and to further their claims to privilege (Francis 1997, 12). But additionally this view has provided 'an important ideological justification for ignoring the patchwork of temporary migration schemes developed by these states since the early 20th century' (Stasiulis 2008, 104). While 'many European countries constructed the migrant labourers as "guest workers" … in settler societies a much larger proportion of immigrants were constructed (through immigration and citizenship policies) as settlers'. Nevertheless, settler societies have also used migrant labour in agricultural work and domestic service and have restricted 'the settlement and citizenship rights of these groups' (Stasiulis and Yuval Davis 1995, 22). Admittedly, the official view of Canada is partial and contested. But I want to suggest that the tension between this dominant view and the everyday lives of current immigrants and temporary migrants in Canada also provides a discursive space that social justice groups and others have used to contest recent directions in immigration policy.

Historically, Canadian nation building attempted to build a white dominion. That is, immigration policies actively worked to attract 'preferred groups' – British men and women and simultaneously worked to exclude or limit access to others. Between 1880 and 1884 Chinese men were recruited to build the Canadian Pacific Railway. Upon its completion the Chinese Immigration Act was introduced and it imposed a 'head tax' on Chinese immigrants making admission more and more expensive until immigration was completed curtailed by legislation in 1923. Similarly, the 1908 continuous journey regulations prevented the entry of South Asians. It should also be noted that while 'less desired' groups, such as Chinese and Asian men, were admitted as cheap labour, women and children were actively discouraged so as to prevent permanent settlement of these groups (Abu-Laban and Gabriel 2002, 37–9). 'Depending on their position in the racial/ethnic pecking order, foreign born workers were differentially incorporated into production relations as unfree temporary/migrant labour, unfree immigrant/settler labour, or free immigrant/settler labour' (Stasiulis 1997, 146). Complex stratifications were apparent from the start.

The explicit racial and gendered preferences within Canadian immigration policy have largely been rejected. The introduction of a points based model was a break with the explicit discrimination that characterized previous Canadian policy. However, the rationales informing the selection model still embodies a number of gender, racialized and class exclusions (Abu-Laban and Gabriel 2002).

Nevertheless, the introduction of this model was followed by a shift in source countries of newcomers to Canada from European countries to those of Asia. Consequently in 2008, China, India and the Philippines were the top three source countries (CIC Facts and Figures 2008). This said, many skilled immigrants from the global south have encountered problems accessing the labour market or are unemployed or underemployed. Consequently, while the earlier explicit racialized and gender barriers have been largely removed what has emerged is a paradox that even as the selection model is more micromanaged than ever before recent skilled workers are not faring as well as their predecessors.

Recent Directions in Canadian Policy: Labour for the Nation

Border controls and immigration policy, both past and present, are deeply implicated in shaping the national labour market insofar as these practices help shape the sale and regulation of labour. The recruitment of labour – whether permanent or temporary – under the auspices of a national immigration regime is predicated on a series of critical policy decisions including 'the *number* of migrants to be admitted; the *selection* of migrants (e.g. by skill or nationality); and the *rights* that migrants are granted after admission' (Ruhs and Martin 2008, 253). Each of these decisions is implicated within broader control claims.

    Whereas in the past people were recruited under various categories to build the 'new' nation today the skills of migrants are seen as a means to allow the nation to compete in a globalizing world. In its *Annual Report to Parliament on Immigration, 2008* Citizenship and Immigration Canada (CIC) states:

> In contributing to Canada's economic prosperity, Citizenship and Immigration
> Canada (CIC) seeks to address the pressing labour market and employer need
> for workers in the short term, while helping to maintain an adaptable and
> competitive labour force in the long term. The world has a limited pool of highly
> skilled labour, and Canada, is in competition with other industrialized countries
> for qualified workers (CIC 2008).

Despite 'skills talk' and the apparent universal acceptance of the desirability of skilled workers 'the definition of what categories of workers are 'skilled' and how the content of 'skills' is delineated is up to debate'. That skill is socially constructed and conceptions of skill are gendered and racialized do not figure in 'skills talk' (Gabriel 2004, 164). However the quest for high-skilled migrant workers, argues Martin Ruhs and Philip Martin, means employers and states are likely to offer them high wages and rights as an inducement. In contrast, countries may offer low-skilled migrant workers fewer rights (2008, 254).

    This section considers some of the recent shifts within Canadian immigration policy. It highlights how a desire for those constructed as 'high skilled' has informed some of the inclusions and exclusions of Canadian immigration policy by focusing on the mechanisms that govern the entry of workers to Canada – specifically the economic class on the permanent side and the foreign worker designation on the temporary side. Those who enter in the former stream are entitled to rights protections guaranteed in the Canadian Charter of Rights and Freedoms, mobility rights, social services as well as employment protections. They can also sponsor members of their family. After a period, currently three years domicile, permanent residents are allowed to apply for Canadian citizenship. And many do at rates higher than immigrants in the United States (Bloemraad 2006, 3). In contrast, temporary foreign workers enter Canada as 'unfree' workers. 'Unfree labour market incorporation means that workers are unable to circulate in a labour market due to legal constraints' (Trumper and Wong 2007, 151). Here status and length of stay is conditional on their work permit; temporary workers are often tied to one employer; and their ability to access rights is often very limited. For many there is no means to move from temporary foreign worker status to that of a permanent resident. In the period 2002 to 2008 the number of temporary work permit applications increased more than 124% (OAG 2009, 28). In some provinces the number of temporary entries exceeded those admitted as permanent residents. Consequently, there are a significant and growing number of people, organized as flexible, temporary workers, who are regulated differently and largely positioned outside the national imaginary. Or to use Sharma's (2006) words they are effectively 'homeless' within the national home.

Permanent Migration: The Economic Class

> Unlike the European model of recruiting 'guest workers', Canada has a history of actively recruiting people who arrive as permanent residents and go on to become citizens. This is a competitive advantage that Canada should not give up easily (Alboim and Maytree 2009, 4).

Under Canadian federalism immigration matters are the concurrent responsibility of the national state and the provinces and territories. For most of Canadian history the national state has played the key role in selection but increasingly provinces are emerging as important players. Immigration is governed by the *Immigration and Refugee Protection Act* which became effective in 2002. It requires that the government, through Citizenship and Immigration Canada (CIC), report on the numbers of people actually admitted in the previous year and outline the plan and target levels for immigration in the upcoming year. Since 2004, as Canada's Auditor General notes, immigration levels have changed little. One measure of the validity of control claims is to consider how well CIC has met its target level for immigration. Certainly, with the exception of 2007, between 2004 and 2008 CIC has been able to realize its numerical goals (OAG 2009, 9). However, a closer examination of the categories of the Economic Class reveal that a more complicated story is unfolding behind the numbers.

Federal Skilled Workers The selection of particular 'desired' skilled labour migrants is a key focus of immigration control. The centrepiece of Canada's immigration program – and by extension its high control claims – is the points based selection model. This model was developed in the 1960s to select independent applicants now called skilled workers under the current system. It was held up as universal, fair and transparent. Initially, points were awarded on the basis of education, occupation and age. Later changes further emphasized education and training, work experience and occupation demand (Li 2003, 24–5). Occupational categories in demand received the most emphasis. In 2001 Canada introduced changes to this selection model by moving away from an occupational demand list to an emphasis on transferable skills and human capital as embodied in individual immigrants (Abu-Laban and Gabriel 2002, 81).

> Up until 2001, 16 units could be assigned to education, 8 units to experience, 10 units to occupation, and 18 units to education and training…[in] the new grid a maximum 25 points could be given to formal education, 20 points to knowledge of official languages, 25 points to a skilled workers experience (Li 2003, 40).

The pass mark for the model has shifted from 75 points at introduction to current 67. The points based system is often held up as a model for other countries and influenced policy developments in Australia (Gabriel 2006, 192). Britain has also introduced a points system that targets the high skilled and skilled workers (*Migration Information Sources* 2008).

In 2008 IRPA was further amended as part of the Federal budget. One of the most significant changes was to give greater power to the Minister of Immigration to 'issue instructions to immigration officers regarding which applications are eligible for processing' (CIC 2008b). This constitutes a significant shift. The government's position was that change was needed to address the immigration backlog. Under IRPA CIC was required to submit all applications it received for processing. By 2008, there was an immigration backlog of 620,000 people – skilled workers and their families – waiting to have their applications processed. 'The average processing time was 63 months' (OAG 2009, 16). Under the new system applications would only be processed if individuals have either:

- have an offer of arranged employment, *or*
- be a foreign national living legally in Canada for one year as a temporary worker or an international student, *or*
- be a skilled worker who has at least one year of experience in one or more of the following [38 listed] occupations (CIC 2009).

The Canadian Council for Refugees (CCR) among others have charged that the amendments gave the Minister of Immigration too much arbitrary power over immigration rules and rendered the selection model vulnerable to political manipulation. It went on to state:

The proposed amendments come in the context of – and contribute to – a disturbing shift towards the use of immigration primarily to meet Canadian employers' needs, without regard to Canadian interest. This includes the problematic increasing reliance on temporary work permits. Canada needs to consider immigrants as full participants in society, not simply as disposable units to fill currently available jobs (CCR 2008).

This said, the points based selection model has always been tied to the needs of the economy. It effectively filters out many people who wish to come to Canada through the use of criteria that many Canadian born citizens would not meet. However, the labour market experiences of recently admitted skilled immigrants raises questions about the efficacy of the selection model's outcomes. It is in this respect that the policy gap between objectives and outcomes (Cornelius et al. 2004) is perhaps most apparent. Statistics Canada, for example, reports that 65.8% of recent immigrants were employed compared to 81.8% of Canadian born and the unemployment rates of recent immigrants were almost twice that of their Canadian equivalents (2003, 12). Numerous other studies have outlined the nature and scope of labour market disadvantage (Alboim, Finnie and Meng 2005; Hawthorne 2008; Weiner 2008). Moreover, many of the 38 occupations that are currently prioritized by the Federal Government are regulated occupations, namely those that are governed by provincial and/or professional associations. Statistics Canada recently noted that 'immigrants who studied outside Canada for a regulated occupation were less likely to be working in that occupation in 2006 than both immigrants who had studied in Canada and persons who were born in Canada' (Statistics Canada 2010). Australia which also uses a human capital approach now engages in an elaborate system of pre-screening in respect to language and mandatory credential assessment. Canada does not and analysts have charged that,

> ... its economic program admitted principal applicants with limited host country
> language ability, nonrecognized credentials and qualifications in fields that have
> weak labour market demand. By 2006, China, the Philippines, India, Pakistan
> and Korea were primary economic category source countries despite major
> potential labour market barriers... (Hawthorne 2008).

In spite of concerns over recent immigrants' labour disadvantage the skilled worker category is prioritized over that of family and humanitarian categories. 'The difference between *selecting* independent class immigrants and *admitting* family-class immigrants and refugees underscores the thinking that economic immigrants are more valuable and desirable' (Li 2003, 40–43). In other words, for many the points based model provides a measure of human capital 'quality control' whereas there is no similar provision for individuals who are sponsored or claim refugee status.

This criteria also effectively erects a barrier that keeps those constructed as low-skilled or those with less (recognized) education and training out of the country. They are by default relegated to low-skilled temporary worker migration programs if they want to work in Canada (Trumper and Wong 2007, 154). Secondly, legal routes of labour mobility and paths to citizenship are increasingly limited to the high skilled. The emphasis on skilled migration is accompanied by the devaluing of those perceived as less skilled and therefore possible drains on the welfare state, and as competitors with national workers (Kofman 2005, 458). Thirdly, in Canada public debate is marked by an almost complete denial of the often-unequal relationships between host countries and sending countries. There is little discussion of how the nation itself may be implicated in the poaching of skilled migrants from the global economic south and the attendant ethical issues this raises (Gabriel 2006, 194).

Provincial Nominee Programs   Permanent labour migration also takes place through Provincial Nominee Programs (PNPs). These programs are framework agreements between the Federal Government and Canadian provinces that allow the latter to put forward candidates for permanent resident status based on specific regional labour needs using provincially established criteria. Since 1998 all provinces have signed federal/ provincial/territorial accords. This system bypasses the national points based selection model and is a quicker route to permanent resident status. It has been observed that these programs were designed to match the federal skilled worker program 'but they are well on its way to replacing it' (Alboim and Maytree 2009, 35). Consider, 'provincial nominees grew by 31% since 2007 and 68% since 2006. In contrast, federal skilled workers grew by only 6% over 2007' (Alboim and Maytree 2009, 15).

The points-based selection model sets a national standard for selection that applies across the country. But the provincial nominee programs vary considerably from one province to another. In 2009, these programs included 'more than 50 different categories each with its own selection approach and criteria' (OAG 2009, 25). It has been pointed out that some provinces charge fees, some accept high skilled only while others also include low-skilled workers in their program. Some jurisdictions require individuals to work in a temporary worker program before being eligible for permanent resident under a provincial nominee program others do not (Alboim 2009, 35). The Auditor General of Canada has recommended that these programs be subject to evaluation to ensure that they are working in conjunction with the objectives of IRPA (OAG 2009, 25–7). It should be emphasized that provincial nominees, like those admitted under the skilled worker category, enjoy all the same rights guaranteed by the Canadian Charter of Rights and Freedoms and can obtain citizenship status. They are also not bound to one employer. Further, their rights of mobility are not circumscribed or compromised by their terms of entry. Consequently, individuals may move from one province to another whether or not their skills are in demand or whether they have the resources necessary to function in a different labour market (Alboim and Maytree 2009, 35).

Canadian Experience Class   In September 2008 the Federal Government added a new program to its Economic Category. The Canadian Experience Class (CEC) allows international students and some categories of temporary foreign workers with Canadian work experience to apply for permanent resident status. The program is designed to attract the best and brightest. Upon its introduction, the Minister of Immigration stated: 'With the Canadian Experience Class fully in place, Canada will be more competitive in attracting and retaining individuals with the skills we need... [it] will go a long way in bringing Canada in line with its global competitors (CIC 2008c). Not surprisingly, this route is only available to temporary workers with professional, managerial and skilled work experience. Under the Immigration Level Plan 2010 the CEC admissions target is 3% of the Economic Class (CIC 2008c).

On the one hand, it is recognized that this program provides an avenue for some select groups of temporary workers to secure permanent residence status and by extension Canadian citizenship. But, on the other hand, critics charge that the selection criteria upon which it is premised – successful labour market attachment is very problematic:

> The two years of work required before being able to apply under the CEC makes workers more vulnerable to employer abuse, as they may be reluctant to report abuse so as not to jeopardize their chances of obtaining permanent status. Experiences with the Live-in Caregiver program provide a concrete basis for these concerns (CCR 2008b).

The Canadian Council for Refugees further pointed out that the provisions of the CEC effectively excluded less skilled temporary foreign workers and refugees (CCR 2008b). In similar vein the Ontario Coalition of Agencies Serving Immigrants (OCASI) charged that the criteria was 'elitist and clearly discriminate on the basis of socio-economic status' and went on to point out 'all temporary foreign workers ... make a significant contribution to Canada's economic, social and cultural life' (2008).

Temporary Foreign Worker Programs

> Immigration is not about filling labour market shortages with just-in-time labour. CIC is not a temp agency. We should be building a nation of active citizens (Victor Wong, Chinese Canadian National Council, Evidence to Standing Committee on Immigration and Citizenship 2008).

Temporary foreign workers are now one of the Federal Government's central concerns. Indeed the Harper government has maintained that the current immigration system is too inflexible and cannot respond to changing labour market needs and shortages (Contenta 2009). In *Advantage Canada*, for example, it pledged to improve the Temporary Foreign Worker Program to address employer requirements. In the 2007 budget $50.5 million over two years was earmarked to fund 'a series of improvements to the TFWP designed to reduce processing delays and more effectively respond to regional labour and skills shortages' (cited by Sutherland 2008). These programs provide flexible labour and are directed at specific sectors and skills shortages. However, as Stasiulis has observed the threat of deportation operates as a key disciplinary mechanism in all temporary worker programs (2008, 103).

CIC reports that 192,519 people came to Canada as temporary workers in 2008 and since 2004 foreign worker arrivals increased by 71% (CIC 2009b). It is speculated that this expansion may be directly related to the backlog of applications in the permanent stream and requirements imposed by the selection model. That is people with lower levels of skill may not qualify under the points based selection model because of lack of language proficiency, level of education or occupational classification (Standing Committee on Citizenship and Immigration 2009, 4). Thus, the Standing Committee on Immigration and Citizenship's 2009 report on temporary and non status workers concluded:

> The expansion of the temporary foreign worker program represents a failure of the economic stream of immigration to bring in the type of workers needed and in a timely fashion ... There was widespread agreement that permanent immigration was more desirable and better for nation building than using increasing numbers of temporary workers (2009, 5).

Temporary workers enter Canada under a number of programs. CIC and Human Resources and Social Development Canada (HRSDC) are jointly responsible for the administration of work visas. Employers must apply to HRSDC for a labour market opinion (LMO) unless excluded by IRPA before any job offer can be made to a foreign worker. The LMO becomes the key to CIC's determination 'if the job offer is genuine and if the employment of the foreign national is likely to have neutral or positive effect on the labour market in Canada' (OAG 2009, 29). Temporary programs differ in terms of requirements imposed on employers and employees, the duration of the visa, and provisions to access permanent residence. Programs recruit at both ends of the skill spectrum but those targeted at high-skilled workers often have fewer requirements.

Of particular note is the shift in the country of origin among temporary workers that reflects what Trumper and Wong refer to as 'a racialization of temporary workers by skill level in that skilled and highly skilled tend to come from the US and Europe and lower skilled workers tend to come from Asia, Pacific and the Americas' (2007, 157). This observation is evident when examining the shifting priorities of the TFWP program. As the Alberta Federation of Labour (AFL) argues as the emphasis in the program shifted from high-skilled workers to low-skilled workers so did the country of origin. Consequently:

> When the program was focused on high-skilled occupations, the bulk of workers came from the US, Japan, United Kingdom and Australia. Today that trend has

reversed itself. The fastest growing source countries are Philippines, Mexico and India (AFL 2009, 11).

This shift as the AFL goes on to argue has a number of consequences for workers. First, 'language and cultural challenges become more pronounced. American or British workers have a relatively easy time acculturating to Alberta'. And second, as workers from the global south are more likely to be racialized minorities issues of racism come to the fore (2009, 11).

Three temporary foreign work programs are discussed briefly here: Seasonal Agricultural Worker Program (SAWP); the Live-in-Caregiver Program (LCP) and the more recent Project for Occupations Requiring Lower Levels of Formal Training.

Seasonal Agricultural Workers Program (SAWP)   The Seasonal Agricultural Workers Program (SAWP) is a longstanding temporary worker program and is 'widely recognized as one of the better administered temporary migration programs' (Basok 2007). Through a series of bilateral agreements migrant labour is recruited to work in particular agricultural sectors including fruits, vegetables, horticulture (Reed 2009, 476). Originally, workers came from the Caribbean (1966) and later from Mexico (1974). 'In 2006, 7806 Mexicans and 7,770 Caribbean workers came to work in Canada. Most workers are men, but about 3% are women, mostly single mothers' (Basok 2007). The program requires workers come for a specified period, anywhere from four to eight months, work 10–12 hours, six days a week (Muller 2005, 44). Source countries are responsible for managing labour recruitment and employers must guarantee hours of work and provide room and board. There are penalties attached to hiring unauthorized workers and for lending migrant workers to other farm employers (Martin 2006, 112). At the end of the period migrant workers must return home and there are no mechanisms to change their status to permanent resident. 'The overstay rate among SAWP workers is negligible' and a 2006 'World Bank report estimates it to be 1.5%' (Basok 2007).

Live-in-Caregiver Program   Temporary migrant labour is also recruited to address certain types of care deficits. Under the provisions of the Live-in-Caregiver Program (LCP) workers come to Canada to provide childcare care, eldercare or personal support in a private household. Two program requirements must be highlighted. First, workers must live in the homes of their employers. Second, the work permit names one specific employer. Numerous studies have outlined how the working conditions of live-in-caregivers are less than desired and are complicated by the live in requirement. Women labour in 'physical and social isolation, with little or no privacy and are often the victims of all kinds of abuse' (Langevin and Belleau 2000, 37). As one assessment noted the live-in-requirement:

... fuels the devaluation of their labour, allowing employers to pay them wages far below those paid to live-out caregivers who perform similar duties. In certain Canadian provinces, live-in caregivers continue to be excluded from basic employment standards such as minimum wage, the standard work week, vacation provisions and overtime pay (Khan 2009, 28).

Like other temporary worker programs, the LCP has grown in numbers. Applications for the LCP received abroad rose from 6,178 in 2002 to 20,799 in 2008 – an increase of more than 236% (OAG 2009, 34). The overwhelming majority of participants are women and figures indicate 95.6% of them in 2005 are from the Philippines (Khan 2009, 29). Unlike the SAWP discussed earlier this program includes a provision where live-in-caregivers can apply for permanent residence status after working 24 months within a 36-month period. Recent evidence from the Standing Committee on Citizenship and Immigration indicated that while this provision was important it also created circumstances where workers were inclined to tolerate poor conditions in order not to jeopardize their ability to apply for permanent residence (2009, 11).

Project for Occupations Requiring Lower Levels of Formal Training   In 2002 the government introduced a Low Skill Pilot Program. It was subsequently modified in 2007 to make LMOs valid for 24 months instead of 12 (Alboim 2009, 38). Its provisions allow employers to hire workers in jobs that require at most a high school diploma or on the job training. Visa can be issued for a period of 24 months. Employers are responsible for recruitment costs, return travel arrangements and ensuring that housing is available and meets a standard. Workers are usually recruited to work in cleaning, hospitality, manufacturing, oil gas and construction (Elgersma 2007).

A number of questions have been raised in respect to this program. Two are particularly noteworthy. First, the Auditor General has pointed out that the program is characterized by 'a lack of systematic assessments of the genuineness of job offers' and 'work permits could be issued for employers or jobs that do not exist' (OAG 2009, 32). This situation renders workers susceptible to unscrupulous recruiters (Alboim and Maytree 2009, 39). Second, workers' vulnerability also

arises because these workers are ineligible for services, subject to mobility restrictions, and dependant on their employer. They also have the added pressure of being unable to bring their families with them or to apply for permanent residence under the Canadian Experience Class (Alboim and Maytree 2009, 40).

Certainly, these concerns are supported by recent evidence given to the House of Commons Standing Committee on Citizenship and Immigration. Others have charged that Canada is on its way to creating its own 'Gastarbeiter Program' that will 'have the clear consequence of formalizing a sub-class of foreign workers who are marginalized from society, [and] vulnerable to exploitation and used by employers to suppress wages and working conditions in certain industries (AFL 2009, 31). To the extent that Canada continues using low-skilled temporary workers to address labour needs these issues will become increasingly pressing.

Conclusion

The control and regulation of labour migration in Canada is marked by an increasing number of programs and categories that sift/filter the population into citizen, partial citizens (permanent residents) non-citizens (low-skilled temporary workers) and those who may 'earn' citizenship (new Canadian Experience Class). This categorical organization of free and unfree labour is accompanied by unequal access to rights and protections. The differential inclusion of (im)migrants more often than not centres on a differentiation between those with skills and those without. A particular valorization of the 'high-skilled worker' dominates the 'skills talk' that imbues immigration debates.

The elaborate migration architecture erected by Canada, including the introduction of new categories within the economic class and the expansion of the temporary worker program, are indicative to the state's attempt to control and manage labour migration. However, as this chapter illustrated this attempt is not without problems. Within the economic category the points based selection model has equated high skill with higher levels of education and training and works on the assumption that selecting high-skilled workers will not only position Canada as a player in the global economy but such individuals will be less costly to integrate. The labour market experience of recent immigrants troubles this assumption. Similarly, the increasing volume and fragmentation of the temporary stream speaks to the shortcoming of the points based selection model, underscores that low-skilled workers are very much in demand and raises broader social justice questions.

The master narrative of the Canadian nation tells the story of a country built on the efforts of immigrants. It's a model home that has opened its doors to newcomers from all over the world and as such is seen as an 'ideal of pluralism and immigration'. Yet recent developments in the regulation of labour migration belie this discourse. Increasingly, the front door is opened to those with high skills. Temporary workers, especially the low skilled, enter as 'guests' and must not overstay their welcome – on terms that circumscribe their mobility, rights and renders them vulnerable. If we return to the title of the government's economic plan *Advantage Canada* perhaps the broader question to be considered is in whose 'advantage' are recent directions in immigration policy.

Bibliography

Abu-Laban, Y. and Gabriel, C. 2002. *Selling Diversity: Immigration, Multiculturalism, Employment Equity and Globalization*. Peterborough: Broadview.

Alberta Federation of Labour (AFL) and Temporary Foreign Worker Advocate. 2009. *Entrenching Exploitation*. Edmonton: AFL, April.

Alboim, N. and Maytree. 2009. *Adjusting the Balance: Fixing Canada's Economic Immigration Policies*. Toronto: Maytree, July, www.maytree.com/policy.

Alboim, N., Finnie, R. and Meng, R. 2005. The Discounting of Immigrants Skills in Canada, IRPP *Choices*, 11(2).

Anderson, J. and Shuttleworth, I. 2004. A New Spatial Fix for Capitalist Crisis? Immigrant Labour, State Borders and the New Ostracising Imperialism, in *Global Regulation. Managing Crises After the Imperial Turn*, edited by K. van der Pijl, L. Assassi and D. Wigan. UK: Palgrave, 145–61.

Arat-Koc, S. 2005. The Politics of Family and Immigration in the Subordination of Domestic Workers in Canada, in *Inequality in Canada*, edited by V. Zawilski and C. Levine-Rasky. Toronto: Oxford.

Basok, T. 2002. *Tortillas and Tomatoes: Transmigrant Mexican Harvesters in Canada*. Kingston-Montreal: McGill-Queens.

Basok, T. 2007 Canada's Temporary Migration Program: A Model Despite Flaws, in *Migration Information Source*. Washington: Migration Policy Institute, November.

Bhattacharjee, A. 1997. The Public/Private Mirage: Mapping Homes and Undomesticating Violence Work in the South Asian Immigrant Community, in *Feminist Genealogies, Colonial Legacies, Democratic Futures*, edited by M.J. Alexander and C.T. Mohanty. New York: Routledge, 308–29.

Bloemraad, I. 2006. *Becoming a Citizen: Incorporating Immigrants and Refugees in the United States and Canada*. Berkeley: University of California Press.

Canadian Council for Refugees (CCR). 2008. 10 Reasons To Be Concerned About Proposed Amendments To Immigration and Refugee Protection Act (IRPA) in Bill C-50, www.ccrweb.ca/documents/c5Otenreasons.htm.

Canadian Council for Refugees (CCR). 2008b. Comments on the Canadian Experience Class, 28 January, www.ccrweb.ca/documents/CECcomments. pdf.

Caplan, E. 2000. Why Immigration will Shape Canada's Future, Text 1749, *Canadian Speeches*, 14(06) (January/February 2001).

Citizenship and Immigration Canada (CIC). 2000. *Building on a Strong Foundation for the 21st Century: The Legislative Review Process*, June, http://cicnet.ci.gc. ca/English/aboutpolicy/lr/e_lro3.html.

Citizenship and Immigration Canada (CIC). 2005. *The Monitor*. Summer.

Citizenship and Immigration Canada (CIC). 2006. *Facts and Figures: Immigration Overview Permanent and Temporary Residents*.

Citizenship and Immigration Canada (CIC). 2008. *Annual Report to Parliament on Immigration 2008*, http://www.cic.gc.ca/English/resources/publications/annual-report2008/.

Citizenship and Immigration Canada (CIC). 2008b. *Backgrounder: Action Plan for Faster Immigration. Ministerial Instructions.* http://www.cic.gc.ca/English/department/media/backgrounders/2008/ 2008/-11-28.

Citizenship and Immigration Canada (CIC). 2008c. *News Release: Canadian Experience Class Now Open For Business*, Ottawa: September, www.cic.gc.ca/English/department/ media/releases/2008/2008-09-05c.asp.

Citizenship and Immigration Canada (CIC). 2009. *Eligibility Criteria for Federal Skilled Worker Applications*, www.cic.gc.ca/English/immigrate/skilled/apply-who-instructions.asp.

Citizenship and Immigration Canada (CIC). 2009b. *Annual Report to Parliament on Immigration, 2009*, www.cic.gc.ca/English/resources/publications/annual-report2009.

Cornelius, W., Tsuda, T., Martin, P. and Hollifield, J. (eds) 2004. *Controlling Immigration: A Global Perspective*. CA: Stanford Press.

Department of Finance Canada. 2006. *Advantage Canada: Building a Strong Economy for Canadians*. Ottawa: Department of Finance.

Elgersma, S. 2007. *Temporary Foreign Workers*. PRB 07-11E. Ottawa: Library of Parliament, www.parl.gc.ca/information/library/PRBpubs/prb0711-e.htm.

Elrick, J. 2007. Country Profile: Canada, *Focus Migration*, 8 (March).

Francis, D. 1997. *National Dreams: Myth, Memory and Canadian History*. Vancouver: Arsenal Pulp Press.

Gabriel, C. 2004. A Question of Skills: Gender, Migration Policy and the Global Political Economy, in *Global Regulation: Managing Crises After the Imperial Turn*, edited by K. van der Pijl, L. Assassi and D. Wigan. UK: Palgrave, 162–76.

Gabriel, C. 2006. Charting Canadian Immigration Policy in the New Millennium, in *Canada Among Nations 2006*, edited by A. Cooper and D. Rowlands. Kingston-Montreal: McGill-Queens.

Gabriel, C. and Pellerin, H. (eds) 2008.*Governing International Labour Migration: Current Issues, Challenges and Dilemmas*. UK: Routledge.

Galabuzi, G.-E. 2005. *Canada's Economic Apartheid: The Social Exclusion of Racialized Groups in the New Century*. Toronto: Canadian Scholars Press.

Hawthorne, L. 2008. The Impact of Economic Selection Policy on Labour Market Outcomes for Degree Qualified Migrants in Canada and Australia, IRPP *Choices* 14(5).

Kofman, E. 2005. Citizenship, Migration and the Reassertion of National Identity. *Citizenship Studies* 9(5), 453–67.

Kofman, E. 2008. Managing Migration and Citizenship in Europe: Towards an Overarching Framework, in *Governing International Labour Migration: Current Issues, Challenges and Dilemmas*, edited by C. Gabriel and H. Pellerin. UK: Routledge, 13–26.

Lavenex, S. 2006. The Competition State and Multilateral Liberalization of Highly Skilled Migration, in *The Human Face of Global Mobility*, edited by M. Smith and A. Favell. New Jersey: Transaction Publishers.

Li, P. 2003. *Destination Canada: Immigration Debates and Issues*. Toronto: Oxford.

Migration Information Source. 2008. *Top 10 Migration Issues of 2008: Issue #2 – The Recession Proof Race for Highly Skilled Migrants*. December, www.migrationinformation.or/Feature/.

Mueller, R.E. 2005. Mexican Immigrants and Temporary Residents in Canada: Current Knowledge and Future Research, *Migraciones Internacionales* 3(1), 32–56.

Office of the Auditor General of Canada. 2009. Chapter 2; Selecting Foreign Workers Under the Immigration Program, in *Report of the Auditor General of Canada to the House of Commons*. Ottawa: Minister of Public Works and Government Services Canada.

Ontario Coalition of Agencies Serving Immigrants. 2008. *OCASI Comments on the Canadian Experience Class Program*, 14 April, www.ocasi-org/index?qid=979.

Reed, A. 2008. Canada's Experience with Managed Migration. *International Journal*, Spring.

Reitz, J. 2004. Canada: Immigration and Nation-Building in the Transition to a Knowledge Economy, in *Controlling Immigration: A Global Perspective*, edited by W. Cornelius et al. CA: Stanford.

Reitz, J. 2005. Tapping Immigrants' Skills. IRPP *Choices* 11(1).

Ruhs, M. and Martin, P. 2008. Numbers vs. Rights: Trade-Offs and Guest Worker Programs, *International Migration Review*, 42(1), 249–65.

Sharma, N. 2006. *Home Economics: Nationalism and the Making of 'Migrant Workers' in Canada*. Toronto: University of Toronto Press.

Standing Committee on Citizenship and Immigration. 2009. *Temporary Foreign Workers and Non-Status Workers: Report of the Standing Committee on Citizenship and Immigration*. 40th Parliament, 2nd Session, May.

Stasiulis, D. 1997. The Political Economy of Race, Ethnicity and Migration, in *Understanding Canada: Building on the New Canadian Political Economy*, edited by W. Clement. Montreal-Kingston: McGill-Queens, 141–71.

Stasiulis, D. and Bakan, A. 2003. *Negotiating Citizenship: Migrant Women in Canada and the Global System*. UK: Palgrave.

Stasiulis, D. and Yuval-Davis, N. (eds) 1995. *Unsettling Settler Societies: Articulations of Gender, Race, Ethnicity and Class*. London: Sage.

Statistics Canada. 2003. The Changing Profile of Canada's Labour Force. *2001 Census Analysis Series*. Ottawa: Statistics Canada, 11 February.

Statistics Canada. 2010. Study: Immigrants Working in Regulated Occupations. *The Daily*, 24 February.

Thobani, S. 2007. *Exalted Subjects: Studies in the Making of Race and Nation in Canada*. Toronto: University of Toronto Press.

Trumper, R. and Wong, L. 2007. Canada's Guest Workers: Racialized, Gendered and Flexible, in *Race and Racism in 21st Century Canada*, edited by S. Hier and B.S. Bolaria. Peterborough: Broadview, 151–70.

Walters, W. 2004. Secure Borders, Safe Haven, Domopolitics, *Citizenship Studies*, 8(3) (September).

Weiner, N. 2008. Breaking Down Barriers to the Labour Market Integration of Newcomers in Toronto. *IRPP Choices* 14(10), September.

Other

Sutherland, J. 2008. HRSDC, Powerpoint Presentation at Policy Research Seminar on Temporary Migration, March 12, 2008.

Chapter 7

Competing Interests in the Europeanization of Labour Migration Rules

Anaïs Faure Atger

Immigration policies, because they imply confronting and reconciling different sovereign interests, are complex issues to be addressed among States. A new actor, the European Union (EU), has nonetheless gained over time both in influence and competence in the area of migration for the purpose of labour. While binding upon all 27[1] Member States of the Union, the rules adopted at the European level can only be implemented insofar as they are transposed and applied at the national level, as the EU has no coercive power. The policy discussions taking place at EU level thus provide an ideal backdrop for examining the current power struggles surrounding the theme of economic migration. By mapping out the different interactions taking place between the EU, the States of origin, those of destination and employers, this contribution aims at bringing to light the position of the individuals involved. Following an overview of national policies on labour migration in Europe, the moves towards the development of an EU labour migration policy are considered. European legislation on migration constitutes a complex regulatory framework which includes conditions for entry and residence, employment, family reunification, as well as for subsequent movement within the European territory. This chapter examines the extent to which the EU is creating a supranational framework for the access by third country nationals to its labour market and the circumstances under which this is taking place.

A National Control Challenged by the EU

Within the EU, the national regimes applicable to labour migration tend to vary from one Member State to another. While those regimes are shaped by national history, demography and geography as well as politics which are specific to each Member State, a cross-country comparison reveals some common principles

---

1   The EU is composed of 27 Member States: Austria, Belgium, Bulgaria, Cyprus, the Czech Republic, Denmark, Estonia, Finland, France, Germany, Greece, Hungary, Ireland, Italy, Latvia, Lithuania, Luxembourg, Malta, the Netherlands, Poland, Portugal, Romania, Slovakia, Slovenia Spain, Sweden and the United Kingdom.

(Faure Atger and Guild 2009). These include the prior identification and bonding of the employee to an employer; exhaustive lists of potential positions open to foreigners; and the designation of privileged groups and jobs for which specific procedures are foreseen. While simplifying national realities and dynamics, such a categorization contributes to uncovering the balance of interests and powers in the European dialogue on labour migration. And even though current bilateral agreements concluded with third countries, as well as more favourable schemes for certain categories of workers, tend to somehow undermine these common trends, the following elements generally characterize standard procedures.

Employers' Authority over Admission

The most salient feature of national regulations on labour migration is the fact that a person wishing to migrate from abroad on professional grounds can do so only with the assistance of the future employer. He/she must have already identified, prior to arrival (thus from the country of origin), a position which he/she can occupy. This implies that for a potential migrant to obtain the necessary documents to enter a Member State for economic purposes, a position needs to be open and suitable, in view of his/her qualifications, his/her desire to apply must be known to the employer and his/her chances of being selected need to be genuine. In some countries such as Denmark, it is even necessary for the migrant to receive the assurance (such as a personalized job offer or a contract) that he/she will be employed in order to be granted an authorization to enter. The role played by the employing company is therefore critical.

Employers are, in a majority of national regimes, the ones who initiate the administrative proceedings. In fact, their prior intervention is generally required before a third country national can contact the consular authorities of the country to which he/she wishes to migrate. Most Member States consider this a requirement for granting the necessary visa or provisional residence permit to access the territory. Such is the situation in the Netherlands where the administrative procedures can only be launched if the employer has made an official declaration in favour of such a process. In Spain, the employer needs to make a subscription to the social welfare system before a third country national can obtain the work authorization necessary for a visa, whereas a Slovenian employer needs to report the identity of the third country national to the national labour department before an entry authorization is granted. The employer is thus empowered by the State to carry out externally control over access to the national territory.

This often complex procedure results in a dependency of the employee on his/her future employer, both prior to entering the country and within it, where this state of affairs continues. The issuing of a work permit and the associated residence rights usually depends upon the continuity of the job for which a third country national has first entered a country. Although documents may not always be delivered at the same time, the validity of the residence permit is made conditional upon the continuity of the employment for which the individual enters the country.

This is the case for instance in Slovenia where the duration of the residence permit matches the duration of the work contract. Such situations imply that conflicts or tensions with an employer will directly affect the employees' administrative status and may involve their immediate return to the country of origin.

State Oversight of the Labour Market

Despite the fact that the employer is the one entrusted to launch the admission process, the State thereafter intervenes in two different ways. First, all Member States require that the proposed remuneration be at least the minimum national salary for an equivalent position. While this requirement ensures equal treatment in pay whether the employee is a national or a third country national, its main purpose is to prevent unfair competition with the local labour force. Second, local workers are always given priority. As we will see in the next section, the European project has led to an adaptation of this principle towards the so-called community preference. Today, following the national test, priority is given to the European labour force before considering applications from third countries.

The task of assessing local labour market availability before recruiting a third country national rests either with the employer or with the State. In Germany, it is a State authority, the federal labour agency, which ensures that no unemployed German national fits the job profile, and that this recruitment will not negatively affect the local labour market. In other countries, the burden of proof remains with the employer, who must demonstrate that the advertised position cannot be filled by a member from the preference groups. A British employer must prove that no jobseeker has the desired profile by making the position public for a sufficient period of time (four weeks) to allow potential local candidates to come forward. In Romania, even if the employer has unsuccessfully taken all necessary steps to recruit at the national level, the local authorities still have the final say as they can subsequently impose a candidate.

The State's aspiration to exclusively control access to its labour market is further reflected in the control of the overall share of third-country nationals entering for labour purposes, though it is often defined with the assistance of employers. Annual quotas determine the maximum number of work permits granted to third country nationals country-wide, or on a sectoral basis. In Slovenia for instance, this quota cannot be greater than 5% of the national labour force. Each year, the Romanian Ministry for Employment proposes quotas which are then approved by the government. In Spain, quotas are established per sector in cooperation with employers and trade unions and, for those positions specified in the tri-annual lists published, it is no longer necessary to assess the availability of the local labour force.

The number and types of positions open to third country nationals can thus also be determined through lists which are revised depending on the perceived needs of the labour market. These correspond to gaps in the local labour force reflecting the lack of attractiveness of some sectors, such as agriculture, services or transport, depending on the country and period of time. In Germany, the *Ausländerbeschäftigungsverordnung* is a detailed catalogue of positions open to third country nationals. Administrative procedures can then be immediately initiated with due respect to the quota criteria. These national safeguards nevertheless tend to become optional for the employment of third country nationals in areas where the labour force is particularly scarce. Filling these positions with third country nationals is considered profitable enough to remove most obstacles to their employment.

Privileged Categories of Workers

Over the years, privileged schemes have emerged when dealing with what is considered as *highly qualified employment*. In several recently modified national legislations, certain types of jobs are open to third country nationals without having to comply with the usual entry requirements. Journalists, language teachers, artists or scientists fall under this category, thereby entitling them to more favourable regimes and treatment. Depending on the Member State, these privileged schemes benefit certain categories of workers, depending on their qualifications, earnings or expertise.

In the United Kingdom, since 2008 an individual must gather 65 points in four different categories (education, experience achieved in past positions, results obtained in the relevant domain) in order to qualify for facilitated access. For professions where the local workforce is particularly scarce, such as the health sector, extra points can be granted. Accumulating a sufficient number of points allows access to Britain without a prior job offer. In Germany, those considered as highly qualified according to the salary earned (€86,400 in 2008 and €63,000 in 2009) can immediately expect to receive a permanent residence permit. In the Netherlands, a university degree combined with a proposed remuneration higher than €49,087 grants a facilitated access to the territory. However, this trend is not a common feature in all Member States; in Slovenia and Poland the current national legislations do not reflect such an approach.

Consequently, some categories of labour migrants benefit from more favourable rules which provide exceptions to the standard, burdensome procedures. Facilitated access is granted through the removal of checks and controls usually exercised by the State. However, the determination of these privileged categories varies from country to country, as the selection operates on the basis of occupation, education, salary or qualifications.

European Rules for the Entry of Third Country Nationals

Migration became an EU competence with the adoption of the Amsterdam Treaty in 1999.[2] This traditionally national prerogative was gradually affected and shaped by the Europeanization of the movement of persons, and particularly the 'freedom of movement' principle applied to an expanding EU (Guild 2009). This now essential aspect of the status of European citizenship was primarily intended for European workers, although it was later extended to all Member State nationals as well as to some categories of third-country nationals. It meant that for certain groups, there was now a right to move across borders, without the prior assent neither of a potential employer nor of the destination state. Three European legislative instruments have further affected national competence over the entry and residence of third country nationals and transferred it to the EU arena.

On 1 May 2004, Directive 2004/38, the so-called 'Citizenship Directive', came into force, thereby strengthening the right to move and reside for all citizens of the Union and their family members and registered partners, whether they are citizens of the Union or not. This Directive expressly entitled the latter to independent rights including employment. However, five years later, the controversial Metock ruling[3] demonstrates the reluctance of Member States to let EU law govern the access to residence and working rights for third country nationals (Carrera and Faure Atger 2009).

Council Directive 2003/86/EC on the right to Family Reunification[4] provides for the granting of rights and benefits to family members of third country nationals legally residing in the EU. These include the right to facilitated access to the territory, a residence permit of at least one year, access to the labour market and to education. As regards the right to employment, equal treatment to the sponsor is provided, although a labour market test may be applied during the first year. For sponsoring a family member, the third country national must legally reside in a Member State, have a valid residence permit for at least one year and have reasonable prospects of obtaining the right of permanent residence. The negotiation of this Directive took three years and considerable discretion was left to the individual States to interpret the Directive, which explains why various limitations and conditions continue to prevail at the national level (Carrera 2009).

At the Tampere Council in 1999,[5] Member States had agreed that the legal status of third country nationals should be approximated to that of nationals. A person who has resided legally in a Member State for a sufficient period of time

---

2   Article 63(3)(a) EC Treaty.

3   European Court of Justice, Case C-127/08, *Metock* [2008].

4   Council Directive 2003/86/EC setting out common rules on the exercise of the right to family reunification by third-country nationals residing lawfully in Member States, OJ L 251/12, 3.10.2003.

5   Tampere Council Conclusions of 15 and 16 October 1999, SN 200/99, Brussels, paragraph 21 (1999).

and who holds a long-term residence permit should have in that country access to a set of uniform rights which are as close as possible to those enjoyed by EU citizens: the right to reside, to receive education, and to work as an employee or self-employed person. The translation of this political commitment into concrete rights led to the adoption of Council Directive 2003/109 on the status of third country nationals who are long-term residents. This instrument covers the status of those non-EU nationals having resided for a period of five years in the territory of a Member State and provides for equal treatment compared with EU citizens as regards employment conditions.

As a consequence of these instruments, for certain categories of third country nationals, Member States are no longer entitled to freely decide which entry and residence criteria to apply. Those are now provided for in European law and subject to supra national review by the European Court of Justice. However, common rules for accessing the EU for the purposes of labour were still lacking. In fact, the various initiatives promoted by the European Commission encountered fierce national resistance which have been hard to overcome and have effectively slowed down legal developments in this field.

Overcoming Member States' Reluctance

Notwithstanding the political consensus demonstrated at the Tampere Council, no substantial steps towards the design of a common European approach to the entry and stay of third country nationals have been taken so far. And even though Member States' reluctance to transfer this sensitive policy area to community level may explain this situation, the progressive Europeanization of rules for entry and residence of certain third country nationals has certainly also played a role. Over the past three years, and following an approach guided by Member States, the Commission has nevertheless submitted a series of proposals, among which the Blue Card[6] and the single framework of rights and procedures[7] constitute the most concrete endeavours. At the same time, discussions taking place under the Global Approach to Migration have provided the means to deal with this topic in a renewed setting and have thus had important implications for the EU agenda on labour migration.

---

6   Proposal for a Council Directive on the conditions of entry and residence of third-country nationals for the purposes of highly qualified employment, COM(2007) 637 final, Brussels, 23.10.2007.

7   Proposal for a Council Directive on a single application procedure for a single permit for third-country nationals to reside and work in the territory of a Member State and on a common set of rights for third-country workers legally residing in a Member State, COM(2007) 638 final, Brussels, 23.10.2007.

Europeanization and the Unanimity Rule

Even though other matters dealt with under Title IV of the EC Treaty have been acted upon since 2004 by means of a qualified majority vote under the rule of co-decision with the European Parliament, the Council has up until the adoption of the Lisbon Treaty managed to keep this focus area under its sole competence.[8] The June 2001 Commission proposal for a Directive on the conditions of entry and residence of third country nationals for the purpose of paid employment and self-employed economic activities[9] provides a good example of the difficulties triggered by the requirement of unanimity. It was so fiercely challenged within the Council that, in view of the lack of consensus, it was finally withdrawn five years later.[10]

In 2004 the European Commission presented a Green Book[11] so as to re-launch a debate on the added value of a European approach to legal migration.[12] This process highlighted the reservations of Member States, as well as their preference for a differentiated approach to legal migration. Such logic implied taking into account the various levels of qualifications of migrant workers when granting them rights. In parallel, the national competence on the issue of quotas was maintained. The Hague programme[13] further compounded this trend, thus encouraging the Commission to submit various legal proposals which would allow speedy response to the fluctuating needs of the Member States. The Commission therefore published in December 2005 a Communication on a Policy Plan for Legal Migration[14] in which it announced the publication of five proposals on labour migration between 2007 and 2009.

The emerging European policy towards labour migration thus moved away from the development of a comprehensive policy, which would involve defining common rules for access to any employment across the European Union, towards sector-specific rules according to the type of activity to be pursued by the migrant

---

8   Decision 2004/927/EC of 22 December 2004 providing for certain areas covered by Title IV of Part Three of the Treaty establishing the European Community to be governed by the procedure set out in Article 251 of that Treaty, OJ L 396/45, 31.12.2004.

9   Proposal for a Council Directive on the conditions of entry and residence of third-country nationals for the purpose of paid employment and self-employed economic activities, COM/2001/0386 final, OJ C 332E/248, 27.11.2001.

10   See Withdrawal of Commission proposals following screening for their general relevance, their impact on competitiveness and other aspects, 52006XC0317(01), OJ C 64, 17.3.2006.

11   Green Paper on an EU approach to managing economic migration, COM (2004)811 final, Brussels, 11.07.2001.

12   The contributions provide an oversight of the various perceptions on the added value an EU approach (http://ec.europa.eu/justice_home/news/consulting_public/economic_migration/news_contributions_economic_migration_en.htm).

13   The Hague Program (OJ C 2005/53, 3.3.2005), item 1.4.

14   Commission Communication, Policy Plan on Legal Migration, COM(2005) 669.

worker. Four different categories were identified: highly qualified workers, seasonal workers, remunerated trainees and intra-corporate transferees. The respective proposals are thus meant to provide for different rules and procedures in each field of occupation, while admission onto European territory remains dependent on what Member States consider to be their 'national absorption capacities'(Guild 2009). By partly reflecting national schemes that favour certain groups, the Commission has focused on reaching a consensus within the Council at the expense of an innovative, rights-based European migration policy. Nevertheless, moving Europeanization forward at all costs might have undermined the already disputed added value of an EU approach towards labour migration (Ryan 2007).

Attracting 'Skills' to the EU

Over the last ten years, increasing competition with other industrial countries has prompted the progressive establishment of legislative frameworks specially targeted at *highly qualified migrants*. The EU Blue Card,[15] designed to send a 'clear signal that highly qualified migrants are welcome in the Union,'[16] is the first proposal to be adopted in the field of labour migration since the publication of the 2005 Policy Plan.

Negotiations towards an agreement have been difficult within the Council, since Member States' perceptions as to who belongs to the category of highly qualified workers or to who should be granted facilitated access to the labour market vary significantly. The scope of the Directive bears evidence of this, in that highly qualified employment is considered as sanctioning an advanced university degree following a minimum of three years of study or relevant professional experience of at least five years. The second criterion, according to which the salary offered in the destination Member State has to be at least 1.5 times the average gross national salary, reveals who the real sponsors of such a framework are, as eligibility depends exclusively on the salary which the company is willing to propose. This aspect puts those countries where the differences in pay are not as pronounced as in others at a disadvantage. As a consequence, some countries will be more accessible than others and intra-European mobility, meant to be one of the main advantages of an EU wide scheme, appears problematic. In fact, access to the whole EU labour market is only granted after one and a half years, provided conditions similar to those for first admission are fulfilled.

To be eligible for a Blue Card,[17] a third country national must be in possession of a work contract or a formal offer of employment of at least one year in a Member

---

15   Council Directive 2009/50/EC on the conditions of entry and residence of third-country nationals for the purposes of highly qualified employment, OJ L 155/17, 18.6.2009.

16   Jose Manuel Barroso's speech of the 23 October 2007, following the publication of the Commission Proposal, COM(2007)637 final.

17   Article 5 of the Directive.

State. The subsequent procedure leading to the issuance of a permit should not last more than a month. After two years of work, the card can be renewed provided a contract exists. Nevertheless, after three consecutive months of unemployment or at least two periods of unemployment, the Blue Card will be cancelled. This provision appears to be inconsistent with the European Convention on the Legal Status of Migrants Workers of 1977, which provides for a minimum of five months of unemployment before the residence permit of the migrant can be revised.

Blue Card holders are to be treated equally with nationals of Member States as regards working conditions which include: pay and dismissal; freedom of association; education, training and recognition of qualifications; a number of provisions in national law regarding social security and pensions; access to goods and services including procedures for obtaining housing; and information and counselling services. With respect to family reunification, it should be noted that Blue Card holders benefit from more favourable rules than those described in the relevant directive. The fact that multiple entries are permitted and access to the other Member States facilitated after 18 months of employment is considered to constitute a unique pull factor for candidates. Companies in particular welcomed the scheme as a valuable tool for enhancing the attractiveness of the EU as compared with the USA and Canada. Nonetheless, small and medium enterprises affirmed that further measures were needed to satisfy the need for other categories of workers. Indeed, the strategy based on attracting high skills and mainly pursued by industry ministries generally benefits powerful transnational companies (Bigo and Guild 2005).

The Blue Card should be greeted as the first real EU instrument for labour migration; however, its added value is jeopardized by the fact that existing national schemes for the highly qualified may remain in force. Furthermore, Member States can again impose national quotas on the number of third country nationals they are willing to accept in this framework and are free to continue applying national admission procedures. In fact, a whole series of provisions are subject to national interpretation, including those relating to the admission procedure, which Member States may leave in the hands of the employer or of the employee, within or outside their territory. Notwithstanding the emergence of an EU labour migration scheme, Member States thus still retain a significant margin of control over the implementation of EU standards, while the exercise of authority for the recruitment of third country nationals is more than ever left in the hands of the employers through the salary criteria.

Establishing EU-wide Rights and Procedures

Aware that a common European procedure would significantly contribute to the establishment and visibility of a European approach to labour migration, the Commission submitted such a proposal in October 2007. Several actors including the European Trade Union Confederation and the European Parliament welcomed the move and highlighted the need to adopt a collective procedural framework before attracting skills.[18] The relevant proposal nevertheless remains under negotiation at the time of writing. By 'aligning and accelerating the procedures necessary for gaining access to the EU labour market for third country nationals,' it aims to simplify access to the EU for labour purposes through the establishment of a common combined residence and work permit with a single application procedure. This permit would provide those third country nationals concerned by the Directive a right to move within and outside the EU, during the time they are carrying out the activity for which the permit has been granted.

In line with the logic currently pursued, it is meant to apply to those third country nationals wishing to be admitted into the European Union in order to work and reside, as well as to those who have already been admitted but do not yet qualify as long-term residents. The scope of the proposal is nevertheless further limited, as seasonal workers, applicants for international protection or temporary protection schemes, third country nationals whose expulsion has been suspended, the highly qualified and those entering under special agreements will not be covered by these procedures. This not only undermines the idea of establishing a *unique* and *uniform* work permit for third country nationals but also further blurs the picture of a common European labour migration scheme.

According to the proposal, *comparable* rights to those of European migrant workers are to be guaranteed in some fields linked to the employment circumstances, such as working conditions, participation in trade unions, social security and health protection. However, equal treatment may be subject to actual employment. This appears extremely problematic when it comes for instance to enforcing labour rights against unfair dismissal. By linking the work and residence permit, administrative procedures for the third country national will be facilitated. This will also reinforce the dependency of the third country national on his/her employer. The interruption of the work contract will immediately have an impact on his/her residence status and related rights.

As regards national control, the one-stop shop will facilitate control by the Member State over migration flows. Furthermore national quotas for the issuance of such permits are maintained. Finally, the length of the permit and the conditions for obtaining, renewing and withdrawing it would continue to be a matter of national competence. As this Directive was originally intended to have a significant impact, it should ideally have been discussed and amended prior to the other proposals. The fact that it has not will undoubtedly limit the scope and effect of this piece of legislation.

---

18   See in particular the position of the European Trade Union Confederation and the EP Report on the Policy Plan on Legal Migration, rapporteur Lili Gruber, 17.9.2007, Final A6-0322/2007.

The Global Approach to Migration

Notwithstanding the adoption of the Lisbon Treaty, which involves a transfer to the co-decision and qualified majority procedure[19] over labour migration, since 2005 further advances in the field were attempted through a more comprehensive European strategy. It was agreed to address the topic of migration along policy concerns other than Justice and Home Affairs, such as Development, External Relations, in particular the European Neighbourhood Policy, and Employment.[20] The driving logic of what strives to be a global approach consists in building a coherent framework and ensuring adapted partnerships with third countries covering the fight against irregular migration, enhanced links between migration and development and legal migration (including for the purpose of labour).

The implementation of this global approach to migration has so far led to two mobility partnerships, with Cape Verde and Moldova, which have been developed and negotiated under the auspices of the EU.[21] Consisting of non-legally binding agreements (Joint Declarations) between certain Member States (15 in the case of Moldova and 5 in the case of Cape Verde) and a particular State of origin, they cover issues of irregular immigration, legal channels of human mobility and cooperation in the area of migration and development. And even though their nature and effect are contentious, the favourable assessment carried out by the Commission, and their endorsement within the Council show that they will most probably become prominent instruments of the EU's external relations and migration agenda (Carrera and Hernandez i Sagrera 2009).

The labour migration provisions revolve to a large extent around capacity building, information sharing and the establishment of paths for mobility mainly of a temporary nature allowing a kind of circular migration. The Member States which have engaged in these frameworks have committed themselves to guarantee nationals of those 'partner' third countries a facilitated access to certain positions, as shows the following excerpt from the Moldovan Mobility Partnership document:

> IV. Access to the Labour Market – Proposal by Italy to further implement its project providing support for potential entrants to the Italian labour market, as it will promote sector-specific projects for Moldovans. Proposal by Sweden to

---

19   Article III-267 of the Lisbon Treaty. As the Lisbon treaty formalizes for the first time the European competence in this area, it does maintain current practice, whereby Member States keep their national prerogative when it comes to determining the number of migrants they are prepared to take in.

20   Commission Communication, *Priority actions for responding to the challenges of migration: First follow-up to Hampton Coutts*, COM(2005) 621 final, 30.11.2005.

21   Council of the EU, Joint Declaration on a Mobility Partnerships between the European Union and the Republic of Moldova, 9460/08, 21 May 2008, Brussels; and Council of the EU, Joint Declaration on a Mobility Partnership between the European Union and the Republic of Cape Verde, 9460/08, Brussels, 21 May 2008.

develop a pilot project to disseminate information in the Republic of Moldova about the impeding Swedish labour migration reform as regards recruitment of workers from third countries in certain sectors. Proposal by Poland to offer admission to the Polish labour market for temporary work without the need to obtain a work permit.[22]

One year later, both mobility partnerships have been evaluated positively by the Commission. Nevertheless, it does warn against the risk of them being a 'collation of new and already planned activities' and calls for further efforts to ensure their added value for the partner country.[23] In the long run, privileged paths for migration will be further developed with other countries depending on the interest demonstrated by Member States and third countries.[24]

Other tangible endeavours in the field of labour migration taken within the framework of the global approach include a migration and information management centre in Mali (CIGEM) and various labour management activities such as capacity building in national employment and migration agencies (ANAPEC in Morocco).[25] As highlighted by the Council, the global approach should enable '*Member States [to ensure], within the framework of their national legislation, the emergence of legal migration opportunities, in particular according to the needs of their labour market.*'[26] Currently, this seems to lead to a proliferation of specific bilateral arrangements, containing provisions on labour migration, migration and development and especially cooperation in the EU efforts against irregular migration. The consistency and coherence of the European approach towards labour migration will be inherently challenged by the development of such schemes. However, in light of the Commission's efforts to develop an EU methodology towards these instruments, this now appears to constitute the main policy setting for discussing economic migration at EU level.

Re-allocation of Power in the Labour Migration Agenda

The move towards the Europeanization of the rules on access to the EU by third country nationals for labour purposes has been hampered by Member States' resolve to maintain their influence over this sensitive topic. However, emphasizing

---

22   Annex on proposed activities, p. 12.

23   European Commission (2009), Staff Working Document, Mobility Partnerships as a tool of the Global Approach to Migration, SEC(2009) 1240, Brussels, 18.9.2009.

24   European Commission, Communication 'An Area of Freedom, Security and Justice serving the Citizen', COM(2009)262, Brussels, 10.6.2009.

25   A migration researcher's network across the Mediterranean (CARIM) has also been established. These initiatives are cited in COM(2008) 611 final, 8.10.2008.

26   2914th General Affairs Council meeting, 8.12.2008.

the need to ensure credibility and economic profitability, the EU has nevertheless developed paths to address this issue at supranational level.

In its Communication on a Common Immigration Policy in Europe: Principles, Actions and Tools,[27] the Commission calls for the achievement of a prosperous union through the enhancement of 'the contribution of legal migration to the socioeconomic development of the EU' as 'appropriate management of economic migration is an essential element of EU competitiveness' and in particular the EU's Lisbon strategy for growth and jobs.[28] This clearly illustrates that the EU is willing to assist in the development of labour migration paths for the benefit of European economies. Whether this has contributed to the transfer of control over the establishment of labour migration opportunities away from the national realm to the European level is far from certain. In spite of the successive shifts in approaches, it indeed appears that the Member States' reluctance has brought about a dispersed and fragmented EU framework where the protection of the rights of third country nationals still depends to a large extent on the prospective employer.

Illusive EU Power over Migration

In the European Union, national legislations in the field of legal migration can be characterized by some common principles – described in the first section of this chapter – which follow a similar logic, i.e. the State's desire to protect local labour markets while satisfying its economic actors. These common features however vary from one Member State to the other at the implementation level.

National policies undergo significant changes as governments come and go and economic priorities are reassessed. Characterized by a high level of State control, the operation of which is often entrusted to employers, these legal frameworks tend in general to severely restrict access to the territory, except for those professions for which labour shortages have been identified. By filtering the movement of third country nationals, the current national legislations also condition access to employment, housing, education and social benefits. In contrast, when it comes to the treatment of those migrants capable of fulfilling positions considered profitable for the economy and for which no candidate can be found at the local level, procedures and access to basic rights are facilitated. The driving force of these policies appears therefore to be both the desire to satisfy perceived needs of economic actors and the protection of internal labour markets, at the expense of an approach based on the rights and security of the individual on the move.

---

27   Communication from the Commission to the European Parliament, the Council, the European Economic and Social Committee and the Committee of the Regions, A Common Immigration Policy for Europe: Principles, Actions and Tools, COM (2008) 359 final, 17.6.2008.

28   Lisbon Strategy, European Council (2000), Lisbon European council, Presidency conclusions, 23–24 March 2000.

At EU level, the only instrument adopted so far in this area is extremely limited both in scope and in terms of benefits because of its closeness to national legislations. The current imbalance between legislative outputs relating to the control of irregular migration and those covering the development of legal channels for facilitating access to the EU shows that Member States' common priority consists of creating the illusion of an inaccessible EU, the admission to which is strictly controlled. In a first phase, legal and physical channels for accessing the EU were reduced and rendered highly complex through the development of enhanced border controls and the imposition of strict visa obligations in an attempt to block passage towards the EU (Bigo and Guild 2005). In parallel, a filtering logic has focused on the development of a selective scheme for labour migration. This may have facilitated agreement among Member States, but the rationale currently pursued by the EU labour migration scheme appears redundant and to lack added value compared to national developments.

In the discussions at EU level, while labour migration is envisaged as a solution to demographic change, to be implemented in the interest of economic growth and fulfilling the Lisbon strategy, the complex scheme which is emerging hardly seems capable of meeting these objectives. Actual economic needs could potentially provide some justification to such utilitarian short-term approach to labour migration. However, the need for low and medium-skilled workers demonstrated by ongoing regularization procedures in some Member States, such as those in favour of care workers introduced in 2009 in Italy, further highlights the current disregard of current labour market requirements in the development of corresponding legislation. In fact, both at national and EU level, employers are given coercive powers over third country nationals; it is also because of their control capacity that the EU has, by means of a Directive, prescribed the cooperation of employers in countering irregular migration for the purpose of employment (Carrera and Guild 2007).[29]

The preamble to the Directive, in effect the first one to sanction an aspect of irregular migration with criminal penalties, justifies its enactment by presenting the possibility of employment without the required legal status as a key pull factor for unregulated entry and stay in the EU. As a penalty to the employers, the Directive foresees financial sanctions and public condemnation. Should this measure be seen as an expression of the reassertion by the EU of its competence over labour migration, a way for Member States to recover the financial benefits they have lost by the related tax avoidance or a manner of demonstrating to their public opinions that they remain in power? With the adoption of this Directive and the extension of a strategy largely based on detention and expulsion, the EU is sustaining an approach which criminalizes irregular migrants. Such an approach seems nonetheless incapable of curbing the phenomena when as a consequence the

---

29   Directive 2009/52/EC of the European Parliament and of the Council of 18 June 2009 providing for minimum standards on sanctions and measures against employers of illegally staying third-country nationals, OJ L 168, 30.6.2009.

migrant is further pushed towards anonymity and invisibility. Maintained in the informal economy, 'the undocumented' or rather those who have failed to comply with the complex framework described above are all the more exposed to abusive labour relations and to violations of their basic social and economic rights.

Interplay of National and Private Stakes

The implementation of the global approach to migration seems to have further fragmented the European endeavour to design a common framework on labour migration. Alongside technical arrangements for facilitating the control and analysis of the labour force present in third countries, it has so far practically resulted in the emergence of various agreements between certain EU Member States and other third countries. The inherent intergovernmentalism of such developments undermines the call for a genuine EU approach. Nonetheless, it appears to now constitute the frame for future discussions on labour migration.

Bargain-type relations have emerged between countries of origin and country of destination, whereby those third countries having the most potential to draw the attention and interests of the EU Member States may benefit from privileged schemes for sending their workers to the EU. So far these have been identified in the immediate vicinity of the EU at the southern Mediterranean border and the eastern neighbouring countries. The channels offered in the mobility partnership demonstrate a desire to have the third state participate in stopping irregular migration towards the EU as well as enable its labour force to contribute to the economy of the European Union. This is considered to be beneficial to the third state as it is supposed to ultimately enhance its development through capacity building and the sending of remittances.

With respect to labour migration rules, the aspiration is still the need to match skills and competences available in countries of origin with the priorities, needs, numbers and volumes determined by each Member State. The related discussions are thus mainly in the interest of the receiving States. While the sending State is called upon to contribute by being made accountable in the European efforts to counter unregulated migration, the pledges made by the Member States in return hardly seem to be balanced: the Member State will inform potential migrants about the risk of travelling irregularly, assist the return of migrants especially of those highly skilled to their country of origin, facilitate the transfer of remittances and provide some limited opportunities for legal migration. The current rhetoric based on *partnerships* and *cooperation* builds upon an illusive role for sending countries. However, the commitments which sending States need to make in the context of these global partnerships appear disproportionate when compared with the benefits they receive from such alliances in a limited number of countries. The bargaining power of the EU as a collective alliance of national interests clearly shifts the control balance away from individual third States.

In this regard, the role given in the implementation phase to new actors with different agendas should not be minimized as it further blurs an already complicated picture. Currently, European agencies such as the European Training Centre, FRONTEX, intergovernmental agencies such as ICMPD and IOM supplement functions traditionally entrusted to employers as they are called upon to implement the strategies developed by Member States within the Global Approach. This proliferation of actors is hardly justified, especially when one considers the little consideration given to trade unions. As to the role given to employers, they are now invited to identify future needs of European economies and to provide employment positions upon the return of the third country national to the country of origin. After Member States formalize the type of desired migration with regard to their economic and political commitments, third, non-state actors with diverse priorities are thus empowered to control the entry and legal status of third country nationals both within national frameworks as well as in the proposed European frameworks.

Traditionally, the definition of labour migration rules was strictly controlled by Member States, while their implementation was left in the hands of economic actors in their position of employers. The EU has progressively sought to gain competence and initiative in this area, but Member States have demonstrated fierce resistance, in effect blocking the adoption of any real European pathways for labour migration. The added value of a European policy in this field would rely upon its autonomy and novelty compared to national legislations. However the approach which is currently envisaged takes the opposite direction, as shown by the adoption of a facilitated scheme for the highly qualified and the move back towards the national realm within the global approach. On the one hand, the Blue Card provides a limited response to current economic interests and is characterized by a rigidity which will prevent it from being adaptable both to fluctuating economic requirements and to the various national settings. On the other hand, the Global Approach emerges as uneven and fails, but for the provisions on irregular migration, to demonstrate a real European dimension. Even though the current rationale is based upon a balance of interests and an exchange between the EU and countries of origin, the bargaining power of the EU as an alliance of national interests enables the development of strict commitments in the efforts against irregular migration and leaves few opportunities for labour migration. The global approach has thus both shifted labour migration opportunities back to bilateral arrangements as well as enabled the emergence of various transnational actors.

Conflicting forces are at play in the EU agenda on labour migration, giving rise to a blurred picture. In this context, the position of the individual moving to the EU for labour migration purposes remains extremely weak, as a fragmented and inefficient set of European labour migration rules has emerged at the expense of a rights-based approach. (Carrera and Faure Atger 2009b). The consistency of EU policy on migration is here at stake and the adoption of a Common Immigration Code, which would provide a consolidated framework of protection respectful of the fundamental rights of the individual on the move could underpin the EU's claims to promote migration opportunities towards its economic area and give those claims more credibility.

References

Bigo, D. and Guild, E. (eds) 2005. *Controlling Frontiers: Free Movement into and within Europe.* Aldershot: Ashgate.

Carrera, S. 2007. *Building a Common Policy on Labour Immigration: Towards a Comprehensive and Global Approach in the EU?* CEPS Working Document. Brussels: Centre for European Policy Studies.

Carrera, S. 2009. *In Search of the Perfect Citizen? The Intersection between Integration, Immigration and Nationality in the EU.* Leiden: Martinus Nijhoff Publishers.

Carrera, S. and Faure Atger, A. 2009a. *Implementation of Directive 2004/38 in the context of EU Enlargement: A Proliferation of Different Forms of Citizenship?* Brussels: Centre for European Policy Studies.

Carrera, S. and Faure Atger, A. 2009b. 'Yes a Rights Based approach to migration is possible!', in *What Future for Justice and Home Affairs within the EU?*, *ENARgy*,29. Brussels: European Network Against Racism.

Carrera, S. and Guild, E. 2007. *An EU Framework on Sanctions against Employers of Irregular Immigrants: Some Reflections on the Scope, Features and Added Value. CEPS Policy Brief.* Brussels: Centre for European Policy Studies.

Carrera, S. and Guild, E. 2008. *The French Presidency's European Pact on Immigration and Asylum: Intergovernmentalism vs. Europeanisation? Security vs. Rights?* CEPS Policy Brief. Brussels: Centre for European Policy Studies.

Carrera, S and Guild, E. 2009. *Towards The Next Phase of the EU's Area of Freedom, Security and Justice: The European Commission's Proposals for the Stockholm Programme.* CEPS Policy Brief. Brussels: Centre for European Policy Studies.

Carrera, S. and Hernandez i Sagrera, R. 2009. *The Externalisation of the EU's Labour Immigration Policy: Towards Mobility or Insecurity Partnerships?* CEPS Working Document. Brussels: Centre for European Policy Studies.

Faure Atger, A. and Guild, E. 2009. L'accès au travail des ressortissants de pays tiers en Europe: Comparaison des législations de 9 états membres, in *Immigration, qualifications et marché du travail*, edited by G. Saint-Paul for the Comité d'Analyse Economique. Paris: La Documentation Française, 131–55.

Guild, E. 2004. Mechanisms of Exclusion: Labour Migration in the European Union, in *Justice and Home Affairs in the EU: Liberty and Security Issues After Enlargement*, edited by J. Apap. Cheltenham: Edward Elgar, 211–55.

Guild, E. 2009. *Security and Migration in the 21st Century.* Cambridge: Polity Press.

Guild, E. and Staples, H. 2003. Labour Migration in the European Union, in *The Emergence of a European Immigration Policy*, edited by P. de Bruycker. Brussels: Bruylant, 171–247.

Ryan, B. 2007. The European Union and Labour Migration: Regulating Admission or Treatment?, in *Whose Freedom, Security and Justice? EU Immigration and Asylum Law and Policy*, edited by A. Baldaccini, E. Guild and H. Toner. Oxford: Hart Publishing, 489–515.

Chapter 8

Australia and Labour Migration

James Jupp

The east coast of Australia was claimed for Britain by Captain James Cook in 1770 and settled by the British government as a convict colony in 1788. Over a period of seventy years, six distinct colonies were created (New South Wales, Tasmania, Western Australia, South Australia, Victoria and Queensland). These came to constitute the six States of federal Australia in 1901. Before federation each colony had its own immigration policy. There was then a transitional period to 1920 until the national Commonwealth government fully assumed its constitutional power over immigration. Immigration policy since then has been centralized and is uniform throughout the entire continent. Between 1788 and 1872 the United Kingdom government exercised an influence over policy. It resumed an interest (though not control) in the 1920s and from 1947 to 1982 through a joint system of assisted migration based on free or subsidized passage costs from Britain to Australia. This was extended to several European states from 1950 (D. of Immigration 2001). In practice the British contribution was minimal during this latter period but the assisted passage terms were favourable to British subjects.

For 150 years emigrants from Britain were helped through this system, which was only extended to non-British immigrants between 1947 and the termination of the system in 1983. Since then only UN Convention refugees, usually selected in agreement with the UNHCR, have had free passages. During the period 1947–1983, non-British immigrants were assisted on the basis of refugee status or by agreement with sending governments. No immigrants or refugees were assisted who were not of 'European descent and culture', until total racial exclusion was ended by 1973. For the entire period from 1901 to the present, immigration has been governed by two frequently amended Acts – the *Immigration Restriction Act 1901–1958* and the *Migration Act* since 1958. There are also a host of frequently changing regulations to implement the legislation and bureaucratic practices which do not necessarily need parliamentary approval. Australia has had a unique Immigration Department at the national level with its own Cabinet minister since 1945. Its name has changed six times to reflect differing priorities, but it is now officially the Department of Immigration and Citizenship (DIAC).

Traditions and Continuities

This brief history is illuminated by some basic popular conceptions of Australia which had long lasting currency. These included its description as 'remote', 'empty' and 'British' in the colonial period; as 'distant', 'empty' and 'white' in the half-century after federation; and as 'insecure', 'underdeveloped' and 'multicultural' over the past 50 years. There is still public debate about the latter descriptions – some claiming, especially in the 1990s, that Australia was 'full up' and had no further need of immigrants, while others denied the description 'multicultural' and criticized policies which departed from the 'white British' traditions of the past. These debates cut across partisan divisions, with governments of both major parties (Labour and Liberal) favouring a steady immigration intake. Public opinion was normally rather sceptical, but oscillated quite significantly between satisfaction and unhappiness with the intake and its sources (Jupp 2007). However the open racism which characterized public debate between the 1880s and the 1960s is now more carefully expressed and in many respects absent. What remains true is that Australia is one of the least densely populated countries in the world, but also one of the driest, with current problems of water usage as in the past (Sloan 2006).

Continuities relevant to *labour migration* need to be understood against this general background. Australia began its settlement history as a convict colony and this system existed in New South Wales until 1840, in Tasmania until 1851 and in Western Australia until 1868. While there was some free settlement during these periods it was not a happy start. Democratic institutions and politics did not become firmly established until the convict system was ended. For the next generation entry to Australia was free to those able to make the lengthy voyage, although legislation was passed in some colonies to restrict the numbers of Chinese arriving in the various gold rushes. The colonial connection with Britain and the assisted passage schemes ensured that nearly all permanent settlers were British or Irish, Germans being the only major exception. Policy was thus directed to remedy the three problems of distance, emptiness and Britishness. Assisted immigrants were mainly recruited from British and Irish rural areas and were expected to go into agricultural labour after arrival. However, in an empty land, there were much greater opportunities for access to land than in Britain or Ireland and many soon became farmers on selections provided by colonial governments. Many others simply settled in the cities, which public policy and official statements deplored but did nothing about (Richards 2008).

There were also important openings in mining, railways and building which manual labour could fill. The controversial exception to all this was the employment of Pacific Islander (*kanaka*) labour on sugar plantations between 1870 and 1900. Slavery was abolished in the British Empire in 1833 but never applied in Australia, where convict labour and Pacific Islander indentured labour took its place. Part of the argument used by campaigners against the convict system in the early years was that it was a form of slavery. A similar attack was launched against the employment of Pacific Islanders later in the 19th century. A tradition was established against bringing anyone into Australia who was subject to controls and limitations on their freedom. This was incorporated into the *Immigration Restriction Act* in a prohibition on indentured labour. The principle was established, with the full support of the strong trade union movement, that immigration was for permanent settlement, not for transitory labour needs. This tradition has now been undermined by governments from both sides of politics favouring employer nominated temporary workers in increasing numbers.

Organized Labour and Labour Recruitment

Middle-class immigrants came to Australia at their own expense and established themselves in commerce and the professions. But the bulk of assisted immigrants were from the rural, and later the industrial, working classes of Britain and Ireland. The shift from rural to urban intakes was apparent by the 1880s and was especially marked in New South Wales. As there was manhood suffrage for British subjects, this meant that the voting population had some experience of British trade unionism or Irish nationalism and was able to use that to press its demands on elected governments to a much greater extent than in the United Kingdom. Trade unions of manual workers were well established by the 1880s and they formed Labour political parties in the 1890s. By 1904 these were able to elect the first 'labour' government in the world and this was repeated more effectively between 1910 and 1914. Similar governments were elected at every State level by 1915. This made industrial issues, including the recruitment of labour through immigration, of continuing importance, especially as Labour governments legislated to protect and advance organized labour. The Australian Labour Party was exceptionally strong among manual labouring rural workers, which gave it a wider electoral basis than its British counterpart. Although founded largely by English and Scottish Protestants, it captured a large part of the large Irish Catholic vote by 1920 and retained it for the next 40 years.

Labour government and trade union influence was marked in the policy towards the largest intake of tied labour, the 171,000 European displaced persons admitted between 1947 and 1953. These were obliged to take any work allocated by the Commonwealth government for the first two years of their settlement. These terms were modified under the post-War Labour government and its successor to stipulate that wages and conditions granted to local workers under the arbitration system must also apply to the DPs. This was significant in gaining union support for the scheme at a time when about 50% of the workforce was unionized. As elsewhere, union membership has declined in recent decades and union influence has been limited under conservative governments. However the election of a Labour Party government nationally in 2007 has increased union influence once again, if not to its levels of 50 years ago (Jupp and Kabala 1993). Of Australia's nine governments, all but one are currently under Labour control.

Selection and Exclusion

Mainly because of its isolation, Australia has been able to effectively control entry since it became a national responsibility in 1901. There are fewer than 20 legal points of entry, all of them with permanent immigration officers. While British subjects could enter without further identification than a passport – and New Zealanders did not even need that – in recent years visa control has been extended to everyone and visas must be obtained outside Australia rather than at the border, except for New Zealanders. This is unusually rigid and more so than for Britain, the United States and Schengen Europe, all of which extend more concessions to Australia than are reciprocated. This allows Australia to vary its intake annually in the light of economic and labour market conditions, although this is limited by the length of time taken to approve permanent residence and family reunion visas. A substantial bureaucracy is kept busy investigating the applications. Flexibility thus becomes a problem if there are sudden gaps in the labour market or an unexpected economic downturn. Both of these problems were becoming acknowledged from 2000. Business visas can now be processed very quickly, while tourist visas from selected countries are issued electronically. Family reunion visas, however, take much longer.

Flexibility has more recently become a problem because of the discovery of serious labour shortages in manual occupations, especially in agriculture and catering. Because policy since 1988 had increasingly favoured the highly skilled and university educated, applicants without these attributes were usually rejected. Pressure from rural employers – close to the then Liberal–National government – was important in opening up the question of attracting labour to rural areas, to which immigrants rarely go. State government pressure from South Australia encouraged a scheme to grant relaxed conditions to 'provincial areas', which included most of Australia outside Sydney, Melbourne and southeast Queensland. The employer nomination scheme was used to tie doctors and other professionals into remote locations, which they could only leave at the risk of losing their visa.

The constitution (s51.xxiiiA) prohibits 'any form of civil conscription'. Bonded labour was used in the post-1947 period for Displaced Persons from Europe in the exceptional circumstances of lingering wartime regulations. Temporary labour visas have not been held to breach this prohibition. In recent years many regionally based visas have preferred location in specific areas, but there is little effective mechanism to implement this. However, loss of employment to a specific employer may invalidate a temporary visa unless an alternative job can be found within a short period. The immigrant may then become an 'unlawful non-citizen' liable to detention and deportation. As a general rule temporary labour visas cannot be renewed for a period exceeding eight years.

Temporary visas became increasingly popular as a way of attracting labour without creating an increased demand for permanent settlement with its implication of citizenship, family reunion and access to publicly funded services. However, overseas students were encouraged to remain because they qualified under the points system. Eventually almost half the skilled intake was already in Australia and completing its courses. This raised the issue of whether students were using the system to gain permanent residence – which they obviously were and, indeed, were encouraged to do. One measurable result was a rise in Chinese and Indian residents with academic qualifications (Khoo and McDonald 2003). However, many of the courses undertaken and the colleges providing them were of dubious economic value. Early in 2010 the new Labour governent began the process of refining qualifications for permanent residence with a strong emphasis on English language skills.

Under the points system introduced in 1979 and frequently modified, tertiary qualifications gained in Australia give a great advantage to former students, who no longer need to return home to change their visa status. What was undesirable was not 'category changing' from temporary to permanent, but the flourishing of substandard colleges and courses offering an easy road to permanence. Another problem was the limitation of paid employment for students to 12 hours a week, which many found inadequate to generate a living wage. Breaching this limit could also lead to the fate of an 'unlawful non-citizen'. A residue of students awaiting removal for this breach was maintained at detention centres such as Villawood in Sydney, though not sent to remote centres reserved for asylum seekers, such as Baxter.

A detailed 'micromanaged' system was developing a complex range of alternative visas which required legal advice to secure the best result. A further complication was the small number of asylum seekers and Convention refugees whose claims to refugee status had to be processed and were open to appeal if unsuccessful. While Convention refugees were chosen in (mainly African) camps, asylum seekers were more random and could not be processed overseas as they had already arrived 'unlawfully' (at least in the eyes of the government if not in the terms of the UN Convention). This created an expanded detention system in prison-like conditions, which became a burning issue from the late 1990s and eventually overshadowed all public discussion of immigration policy. Australia became internationally notorious for its drastic policies. Even when recognized as genuine refugees – as most asylum seekers were – they were only granted temporary protection visas, creating an uncertain and disadvantaged minority. One side-effect of this was to utilize Afghan refugees as rural abattoir workers, at which they excelled. This suggested to rural employers that immigrants could be recruited to their industries, many of which had severe labour shortages in thinly peopled districts. These temporary protection visas were replaced by permanent residence visas by the Labour government elected in November 2007. The government sought to process asylum seekers within the terms of the UN Convention and ended the process of detaining them in distant and independent Nauru rather than in the Australian territory of Christmas Island. These changes coincided with an increased intake due to the Sri Lankan political situation.

Public policy was thus faced with a dilemma. Great efforts and expense had gone into discouraging asylum seekers coming by boat, while unskilled applicants for permanent residence were routinely rejected under the points system. Thus less-skilled vacancies could not be filled either by refugee applicants or by other immigrants not favoured as permanent settlers. The solution was seen to be the major departure from the tradition of authorizing temporary residence for semiskilled workers with employer nomination. Temporary skilled workers had always been welcomed and were essential in many industries such as mining, which drew on skills for special tasks. But anything like a 'guest worker' system had been so consistently rejected by Australia for decades that the new '457' visa scheme raised potential opposition. In fact it did not arouse much, as there was full employment and widespread recognition of shortages in many industries. A further variant on past practice was a proposed scheme to bring in Pacific Island workers for agriculture, at the request of Pacific Island governments. This emulated a long standing New Zealand scheme and is yet to become fully operational. For many years Australia has also operated a working holiday scheme for young people from selected countries, who have proved vital in some areas of agricultural harvesting. This has recently been expanded. The largest intake has been British. Temporary migrants now exceed the family and humanitarian component by far and the total numbers being admitted are higher than in any post-War period.

The rapid expansion of the immigration intake on the basis of temporary visas (457), was the response of the Howard Liberal Coalition to the demands of its employer and rural constituencies. Coming into office in 1996 unconvinced of the need for expanded immigration, Howard's government cut the intake for the next two years. However, it left office in 2007 with the highest intake for a generation, much of it based on temporary entrants. The central feature of the scheme is sponsorship by employers, although State governments may also nominate. Subclass 457 visas are available for 'primary' workers and their 'secondary' dependents in roughly equal numbers. Secondary dependents are spouses and school age children, who are eligible for paid employment but not welfare and medical benefits. Temporary labour immigrants numbered under 40,000 per year until 2005–5, when they took off rapidly towards 115,000 in 2007–8. In the latter year 58,050 primary visas were granted, of which the largest numbers were in New South Wales, Victoria and Western Australia. The projected intake of 130,000 for 2008–9 included both 457 entrants and Working Holiday youths at record levels higher than for 40 years (DIAC 2008).

The Deegan Report of 2008

The incoming Rudd Labour government accepted this expansion, but was less sympathetic to demands from employers to ease restrictions. With a strong and vocal union base, the Labour Party had traditionally suspected the motivation and ongoing practices of employers. The most recent official investigation into the 457 scheme is within that tradition. The final report *Visa Subclass 57 Integrity Review* by Barbara Deegan (an industrial relations expert and former public servant) was presented to the Rudd government in October 2008 (Deegan 2008). The Deegan report drew on widespread submissions and interviews with many interested parties and was strongly influenced by some major unions. The peak body – the Australian Council of Trade Unions – 'welcomes this review into the integrity of Australia's Temporary Business Long Stay – Standard Business Sponsorship (Subclass 457) Visa... The current scheme fails to adequately protect the rights of temporary overseas workers.' The report was presented to the Deputy Prime Minister and the Minister for Immigration and Citizenship, but has an excessive number of 57 recommendations, many of which are unlikely to be implemented.

The report draws attention to complaints already recorded by the Australian Human Rights Commission. These included:

- not being paid overtime
- working longer hours than other employees
- limited access to sick leave and dismissal if leave is taken
- dismissal because of pregnancy
- dismissal for taking carer leave
- rent overcharging for employer provided facilities
- sexual harassment.

Among the report's particular concerns were that the 457 visa program should not damage existing conditions and thus lose public support. The Queensland government argued for 'the clear understanding that it does not undermine Australian employment opportunities, wages or working conditions'. New South Wales echoed this in calling for respect for 'the rights and dignity of employer sponsored migrants'. These approaches were endorsed in the first recommendation that 'so far as possible ... Subclass 457 visa holders should have the same terms and conditions of employment as all other employees in the workplace'. The terms of reference focus on the same concerns:

- measures to strengthen the integrity of the 457 program;
- the employment conditions applying to workers under the program;
- the adequacy of measures to protect employees from exploitation;
- health safety and training measures
- English language requirements
- opportunities for Labour Agreements between workers and employers.

The inquiry was not asked to examine the terms and conditions under which 457 entrants might convert their visas to permanent residence. This had become very common for those on overseas student visas after their local graduation. The report was most concerned with those recruited on lower wages rather than those on high professional salaries, who were assumed to command secure and superior positions. Even those on the lower scales had skills and unskilled, non-English-speaking entrants were not being sought. However some of the skills, for example in catering and construction, were noted for their breaches of conditions. A minimum wage was required for 457 visas, but this was not always being met in practice.

Other concerns were about the integrity of migration agents and the danger of overseas recruiters giving false information and extracting extra payments, a practice common in China from the 19th century. Employers were also to be forbidden to deduct payments in exchange for approving visa applicants. Secondary applicants (wives and dependent children) were to enjoy the right to employment and employers should be levied to cover costs of access to the public health system Medicare. Dependents would also be eligible for English language training as would principle applicants, allowing them access to existing provision for permanent immigrants under the Adult Migrant English Program.

Some Issues and Potential Problems

The recent shift towards temporary labour recruitment is a complete reversal of the principles established a century ago. These prohibited indentured labour and the recruitment of manual workers from Asia and the Pacific. Nation building, on the basis of permanent residence leading to citizenship, assumed both that immigrants should come from similar (i.e. British) cultures and should remain. In practice neither of these principles was applied as rigorously as the White Australia policy (1901–1973) which was based on race. There was always an element of movement back to original homelands or onwards to North America. There were occasional waves of European migration, especially following the United States restrictions of 1924 and the rise of Nazism after 1933. These became much more common from 1947 to 1975. Citizenship was eventually made easy, with a waiting period of only two years after arrival (now raised to four years). Until 1982 many immigrants (and the majority of the British) were assisted generously with their fares. Only since then have British citizens been treated on the same basis as others. One consequence has been a shift from Europe to Asia as the main source of settlers (Hugo 1986). Declining numbers from Britain were replaced to some extent by increasing numbers from New Zealand and South Africa and the decline was slightly reversed in the last years of the Liberal government, mainly due to increased temporary migration.

The changes introduced in the 21st century reverse much of these traditions. It is still expected that the majority allowed in for permanent residence will remain and become Australian citizens. The majority are still selected on the basis of their skills, education, language facility and employability and the trend away from family reunion to skilled intake was already consolidated by the 1990s. The humanitarian intake under the UN Convention on Refugees has remained at a very modest and relatively declining level. Asylum seekers arriving from outside the approved intake were detained in a manner increasingly draconian and controversial until changes introduced by the new Labour government in 2008.

Those arriving by sea are still detained for inspection on remote Christmas Island, an Australian territory close to Indonesia. An upsurge in arrivals from Sri Lanka late in 2009 led to arrangements for processing to be made with Indonesia, as Christmas Island was becoming full up. The government had to resist Opposition attacks but, in reaction, foreshadowed severe penalties for people smugglers (if caught) in its defence and terrorism programme announced in February 2010.

All of this has sustained an immigration system which is remarkably tight (IOM 2008). Apart from New Zealanders, all arrivals are required to have a visa issued overseas, whether settlers, tourists or temporary workers and students. Even New Zealanders were divided in 2001 into those eligible for permanent residence and those who were not, another departure from more than a century of unlimited trans-Tasman movement. Mass tourism, mainly from Asia, has expedited the issuing of electronic visas at the point of departure. But the ideal remains that nobody can enter Australia without permission, and that all permanent settlers must be effectively scrutinized before they arrive (Cobb-Clark and Khoo 2006). The major 'unlawful' residue left in Australia, of about 45,000, are visa overstayers, of whom the largest numbers are British, American and Chinese. Over 20,000 are removed each year, most leaving voluntarily.

A Harmonious Multicultural Society with a Flexible Labour Intake?

Immigration control has been a function of the national Commonwealth government since 1901, with some settlement services left to the component six states and two territories of the federation. As an island, Australia is particularly protected by its environment, even if anxiety has often been ascribed to its relations with its neighbours. The long-term objectives of immigration policy have been to create a successful and harmonious society from scratch; to build a modern urban economy; to improve the calibre of the labour force; and to retain detailed control of who enters and resides in Australia for whatever reason (McDonald and Withers 2008). In general these objectives have been met, although the methods for their achievement have changed with circumstances. The population base remains derived from the British Isles, with Irish Australians distinctive mainly by their religion. However the composition has changed quite substantially since 1950, from being '90% British and 99% white' (an official if exaggerated description). It could now be more accurately described as '65% British and 85% white'. Racial data are no longer produced, as they were in detail between 1901 and 1966. Less than 10% subscribe to religions other than Christianity, although twice that proportion claim to have 'no religion'. The proportion of Muslims, at 1.5%, is lower than in France, Britain, Germany or Canada, despite the close proximity of Indonesia and Malaysia.

This is, then, not the most multicultural country in the world but, rather, one that has seen fairly rapid and recently escalating change. Almost 25% are now born overseas, among the highest proportions in the world. Another major shift has been from a predominantly manual labour force and migrant intake up to the 1920s, to a well educated and skilled intake since the 1980s. This is sustained by a large intake of overseas students, the majority coming from China, India and other Asian sources. These are not only allowed, but are encouraged, to remain and become citizens, whereas temporary labour immigrants, although entitled to apply, might find it more difficult to secure permanence and then citizenship without tertiary qualifications and good English. These shifts in policy have greatly increased the number of applications for permanence made within Australia rather than, as previously, overseas.

This, then, is the basis for a harmonious multicultural society with a well educated population and a sound economy. What has recently happened is a departure from some long-term traditions of recruitment which has yet to show its impact. These changes include the attraction of temporary unskilled labour to industries such as agriculture, catering and construction; and the attraction of highly skilled immigrants in medicine, accounting, information technology and mining. These are treated differently, with the unskilled to be limited to a maximum period of eight years residence and to be denied the prospect of citizenship, while the skilled are encouraged to remain, bring their families and become Australians. This presents two problems; the unskilled will also want to remain; while the skilled will be enticed to other states, especially in Europe and North America, where their new Australian passports and experience will make them welcome. Moreover, the recent drive to test the 'Australian values' of immigrants can hardly apply so rigorously to those unable to become citizens. Eventually it is probable that many temporary immigrants will, in fact, become permanent and then citizens as in the past.

A major problem for the unskilled, now subject to official review, is that employers cannot be trusted to treat them fairly, and have the power to dismiss them, leading to their possible deportation. Whether coming from the Pacific Islands or from China and India, many have no knowledge of their rights or even of the legally determined wages and conditions under which they will work. A similar problem arises for the humanitarian intake, which has a higher level of unemployment than the skilled majority and usually comes from states where wages, conditions and human rights are all very inferior to Australia. Those on humanitarian visas have nowhere else to go. Until they gain citizenship they cannot leave Australia without endangering their right to return, nor are they likely to be accepted as settlers anywhere else. There is a public policy challenge in ensuring that an underclass is not created from refugees and temporary entrants. Australian policy for a century has set itself against such a possibility, with some success. But the reduction in legally arbitrated labour conditions and of trade unionism in the past two decades should be a matter of concern. Among the first acts of the incoming Labour government was a reversal of some of the basic features of the Howard changes to industrial law. But some aspects remain or are being phased out slowly. In particular the right of unions to access work sites has been especially relevant in construction and catering and is strongly opposed by employer organizations. While illegal recruiting and fraudulent documents through overseas agents is not a major problem within Australia, it does apply in such source countries as China and India.

Temporary labour immigration sponsored by employers is obviously superior to the widespread practice elsewhere of illegal entry, creating a pool of labour which has no significant rights against its employer or the state. That 'system' has the advantage to the employer of flexibility, in the sense that labour can be paid at a rate determined by the lack of civil rights or trade union protection to workers, for whom there is little public sympathy and even some hostility. Such workers are liable to deportation in times of economic downturn, a fate which befell many thousands of Indonesians illegally living in Malaysia some years ago. Such 'unlawful' workers are not normally covered by occupational health and safety provisions, by insurance, or even by basic welfare and health provisions generally available to local citizens. One disturbing feature of the Australian temporary system is that it excludes provision for access to Medicare, the national health system. However, a strong point is that principal workers are allowed to bring in wives and dependent children who are entitled to seek work and to participate in education. This should modify the problem of large numbers of unattached males with no roots in the community.

Several Australian economic enterprises have become dependent on temporary migration, most notably higher education, catering, building and construction and non-pastoral agriculture (Lester 2007). Transitory demand in each calls for transitory migrants. But these are not always a reliable or predictable source. The recent rapid expansion of Indian student arrivals has made many educational institutions very dependent on this continuing. But a number of events have touched Indian sensitivities and led recently to a marked drop in applications. These included the mismanaged attempt to prosecute an Indian Muslim doctor, following the attack on Glasgow airport in 2007. He became a national hero in India when the charges were seen to be totally unfounded and based only on a family connection with one of the terrorists. Two years later frequent attacks and robberies against Indian students in Melbourne raised the anxiety of Indian parents and, once again, were widely reported in the Indian media. The illogical official response was to criticize the use of student visas to lead on to permanent residence once graduation was achieved. Apart from many colleges, some of them quite dubious, several universities draw so many of their students from India, China and elsewhere overseas that they face economic disaster if there are falls in demands or stricter regulations. Lingering elements of racism cannot be excluded from the preference for British, New Zealanders and South Africans in schemes like the working holiday programme or temporary ('457') work visas, which have raised the level of 'Anglo' immigration previously declining.

The whole history of Australian social and industrial policy for over a century has been to avoid and eliminate inequity and exploitation in employment and to prevent the use of immigration to reduce wages and conditions. But in recent years the decline in union influence, and the election of a national government dedicated to free enterprise and labour market flexibility, changed the situation. So has a more rigorous dedication to market economics and consequent state policies towards industrial relations. With the defeat of the Howard government in 2007 there should be a change back to some previous principles from a government more sensitive to union influence. But the new government is keeping the immigration level at a record high and within it temporary labour migration has an even larger role (Markus, Jupp and McDonald 2009).

By the end of 2009 there were no immediate signs that the level of immigration will be reduced in the light of the world economic downturn. So far this has not affected the relatively low level of unemployment in Australia at below 6% of the workforce. However the evidence of history and of public opinion research both suggest an inverse relationship between rising unemployment, government popularity and levels of immigration. Because of its isolation and tradition of micromanaged selection, Australia is in a strong position to turn the flow on and off as government thinks fit. The temporary labour intake would be an obvious target for reduction as it has no electoral influence. But this has yet to happen and immigration is at a level unprecedented since the immediate post-1945 levels, but with a much larger temporary component.

Bibliography

(Detailed Population Statistics appear in the five-yearly Census – most recently 2006. Immigration Statistics appear in the Annual Report of the Department of Immigration and Citizenship, Canberra and in their research reports.)

Cobb-Clark, D. and Khoo, S.-E. 2006. *Public Policy and Immigration Settlement*. Cheltenham: Edward Elgar.

Deegan, B. 2008. *Visa Subclass 457 Integrity Review: Final Report*. October.

Department of Immigration (Australia). 2001. *Immigration; Federation to Century's End 1901–2000*. Canberra: DIMIA.

Department of Immigration and Citizenship. 2008. *Visa Subclass 457 Integrity Review: Final Report*. Canberra: DIAC.

Hugo, G. 1986. *Australia's Changing Population*. Melbourne: Oxford University Press.

International Organization for Migration. 2008. *World Migration 2008: Managing Labour Mobility in the Evolving Global Economy*. Geneva: IOM.

Jupp, J. 2007. *From White Australia to Woomera*. Melbourne: Cambridge University Press.

Jupp, J. and Kabala. M. (eds) 1993. *The Politics of Australian Immigration*. Canberra: Australian Government Publishing Service.

Khoo, S.-E. and McDonald, P. 2003. *The Transformation of Australia's Population, 1970–2030*. Sydney: University of New South Wales Press.

Lester, L. 2007. *Immigrant Labour Market Success: Working Paper No. 159.* Adelaide, National Institute of Labour Studies (http://www.ssn.flinders.edu.au/nils/).

Markus, A., Jupp, J. and McDonald, P. 2009. *Australia's Immigration Revolution.* Sydney: Allen & Unwin.

McDonald, P. and Withers, G. 2008. *Population and Australia's Future Labour Force: Policy Paper 7.* Canberra: Academy of the Social Sciences in Australia.

Richards, E. 2008. *Destination Australia.* Sydney: University of New South Wales Press.

Sloan, J. 2006. *Economic Impacts of Migration and Population Growth.* Melbourne: Productivity Commission (http://www.pc.gov.au/study/migrationandpopulation/index.html).

Chapter 9

The 'Outside-In' –An Overview of Japanese Immigration Policy from the Perspective of International Relations[1]

Midori Okabe

Introduction: The Fallacy of Human Rights Protection Across Borders

The increased degree of interdependence among states has created factor endowments of various forms for changes in national politics. The enormous volume of studies on globalization shows that transnational outcomes of intense interaction among state and non-state actors have yielded a significant impact on domestic policy formation.[2]

Studies on human migration also deal with global dynamics incorporated into the national political space. Recently, the focus of the analysis has been the emerging global migration regime. Often, this phenomenon is understood as the creation of a transnational space associated with the protective institution of human rights.[3] Many studies on Japanese policy deal with globalization, both as a potential trigger of change in domestic politics and also as an influence in international policymaking.[4] What is remarkable is that the global impact they are empirically or theoretically examining is quite often misinterpreted in Japanese society.

---

1 An earlier version of the chapter was prepared for the 2009 ISA Workshop Constructing and Imagining Labour Migration. This is also part of a research project sponsored by the JSPS Grants-in-Aid for Scientific Research (2007–2009). The author greatly appreciates Elspeth Guild and James F. Hollifield for their assistance. Alexandra Delano and Prem Kumar Rajara provided me with truly insightful commentary during the workshop, for which I am very much grateful. Last but not least, remarks made by Martin O. Heisler for the general discussion have been the driving force behind my major revisions of this work; I am sincerely obliged to them.

2 The effects of globalization to the national politics have so far been studied by many scholars, including Peter Evans, David Held, John L. Cambell, and many others.

3 Sassen 2002. A more focused viewpoint on human rights is assumed by Donnely 1986, 3. Stephen Castles (for instance, among his other magnificent works, 2000) deals more directly with the linkage of the two.

4 Komai 1999; Iyotani 2001; Kondo 2002; Oishi 2005, etc.

Some of the advocates of immigration tend to imply (although it may not be by their intention) that Japan should pursue full protection of foreigners' human rights often at the expense of its national citizen. From this standpoint, the Japanese government is criticized for its (mis)management of foreign residents. Under the current policy, foreign residents are not given the right to work as unskilled labourers, not guaranteed a sufficient social security scheme even when they are unemployed, compelled to leave when their stay is not authorized, and barred from political rights that are not established on the basis of nationality. All of them are criticized by such immigrant advocacies on the ground that they do not fulfil the ideal of universal human rights protection. Meanwhile the problem of why and how native citizen and foreign nationals are evenly treated in the society is not yet seriously tackled with, let alone by the government but more strikingly on the part of such human rights protector.

Their criticism does originate from a worthy ideal, but it is very difficult (if not impossible) to solve all these problems. What is more necessary to seriously consider, above all in the field of political science, is how this noble idea is distorted when it becomes incorporated into the structure of immigration policy. The official message, increasingly visible since around the turn of the century, is that Japan should meet global standards in terms of human right protection and hence receive a larger volume of legal immigrants (not just directly but also through the regularization of irregular immigrants). It is said that their integration into society should also be better facilitated.[5] This statement seems quite reasonable, but in the Japanese context, this kind of human rights protection movement has the potential to be quite misleading, especially in terms of immigration policy-making.

The amnesty issue is one example. In 2008, the Ministry of Justice decided to expel a Filipino couple that had entered Japan using fraudulent passports and stayed in Japan illegally thereafter.[6] They had a child who was born in Japan and brought up in Japan until her mid-teens. While ruling that the parents must be deported, the Minister of Justice extended amnesty to the child by allowing her two options: she could fly to the Philippines with her parents or remain in Japan alone. The decision was made on the grounds that she speaks Japanese only and that her aunt and uncle, who lived in Japan as legal immigrants, had expressed the intention to care for her during her stay if she so chose.

The amnesty agreement was unexpectedly criticized by major human rights advocacy groups. Newspapers and broadcast programs objected that it was against children's rights agreements to separate the family. However, their claim was not that the family should move together and start their new life in the Philippines, even though the government in Manila had expressed that they were ready 'to

---

5   Some argue that Japan should (or could) increase immigration intake because only 1.5% of its population is made up of foreigners.

6   *Asahi Shinbun* (Asahi Newspaper), 9 March 2009.

send humanitarian assistance' to them.[7] Instead, the advocacy groups protested the deportation decision as being a human rights violation.[8]

The issue indicates problems that are not easy to solve. This includes not only the problem of whether or not the Japanese government's decision (including the way in which amnesty was granted) was acceptable from a moral perspective. The problem of legitimacy as applied to the transnational space also arises; essentially, the question is whether international (or global) moral rights are to be interpreted in domestic politics using universal reasoning. Human rights, like many other forms of rights, are the reflection of the will of every individual. Nevertheless, when the will of an individual is authorized by a rights protection regime, this sometimes causes instability throughout the world. If the Filipino family expressed their desire not to return to the Philippines, this was their choice. However, when their return to the Philippines was decided by the Japanese government – when they refused and the refusal was supported by the human rights advocacy groups that condemned the Japanese government for the violation of human rights – this had the capacity to yield many other consequences. It could imply that the advocacy groups feel that the family has been ill-treated by the Filipino government.[9] This point would lead to an essential problem: whether the economic situation of a country can be the basis of an international protection regime. As with refugee assistance, the reception of foreign nationals on the grounds of human rights protection standards may cause the country of origin to be perceived as failing in one respect or the other, which could cause serious problems if the country is fairly sensitive to be perceived as such. It could hamper the effort of confidence building between the two countries concerned.

Another example of human rights' relevance to immigration policy in the Japanese context is the question of whether or not to give political rights to non-Japanese nationals. This is a challenging question that is being highlighted in the context of a significant change in contemporary Japanese politics.[10] Debate has intensified since around 2000, when the Research Commission on the Election

7 *Manila Bulletin*, 11 March 2009.

8 *Mainichi Shinbun* (Mainichi Newspaper), 13 March 2009.

9 The Department of Foreign Affairs at Manila expresses their concern that the family's pledge will invoke misunderstanding of their treatment in the international society. Cf. *Manila Bulletin*, 11 March 2009.

10 The ruling Democratic Party of Japan is reported to favour the concept (though it is not yet fully committed to the idea) of giving foreign residents with permanent visas voting rights in local elections. Cf. *The Japan Times*, 3 May 2008. Also, there is growing political anticipation (often across political parties) that Japan will regain international credibility by expanding its 'humanitarian power'. The regularization of illegal entrants might become an option in the near future on this basis.

System of the LDP (then the ruling party) raised this issue for discussion.[11] In September 2000, Hiromu Nonaka, the then secretary-general of LDP, stated in front of the press about the Koreans and Taiwanese who had remained in Japan even after their independence from Japanese colonial rule were achieved, as well as their descendants who resided in Japan., He claimed they were entitled to voting rights in local elections *because they were victims of Japanese war crimes*.[12] What is critical in this argument is not that they are minority groups most often discriminated against in Japanese society, even though this is something that the Japanese should be ashamed of. What is to be noticed is that the focus has shifted. The issue of post-war reparations is in this context connected with immigration problem because international relations are being mixed with domestic politics. Besides, the likelihood of a referendum or equivalent democratic procedure in the process of immigration policy-making is very low in this setting, because the immigrants' integration problem has become a 'diplomatic' issue here. In particular, the issue is regarded as one of human rights protection across borders in the Japanese case, which is closely connected with post-war compensation. Hence, voices against the local voting rights for them could be perceived as expressing a sense of disregard for universal human rights and of refusal to post-war reparations.[13]

The purpose of this chapter is to provide a new theoretical framework for the analysis of Japanese immigration policy and to assert the relevance of an international relations perspective in the study of immigration. It has an aim to shed light of the role of state to control labour migration by seeing through the relevant politics that surround it. This study does not claim any particular ideological stance regarding immigration policy, and it attempts to depict as non-biased analysis the mechanisms through which the policy is constructed. Values and ideals are important to consider, but they are definitely not appropriate tools for evaluating Japanese immigration policy here, whether past, present, or future; they are only considered as factors that influence the political process.

---

11   The root cause lies in the discriminatory tendencies of Japanese society with respect to Koreans (and Chinese) as minorities since the era of Japanese colonial occupation in the early 20th century. Cf. Weiner 1997.

12   *Japan Times*, 20 September 2000. Nonaka also referred to a forced migration of Koreans to Japan during the colonization period, but a consensus has not developed regarding this issue among historians, partly because of evidence that refutes it.

13   The internal-external security nexus is very much different in its character from that which exists in the European Union. In the Japanese case, international relations per se are projected onto domestic politics, which often creates conflict. The EU, on the other hand, holds it as a result of its experiment to alter border relations as witnessed in the Schengen regime. Cf. Bigo 2001; Huysmans 2006; Buzan and Waever 2009, etc.

International Relations Perspective

The study of migration with the approach of international relations (IR) understands the global migration regime as based on inter-state cooperation and sharing of 'control'.[14] The major works of literature that give a sociological account of international migration have either ignored or undervalued the role of the state, but the IR-oriented immigration studies do emphasize the state's relevance.[15] James F. Hollifield puts it as follows: 'The biggest shortcoming of the globalist thesis … is the weakness or in some cases the absence of any political explanation of migration. The locus of power and change is in society and the economy. There is little place for states and national regulations in this framework.'[16]

The shift in focus that regards immigration as a state method of control helps one understand why the shape, design, and conflict involved in the making of immigration policy are different from one state to another. This viewpoint is of primary importance in the age of developed interdependency among states and the era of globalization. Many states that enjoy neoliberal political systems are increasingly finding that not just political asylum but also economic migration is an issue of political concern. The enormous volume of economic (and social) interaction across borders has conferred tremendous benefits to contemporary states, but it has also spawned by-products, such as transnational crimes, the shared risk of instability on the occasion of sudden economic or political shocks, environmental problems, and so forth. The larger volume of more frequent human migration across borders is also a consequence of this development, but whether it is included in the category of 'by-products' is a highly sensitive question. This is where the public justice (of the state) and human rights (of a transnational nature) conflict.[17]

Japan has traced the same path to a certain extent. Contemporary immigration to Japan has significant relevance to the closer-knit regional cooperation in Asia that had made Japan, as the core of the network, gradually adjust its industrial structure to adapt to the global division of labour.[18] However, the major difference

---

14   Note that the viewpoint originates from Stephen Krasner's panoptic definition of an international regime, described as 'sets of implicit or explicit principles, norms, rules, and decision-making procedures around which actors' expectations converge in a given area of international relations.' (Krasner 1983, 2). It also refers to such major, pioneering works in the study of international regimes as that of Haas 1975; Keohane and Nye Jr. 1977; Young 1980; Rittberger 1993; and so forth. The concept of the global migration regime along these lines is shaped by a neoliberal approach in the works of James F. Hollifield (1992 and 2007), etc.

15   With a few exceptions, such as Torpey 2000, etc.

16   Brettel and Hollifield 2000, 158.

17   The school of thought has developed this argument of the 'liberal dilemma', as is often described. Cf. Freeman 1995; Joppke 1998, Hollifield1999; etc.

18   Toshio Iyotani (2001) claims that the relevance of the 'global approach' to immigration studies lies in understanding (im)migration not as a set of relations between

between Japan and other countries in the area of immigration politics is that national security concerns have a non-negligible impact in domestic politics. In other words, from an IR perspective, Japanese immigration policy is understood as the optimal point of international political dynamics at which non-economic (traditional) and economic-derived security situations can both be factors of its development.

Why Still Seen as Less Generous? The Low Profile of Government

It is already a commonly shared view that Japan is one of the least generous countries when it comes to immigration, including asylum acceptance. However, it is not entirely true that Japan has remained isolationist. There are already over 2.2 million foreigners (roughly three times more than three decades ago) living in Japan at present, and they come from more than 180 countries, according to the Immigration Bureau.[19] Few Japanese people would have imagined in early 1970s that their local government office, after a few decades, would begin to prepare information not only in Japanese but also in Chinese, Korean, and Portuguese. Nevertheless, the isolationist image of Japanese immigration policy persists.

The notion of isolationism does not necessarily reflect the fact that Japan has gradually opened its door to enable larger-scale immigration over the past few decades, and it continues to do so even today. Although it had a slow start compared to other major countries in terms of receiving immigration, Japan had already become a de facto multi-ethnic and multi-cultural country by the latter half of the 1980s.

Immigration to Japan began along with a change in international relations in the Asian regional context. The 1985 Plaza Accord has produced an investment-driven economic system in Asia, with Japan becoming the primary source of FDI in almost all other countries in the region, thanks to the greater appreciation of Yen.[20] The regional trade and production network has grown significantly stronger, and Japan has become one of the most attractive destinations for would-be immigrants in Asia.

Immigration to Japan has been enabled by the economic circumstances, and this tendency continues as the business sector demands more unskilled immigrants.[21]

---

relevant states, but instead in the context of a global capital economy. The author finds his insights very useful, but also sees the role of the state as an independent variable.

19   The exact number of foreign residents in 2008 was 2,217,426, according to the Immigration Bureau, Ministry of Justice, Japan.

20   Cornelious, Martin and Hollifield 1992.

21   The Japan Federation of Economic Organisations ('Keidanren') officially claims that accepting unskilled labour is not desirable, but at the same time, it has demanded a broader (and thus more ambiguous) definition of the category 'highly skilled'. (Interview with the personnel at Keidanren, October 2008.) Also, the Ministry of Economy, Trade

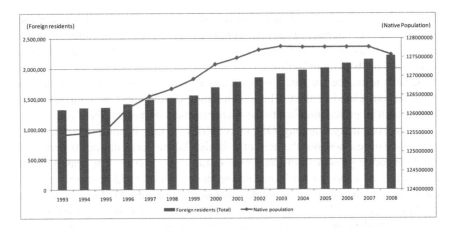

Figure 9.1   Foreign residents in Japan 1993–2008

Sources: Statistics on the number of foreign residents, Immigration Bureau, Ministry of Justice, Japan (2003 and 2009). Also, *Population of Japan*, Statistic Bureau, Cabinet Office, Japan (2008).

Notes: 1. The Japanese government requires all foreigners to register within 90 days of entry into its territory. The number of 'foreign residents', therefore, does not technically correspond to what the Japanese government describes as 'permanent residents' (nor does it fit the United Nations definition of 'immigrants'.* However, in reality, there are only a few people who register for travel less than 90 days, and those who register tend to stay longer (for more than one year), which implies that the number is more or less equivalent to that of long-term residents.

2. The figure for the native population in 2008 is estimated.

* Cf. United Nations, Recommendations on Statistics of International Migration, ST/ESA/STAT/SER.M/58/Rev.1, 1998.

This does not mean that immigration control is entirely out of the hands of the political sector.

However, the government has kept a low profile; it has never demonstrated an ambitious level of engagement in the field of immigration 'management'. All that has been accomplished is the development of precise legal entry regulations, with poor institutional capability to cooperate with other divisions that could handle matters related to immigration, such Ministries as of Economy, Health, Labour, and Education, and so forth.[22] This governmental position has given the impression

---

and Industry (METI) is aware that despite the existent immigration regulations, which only welcome skilled workers, many domestic industries need more unskilled workers to increase their profits. (Interview with an official from METI, March 2008; cf. as written references, METI 2005 and 2008.)

22   Takamichi Kajita (2001) suggests that ministerial rivalries (notably that between the Ministry of Labour and the Ministry of Justice) have been one of the elements hampering

that Japanese society is indifferent to the plight of foreigners.[23] However, the government has tolerated unskilled foreign workers' coming to Japan. In most cases, they work around law enforcement barriers through what is described as 'side-door' or 'back-door' inflows.[24]

Japan's tolerance for foreign population intake can also be understood in a globalization-related context. The underpinning development was Japan's shift from industrial protectionalism to the encouragement of market liberalism.

Japan was unique among OECD countries in that it achieved significant economic success without the help of a foreign labour force during its period of rapid economic growth from late 1950s to the early 1970s.[25] The reason Japan did not recruit a foreign workforce during the period of rapid economic growth cannot be explained in terms of market mechanisms because the fact is that Japan did have a demand for labour at the time.[26] It is argued that the government's reluctance to develop an open policy at the time is better explained in the context of domestic politics.[27] The main goal of Japanese politics at the time was economic recovery and, with an incompletely developed infrastructure for the enhancement of democracy, no steps were taken to reflect the will of the constituencies on labour immigration for policy-making on a national level. The recruitment of (alien) cheap labour could not possibly be on politicians' agenda as they sought votes in the context of government-led domestic demand expansion policies. Also, the labour policy at the time was closely linked with the policy regarding industrial development.[28] The Japanese government believed that the open recruitment of a labour force could negatively affect Japanese industries that were not competitive enough, especially in terms of technical innovation. Immigration control at the time was pursued and linked with the protectionism as above. In addition, there was a certain amount of flexible labour in Japan as a result of rural-urban migration, in

---

functional cross-ministerial cooperation.

23　The author reserves judgment regarding arguments about how immigration control in Japan is, to a large extent, intended to help Japan retain its ethnic/cultural homogeneity. It is assumed that proactive (regulatory) control would contradict the authority's tacit approval of illegal patterns in the workforce that have appeared since the latter half of 1980s and throughout the 1990s. What should be pointed out with regard to that period is the government's reluctance to develop a control policy, which is the main argument of this chapter.

24　'Back-door' means illegal entry, mainly conducted by people from the Middle East and other parts of Asia from the 1980s throughout the 1990s. The term 'side-door' refers to those people who entered Japan via legal procedures (in categories such as 'entertainer', 'technician', 'student', etc.) and became illegal afterwards, simply because they were working in businesses that were not authorized, including unlawful jobs. These people were often the victims of human smuggling. Iyotani 2001.

25　Iyotani 2001.

26　Bartram 2000.

27　See Bartram 2000; Iyotani 2001; Kajita 2001.

28　Iyotani 2001.

many cases including resettlement, but also including a seasonal migration pattern called 'dekasegi'.[29]

Moreover, the discussion of labour immigration has generally been held because voices from small and medium-sized industries were not heard in the decision-making process. Large industries did have the ability to influence national policy to a certain extent (though not to the extent that they have been able to since the mid-1980s), yet their major concern at the time was not focused on the use of foreign labour intake. Rather, they were more interested in extending their businesses across the border.

In parallel, however, globalization triggered a move away from a subsistence economy and necessitated the settlement of immigrants in place of simple chain migration.[30] Increased FDI and the ever more complex global production network subsequently enabled the separation of working procedures, and at the same time, it led to a 'border-less' labour paradigm in the transnational context.[31] The establishment of production networks across borders in part broadened the opportunity for Asian (would-be) migrant workers to come.

The early 1990s were when Japan felt the need to change the structures of its state and society for two reasons, one of them being the bursting of its bubble economy.

The collapse of the asset-oriented economy has created serious and long-lasting recession in Japan. This time period is called 'the loss of 10 years,' but in fact, this 'lost' period extends over 20 years. Deregulation is one of the measures for economic revival and is closely linked with changes in employers' and employees' mindsets regarding working style as career employment and labour costs. The Koizumi administration (2001–2006) pushed for regulatory reform and yielded results in the form of drastic structural changes. This reform plan aimed to reduce the government's commitment in the market while altering the composition of the working class. A huge divide had emerged between the upper and lower classes, and people were no longer regarding themselves as part of 'among the millions of the Japanese middle class'. This is in large part due to changes in working styles and conditions. The 'sacredness' of the lifelong employment system began to be questioned, and more and more irregular employment cases were legally adopted.[32] Management started to demand a more adaptable (and flexible) labour force to maximize profits and minimize costs.

---

29   The domestic migrants, most of whom were farmers from regions that were very snowy in winter, came to the urban cities during the winter when they could not engage in agricultural work. These 'dekasegi' were sufficiently flexible and in many cases low-end. Hence, they were most likely to substitute for foreign workers.

30   Iyotani 2001. Also, see Sassen 2002.

31   Iguchi 1997.

32   Previously, irregular employment was acceptable only in limited occupations (e.g., interpreters, translators, etc.). Nevertheless, during the course of the deregulation process, the range of occupations for which this was allowed was gradually broadened

It is interesting to contrast this with the stubborn refusal to accept foreign labour in the early 1970s as well as in the 1990s. Both periods were marked by low unemployment, but starting in the late 1990s, the unemployment rate began to rise. This parallels a change in the perspective of employers, who began to regard labour cost as a variable rather than as a fixed cost.[33] It seems that foreign labour needs to be flexible so that it can act as a safety valve for company management in times of economic hardship.

Along with the socioeconomic structural changes, migration issues were on the political agenda. In 2004, a taskforce was set up by the Committee for Regulatory Reform in the Cabinet Office. The group initially served within the framework of international economic cooperation, and later it began to deal directly with the recruitment of foreign nationals. The debate dealt with smoothing the international movement of people across Japan's borders. Immigration policy and integration came under review. Throughout this discussion, Japanese 'society' came to be seen as a major problem. The closed corporate culture, the infrastructure's unsuitability for highly skilled workers, and the inadequate provision of public services by local governments were the main issues. Deregulation was seen as a way to overcome these 'problems.'

These trends continue to the present. Business organizations, economic ministries, demographic planning institutions and the like are in support of a larger scale of labour migration. The idea of highly skilled immigrants has emerged from this context. There is indeed substantial concern regarding how Japan can remain a 'competent state' in the battle among nations over the acquisition of highly skilled human resources, but the concern is not the main pillar of the policy, nor is it directly realized in the concrete program of foreign labour recruitment. The Cabinet launched 'the Committee on the Recruitment of Highly Skilled Foreign Labour' on December 2, 2008. Its role will be to find a way to encourage more highly skilled immigrants to choose Japan as their destination country. The debate, however, will most likely be based on the existing opinion put forth by business interests, which favours less immigration control, to the point of accepting less-skilled labourers. Meanwhile, there are already a large number of foreign students at Japanese universities, and a major goal in this policy is in fact not to recruit scholars or innovators directly from abroad so much as to 'keep them from leaving' after they have been educated in Japan and supported by generous scholarships from the Japanese government.

The major concern of supporters for larger-scale labour recruitment is that their appeal is not fully reflected in the current immigration policy. While the business sector needs more unskilled labourers than it does skilled labourers, the current immigration law only allows skilled labourers to reside and work in Japan.

---

until it came to include technically skilled workers in the automotive industry and in other manufacturing industries. University professors and schoolteachers today are also employed on an irregular basis.

33   *Seidosha* 2007.

The reasons for this lay not in rational economic logic but rather with international security concerns.

Unsettled Problem: Security Aspect

There is another reason not yet mentioned in this chapter why the early 1990s is the time period when Japan moved to change the structures of its state and society: the demise of the Cold War.

The end of the Cold War did not bring regional conflict in Asia as was expected. However, it did move Japan to change its diplomatic policy stance, particularly in terms of prioritization. As in the realm of international political economy, the review of the 'hub' and 'spoke' structure in the Asian region has enabled less dependency on the United States for many Asian countries, fostering closer intra-regional ties.[34] Japan, China, and Korea have gradually been incorporated into the ASEAN regional framework, and with increased interaction across borders, some have begun to consider that increased political coordination among these countries is needed. Security concerns caused by transnational commerce have been raised. This is a process that to a certain extent is very similar with the foundation of the European Union and other possible paths of regional integrations.

The Asian regional context, however, also contains some cleavages that are not entirely filled by a 'borderless' economic framework.[35] The confrontation with North Korea is by all means the greatest security concern, not only for Japan but also for other Asian countries. Territorial disputes taking place between Japan and South Korea, between Japan, China, and Taiwan, between China, Taiwan, Vietnam, the Philippines, Malaysia, and Brunei, and many other cases hamper further efforts for regional integration.[36]

Above all, the unresolved issue of international relations over post-war reparation has made the Japanese hesitate in assuming diplomatic leadership in the region.[37] The attitude is not entirely one of self-discipline on the part of Japan but is also a reflection of political reactions from China and Korea that Japanese pro-activeness in international relations is quite often perceived as a security threat by these countries. As David Forsythe notes, in such occasions Japan 'was forced

---

34 Of course this does not imply the decay of the relevance of the US to this region, nor does it negate the fact that bilateral agreements (FTAs and EPAs) are still the dominant pattern of international cooperation. However, these important points are not the primary subject to be addressed in this chapter.

35 Kent E. Calder and Francis Fukuyama, *East Asian Multilateralism: Prospects for Regional Stability*, Johns Hopkins University Press, 2008.

36 This may be an interesting subject for comparative analysis with the case of the European Union, where the Gibraltar issue did block the ratification of the external treaty but not the entire process of establishing the Schengen regime.

37 Katzenstein 2008.

to face its tarnished past' out of context.[38] The troublesome matter is that inter-state competition is often reflected in the confrontational structure of domestic politics, where cleavages between the conservative and the liberal takes almost a one-to-one correspondence with the international dispute between Japan and China, South Korea, or even North Korea. The liberal advocacy for immigrant rights is, in most cases, for the purpose of liberating them from an oppressive society. However, the accusations of domestic political failure and the support for these immigrants' countries of origin against the country of their residence in light of international rivalries are not distinctive in the eyes of Japanese native citizens. Authorities shaping immigration policy must do anything but remain silent in the face of this situation, even with little possibility of cooperating with foreign ministries and politicians. The relevance of internal and external security contact needs to be considered seriously, but the nexus can be a strong impediment for the government to take action. Recruiting nurses and caregivers from the Philippines and Indonesia via Economic Partnership Agreements may be a compromise out of bilateral (political) economic dispute, but it may create social problems in future Japanese society because they are gone after their contracts expire even when the market still needs them. Voting rights only in local elections could improve the international relations between South Korea and Japan, but may cause disputes in society where solidarity between native and non-native citizens is not yet strong enough.

In reality, the Japanese version of internal-external nexus has not yet provided leverages to take political actions. The National Police Agency, in partnership with the Immigration Bureau, has made remarkable improvements in combating illegal immigration with the help of technology and improved detective work. An inter-ministerial taskforce to combat terrorism has also been launched following the events in the US on 11 September 2001. However, these measures are separately discussed in the immigration policy framework. The security aspect has yet to be associated with migration itself, and thus Japan has not yet witnessed the 'securitization' of migration.[39] We note that the process is not aligned with security discourse. Policymakers rarely combine the argument of controlling illegal migration with the open policy of recruiting (skilled) migration. Indeed, the international cooperative framework is lacking on both a regional and a bilateral basis.

There are several reasons for this situation. First, as was explained earlier in this discussion, there is a constant need for highly skilled labourers in Japan (and possibly in other countries). However, most highly skilled immigrants head for the US or Europe and not for Japan. In this context, the regulatory political discourse regarding human migration has an adverse effect. Second, international cooperation of this kind has focused on organized crime facilitating human

---

38   Forsythe 2006, 177.

39   For the debate on the 'securitization' of immigration, cf. Huysmans 2000; Waever 1995, etc.

trafficking and illegal migration, and it (a) has been regarded as issues separate from open migration policies, and (b) has evolved from the global multilateral framework and not the regional reality.

In December 2004, the government adopted an action plan for the prevention of terrorism. This preventive mechanism is consistent with issues discussed in the 1997 G8 Summit of Justice and Interior Ministers. It has been strongly affected by international cooperation since 2001, and the stricter entry procedures (including the fingerprinting of all foreign nationals over the age of 16) undertaken by the Immigration Bureau should be viewed in this context. The increased deployment of crisis management officials at major ports and airports is also a result of international political development.

There also exists a regional form of cooperation, which was endorsed under the terms of the ASEAN framework in 2002.[40] This policy initiative was, however, encouraged by the US upon assessing the Asian–EU dialogue. In other words, cooperation of this kind is a reaction to the global security-sensitive discourse mainly generated by non-Asian countries, and it is not the result of spontaneous political evolution within Asia.

The same logic can be applied to human trafficking. Japan signed the UN Convention against Transnational Organized Crime in December 2000, which was followed by several relevant international agreements to tackle human trafficking and smuggling.[41] The resulting regional cooperative framework again serves only to enforce these international mechanisms.

The Asian coexistence of regional and global cooperation frameworks represents the missing conceptual link between migration and security issues. Human trafficking and smuggling, and terrorism in general, do have significant relevance to cross-border movement, but they are seen as politically distinct from one another. This is because the coordination of migration policies in the context of regional integration has so many stakeholders with inconsistent viewpoints and perspectives. For Asia, the influx of people into a country results in a decrease in another country's population, as the former is the immigrant-receiving country and the latter is the immigrant-sending country, and both exist in the same region. Security measures enacted to decrease the number of immigrants may be a higher priority in one country than it is in another, as viewpoints regarding the influx of foreign nationals are not (and need not be) harmonized. Contrary to the immigration-promotion standpoint, there exist few common approaches to 'secure' immigration in a regional context. Global cooperation does help mitigate some of the possible negative consequences, but it is far from a full-fledged protection measure.

---

40   ASEM Copenhagen Declaration on International Cooperation to Combat International Terrorism, September, 2002.

41   Kashiwazaki and Akaha 2006 (http://www.migrationinformation.org/Profiles/display.cfm?ID=487).

...

Conclusion

This chapter so far has discussed the structural dynamics of the formation of immigration policy. Japanese authorities once tried to claim a high degree of control in labour migration in the post-WWII period, which explains the surprisingly 'isolationist' policy during periods of high labour demand throughout the 1960s. However, their zest to take hold of this issue has lost over time in parallel with its function declines sharply, as Japan has become *de facto* a country of receiving immigration through channels from 'side' and from 'back'. While labour migration is kept less important as an issue for open political debate, the challenges to the state authorities claim to control labour migration come in the form of human rights claims as is juxtaposed with the 'fallacy' that Japan is still a country of non-migration.

The government position towards political development in this area is still modest, in part because of its failure to perceive its importance, but also because of the failure to address the internal-external security nexus that characterizes Japan's struggle with immigration. Japan's challenge regarding immigration is not only to balance out the protection of transnational human rights with the legitimacy of the state's sovereignty. It is also to address long-lasting international confrontation that goes through transformation by the global political dynamics but still requires conventional wisdom for its resolution. The tactful handling of the immigration problem only starts with this recognition, and the rational reconciliation of international and transnational demands would lead to the successful management of all people in Japanese society. Human rights issue by all means needs to be tackled with but it should not be regarded as a tool of diplomatic compromise. What is at stake is not only the right of minorities but also that of native citizen.

Bibliography

Bartram, D. 2000. Japan and Labour Migration: Theoretical and Methodological Implication of Negative Cases, *International Migration Review*, 34(1).

Bigo, D. 2001. The Möbius Ribbon of Internal and External Security(ies), in *Identities Borders Orders: Rethinking International Relations Theory*, edited by M. Albert et al. Minneapolis: University of Minnesota Press.

Brettel, C.B. and Hollifield, J.F. (eds) 2000. *Migration Theory: Talking across Disciplines*. New York and London: Routledge.

Buzan, B. and Waever, O. 2009. Macrosecuritization and Security Constellations: Reconsidering Scale in Securitization Theory, *Review of International Studies*, 35.

Cambell, J.L. 2004. *Institutional Change and Globalization*. Princeton: Princeton University Press.

Castles, S. 2000. *Citizenship and Migration: Globalization and the Politics of Belonging*. New York and London: Routledge.

Cornelius, W.A., Martin, P.L. and Hollifield, J.F. (eds) 1992. *Controlling Immigration: A Global Perspective*. Stanford: Stanford University Press.

Donnely, J. 1986. International Human Rights: A Regime Analysis, *International Organization*, 40(3).

Evans, P. 1997. The Eclipse of The State? Reflections on Stateness in an Era of Globalization, *World Politics*, 50.

Forsythe, D.P. 2006. *Human Rights in International Relations*. Cambridge: Cambridge University Press.

Freeman, G. 1995. Mode of Immigration Politics in Liberal Democratic States. *International Migration Review*, 29(4).

Haas, E.B. 1975. Is There a Hole in the Whole? Knowledge, Technology, Interdependence and the Construction of International Regimes, *International Organization*, 29.

Held, D. 1999. *Global Transformations*. Cambridge: Polity Press.

Hollifield, J.F. 1992. *Immigrants, Markets, and States: The Political Economy of Postwar Europe*. Cambridge: Harvard University Press.

Hollifield, J.F. 1999. Ideas, Institutions and Civil Society: On the Limits of Immigration Control in Liberal Democracies, *IMIS-Beiträge*, 10, 57–90.

Hollifield, J.F. 2007. The Emerging Migration State, in *Rethinking Migration: New Theoretical and Empirical Perspective*, edited by A. Portes and J. DeWind. Oxford: Berghahn Books.

Huysmans, J. 2000. The European Union and the Securitization of Migration, *Journal of Common Market Studies*, 38(5).

Huysmans, J. 2006. *The Politics of Insecurity: Fear, Migration and Asylum in the EU*, New York and London: Routledge.

Iguchi, Y. 1997. *Kokusaiteki na Hito no Ido to Roudou Shijo: Keizai no Global-ka no Eikyo (International Migration and Labour Markets: The Effects of a Globalized Economy)*. Tokyo: Japanese Institute for Labour Policy.

Iyotani, T. 2001. *Globalization to Imin (Globalization and Immigrants)*. Tokyo: Yushindo.

Iyotani, T. 2001. *Immigration in an Age of Globalization (Globalization to Imin)*, Tokyo: Yushindo.

The Japan Times. 3 May 2008. DPJ Weighs Voting Rights for All Permanent Residents.

Joppke, C. 1998. Why Liberal States Accept Unwanted Migration, *World Politics*, 50(2).

Kajita, T. (ed.) 2001. *Internationalization and Identity*. Tokyo: Minerva Shobo.

Kashiwazaki, C. and Akaha, T. 2006. Japanese Immigration Policy: Responding to Conflicting Pressures. *Migration Information Source*, November.

Katzenstein, P.J. 2008. *Rethinking Japanese Security: Internal and External Dimensions*. New York and London: Routledge.

Keohane, R.O. and Nye, J.S. Jr. 1977. *Power and Interdependence: World Politics in Transition*. Boston: Little, Brown.

Komai, H. 1999. *Nihon no Gaikokujin Imin (Foreign Migrants in Contemporary Japan)*. Tokyo: Akashi Shoten.

Kondo, A. 2002. The Development of Immigration Policy in Japan, *Asian and Pacific Migration Journal*, 11(4).

Krasner, S. 1983. *International Regimes*. Ithaca: Cornell University Press.

METI. 2005. *Gaikokujin Roudousya Mondai (Foreign Workers Problem)*, October.

METI. 2008. *Keidanren, Keizai Trend (Economic Trend)*, December.

Oishi, N. 2005. *Woman in Motion: Globalization, State Policies, and Labour Migration in Asia*. Stanford: Stanford University Press.

Rittberger, V. 1993. *Regime Theory and International Relations*. Oxford: Clarendon Press.

Sassen, S. 2002. *Global Networks: Linked Cities*. New York and London: Routledge.

Seidosha. 2007. *Gendai Shiso (Contemporary Thought)*, 35(7).

Torpey. J. 2000. *The Invention of Passport: Surveillance, Citizenship and the State*. Cambridge: Cambridge University Press.

Waever, O. 1995. Securitization and Desecuritization, in *On Security*, edited by R. Lipschutz. New York: Columbia University Press.

Weiner, M. (ed.) 1997. *Japan's Minorities: The Illusion of Homogeneity*. New York and London: Routledge.

Young, O. 1980. International Regimes: Problems of Concept Formation. *World Politics*, 32.

SECTION III
Equivocal Claims: Examining Labour Migration Regimes with Ambivalent Control Claims

Elspeth Guild and Sandra Mantu

This last section of the book investigates areas of the world where state authorities' claims about controlling labour migration are limited or tempered by regional agreements, which exclude from control mechanisms groups of people based on criteria unrelated to their status as labour migrants. The other two sections have focused on state authorities which invest politically or otherwise in claims about migration control, although the results they obtain are not necessarily matching their expectations. This section examines the migration control mechanisms developed in the European Union, the US–Mexico migration in the context of NAFTA and the Central Asian region, which is a new actor on the migration scene. The final chapter by Didier Bigo, although located in the context of the EU, serves also as a reflection on the successes and failures of control based paradigms of labour migration. Unlike the NAFTA or the Central Asian approach, the EU has premised its labour migration regime on free movement which is no longer treated as a security issue, at least, as far as intra-community labour migration is concerned. The EU's experience as a de-securitization project shows that abolishing labour migration controls even among countries which differ in terms of their wealth, social benefits, minimum wages etc. does not result in significant movement, a reduction of social solidarity, nor a rise in xenophobia. The US–Mexican relations within the framework of NAFTA have not managed to surpass the identification of labour migration as a security issue, whereas the 'war on terror' has, for the time being, inscribed the migration debate within the logic of counter-terrorism and the fight against drug smuggling. National security priorities have also impeded the achievement of a regional free movement regime in the Central Asian region, which is mainly characterized by conflicting migration interests. The de-securitization of labour has proven to foster positive developments in the case of the EU but the underlying issue remains the likelihood of imagining such a migration paradigm.

Chapter 10

Equivocal Claims? Ambivalent Controls? Labour Migration Regimes in the European Union

Elspeth Guild

Introduction

The objective of this chapter is to examine claims about labour migration regimes in the European Union (EU). The European context is a particularly interesting one as it is highly dynamic and reveals deep cleavages in perceptions and meanings of control. I will examine the subject under the following headings:

1. The European integration dynamic;
2. Fragmentation and the foreigner;
3. Tools of control and control of tools.

This is an examination of a labour migration scheme, which is designed around the abolition of controls on economic migration of all kinds on persons depending on reciprocity on the basis of nationality. It reveals a number of features which confound many commonly held premises about labour migration:

- The abolition of controls on labour migration has had a minimal effect on movement of workers in the EU notwithstanding the EU's latest enlargements to relatively poor states in Southern and Central and Eastern Europe;[1]
- The entitlement of intra-EU labour migrants to equal treatment with nationals and full access to social benefits has not resulted in widespread abuse nor in a diminution by Member States of their social benefits or concerted attempts to limit access by labour migrants (with notable exceptions such as the UK);[2]
- Very generous rules on family reunification have not resulted in widespread 'abuse'; in fact, notwithstanding the right to be joined by a wide range of family members, most labour migrants are joined only by spouses and young children only;

---

1   Galgoczi, Leschke and Watt 2009.
2   Triandafillidou and Gropas 2007.

- The identity move from discriminated against ethnic minority foreigner/ migrant to individual entitled to equality and increasingly invisible as a target of racism can take place very quickly. The key appears to be public leadership committed to equality;
- When labour migrants are beneficiaries of full equal treatment rights in wages and working conditions, secure residence rights and a right to family reunification, they cease to be categorized as 'unwanted' migrants even if they work in disfavoured sectors which are relatively poorly paid; the discourse of highly skilled workers as welcome and low-skilled migrant workers as unwanted disappears;
- When states lift their hand off labour migration allowing people to make their own choices neither does this operate as a solution to labour needs nor unemployment. People do not necessarily or, in the EU example, even normally or usually move from countries of high unemployment and low social benefits to countries with low unemployment and high social benefits. Where states have labour shortages their administrations are still required to take active efforts to recruit labour migrants as only statistically low numbers of persons move spontaneously;
- This experience characterized by high and rapid achievement of social inclusion and harmony tends to be disregarded when EU policy makers come to address the question of labour migration from outside the EU;
- The lesson which the EU does seem to have retained from the abolition of controls on movement of persons for economic purposes is territorial. The completion of the Schengen area without internal border controls on the movement of persons has been a substantial success for the participating countries (which do not include Ireland and the UK).

The European Integration Dynamic

The European Union is founded on three international treaties which have been subject to regular amendment and addition but which have retained their primary objective – the creation of an internal market – and added to it the establishment of monetary union. The creation of the internal market means, according to these treaties, the abolition on the control of persons crossing intra Member State borders and free access to the labour market and self employment for nationals of the Member States.[3] Thus, in labour migration terms, the purpose which the EU was given in 1957 (and which has remained with it) has been to oblige Member States

---

3 And their third country national family members who accompany or join them there.

to abandon control over labour migration of nationals of the participating states.[4] In this regard the EU is a de-securitization project as regards labour migration.[5]

In order to achieve the project, a series of activities along the way were necessary and surprisingly often engaged the vexed question of labour migration. First, the EU had to establish its law as taking precedence over national law. This was a monumental task which required civil servants in the Member States to be persuaded to apply EU law rather than national labour migration rules in respect of nationals of the Member States.[6] To succeed in this objective, the national courts of the Member States were engaged – first to accept that EU law has priority, secondly that the decisions of the European Court of Justice which interpret EU law take priority over decisions of their national courts (supreme courts etc.) and thirdly to discipline civil servants who failed to apply EU law.[7] This process took place gradually over a period of about 30 years from 1957–1987 with many set backs along the way but eventually arriving more or less at the objective. There are still examples of Member States failing properly to implement EU free movement of persons rules and the ECJ judicially slapping their wrists for failure to fulfil their obligations. Generally, however, where caught misapplying EU free movement rules, Member States change their rules and practices to conform, even where there has been substantial political investment in the issue.[8]

The loss of control over labour migration of nationals of the EU Member States is fairly complete. EU nationals know they are entitled to move and look for work anywhere in the EU. Employers know that they can hire EU nationals without checking for work or residence permits.[9] State authorities are often unaware of who is on their territory or only become aware of the economic migrant some time well after he or she has begun working there for some time, for instance when the EU migrant worker files a tax return. Even those states which keep an eye on who is on the territory through population registers do not always capture EU nationals. When one such state, Germany argued that it was entitled to include in its database on foreign nationals, details of EU citizens exercising their rights, the ECJ retorted that this was unnecessary as anonymous information was sufficient for the purpose and was less intrusive on the data protection rights of individuals. Further the ECJ

---

4   Guild 2004.

5   Waever, Buzan, Kelstrup and Lemaitre 1993.

6   Majone 1994.

7   Burley, and Mattli 1993.

8   A good example of this relates to the attempt by a number of EU states to regain control over the migration of third country national family members of migrant EU nationals. The ECJ found these efforts inconsistent with the EC Treaty and required the states to abandon their control practices. Within six months, all the offending states had changed their policies and practices (*Metock*, ECJ 25 July 2008). Handoll 2009.

9   Enlargement of the EU creates ambiguities when nationals from accession states are usually not permitted free movement as workers immediately but have to wait a specified number of years before enjoying that status. Nonetheless, there has never been a limitation on free movement for other purposes including self-employment – Huysmans 2000.

held illegal the German argument that the personalized data was necessary for fighting crime as it discriminated between EU citizens from other Member States and German citizens who were not subject to inclusion on the database.[10]

While the grip of Member State bureaucracies was being prized off labour migrants who were nationals of other Member States, so too the number of Member States was changing. While the EU began with six Member States (Belgium, France, Germany, Italy, Luxembourg and the Netherlands) it gained:

- Denmark, Ireland and the UK in 1973 (current populations: 5.5 million, 4.5 million and 61 million);
- Greece in 1981 (current population: 11.2 million);
- Portugal and Spain in 1986 (current populations: 10.6 million and 45.8 million);
- Austria, Finland and Sweden in 1995 (current populations: 8.3 million; 5.3 million; 9.2 million);
- Cyprus, the Czech Republic, Estonia, Hungary, Latvia, Lithuania, Malta, Poland, Slovakia and Slovenia in 2004 (current populations: 0.8 million, 10.4 million, 1.3 million, 10.0 million, 2.2 million, 3.3 million, 0.4 million, 38.1 million, 5.4 million and 2.0 million) and
- Bulgaria and Romania in 2007 (current populations 7.6 million and 21.5 million).[11]

The enlargement process is not yet over.[12] There are currently three candidate countries: Croatia, Macedonia and Turkey and five potential candidate countries: Albania, Bosnia, Kosovo, Montenegro and Serbia (not to mention Iceland). Each has its own timetable and action plan. The combined population of the EU is just under 500 million ranging from 82.5 million in Germany (though the population was increased by a third when reunification of East and West Germany took place in 1990) to under 0.5 million in Malta. Of the candidate and potential candidate states, the only one with a population over 7.5 million (Serbia) is Turkey with a population of 72.5 million people.

As regards labour migration, the control claims of the Member States are gradually abandoned in the context of enlargement. Twice, in 1973 and in 1995, the nationals of the Member States joining the EU were not subject to any temporary restriction on free movement of workers. From one day to the next, all the states had to abandon their control claims over migrant workers from Denmark, Ireland and the UK in 1973 and Austria, Finland and Sweden in 1995. In the 2004 enlargement, workers from Cyprus and Malta were accorded immediate free labour migration rights. However, for all the other states engaged in the enlargements there has been a delay in the abandonment of labour migration controls over their nationals.

---

10   C-524/06 *Huber* 16 December 2008.
11   Verdun and Croce 2005.
12   House of Lords 2006.

The usual period for the delay is five to eight years. The end of the delay period arrived on 1 May 2009 for the Member States which joined on 1 May 2004 (with an exceptional extra two years for Austria, Germany and the UK). For Bulgaria and Romania, 2012 will be the final date for lifting controls (other than a possible exceptional two-year period).

For the purposes of European integration, it makes no sense to discuss integration without bearing in mind the dramatically changing composition of the EU-integration into what is a more useful question. Each Member State has a vote at the Council, sends a Commissioner to the European Commission, a judge to the European Court of Justice and participates in the European Parliament by way of direct suffrage which while taking into account the populations of the Member States also ensures that the small Member States are entitled to elect deputies. It is not just the space and population which is transformed by enlargement, the institutions as well undergo substantial changes.[13]

Regarding workers, however, it is worth remembering that on 9 December 2004 the UK's final judicial instance, the House of Lords, gave its judgment[14] regarding the legality of the UK immigration authorities stationing their officers at Prague airport (Czech Republic) to advise airlines not to permit some passengers to board planes bound for the UK. The reason for UK immigration officers to advise airline staff to prohibit boarding to some persons was on the basis of ethnic origin and immigration suspicions. The UK authorities feared that some passengers who were Czech nationals but ethnically Roma might make asylum applications which the UK authorities considered unfounded as they deemed the Czech Roma to be disguised economic migrants, if these passengers arrived in the UK. The UK government fears were fully described in terms of percentages of asylum applications and rejection rates for Czech Roma over the preceding years. The UK court found the checks illegal on grounds of racial discrimination. However, on 1 May 2004, all Czech nationals, including ethnic minorities, became citizens of the European Union and entitled to free movement as workers or to seek jobs and self employment in the UK or anywhere else in the EU. The same people, Czech Roma, who had been the subject of very intrusive exclusion policies of the UK authorities (unlawfully on the grounds of ethnic origin) had the right to move to work in the UK even before the UK's highest court found the state exclusionary activity unlawful.[15] While the UK court only found that the extraterritorial controls were illegal because they constituted racial and ethnic origin discrimination (in other words not condemning the UK authorities for the practice of extraterritorial controls in general) the membership of the Czech Republic to the EU freed Czech Roma from any controls on labour migration at all. One might say that the court was extremely timid in comparison with the UK state authorities which abolished labour migration control altogether for the persons in respect of whom, only shortly

---

13 Meunier and McNamara 2007.
14 *R v SSHD* ex p ERRC [2004] UKHL 55.
15 Goodwin-Gill 2005.

before, they had been spending substantial public resources to prevent their labour migration.[16]

Loosening the grip of EU state authorities over labour migration by nationals of newer Member States is not self evidently easy. It must happen, but as the above example shows, it is often contested. Nonetheless it does happen because Member State authorities accept that it must happen.[17] For instance, not only have almost all of the Member States which joined the EU in 2004 opened their labour markets to workers from Bulgaria and Romania but so have Sweden, Greece, Spain and Portugal (in that order). In the context of candidate states, only Turkey presents a challenge as regards workers' rights mainly because of migration politics in Austria and Germany. The other candidate states do not have populations sufficiently large to have been perceived by policy makers in the EU as an issue sufficiently serious to engage with.[18]

Once the emphasis is on a *right* to free movement to work and the Member State authorities are prohibited from interfering with that right: they may not require nationals of other Member States to seek work permits, are barred from requiring nationals of other Member States to obtain residence permits etc., the question is why do people not move. According to the European Commission, approximately 2% of the inhabitants of the EU live in a country other than that of their nationality. For the 2004 Member State nationals, the figure rose from 0.2% in 2003 to 0.5% by the end of 2007. A similar increase has occurred as regards Bulgarians and Romanians. As the Commission points out, of the 2004 Member States, mostly Poles, Lithuanians and Slovaks have moved, nationals of the rest of those states have mainly stayed at home. Of those who have moved, their main destination countries have been Ireland and the UK. Of the 2007 Member State nationals, most have gone to Spain and Italy.[19] Claims that there is a bottomless pool of labour migrants waiting to move as soon as controls are lifted are not substantiated by the EU experience. In fact, there are very few migrant workers available as most people will stay at home even though the unemployment and wage differentials are impressive.

According to Eurostat, the EU's statistical agency, in December 2008 unemployment stood at 2.7% in the Netherlands and 14.4% in Spain. Statutory minimum wages are under 300 Euros per month in Bulgaria, Estonia, Latvia, Lithuania, Hungary, Poland and Romania; between 301 and 999 Euros per month in the Czech Republic, Greece, Malta, Portugal, Slovenia and Spain and more than 1,000 Euros per month in the rest (at least the rest of those states which have

---

16   Zaiceva and Zimmermann 2008.

17   Border controls have been a particularly contested area, see Atger-Faure 2008.

18   European Commission, http://ec.europa.eu/enlargement/press_corner/key-documents/reports_nov_2006_en.htm and http://ec.europa.eu/social/main.jsp?catId=466&langId=en.

19   Press Release, European Commission 'Free Movement of workers is good for Europe's economy', 18 November 2008.

minimum wages). The highest minimum wage is in Luxembourg at 1,570 Euros per month.

The average minimum salary in Denmark is the equivalent of 1,850 Euros per month, 1,277 Euros in Germany and 1,258 Euros in France. But the average salary in Portugal is 470 Euros per month, 246 Euros in Poland and 92 Euros in Bulgaria (for some of these countries there is a narrow range).[20] Money does not explain EU migration patterns any more satisfactorily than unemployment rates. Further, notwithstanding the relative levels of movement of Romanians and Bulgarians to Spain since 1 January 2007 and the relatively high unemployment rate in that country, Spain lifted restrictions on movement of workers from the two countries as from 1 January 2009. Thus the decisions on labour migration which EU Member States make cannot be explained by the application of simplistic economic rational choice theory. What is original about the EU labour migration system is that it is based on reducing to the point of vestigial the labour migration control claims of the Member States and leaves in the hands of the individual the choice whether to move or not.[21] At the same time, the system is characterized by substantial worker protection – maximum working hours, minimum holiday entitlements etc. Further, the Member States have comprehensive sickness insurance and health care systems, unemployment and social benefits for the elderly and their care. Social solidarity has not been impaired as a result of permitting unlimited labour migration in an ever larger EU.

Fragmentation and the Foreigner

As outlined above, in a fairly short period of time, the EU has changed its size and shape and the status of people living within it.[22] Many people move seamlessly from irregular status in one country to citizen of a Member State entitled to residence, work (and social benefits) without crossing any border or making any application. They are embraced by EU law which transforms their status from irregular labour migrant in national law to EU citizen with an entitlement to unimpeded labour migration. The same is likely to happen again as enlargement continues. This means that the border between legality and irregularly, between state immigration control over labour market access and a prohibition on state control is fluid. However, fluidity does not end there. Third country nationals who are family members of EU migrant workers are entitled to residence and access to employment which the host Member State is not permitted to question or restrict. While third country national family members can be required to obtain visas for entry and residence cards (according to EU law rules) so long as their

---

20   European Union, Minimum Monthly Salaries 2008 http://eeuropeanrussianaffairs. suite101.com/article.cfm/european_union_minimum_monthly_salaries_2008.

21   Guild 1999.

22   Mantu 2008.

principal is a worker there can be no resources requirement, no health insurance requirement and a right to equal treatment. Even if the third country national was irregularly in the host state before the marriage to an EU national, the state cannot 'punish' the couple for that irregularity by requiring the third country national to leave to obtain a visa (this, according to the European Court of Justice would be disproportionate).[23] Third country national family members of EU nationals who have exercised their working rights are defined by EU law – all spouses, children under 21 or over that age if dependent (it does not matter if children are married etc.), ascending and descending relatives who are dependent on the worker and or his or her spouse. There is a duty to facilitate the admission of wider family members if they are dependent and in need.[24] On the basis of equal treatment with that of own nationals, unmarried partners, civil partnership and same sex relationships must be recognized for the purpose of residence and work of the third country national partner.[25] Thus the state's control over third country nationals is also fluid as they too move from the grip of national law to rights holders in EU law.

There are a number of agreements with third countries (ie countries which are not EU Member States) which give their nationals the right to move to and work in the EU on the same basis as nationals of EU Member States. These countries are Iceland, Norway and Switzerland. An agreement with Turkey gives its citizens who have gained lawful access to the labour market of a Member State the right to retain that labour market access and after four years to have free access to the labour market of that Member State. Some agreements with other third countries, such as Croatia and Macedonia, include provisions which permit their nationals to have access to self employment in any Member State. However, under these agreements, the individual must obtain a residence permit though the rules on the issue of the residence permit must not add further (national) criteria to those contained in the agreements themselves. A variety of other agreements with third countries provide a right for companies of the third country to send their workers to an EU Member State to carry out services, while still more agreements provide a right to equal treatment in wages and working conditions and in social security for their workers who are working (lawfully) in the EU.[26]

From 1999, the EU was accorded a series of powers to adopt legislation regulating the status of foreigners who are third country nationals (ie not nationals of any EU state). These powers cover asylum, border controls and migration.[27] Statistically, the largest single group of third country nationals who gain access to the EU labour market are people granted entry on the basis of family reunification. As regards family reunification of third country nationals with other third country

---

23   Kofman 2004.
24   Carrera 2005.
25   Article 2 Directive 2004/38.
26   Billet 2009 (forthcoming).
27   Peers and Rogers 2006.

nationals who are already resident in the EU, Member States no longer are entitled to apply their national laws. An EU directive sets out the conditions which can be applied. While the threshold for family reunification of third country nationals is higher in terms of the conditions which must be fulfilled than its counterpart for EU nationals who exercise their treaty rights, nonetheless, it is EU law not national law.[28] The loss of control over access to the territory and labour market of third country nationals which is inherent in the family reunification directive was sufficient to inspire three Member States, Denmark, Ireland and the UK to refuse to participate. They remain in splendid isolation running their own immigration systems regarding family reunification.

For family reunification of third country nationals there is still the appearance of national control. Family members may still be required to obtain visas from national consulates, they are required to obtain work and residence permits when they arrive in the destination EU state. For the individual, it appears as if the state is still very much in control – applying its laws, requiring national rules to be complied with. But the reality is somewhat different. EU law defines the conditions for family reunification of third country nationals with third country nationals already in the EU. Member States no longer have the power to change the rules of family reunification. They have a few discretionary clauses (like the much discussed provision on integration measures and tests)[29] which were inserted, often at the last minute into the EU measures to provide an assurance to national officials that they are still in charge.[30] But as Groenendijk has pointed out, because these provisions exist in EU measures, they are subject to interpretation by the European Court of Justice – the Member States no longer have the last word even on these little 'sovereignty' cards.[31] While it will be some time before the full effect of the transformation of state sovereignty will become apparent, it is already in practice. In a debate in the Netherlands in 2008, some political actors wanted to raise the age limit for spouses to be able to join third country national sponsors there. Denmark had recently done just this.[32] The matter never even became a serious part of the debate on family reunification as the EU Directive does not permit Member States to add new obstacles to family reunification.

Similarly, the EU adopted a measure creating a common status of EU third country national who has been resident for five years lawfully on the territory of a Member State. For these persons, not only is there a common EU status which protects labour rights and excludes their expulsion except on the limited grounds permitted in the Directive, but it also extends the possibility for long-term resident third country nationals to move and exercise economic activities in other Member States. Once again, in the Directive there are a number of 'sovereignty' card

---

28   Oosterom-Staples 2007.
29   Oers, R. van 2009.
30   Groenendijk, Fernhout, Van Dam, Van Oers and Strik 2006.
31   Groenendijk 2007.
32   Walter 2008.

provisions which provide the appearance of control by Member State authorities. But the matter is now EU law and no longer sovereign to the Member States. Again, for labour migrants, it may appear that it is still the Member States that are in charge, but the Member States' margin of action is highly diminished, their authorities are bound to apply the EU directive (except for Denmark, Ireland and the UK which, once again, chose not to participate). The odd result of this measure in the context of enlargement is that, for instance, a Russian national who has lived and worked for five years in Romania and obtained a long-term resident card will have a right to access to the Germany labour market (subject to delays which Germany can apply for up to 12 months) sooner than a Romanian national.[33]

The most complicated issue in the EU as regards national control over extra Union labour migration is first access to the labour market. Here, notwithstanding proposals first put forward by the European Commission in 2001, it was only in 2009 that a measure was adopted on the subject.[34] For my purposes, what is important is what it means for sovereignty and the right of states to control migration. The decision of the European Commission to break economic migration into different strands – highly skilled, researchers and students, inter-company transferees and low-skilled seasonal workers – and to make different sets of rules of each of the categories is very significant regarding the way in which labour migration control is perceived among the Member States. This is because it heralds the allocation of different rights to third country national workers depending on their value to the EU labour market. Unlike the lesson of EU national labour migration where all workers are entitled to the highest level of rights available to national workers, when it comes to third country national migrant workers it looks like there will be substantial differences. Highly qualified third country national workers are given better rights than lower skilled workers. The principle appears to be that the economically stronger should be privileged and the equally needed but economically weaker migrant workers should be deprived of rights. These rights take the form of security of residence, equality of wages, access to social benefits and family reunification.

The illusion of control (to which I will return below under tools of control) is compounded by the illusion of capacity to choose. The mantra of 'managed migration' based on rational choices about labour market needs drives the vision that state authorities are capable of choosing 'good' labour migrants and rejecting 'poor' labour migrants. Indeed, good usually means highly skilled and poor means exactly those without resources. In the European context there are traditionally three mechanisms which have been applied to separate the good from the poor labour migrants and thus to achieve what is considered a beneficial managed migration system. First, potential labour migrants must fulfil criteria on skills – unless they meet skills levels established by national legislation they will not be

---

33   Carlier and Guild 2006.
34   Directive 2009/50 on the conditions of entry and residence of third-country nationals for the purposes of highly qualified employment.

permitted to migrate. Secondly, the authorities apply a labour market test – is there anyone in the EU labour market already who could take the job – if so the labour migrant should be rejected. Thirdly, salary levels – only labour migrants who will be paid over a certain salary will be admitted. The skills criteria has been subject to endless discussion about what kind of skills are needed – should there be priority lists of skills in short supply, how are such lists to be determined. Regarding the labour market test, the fairly obviously illusory nature of such a test which must be applied to the labour market of 27 Member States with a population just short of 500 million is hard to disguise. The local nature of so many labour markets is evidenced by the low movement rates of nationals of EU Member States. The salary requirement has been very seductive to some Member States but then has fallen out of favour to some extent as it means the potential migrant must already have a job offer which could stifle initiative and self employment which would create jobs. Also, some jobs carry high salaries but not high social acceptance. Under the Dutch skilled migrant programme a salary level is determinant for the issue of labour migration authorizations except for three categories of workers: football players, Imams and prostitutes. The three sit uncomfortably beside one another as a class of their own.

Another problematic aspect of the good and poor labour migrant approach in the EU is that Member States acknowledge very different labour market needs. For instance, in Spain and Poland, the authorities acknowledge that their economies need agricultural workers in substantial numbers. While other Member States also need agricultural workers they are often less honest about the fact. Thus, a good labour migrant in Poland is not necessarily the highly skilled Indian IT worker who was the object of Germany's Green Card system launched in 2000 (and revised in 2004) but the low-skilled Ukrainian agricultural worker. Further, with the ageing of Europe, more and more care workers willing to work in the home with the elderly are needed.[35] In Italy there is substantial labour migration from the Philippines and elsewhere to fulfil this need.[36] But these workers are not classified as the good migrants according to the scheme of directives even though they are the ones which the economy may need most. The dominance of the managed migration discourse means that the good labour migrant is always defined as the highly skilled/paid. Because he or she is classified as desirable, there is an assumption that there is competition among states to encourage the individual to move to their country. This assumption then justifies the differential treatment of the desirable labour migrant. In order to encourage him or her to come to the EU the rules of migration must include entitlements to good conditions of entry, family reunification, labour market access, social conditions and access to social benefits.[37]

---

35 Johnson and Zimmermann 1993.
36 Castles and Miller 2005.
37 Bigo and Guild 2005.

However, the contrary assumption applies to the poor labour migrant, although he or she may be even more valuable to the economy than the highly skilled/ paid labour migrant. Because he or she has been classified as poor, it is assumed that there is an enormous pool of such migrants available to come to the host state to do the work. Thus, according to the market approach to human beings, there is no need to provide good conditions of entry, family reunification, labour market access, social conditions or access to social benefits to these persons. The assumption about the nature of the work and its value to the economy justifies that discriminatory treatment of the labour migrant. So-called low-skilled workers are made subject to restrictions so that their residence will be temporary and when they leave the assumption is that there will be others to take their place. These workers are then accorded a more precarious work and residence permit, excluded from social benefits and often excluded also from long-term residence status.[38]

As has been extensively examined in gender studies, the allocation of the titles highly skilled and low-skilled tend to have gender consequences. They are used to justify differentials in treatment which reinforce gender stereotypes and have the consequence of limiting women's access to economic stability. Ann Tickner's work in particular has focused on the intersection of migration and the precariousness of women's economic status.[39] In the European labour migration context, it is also interesting to note that many of the jobs most likely to fulfil the highly skilled categories are those where there is a differential in gender privileging men. Some of the medical sciences and teaching are an exception to this norm but those exceptions only emphasis the generality of the gender element in the determination of high-skilled versus low-skilled labour migrants.

Tools of Control and Control of Tools

The mechanisms of labour migration have been changing in the EU over the last ten years. Two developments are particularly important. The first has been a trend to carry out labour migration control outside the state. Thus, EU states require labour migrants to be outside the country when they or their employer makes an application for a work permit and that the labour migrant obtain a visa before travelling to the state. Paradoxically, this externalization of labour migration control has the effect of putting the individual much farther from the officials who must apply a labour market test (if one is applied at all). One solution which the UK has adopted is to move the decision making abroad as well in order to follow the externalization of the control process. So instead of officials with knowledge of the labour market making the decision on access for a potential immigrant, it is officials in the UK consulates in the country of origin who make the decision. In terms of ministerial competence, the employment and trade ministries are edged

---

38   Groenendijk 2007.
39   Tickner 1999.

out of the equation and the interior ministry seeks to embed itself in the consulates which belong to the foreign ministry. As the externalization takes hold, the control of the foreign ministries becomes more evident. In order to diminish this rather troublesome formula, many of the labour migration control mechanisms are transferred to agencies – in the UK case the job of assessing and issuing visas was hived off to the UK Visas Agency (under joint foreign and interior ministry control) and dealing with immigration controls to UKBA (UK Borders Agency).

The second development is the identity of those engaged in controlling labour migration. As Guiraudon has developed, the move of mechanisms of control has not only moved out beyond the borders it has also moved within the state. The introduction of sanctions against employers for hiring workers who have not been authorized by the state has been a regular feature of EU state labour market control over the past ten years.[40] In 2009, the EU adopted a Directive on sanctions against employers for employing undocumented migrants. This has the interesting effect of once again changing the nature of sovereignty as regards this type of tool in relation to labour migration. On the one hand, the private sector is obliged to take on the task of labour migration control on pain of sanctions, usually financial penalties, for failure to correctly to carry out the task, on the other hand, the power to make rules about those sanctions moves away from that of the Member State into the hands of the EU authorities.

This change in the nature of the actors is not exclusive to the way in which labour migration is controlled within the state. It also applies in the extraterritorial move as well in the form of carriers' sanctions. The development of private sector controls sanctioning employers accompanies the measures which have already been adopted at EU level sanctioning travel companies (excluding train companies) which bring to the external border of the EU persons who are not then admitted.[41] These sanctions have been put into place as a mechanism to make sure that visa rules are respected – the transport companies are required to make sure that travellers have the right documents for entry into the EU so that those who do arrive at the borders are likely to be admitted on pain of a sanction against the transport company.

The place of the controls bears attention. The tools of control in the EU are primarily:

- visas, which must be obtained abroad, accompanied by sanctions on transporters;
- external border controls, which may be carried out at external borders or more often just beyond the borders of EU states;
- work and residence permits, which must be obtained in the state, accompanied by sanctions on employers;
- police registration systems, whereby the worker must provide personal details.

---

40   Guild and 2006.
41   Scholten and Minderhoud 2008.

The disciplining measures are refusal of visas, entry, work or residence permits, police investigations, fines on transport companies, employers and expulsion of the worker. The measures take place in a variety of different places and are carried out by an increasingly diverse number of actors. There is a division of powers to make law between the EU and the Member States. As the Member States seek more consistency in how labour migration rules in other Member States are applied and carried out, so in the process they relinquish increasing power themselves to control labour migration. As the idea of making the private sector take more responsibility for labour migration in the form of transport companies checking work permits and employers subject to fines for employing migrants without the necessary documents, so too the capacity of the state to control labour migration is paradoxically weakened. Where the state previously took a more important role in certifying labour migrants one by one, as the control function is hived off to the private sector the capacity to know exactly what is going on is not necessarily enhanced. If one of the justifications for the move is that there will be public financial savings, then the commensurate increase in the number of labour inspectors is unlikely to take place.

The EU is struggling at the moment with the question of where the tools are controlled. While the three 'opted out' Member States – Denmark, Ireland and the UK remain strictly sovereignist in respect of all the activities, the rest of the EU is moving in quite a different direction. Increasingly, measures on labour migration, border control, extra-territorial controls on movement of persons and visa issuing are all moving into the exclusive competence of the EU. The tools which Member States have, but also which they are obliged to use, are formulated within the EU institutions. Once the measures are adopted the Member States are obliged to carry them out faithfully. Some activities have been hived off into EU agencies – specifically FRONTEX to which I will return below in greater depth. The control of the tools has moved to the EU though the tools of control must be carried out primarily by the Member States.

As regards visas, short stay visas are a matter of EU law. The reasons for issuing or refusing to issue a short stay visa (Schengen visa) is a matter covered by the EU's Common Visa Code, which became effective on 5 April 2010.[42] As regards long stay visas, some are covered exclusively by EU law rules – such as those for family reunification others are partially covered for instance in the highly skilled migrant directive though Member States retain the right to issue national visas. There are still very substantial variations among the Member States in how they apply EU law even on the issue even of short stay visas – while the overall refusal rate of short stay visas in the EU is about 10% the variations between Member State consulates in the same country can be very substantial indeed.[43] For instance, as regards applications for short stay visas made in Nairobi, Kenya in 2007:[44]

---

42   Regulation 810/2009.
43   Beaudu 2007.
44   http://register.consilium.europa.eu/pdf/en/08/st08/st08215.en08.pdf.

- Germany: 4687 applications, 740 refusals;
- France: 2808 applications, 248 refusals;
- Italy: 2634 applications, 74 refusals;
- Netherlands: 2556 applications, 247 refusals.[45]

At the EU's external border, there is a clearer picture of the changing control of the tools. On the one hand there is an EU regulation on admission and refusal of individuals at the external borders of the EU.[46] This regulation has been in force since 2006 and requires officials carrying out border controls to do so in a manner which does not discriminate on the basis of race, ethnicity, religion or gender. Further, where an official refuses admission to an individual this must be in accordance with the rules set out in the regulation. The individual must be given notice of refusal in writing and informed of his or her right of appeal against that decision.

The control of the EU's external border is coordinated by an EU agency, FRONTEX, which is charged with ensuring the proper coordination of the maintenance of external border controls.[47] It is not charged with ensuring that the EU's border control law is correctly carried out. FRONTEX has been very much in the news on account of its role coordinating maritime actions to prevent irregular migration into the EU in the Atlantic around the Canary Islands (part of Spain) and in the Mediterranean around Malta and the Italian island of Lampedusa which is closest to the African coast.[48] The activities of FRONTEX and the manner in which the operations it has been coordinating have been carried out are controversial. As its role is one of coordination, it depends on the Member States making available for actions their coast guard boats and personnel. These personnel and boats continue to be regulated according to national law rather than EU law resulting in fairly substantial incoherence among the actors. UNHCR has been particularly concerned about the activities as it is not clear that refugees are able to make their claims to asylum under the conditions of these controls.[49]

---

45   See UNHCR Statistics on Refugee Protection 2007, table 13.

46   The Schengen Borders Code: Regulation 562/2006.

47   Regulation 2007/2004 establishing External Borders Agency.

48   http://www.frontex.europa.eu/newsroom/news_releases/art40.html; Carrera 2007; Human Rights Watch September 2009.

49   'UNHCR and Frontex have begun discussions on cooperation, as foreseen in the Frontex Regulation and proposed by the Commission in its Communication on Reinforcing Management of the EU's Southern Maritime Borders. UNHCR is willing to collaborate with Frontex to ensure that personnel deployed on joint operations are trained in the essential principles of international law and refugee protection. Guidance would appear also to be necessary on how border operations can be carried out in a way that ensures consistent respect for international refugee law. UNHCR calls on the Presidency and other Member States to support development of this cooperation in relevant priority areas, including training, exchange of information relevant to risk analysis, and others.' UNHCR, July 2007, http://www.unhcr.org.ua/news.php?in=1&news_id=112.

As regards work and residence permits, a directive has been adopted on highly qualified migration only.[50] The main weakness of the directive is that it neither sets a minimum standard nor a maximum one for the admission of highly qualified migrants to the EU. Thus Member States are not constrained either by upper or lower limits to issue work and residence permits in accordance with the Directive.[51] For the moment this is still a matter of Member State control as regards first admission and residence for other categories of labour migrants. However, as mentioned above, there are agreements with third countries which require Member States to privilege the treatment of nationals of the other party.[52] EU law, of course, regulates the issue of work and residence permits for third country national family members admitted under the Directive.[53] Further, once the labour migrant has lived for five years in the EU he or she will be eligible for long-term residence status and access to the whole of the EU labour market thus control passes to the EU to make the rules and ensure that national officials apply them consistently and correctly.[54]

Once inside the EU the border control picture changes again. The same regulation which establishes the common external border control regime also requires all EU states (except Denmark, Ireland and the UK) to abolish all internal controls on the movement of persons. It does not matter whether those persons are EU nationals or third country nationals. The power of the state to control is prohibited. While at airports this is hard to see as security controls on identity carried out by airways replaces the identity controls which had been carried out by officials, the difference is important.[55] On trains, roads and buses across Europe the change is immediately evident. In fact it is so evident that there is great annoyance when state officials carry out identity checks inside their borders on travellers. These checks are still permitted under the EU rules which require the abolition of intra Member State border controls but they must not replace border controls.[56] Their objective must be exclusively police measures and they must be justified. Thus these controls, in law, are very different from immigration controls. In practice they are gradually becoming so as well. The EU labour migrant whether an EU citizen or third country national does not (normally) encounter the state at the EU's intra Member State borders. The encounter, if it occurs at all, will happen well after the individual has arrived and may never happen.[57]

A further restriction on the Member States' right to control labour migration within the EU takes the form of the EU rules on service provision. If the third

---

50   Directive 2009/50 adopted on 25 May 2009.
51   For a more substantial analysis of the proposal before adoption see Guild 2007.
52   Gutmann 2000.
53   Condinanzi, Lang and Nascimbene 2008.
54   Groenendijk 2007.
55   Hobbing 2005.
56   Article 21 Schengen Borders Code.
57   Bertozzi 2008

country national is working in one Member State and is sent to another by his or her employer to carry out a contract (even if this takes some time) EU rules protect the right of the business to send its employee across the EU border for this purpose. As there is no intra Member State border control, the individual moves to where the work is to be carried out, carries out the activity and generally returns home. The state may never be aware of the fact that the individual was on the territory. This has caused some Member States substantial anguish about who is on their territory but also about the collection of taxes in respect of work carried out on their territory. The Belgian authorities have put in place an on line registration system where enterprises must notify the state when any worker from outside Belgium comes to carry out services for more than three days in the country so that the state can impose social charges, taxes etc. it is unclear just how successful this system is.[58]

In the 2010 climate of rising unemployment and great job insecurity, the possibility of posted workers arriving from other Member States to carry out contracts has become increasing politically charged. In Sweden, a highly controversial case of a company which engaged Estonian workers and posted them to Sweden to carry out works without fulfilling the social and wage conditions applicable to Swedish workers was determined by the European Court of Justice in 2007.[59] Notwithstanding rage on the part of the trade unions, the ECJ upheld the right of companies to send their workers to carry out services across EU borders. The actual reasoning of the ECJ perhaps does not merit all the antagonism which it has elicited. The court did not exclude the right of the state to ensure the wage and social standards are equivalent for posted workers as for national workers but found that Swedish legislation did not provide for the application of this power in accordance with EU law. In the UK, in February 2009, the posting of Italian and Portuguese workers to carry out works in Lincolnshire at the oil company Total's refinery there gave rise to unauthorized industrial action by workers demanding 'British jobs for British workers'. But most posting of workers passes unnoticed because there are no border controls on movement of persons within the territory (the UK excepted of course). The numbers and impact of posted workers also seems to militate against state authorities becoming aware of their presence except when there are substantial teams of workers who move together to a worksite.

While the right of Member States to control labour migration within the EU and increasingly into it has diminished, the desire to control has not. Within the part of Member States interior and justice ministries there continues to be substantial concern about the loss of control and the consequences which this has, not least on the professional futures of the individuals involved. On the one hand, the explosion of interest in all matters even tangentially connected with security which followed the 11 September 2001 attacks in the USA provided legitimacy to those expressing concern about the loss of control over movement of

---

58 Watson 1983.
59 Tans 2008.

persons, including labour migrants in the EU. On the other hand, the exponential growth of technical capacity in information technology provided undreamt of possibilities for collecting, storing and using information, including information about individuals. Interest in security as an issue of movement of persons and the possibility to collect and use information collided over the first ten years of the new millennium leading towards new ways of controlling movement of persons.[60] The European Commission proposed a border package on 13 February 2008 aiming at establishing an EU entry/exist system registering the movement of specific categories of third country nationals at the external borders of the EU, as well as a border control mechanism (Automated Border Control System) enabling the automated verification of travellers' identity based on biometric technology.[61] The idea is that people will swipe themselves in and out of the EU under the watchful eye of border guards. Their information will be checked against the widest possible group of EU databases (for asylum seekers, criminals etc.).[62]

The security tools and techniques envisaged by the Commission are threefold:

1. The setting up of a new European-wide database containing specific information on certain categories of non EU-nationals.
2. Interoperability of the database with other already existing and planned EU databases and biometric systems.
3. The systematic checking of everyone entering and leaving the EU with at least three categories of persons: those third country nationals who have visas containing biometric data which will be checked at the border; third country nationals who do not need visas for a short stay in the EU whose biometric data will be taken at the border; citizens of the Union whose biometric data will be incorporated into their passports which will be swiped on entry and exit.

It shows most starkly the changing nature of the ambition of control. What is new in the package is a three fold change in thinking about migration control. First, it is no longer about sovereignty and its cut free from state borders. Instead it may take place anywhere no longer tied to the purpose of marking the border between places and states. Secondly, it is no longer about the division of persons between citizens and foreigners. All persons would be subject to the system of control irrespective of nationality. Everyone is controlled when he or she is in the process of moving. Thirdly, control is intrinsically linked to the allocation of an identity which is held in a database (probably centralized). The individual is

---

60   Brouwer 2008.

61   Commission Communication, on an entry/exist system at the external borders of the European Union, facilitation of border crossings for bona fide travellers, and an electronic travel authorization system, COM(2008) final, Brussels.

62   Guild 2008.

subject to a control of his or her identity against the prototype which is held by the control authority. Of course, the proposal raises a whole series of issues about protection of personal data. But more centrally, it indicates a change in the way the EU perceives migration and people. The vocation to control the foreigner is able to morph into an ambition to allocate identity and control any individual against the official, ideal identity. Labour migration control appears to give way, in this scenario to control which is no longer about labour nor even about migration as the citizen and the foreigner are equally subject to control. Nor is it ultimately related to the state and sovereignty, as the actor at the heart of the control is the EU. It points towards a change in governmentality, to use Foucault's term. There is a ground shift in the way in which the exercise of power constitutes authority and is inscribed on the body of the individual.

Conclusions

At the outset of this chapter I set out a number of contentions to be exemplified. Now at the end of the chapters I will asses those contentions on the basis of the research. First, regarding free movement of workers, the EU experience indicates that abolishing controls on labour migration based on reciprocity even among countries with very different standards of living, minimum wages, standards of social benefits and unemployment rates does not result in (a) significant movement (b) a reduction of social solidarity or (c) a rise in xenophobia.

Secondly, the EU experience of developing a labour migration system beyond national sovereignty and no longer on a reciprocal basis shows much greater fears of foreign workers which result in the diminution of rights and a restrictive approach. Thirdly, the move of power to control labour migration from state borders and sovereign decisions to EU mechanisms appears to facilitate the move beyond the borders to mechanisms of immigration control embedded in third countries, the high seas (ie beyond sovereign territory) and into the private sector. The burden of carrying out controls is moved to carriers and employers, in other words the private sector. Fourthly, while security claims around hard state sovereign border controls have lost much of their appeal in the EU, instead, the security claims have fuelled the development of supranational electronic control systems replete with large scale data bases filled with personal data on people on the move.

What the EU experiences seem to indicate for the future is an increasing irrelevance of state borders for the movement of labour migrants and an increase of electronic surveillance detached from specific territorially symbolic places. The objective of the new forms of surveillance appear to be to track the individual and his or her economic activities in order to discipline a substantial array of actors inside and outside the remit of state sovereignty as it is usually visualized on maps.

References

Beaudu, G. 2007. L'externalisation dans le domaine des visas Schengen. *Cultures & Conflits*, 68, 85–109.

Bertozzi, S. 2008. *Schengen: Achievements and Challenges in Managing an Area Encompassing 3.6 million km²*. CEPS Working Document No. 284. Brussels: CEPS, February.

Bigo, D. and Guild, E. 2005. *Controlling Frontiers: Free Movement Into and Within Europe*. Aldershot: Ashgate.

Billet, C. 2009. EC Readmission Agreements: A Prime Instrument of the External Dimension of the EU's Fight Against Irregular Immigration: Assessment After Ten Years of Practice. *EJML* (forthcoming).

Brouwer, E. 2008. *Digital Borders and Real Rights: Effective Remedies for Third-country Nationals in the Schengen Information System*. Leiden/Boston: Martinus Nijhoff.

Burley, A. and Mattli, W. 1993. Europe Before the Court: A Political Theory of Legal Integration. *International Organization*, 47(1), 41–76.

Carlier, J.-Y. and Guild, E. 2006. *L'avenir de la libre circulation des personnes dans l'UE (The Future of Free Movement of Persons in the EU)*. Brussels: Bruylant.

Carrera, S. 2005. What Does Free Movement Mean in Theory and Practice in an Enlarged EU? *European Law Journal*, 11(6), 699–721.

Carrera, S. 2007. *The EU Border Management Strategy: FRONTEX and the Challenges of Irregular Immigration in the Canary Islands*. Brussels: CEPS.

Castles, S. and Miller, M. 2005. *The Age of Migration*, 3rd edition. Houndsmill: Palgrave McMillan.

Condinanzi, M., Lang, A. and Nascimbene, B. 2008. *Citizenship of the Union and Freedom of Movement of Persons*. The Hague: Martinus Nijhoff.

Faure Atger, A. 2008. *The Abolition of Internal Border Checks in an Enlarged Schengen Area: Freedom of Movement or a Scattered Web of Security Checks?* Brussels: CEPS.

Galgoczi, B., Leschke, J. and Watt, A. 2009. *EU Labour Migration since Enlargement: Trends, Impacts and Policies*. Aldershot: Ashgate.

Goodwin-Gill, G.S. 2005. R (ex parte European Roma Rights Centre et al.) v. Immigration Officer at Prague Airport and another (UNHCR intervening). *International Journal of Refugee Law*, 17, 427–453.

Groenendijk, K. 2007. The Long Term Residents' Directive, Denizenship and Integration, in *Whose Freedom, Security and Justice? EU Immigration and Asylum Law and Policy*, edited by A. Baldaccini, E. Guild, and H. Toner. Oxford: Hart, 429–50.

Groenendijk, K., Fernhout, R., Dam, D. van, Oers, R van and Strik, T. 2006. *The Family Reunification Directive in EU Member States*. Nijmegen: Wolf Legal Publishers.

Guild, E. 1999. *Immigration Law in the European Union*. The Hague: Kluwer Law International.

Guild, E. 2004. *Legal Elements of European Identity Citizenship and Migration Law*. The Hague: Kluwer Law International.

Guild, E. 2007. *EU Policy on Labour Migration: A First Look at the Commission's Blue Card Initiative*. Brussels: CEPS.

Guild, E. 2008. *The Commission's New Border Package: Does it Take us One Step Closer to a 'Cyber-fortress Europe'?* Brussels: CEPS.

Guild, E. and Minderhoud, P. (eds) 2006. *Immigration and Criminal Law in the European Union: The Legal Measures and Social Consequences of Criminal Law in Member States on Trafficking and Smuggling in Human Beings*. The Hague: Martinus Nijhoff.

Gutmann, R. 2000. *Die Assoziationsfreizügigkeit türkischer Staatsangehöriger: Ihre Entdeckung und ihr Inhalt*. Baden-Baden: Nomos Verlagsgesellschaft.

Handoll, J. 2009. Family Reunification after *Metock*, in *Rethinking Free Movement of Workers: The European Challenges Ahead*, edited by P. Minderhoud and N. Trimikliniotis. Nijmegen: Wolf Legal Publishers, 173–89.

Hobbing, P. 2005. *Integrated Border Management at the EU Level*. CEPS Working Document No. 227, Brussels: CEPS.

House of Lords (UK) 2006. *The Future Enlargement of the European Union, 24th Report*. 7th Session.

Human Rights Watch. 2009. *Pushed Back, Pushed Around: Italy's Forced Return of Boat Migrants and Asylum Seekers, Libya's Mistreatment of Migrants and Asylum Seekers*, September.

Huysmans, J. 2000. The European Union and the Securitization of Migration, *JCMS* 38(5), 751–77.

Johnson, P. and Zimmermann, A. 1993. *Labour Markets in an Ageing Europe*. Cambridge: Cambridge University Press.

Kofman, E. 2004. Family-related Migration: A Critical Review of European Studies, *Journal of Ethnic and Migration Studies*, 30(2), 243–62.

Majone, G. 1994. The European Community: An 'Independent Fourth Branch of Government'?, in *Verfassungen für ein ziviles Europa*, edited by G. Bruggemeier. Baden-Baden: Nomos, 23–43.

Mantu, S. 2008. *The Boundaries of European Social Citizenship*. Nijmegen: Wolf Legal Publishers.

Meunier, S. and McNamara, K. 2007. *Making History: European Integration and Institutional Change at Fifty*. Oxford: Oxford University Press.

Oers, R. van. 2009. Justifying Citizenship Tests in the Netherlands and the UK, in *Illiberal Liberal States: Immigration, Citizenship and Integration in the EU*, edited by E. Guild, C.A. Groenendijk and S. Carrera. Aldershot: Ashgate, 113–30.

Oosterom-Staples, H. 2007. The Family Reunification Directive: A Tool Preserving Member State Interest or Conducive to Family Unity?, in *Whose Freedom,*

228 Constructing and Imagining Labour Migration

Security and Justice? EU Immigration and Asylum Law and Policy, edited by A. Baldaccini, E. Guild and H. Toner. Oxford: Hart, 451–88.

Peers, S. and Rogers, N. 2006. *EU Immigration and Asylum Law*. Leiden: Martinus Nijhoff.

Scholten, S. and Minderhoud, P. 2008. Regulating Immigration Control: Carrier Sanctions in the Netherlands, *EJML*, 10(2), 123–47.

Tans, S. 2008. Case Note on *Laval*, 18 December 2007 (Case C-341/05) and *Viking*, 11 December 2007 (Case C-438/05), *EJML* 10(2), 249–75.

Tickner, J.A. 1999. Why Women Can't Run the World: International Politics According to Francis Fukuyama, *International Studies Perspectives*, 3–11.

Triandafillidou, A. and Gropas, R. 2007. *European Immigration: A Sourcebook*. Aldershot: Ashgate.

Verdun, A. and Croce, O. 2005. *The European Union in the Wake of Eastern Enlargement*. Manchester: Manchester University Press 2005.

Waever, O., Buzan, B., Kelstrup, M. and Lemaitre, P. 1993. *Identity, Migration and the New Security Agenda in Europe*. New York: St Martin's Press.

Walter, A. 2008. *Reverse Discrimination and Family Reunification.* Nijmegen: Wolf Legal Publishers.

Watson, P. 1983. Freedom of Establishment and Freedom to Provide Services: Some Recent Developments, *CML Rev*, 20, 767–824.

Zaiceva, A. and Zimmermann, K. 2008. Scale, Diversity, and Determinants of Labour Migration in Europe, *Oxford Review of Economic Policy*, 24(3), 427–51.

Chapter 11

Nationality:
An Alternative Control Mechanism in
an Area of Free Movement?

Sandra Mantu

Introduction: Free Movement, The 'Right' Nationality and Control

Migration studies abound in examples of how states, either on their own or in cooperation with others, try to control or manage the movement of persons across borders. In comparison to family reunification or asylum seeking, labour migration is labelled by state discourse on migration as a legitimate and 'wanted' form of movement. The European Union (EU) has, as such, acknowledged that labour migration is economically desirable and that previous restrictive policies are no longer appropriate.[1] Yet, in spite of this admission, as the chapters by Faure Atger and Guild in this book show, it continues to operate with two distinctive paradigms of control, one applicable to European Union citizens and a second one to third country nationals (TCNs). Among the many issues involved in the control of labour migration, who is entitled to move in order to seek work or take up employment is highly relevant. In negotiating the identity of the subject allowed to cross borders, nationality plays an important part as some nationals will be preferred over others. In the context of the EU, for example, this is made clear by the rule that Community nationals will be preferred with the occasion of filling vacant work positions. In a less visible manner than border controls, for instance, nationality informs the construction of labour migration control mechanisms by setting in place the preconditions that make possible the drawing of distinctions between individuals allowed to move and those whose mobility is restricted or denied. This chapter will focus on the paradigm of control around the movement of Union citizens for whom European citizenship operates as a mechanism reinforcing the ceasing of control over labour migration by state authorities. By analysing the case law of the European Court of Justice (CJEU) on issues relating to the nationality of the Member States it is suggested that the EU project requires the rethinking of state sovereignty and control narratives.

The European Union started its existence as a primarily economic community based on a set of fundamental freedoms that included, albeit in a rather primitive

---

1   Bernard Ryan in Baldaccini, Guild and Toner (eds) 2007.

manner, the free movement of persons. The initial ECSC Treaty (Article 69) equated this freedom with the movement of labour in the few economic sectors covered by that Treaty. The Treaty of Rome took the idea of free movement one step further and called for the establishment of a common market but provided again for a limited version of the free movement of persons, as it equated persons with workers and producers.[2] More importantly for this analysis is that the notion of 'persons' benefiting from free movement has always been understood to mean nationals of the Member States. Economically irrelevant persons, even if nationals of the Member States, and those holding the nationality of states outside the European project were initially excluded. The further changes operated to the Treaties have not abandoned the economic dimension of the European project; rather they have expanded and refined it. The fulfilment of the economic goals of the EU has required that Member States give up at least some attributes of their sovereign right to control the movement across their national borders regarding certain persons (nationals of the other Member States) as well as abolish employment restrictions based on nationality for Community workers. The achievement and smooth functioning of the common market appear intrinsically coupled with a process of redrawing the boundaries of Member State sovereignty in certain areas. Yet, the creation of a space without internal frontiers, in which the free movement of persons, goods, services and capital are guaranteed, has more than once met with the Member States' reluctance regarding the loss of control over their territories towards the Community. In the context of the Schengen agreement, Sergio Carrera has pointed out 'It was felt that the right to move and reside freely within the EU (openness) needed to be accompanied by a security framework (control)', precisely because the idea of an area without internal borders and checks raised concerns about migration control and security issues.[3]

The process of abandoning control over the movement of nationals of other Member States, albeit seen primarily as economically productive individuals, has been aided by the case law of the European Court of Justice interpreting the free movement of workers and the secondary legislation adopted for its practical implementation and realization.[4] The Court's approach stresses that the source of control over labour migration is situated outside the state, and in theory, outside the reach of its influence. The Court of Justice of the European Union (CJEU) has declared that the notion of 'worker' is an autonomous one; national definitions

---

2   Olsen 2006, 5–6.

3   Carrera 2005, 700.

4   Regulation 1612/68 of 15.10.1968 on freedom of movement for workers within the Community (OJ No L 257, 19.10.1968); Directive 2004/38/EC of 29.04.2004 on the right of citizens of the Union and their family members to move and reside freely within the territory of the Member States (OJ No L158, 30.04.2004); Directive 98/49/EC of 29 June 1998 on safeguarding the supplementary pension rights of employed and self-employed persons moving within the Community (OJ No L 209, 25.07.1998).

are irrelevant as long as the conditions identified by the CJEU are met.[5] Because of this case law, being a worker and a national of another Member State secures a strong position for the individual migrant. Access to this secure and attractive position is based on meeting two conditions: holding the 'right' nationality and meeting the conditions of the worker definition spelled out by the CJEU. While the second condition has been progressively relaxed by the Court in order to capture atypical workers, the first condition has not benefited from a similar intense judicialization as the personal scope of Community law has been mainly expanded via enlargements, i.e. the accession of new countries to the European Union.

While it is possible to read the European Union as a de-securitizing project built around the abandonment of control over labour migration as Elspeth Guild does in her chapter, it can also be argued that there is a level at which the Member States have not officially and formally lost control, as they are free to determine the criteria of nationality attribution, therefore directly controlling the personal scope of European Union law as far as free movement of persons, including workers, goes. One must add that this is a jealously guarded power, one of the last bastions of sovereignty in the context of the EU. The borders of identity embedded in the legal concept of nationality have proven more difficult to dismantle than the territorial ones.

The introduction of Union citizenship in 1992 has not formally changed the situation. What's more, the free movement of persons understood as the free movement of the economically active seemed to go relatively unchallenged by this new citizenship status.[6] The exclusion of TCN's from the personal scope of EU citizenship and the lack of influence of the EU over who is entitled to be a European citizen function as mechanisms of migration control. There are signs that this status quo is currently being challenged in various ways. What this chapter intends to do is show how nationality attribution as a sovereign prerogative of the nation state is itself being challenged and transformed in the EU context and mainly via the case law of the CJEU. My aim is to examine if the interpretation of EU citizenship and of the condition to hold the nationality of a Member State by the Court has created 'micro-transformations'[7] in the relationship between state nationality, EU citizenship and entitlement to rights in a supranational context.

---

5   See for example, Rogers and Scannell 2005, 101–20; Condinanzi, Lang and Nascimbene 2008, 65–105.

6   Free movement rights had been extended via secondary legislation to include only those economically inactive persons sufficiently rich to be able to provide for themselves.

7   Sassen 2003, available online at http://www.aacu.org/liberaleducation/le–sp03/le–sp03feature2.cfm.

Union Citizenship: The Maastricht 'Innovation'

When first introduced, citizenship of the Union was seen as the answer to the democratic deficit that the Union as a whole was supposed to be experiencing. It was also intended to provide the popular basis that would further the European project and lend it a much needed legitimacy.[8] The Amsterdam Treaty later confirmed what EU citizenship was definitely not intended to be, namely, a substitute for national citizenship. Any fears that certain Member States might have had regarding the evolution of the Union towards statehood seemed properly addressed. The debate on the advancement towards a state-like form has continued in the years to come, despite the reassurance of the Amsterdam Treaty[9] that there was not going to be one European people, in the sense of a European nation, but rather, several European peoples sharing certain common traditions and possibly more important, a joint vision of the area's future.[10]

According to Article 20 TFEU (former Article 17 TEC) every person holding the nationality of a Member state shall be a citizen of the Union and in this capacity he/she will enjoy the rights conferred by the Treaty and shall be subject to the duties imposed thereby. At first sight, it would appear that any questions regarding acquisition and withdrawal of EU citizenship are decided by the Member States. In practice, this means that there are currently 27 ways of becoming an EU citizen and 27 ways of losing the same status; in case of future enlargements the numbers will increase. Harmonization of the rules of nationality currently in force in the various Member States seems to be a delicate issue, the explanation lying in the importance attached to nationality determination in general. Who is allowed to become a 'club member' is, at least, from the perspective of international law, a matter of national sovereignty and one that states are keen on controlling.

Yet, what is the function of nationality in the context of the European Union? If, indeed, Union citizenship is meant to voice the relationship that exists between the Union, on one hand and on the other, the nationals of the Member States as citizens of the said Union, then the rules defining this status should not be entirely within the ambit of national legislation on nationality determination, since this relationship is meant to transcend the boundaries of the nation state. Up to now the Member States have shown extreme reluctance in thinking beyond the national level of identity. The downside to a more open-minded approach to determining who is a citizen of the Union impacts the position of TCNs who currently are

---

8   See, Jessurun d'Oliveira 1995; Evans1995; O'Leary 1992; O'Leary 1998.

9   In the same line of argument there are various Council declarations issued around that time stressing that despite the fact that citizenship of the Union brings additional rights and protection, it does not replace national citizenship. See, Bull EC 10–1992 pt I.8, 9 and Bull EC 12–1992 pt I.35 at 25.

10   See Jessurun d'Oliveira's discussion of the idea of one single European nation or demos and the Treaty's pledge that the Union shall respect the national identities of the Member States, Jessurun d'Oliveira 1995, 73.

excluded from Union citizenship unless they naturalize in one of the Member States.[11] Thus, the topic of Union citizenship is entangled with migration since by controlling the rules for determination of Union citizenship, the Member States indirectly control migration towards the Union and access to the EU labour market. The paradigm of control used in the case of intra-Community migration transgresses the traditional form of control at the border in favour of more subtle forms of exclusion, centred around the pivotal issue of whom is allowed to join what, up to now, has been a privileged status that entitles its holder to a series of rights through out the entire territory of the Union.

The introduction of Union citizenship has been seen as the successful coronation of a longer process that started with the idea of free movement of workers, described as an 'incipient form of European citizenship'.[12] Despite this long deliberation process, the actual promises of EU citizenship have been received by some scholars with reservations due to its restrictive personal scope, which left outside TCN's, and because it did not seem to constructively enhance the catalogue of rights that Member State nationals could enjoy on the basis of the Treaty and its implementing legislation. Nationals who were economically inactive were able to enjoy the right to free movement on the basis of three Residency Directives (now replaced by Directive 2004/38) adopted prior to the introduction of Union citizenship, if they had sufficient resources and extensive health insurance in their host state. Workers already enjoyed extended rights of movement and more importantly, the same treatment as the nationals of their host state with regard to, among others, social and economic benefits. A further criticism related to the failure to include fundamental rights in the concept of EU citizenship, although they were to be respected as general principles of Community law under the scrutiny of the Court.[13]

While the status of EU citizenship was made dependent on the person holding the nationality of one of the Member States, there were provisions suggesting the possibility of future review of the actual content of Union citizenship but the Treaty left the ultimate call with the Member States.[14] Moreover, the 'Declaration of Nationality of a Member State' attached to the EC Treaty stated:

---

11 According to data available from Eurostat, the number of acquisitions of citizenship by persons previously stateless or holding the nationality of another country is relatively small. For example, in 2006 the largest number of acquisitions of citizenship has occurred in the UK – 154,015, Germany – 124,566, France – 147,868. Even so, the number of resident citizens holding a different nationality is much higher. More info, http://epp.eurostat.ec.europa.eu.

12 d'Oliveira, op cit p. 87.

13 See Alston 1999; Peers 2006. The Lisbon Treaty has made the EU Charter on Fundamental rights binding.

14 Former Article 22 EC stated 'The Commission shall report to the European Parliament, to the Council and to the Economic and Social Committee every three years on the application of the provisions of this Part. This report shall take account of the development of the Union. On this basis, and without prejudice to the other provisions

wherever in the Treaty establishing the European Community reference is made to nationals of the Member States, the question whether an individual possesses the nationality of a Member State shall be settled solely by reference to the national law of the Member State concerned. Member States concerned may declare, for information, which are to be considered their nationals for Community purposes by way of declaration lodged with the Presidency and may amend such declaration when necessary.[15]

Germany and the United Kingdom have made such declarations on nationality, testifying that nationality attribution was, in their view, not a Community competence.[16] As a result, it seemed that if the personal scope of Union citizenship was to be changed, it would be the result of Member States' will, leaving little scope for the Court.

Revisiting the Relationship between EU Citizenship and Member State Nationality

This initial lack of enthusiasm regarding EU citizenship and its impact on Member State nationality was also connected with a lack of faith in the concept's substantial content, that is, in the panoply of rights and, possibly, duties that it bestowed upon EU citizens. Yet, as Besson and Utzinger point out, around 2000 this *status quo* is transformed as the CJEU starts to interpret the concept of EU citizenship in a novel manner.[17] They argue that the CJEU started to address in a consistent manner three essential aspects of the concept: the rights-based nature of EU citizenship,

---

of this Treaty, the Council, acting unanimously on a proposal from the Commission and after consulting the European Parliament, may adopt provisions to strengthened or add to the rights laid down in this Part, which it shall recommend to the Member States for the adoption in accordance with their respective constitutional requirements.'

15   Declaration on Nationality of a Member State, attached to the EC Treaty by the operation of the Maastricht Treaty.

16   The German declaration stated that 'All Germans as defined in the Basic Law of the Federal Republic of Germany shall be considered nationals of the Federal Republic of Germany', a provision meant to include also those German ethnics not necessarily citizens of the Republic. The UK government has made two declarations, one in 1972 upon its accession and a second one in 1982 meant to reflect the changes introduced with respect to UK's nationality legislation. The second declaration states that only certain categories of citizens qualify for free movement of persons within the Union and are thus to be considered as nationals of the UK for Union purposes: British citizens, persons who are British subjects and have the right of abode in the United Kingdom and British Dependent Territories citizens who acquire their citizenship from a connection with Gibraltar. The compatibility of UK's declaration with regard to its nationality has been scrutinized by the ECJ in the *Kaur* case which will be discussed later.

17   Besson and Utzinger 2007, 577.

the material scope of EU citizenship rights and the personal scope of the same rights.[18] This case law has improved the mobility possibilities of economically inactive citizens who previously had to meet stringent requirements and increased their security of residence in case of economic distress.[19] The transformation of EU citizenship from a purely market oriented one, to a more social citizenship has explicitly affected the manner in which the personal scope of the Treaty has to be interpreted. It no longer covers nationals of the Member States *qua* workers, but nationals of the Member States *qua* citizens of the Union. This also marks the start of a qualitative leap towards membership in a social unit as opposed to membership in a merely economic and liberalized market. Currently, this leap falls short of completeness, although the idea of solidarity between EU citizens has started to permeate the case law of the Court.[20] In the national setting, the structuring principle of citizenship is that of equality between those holding it, where as citizenship of the Union is structured around the right to free movement and residence, a right which is enjoyed differently by citizens according to their economic contribution (at least for movement and residence beyond three months).[21]

Related to these developments, the Court has also expanded the material scope of the Treaty for the purpose of the citizenship provisions, mucking up the relatively well-established division between areas where the EC had exclusive competence and areas that belonged to the discretion of the Member States and prompting some authors to argue that any subject-matter could be considered to be covered by the scope *ratione materiae* of the Treaty as long as it had any connection, however dim, with the exercise of free movement.[22] The expansion of the concept of Union citizenship has not been as linear as presented above, the Member States being at times quite discontent with the Court's approach to social rights and the inclusion of the economically inactive into the body of citizenry that could benefit from free movement rights, although their entitlements have always been somewhat less well appointed than those of their economically active counterparts. Yet, the Court has maintained its position that the introduction of Union citizenship suggests the existence of a certain degree of financial solidarity between the nationals of the Members States, which requires, for instance, that those mobile citizens in financial distress should not be automatically expelled. This development opens interesting parallels with the initial enactment of the intra-community labour migration and the loss of control experienced by the Member States. While one cannot speak of the same impact as in the last case, it should be noted that since the introduction of Directive 2004/38 and the case law of the CJEU on European citizenship, the intensity of control that Member States

---

18   *Ibid.*

19   Mantu 2008.

20   See among others Joined Cases C–22/08 and C–23/08 *Vatsouras and Koupatantze v. ARGE Nurnberg 900.*

21   See Article 24 of Directive 2004/38.

22   In the context of social rights, see Hailbronner 2005.

are allowed to exercise over the intra-community migration of other categories of nationals than workers has lost in intensity, while the idea of solidarity between Union citizens has been simultaneously promoted.

Tensions between the Member States' desire to protect their supremacy as regards, among others, the administration of national systems of social protection on one hand, and the Court's expansive interpretation of the citizenship provisions on the other hand point towards the qualitative changes brought by Union citizenship. Moreover, it is here that the rights-based nature of EU citizenship reveals its importance, since the Member States are no longer allowed to be the ultimate factor of decision as regards the possibility of their national citizens to enjoy the rights attached to the status of European citizen.

The description of the evolution of EU citizenship is by no means exhaustive but it does point out how this status challenges in imaginative ways nationality as the basis of national and EU citizenship and the migration narrative of the Member States. Since non-national EU citizens can benefit in other Member States than their own, from rights and privileges previously exclusively reserved to national citizens or EU workers, nationality itself as the main criteria of membership attribution is being challenged. Furthermore, what is also challenged is the exclusivity of the relationship between nationality and national citizenship upon which most national states in the EU are built.[23] States in general are keen on maintaining control over nationality because as a concept, it structures the spatial and temporal legal imaginary within which immigration discourse is then constructed. By eroding the borders of identity embedded in national citizenship, EU citizenship creates the possibility of thinking about migration otherwise than in control oriented fashions and beyond economically viable types of movement; it offers the glimpse of a paradigm that is built around solidarity and human beings as opposed to persons seen in their economic capacity and viability.

Because of the role played by EU citizenship in expanding the personal and material scopes of the Treaty, one can ask whether it has also managed to change the understanding of the relationship between national citizenship constructed on nationality and the personal scope of the Treaty. In other words, do Member States enjoy unlimited freedom in determining who their nationals are, and therefore, what individuals are entitled to benefit from free movement and labour access across the Union? Based on the developments taking place in the CJEU's case law on EU citizenship, mainly regarding access to social benefits, the dialectic evolution of Union citizenship starts to be acknowledged: when first introduced it was being influenced by national paradigms of citizenship, while now it is affecting national citizenship in return, despite the Member States' attempts to limit this by making it dependent on national citizenship.[24] One can trace these changes in various developments, for example the already

---

23   Besson and Utzinger 2007, 589.
24   Ibid., 583. Also, Rostek and Davies 2007; Kochenov 2004; www.ciaonet.org.

mentioned de-coupling of nationality from rights' entitlement. Similarly, in their study on the influence of European citizenship on national citizenship policies, Rostek and Davies argue that there is a growing interdependence between the nationality legislations of the different Member States. They explain this trend as partly due to the introduction of Union citizenship since 'granting national citizenship no longer concerns only one country, but also affects other members of the Community'[25] as the person becomes entitled to free movement rights.[26] A further factor that needs to be considered is the creation of a common immigration policy at the EU level and the subsequent subordination of national immigration policies.[27] Rostek and Davies concluded that 'notwithstanding the provisions agreed on in Maastricht, the EU aspires to gain control over the setting of conditions determining access to national citizenship'.[28] If their assumption is correct, one would expect to see a rise in the number of naturalizations taking place across the EU, yet this is not supported by naturalization rates in the Member States.[29] Their conclusion somewhat ignores the complexity of the EU, since it may be plausible that the idea of European citizenship independent from nationality of the Member States, will find more favour with the Court, than with the Council.

25 Ibid., 118–19.

26 It is interesting to note that in its last *Report on Citizenship of the Union* (covering the period from 1 May 2004 to 30 June 2007), the Commission lists as a possible subject-matter of worry 'the extension of citizenship to nationals of another country on the basis of, inter alia, membership in an ethnic community'. It is not clear what country or countries the Commission had in mind when making this claim. From Rostek and Davies' study, it can be inferred that Spain could be such an example, especially in light of the regularizations that have taken place here. However, one should not forget that the German declaration on nationality attached to the TEC included in the definition of German nationals a much wider category of German ethnics than German citizens and that this extension of the EU citizenship status has not been lamented by the rest of the MS nor by the European institutions. Furthermore, Spanish nationality legislations allow for easier naturalization procedures for nationals of certain countries in Southern America with whom Spain has special ties. Again, these provisions have not been challenged by other Member States. Thus, it becomes apparent that the real issue in the Spanish regularizations is, in fact, the position of irregular TCN's which manage to escape the normal immigration channels.

27 See for example, Withol de Wenden 2002.

28 Ibid.

29 One can also argue that the harmonization of the status of long-term TCN's by the Union is a direct response to the same institutions' lack of success in convincing the Member States to relax their naturalization procedures and possibly harmonize them (thus, more of an acknowledgment of their failure).

The CJEU's Case Law on Nationality: Before and After the Introduction of Union Citizenship

Considering that the Court has managed through its case law to give substance to the provisions on EU citizenship, it is interesting to review its position in relation to nationality issues that could influence the interpretation of the personal scope of the Treaty. Most scholars argue that the Court has maintained a rather neutral position in the rare occasions when it has had to adjudicate on the effectiveness of the nationality granted by one of the Member States.[30] Yet this neutral position does not necessarily equal with a complete lack of legal influence on the competences of the Member States.[31]

One of the first cases in which the Court has dealt with the effects of the nationality legislation of one of the Member States is *Airola*.[32] This case dates before the introduction of Union citizenship and it involved the entitlement to an expatriation allowance that was under dispute after the complainant had involuntarily acquired a second nationality upon her marriage. The Court has stated that the concept of nationals contained in Article 4(A) of Annex II of the Staff Regulations of Officials was to be interpreted in such a manner that would exclude discrimination on the basis of sex. Based on Italian law, a woman marrying an Italian man automatically acquired Italian citizenship and moreover, was unable to renounce it. The same was not true of men marrying Italian women. The Court held that the applicant's second nationality should not be taken into account since the opposite led to a violation of the principle of equal treatment of sexes in the Community context. One can thus conclude that there are situations when EC law, despite the fact that Member States are, theoretically, free to set their own rules on nationality, will invalidate the effect of national rules on acquisition of nationality.

In *Auer* the ECJ clarified that the manner in which the nationality of one of the Member States has been acquired is irrelevant since 'there is no provision of the Treaty which, within the field of application of the Treaty, makes it possible to treat nationals of a Member State differently according to the time at which or the manner in which they acquired the nationality of that state, as long as, at the time at which they rely on the benefit of the provisions of Community law, they posses the nationality of one of the Member States and that, in addition, the other conditions for the applications of the rule upon which they rely are fulfilled'.[33]

---

30   Condinanzi et al. 2008, 11.

31   Interestingly enough, the Treaty provisions on free movement contained no direct reference as to the nationality of those entitled to it. It seems to have seen self-understood that it was limited only to nationals of the than Member States.

32   Case 21–74 *Airola*; ECR 1975 – 00221.

33   Case 136/78 *Auer*; ECR 1979 – 00437, paragraph 28. The case deals with the interpretation of the conditions that need to be fulfilled in order to benefit from the freedom of establishment and the approximation of diplomas in the Community context. Mr. Auer, an

This seems a logical application of the principle of non-discrimination on the basis of nationality. It would be inconsistent with this principle if Community law would apply differently based upon the manner in which the citizen had obtained his nationality.

Gullung is another case dealing with dual nationality.[34] Mr. Gullung was a lawyer holding dual nationality, French and German. He was registered as a lawyer in Germany and wanted to practice the same profession in France based on the freedom of establishment and in spite of the fact that the French authorities had refused him on grounds connected with his character. Regarding dual nationality, the Court had to assess whether a person who is a national of two Member States and who is admitted to the legal profession in one of those states may rely on the provisions of the specific directive in the territory of the other Member State. The Court upheld its previous decision in *Knoors*[35] and answered in the affirmative, since a different answer would have undermined the realization of the free movement of services. Again, this outcome can be interpreted as a practical application of the principle of non-discrimination on the basis of nationality. A.G. Darmon argued in this sense citing *Auer* and *Knoors* and stated that as long as the issue is not purely internal, then the fact

---

Austrian national had obtained his diploma in veterinary medicine in Italy; he was pursuing this profession in France, where he was not complying with the French requirements for the practice of veterinary medicine. Regarding nationality the referring court wanted to assert whether 'the fact that the person concerned had acquired French nationality by naturalization at a date subsequent to that on which he had obtained the Italian degrees and qualifications on which he relies, was such a nature as to influence the outcome of the case' (paragraph 27).

34   Case 292/86 *Gullung*; ECR 1988 – 00111.

35   Case 115/78 *Knoors*; ECR 1979 – 00399. This case deals with the interpretation of Community law when a person tries to make use of Community based rights against his own state. Mr. Knoors, a Dutch national, had been employed for a long time in Belgium as a plumber and head of an independent business. He applied several times in Netherlands in order to carry out the same activity there but was refused. The case deals with the correct interpretation of who are to be considered beneficiaries of Community law since Knoors had possessed his entire life only one nationality, Dutch. The ECJ has stated that beneficiaries of the right to freedom of establishment are nationals of a Member State without any distinction as regards nationality or residence. As long as they come objectively within one of the situations provided for in the Directive, which lays down the rules on freedom of establishment (paragraphs 16–17). Moreover, the nationals of the host state will come under the auspices of the relevant EC legislation when 'owing to the fact that they have been lawfully resident on the territory of another Member State and have there acquired a trade qualification which is recognized by the provisions of Community law are, with regard to their state of origin in a situation which may be assimilated to that of any other person enjoying the rights and liberties guaranteed by the Treaty'.

that the applicant holds dual nationality of two Member States does not preclude the application of EC law against the state of whom he is a national.[36]

It is interesting to point out that the ECJ has declined to apply the so-called principle of effective nationality established by the *Nottebohm* case.[37] Although this principle of international law is disputed among scholars, it is considered by some as one of the international standards on the subject of nationality. Moreover, according to the internationally agreed standards on nationality matters, in case of dual nationals, once they are on the territory of one of their states of nationality, they are to be considered as nationals of that state; likewise, the international standards on diplomatic protection in case of dual nationals entail that diplomatic protection cannot be exercised by the state of first nationality against the state of second nationality.

Thus, in the context of the Community legal order, the protection of the main principles upon which the Community was build requires a different interpretation of certain principles of international law, regardless of the fact that the said principles bind the Member States. The uniqueness and proper functioning of this new legal space[38] implies that the sovereignty of its Member States in areas of nationality attribution and conflicts of nationality will occasionally be trumped upon. What was not necessarily clear before the establishment of European citizenship was whether Community law had the power to set aside national rules beyond cases involving dual nationality and move into more thorny issues of nationality attribution and, for example, prevent loss of nationality of a Member State or impose the acquisition of such a nationality.

---

36   Opinion of A.G. Darmon in *Gullung* delivered on 18 November 1987, paragraphs 6–9.

37   The *Nottebohm* Case (*Liechtenstein v. Guatemala*) International Court of Justice April 6, 1955 (1955 I.C.J. 4). The naturalization of Mr. Nottebohm by Lichtenstein has been found to be non-opposable to Guatemala as it had been done in the absence of any 'bond of attachment' between Nottebohm and Lichtenstein. The International Court of Justice defined nationality in this case as being 'a legal bond having as its basis a social fact of attachment, a genuine connection of existence, interests and sentiments, together with the existence of reciprocal rights and duties. It may be said to constitute the juridical expression of the fact that the individual upon whom it is conferred, either directly by the law or as the result of an act of the authorities, is in fact more closely connected with the population of the State conferring nationality than with that of any other State'.

38   Since *Costa v. ENEL*, the Court has been constantly reminding that the Member States have created a new legal order, 'a Community of unlimited duration, having its own institutions, its own legal capacity ... and real powers stemming from a limitation of sovereignty or a transfer of power from the states to the Community, the Member States have limited their sovereign rights and have thus created a body of law which binds both their nationals and themselves.' Case 6/64 *Costa v. ENEL* [1964] ECR 1141.

Decided in 1992, *Micheletti*[39] deals again with the issue of dual nationality and asks whether the relevant provisions of EC law permit a Member State to deny the holder of dual nationality, where one nationality has been conferred by a Member State and the other by a non-member country, the right to exercise freedom of establishment on the ground that the law of the host Member State considers him to be a national of the non-member country.[40] The Court has upheld its previous case law and stated that while

> under international law, it is for each Member State, having due regard to Community law to lay down the conditions for the acquisition and loss of nationality [...] it is not permissible for the legislation of a Member State to restrict the effects of the grant of nationality of another Member State by imposing an additional condition for recognition of that nationality with a view to the exercise of the fundamental freedoms provided for in the Treaty.[41]

Thus, the Court has refused once again to use the *Nottebohm* doctrine of effective nationality[42] in the Community context while stressing that the internal laws of the Member States may not override or condition the enjoyment of rights granted by Community law. In order to reach this conclusion it did not use the concept of Union citizenship; instead it has emphasized the principle of non-discrimination and the negative and variable effects of admitting that the Member States are allowed to apply their own interpretations of effective nationality in the case of dual nationals. One might add that the application of the principle of effective nationality would be at odds with the entire philosophy of an area of free movement where nationality is irrelevant (at least concerning the nationals of the Member States) when it comes to the enjoyment of Treaty guaranteed rights.[43]

---

39 Case C–369/90 ECR [1992] I–0423. Mario Micheletti was born in Argentina of Italian parents and since his birth he had possessed dual nationality, Argentinean and Italian. The applicant arrived in Spain where he intended to establish himself as a dentist. His application was denied since according to the Spanish Civil Code in case of dual nationals, Spanish law recognized the nationality of the country where the person last had his habitual residence. Based on these provisions, Micheletti was considered an Argentinean national and not an Italian one, thus he could not benefit from the freedom of establishment that the Treaty reserves for nationals of the Member States.

40 Case C–369/90 *Micheletti* , paragraph 9.

41 Idem, paragraph 10.

42 In his opinion in *Micheletti*, AG Tesauro argued against the use of this particular doctrine whose origins lie according to him in a 'romantic period' of international relations and, in particular, in the concept of diplomatic protection. See Opinion of AG Tesauro, ECR [1992] I–04239, paragraph 5.

43 For a different reading than in *Micheletti*, see Case C–179/98 *Belgian State v. Fatna Meshbah*, ECR [1999] I–07955.

The position of the Court has been further nuanced in the case of *Garcia Avello*[44] that shows the manner in which Community law and more particularly, Union citizenship coupled with the principle of non-discrimination can limit the application of national rules on the change of surnames. The case concerns the surname of children born in Belgium to a married couple resident there. The father, Garcia Avello was a Spanish national; the mother was Belgian, while both children had dual nationality; the children had been registered in Belgium as having only one surname according to the relevant national law. The Belgian authorities refused the application launched by the couple to have the surname of their children changed to 'Garcia Avello' which would have respected the Spanish rules on surnames. The Belgian authorities argued that despite being dual nationals, as long as they were in Belgium, the children would be treated as Belgian nationals alone, thus their surname had to be determined according to the relevant Belgian rules.

The Court argued that despite the fact that the rules governing a person's surname were at that time matters coming within the competence of the Member States, the latter must none the less, when exercising that competence comply with Community law and in particular the Treaty provisions dealing with free movement.[45] This meant that read together, Articles 18 and 20 TFEU [former Articles 12 and 17 EC] had to be interpreted as precluding Belgium from denying the application for a change of surnames of children holding dual nationality, Belgian and Spanish, thus allowing them to hold a surname formed according to Spanish rules. What is remarkable is that the CJEU held that Spain's defence based on the 1930 Hague Convention which provided that in case of dual nationality the law of the forum applies (in this case Belgian law) is not appropriate in this case as 'it is not permissible for a Member State to restrict the effects of the grant of nationality of another Member State by imposing an additional conditions for recognition of that nationality with a view to the exercise of the fundamental freedoms provided for it the Treaty'.[46] The conclusion that can be put forward is that the Union created by the Member States, based on the principle of equality and in which Union citizenship is destined to be the fundamental status of its Members, might require different principles of membership recognition and attribution or, at the very least, their rethinking in order to put them in accord with the special features of this new legal space.[47]

---

44 Case C–148/02 *Garcia Avello*, http://curia.europa.eu.
45 Idem, paragraph 25.
46 Idem, paragraph 28.
47 A.G. Jacobs made an interesting remark that the Court left aside. He argued that once it is clear that there is discriminatory treatment on the basis of Article 12 EC (now Article 18 TFEU) it is not important to analyse possible infringements to the children's private life on the basis of Article 8 ECHR. He argues that *in the Community context*, it is irrelevant that the ECHR has held that legal restrictions to the possibility of changing surnames might be justified in the public interest. Thus the existence of a wide margin of appreciation in the context of the ECHR does not have any direct bearing on the breadth

The Court has reconfirmed that national rules regarding the attribution of names have to be applied in conformity with Community law, in the sense that, their application must not lead to situations that would violate the principle of free movement by hampering the exercise of that right. In the case of Grunkin,[48] the CJEU has had to rule again on the compatibility of the non-discrimination principle and the rights embodied in the EC Treaty with a national rule on the determination of the surname borne by a child.[49] The German authorities had refused to recognize the surname given to a child in accordance with Danish law, the law of the place of his residence at the time of birth, arguing that according to German law the surname of a person is determined solely by the law of his state of nationality, in this case Germany. The Court has decided against this interpretation since it would have lead to the existence of two different surnames for the same person, a situation which would hamper the exercise of the free movement rights of the child. It is important to point out that unlike *Garcia Avello*, in this case the baby was not a dual national and that EC rules can influence the applicability of national rules, if these negatively impact on the Community rights of the EU citizen concerned.

The Politics of Nationality and Migration

When considering the above mentioned cases, it becomes evident that while the Court has had to rule on issues of nationality, they mostly involve the effects that a grant of nationality by a Member State have in the Community legal order. The Court has not scrutinized the principles used by Member States for nationality attribution or why they opt for particular criteria. One would argue that if the Court would choose to follow this path, it would face serious contestations as to its competence to engage with such issues. Nevertheless, the Court has been asked to perform such a control in the *Kaur* case but as it will become apparent it has failed to face up to the challenge.[50] The case brought to the forum questions regarding the legal value of the Declarations on nationality attached to the Treaty and the proper definition of whom qualifies as an UK national for the purpose of Community law. The relevant

---

of the margin of appreciation available in the different context of citizenship of the Union. If one does not accept that Union citizenship has brought a qualitative change to the legal space of the Union than this statement would not make any sense since we are talking about more or less the same states, with the same notions of public policy and so on.

48   Case C–353/06 *Stefan Grunkin and Dorothee Regina Paul v. Standesamt Niebull, 14 Oct 2008.*

49   Baby Leonhard Matthias-Grunkin Paul was born in Denmark to a German couple residing there; he was registered in Denmark under the joint surname of the parents, although they did not use that joint surname.

50   Case C–192/99 *The Queen v. Secretary of State for the Home Department ex parte: Manjit Kau.* See also Shah 2001.

piece of national legislation at that time was the British Nationality Act of 1981 that differentiated between several types of British nationals, who enjoyed different sets of rights. The most important difference was between those enjoying the right of entry and abode in the UK and those who like Mrs Kaur did not.[51] The referring court asked the CJEU to clarify the legal effects of the declarations on nationality issued by UK in 1972, 1982 and 1992 especially since its nationality law identifies only some of its nationals as having the right to enter and remain in that state as well as the relevance of Article 3/2 of the Fourth Protocol to the ECHR.[52] More importantly, the Court has been asked to decide whether the provisions on Union citizenship have any impact on the nationality legislation of the UK since according to *Micheletti* 'a Member State can define the concept of national only if it has due regard to Community law and, consequently, only if it observes the fundamental rights which form an integral part of Community law'.[53] In this case the applicant argued that the UK legislation infringes fundamental rights inasmuch as it has the effect either of depriving Britons of Asian origin of the right to enter the territory of which they are nationals or, of rendering them effectively stateless.[54]

At the end of the day, the Court has refused to analyse the UK legislation either in the light of Community law or human rights principles. It has decided to focus on the value of the Declarations on nationality attached to the Treaty that the UK had made in 1972 and 1982; it finds them to have been made with due regard to Community law.[55] The court argues that the United Kingdom in accordance with

---

51   Born in Kenya in 1949, Mrs. Kaur became a citizen of the United Kingdom and Colonies under the terms of the 1948 Act. Following the entry of the 1981 Act, her status changed to that of a British Overseas Citizen who had no right to enter or remain in the UK without the authorization of the State Department. After several periods of temporary residence in the UK, in 1996 she applied again for leave to remain which was denied this time. She appealed and stated that she would like to work in the UK and periodically travel to other Member States in order to receive services and possibly work there. This is why the court of appeal considering that the case involves issues of Community law referred questions to the ECJ. For more details on the background and discriminatory character of the UK legislation in question see Shah 2001.

52   This article provides that no one shall be deprived of the right to enter the territory of which he is a national. The UK is not part to this Protocol but its applicability in the Community legal order would have been possible as a matter of general principles of law that the Community respects. However, the Court has left the question of the impact of human rights norms in the EC legal order untouched.

53   *Kaur*, paragraph 17.

54   Ibid. A similar case has been decided on the basis of the ECHR by the former Commission that has found a similar UK legislation discriminatory on the basis of race and colour; see the *East African Asians v. UK* case.

55   In reality, the Court does not explain how it came to this conclusion. The only argument that seems to be put forward is that when the declarations have been made, the rest of the Member States have accepted them without questioning their content, which in itself is not a very convincing argument to start with.

the relevant principles of international law and in light of its imperial and colonial past, has defined several categories of British citizens whom it has recognized as having rights which differ according to the nature of the ties connecting them to the Kingdom.[56] As to the 1972 Declaration attached to the Accession Treaty to the EC, the Court argued that it must be taken into consideration as an instrument relating to the Treaty for the purpose of its interpretation and, more particularly, for determining the scope of the Treaty *ratio personae*. Moreover, the declaration did not have the effect of depriving of Community law rights any person who did not satisfy the definition of a national of the UK. The point the Court was trying to make is that for persons such as Mrs Kaur Community law rights never arose in the first place. It becomes thus clear that the Court has refused to engage in any sort of substantial review of the nationality laws of the UK, while at the same time leaving the impression that Union citizenship has no impact on member states' nationality legislations.

The *Chen* case[57] is yet another reminder of the political charges that nationality issues carry along and of the manner in which nationality legislation intersects migration control. The ultimate question in this case regarded the effects of an acquisition of nationality with the sole purpose of obtaining the status of Union citizen and the rights attached to it, in order to evade regular migration control. Mrs. Man Chen, a Chinese national married to another Chinese national, arranged for the second daughter of the couple, Catherine, to be born in Ireland and thus, acquire Irish nationality. At that time, Ireland used *ius soli* as its principle of nationality acquisition Ms. Chen's aim was for her daughter to become a Union citizen and in this capacity, by making use of the right to freedom of movement that is incumbent for each citizen of the Union, to move and take up residence in the UK. The case delved around issues related to the right of free movement for Union citizens but, for the present discussion, the most interesting element relates to the claim of the UK government that the acquisition of Irish nationality by the baby is in fact an abuse of Community rights, as it abuses the scope of the Community rules on free movement of persons.

The UK government tried to argue that the attribution of Irish nationality and the effects that it has generated in the Community legal order (namely, Catherine's Union citizenship and entitlement to make use of the rights attached to it) should not be opposable to it. Both the Court and AG Tizzano rebutted the hypothesis where the UK might be allowed as a matter of Community law to deem the acquisition of Irish nationality as not effective for certain purposes, in this case for the issuing of a residence permit in the UK, on the basis of EC law. AG Tizzano argued that as long as 'the legality, from the point of view of international or Community law, of the grant of nationality by the Irish state' has not been challenged, 'it is not

---

56   *Kaur*, paragraphs 19–20.

57   Case C–200/02 *Chen Kunqian Catherine Zhu and Man Lavette Chen v. Secretary of State for the Home Department* [2004] ECR I–9925. See also, Kunoy 2006; Carlier 2005.

necessary to express any view as to the existence or otherwise of any provision of general law to the effect that no state is required to recognize nationality granted to an individual by another state in the absence of a real and effective link between the individual and the state'.[58] The Court has used the same line of argument stressing that based on its previous case-law, the Member States are not allowed to restrict the effects of a grant of nationality by another Member State by imposing additional criteria. Moreover, the Court has also refused to acknowledge that the actions of Mrs. Chen could be considered as amounting to a misuse of Community law. The prudent tone adopted by the Court in the *Chen* case has been explained as the 'court's reluctance to encroach on the competence of the Member States to decide on the criteria on which nationality is conferred and whether or not all nationals are European citizens'.[59] It points to the difficulty of separating the discussion of the attribution of nationality at the national sphere from its wider Community implications.

Is it possible to systemize and make some sense of the Court's case law? On one hand, there are cases where the Court argues that since the application of national rules on nationality limits or denies the enjoyment of Community based rights, it should be set aside, while on the other hand, there are cases where the Court refuses to censor the same national rules. To the first type belong most cases involving dual nationals denied the use of their Community rights. Initially, these cases were related to the exercise of labour migration while later, the scenarios escape the mere economical dimension and start engaging issues of identity (a person's name) and human rights. It is clear that the principle of non-discrimination on the basis of nationality or the principle of equality between men and women take precedence over national rules.[60] The second situation involves cases where nationality is more of a politically sensitive category as well as involves qualitatively different human rights issues, such as what is the minimum content of national citizenship, the rights without which one could be labelled stateless; whether or not Community law prevents the Member States from emptying their national citizenship status of the rights that define it. The Court's answers to this second category have been tamer. Yet, it is clear that the doctrine of effective nationality is rejected in the Community legal order. Moreover, it is no longer possible to assert that the Member States are completely free to set their own nationality rules based on their position as sovereign actors in the international legal order.[61] Even if their obligation to apply nationality law having due regard

---

58   Opinion of A.G. Tizzano, paragraphs 36–7.

59   Kunoy 2006, 184–5.

60   The *Grunkin* case suggests that not only dual nationality as a criterion for discrimination will be treated as suspicious by the Court but also the simple fact of having a different place of residence as a result of the exercise of the right to free movement.

61   Jessurun d'Oliveira has argued that in effect the Court statement in *Micheletti* which it has repeated ever since is not that exceptional. He claims that the Court glossed over Article 1 of the 1930 Hague Convention which mentions that the exercise of nationality

to Community law is translated only as 'a necessary corollary of the obligation of Member States to recognize the Treaty rights of nationals of other Member states and thus as a necessary condition to ensure that the application of the free movement did not vary from member State to Member State',[62] the first steps towards the dismantling of state autonomy in nationality matters have been firmly made. It is interesting to observe that all the cases discussed above involve persons trying desperately to evade the constraints imposed by their own states by invoking more favourable EU provisions.

Testing the Limits of European Union Citizenship

What constitute the outer limits of the court's influence on national policies and rules on nationality, since up to now the core issues of nationality attribution, that is, the conditions for acquisition and loss have escaped the scrutiny of the ECJ? It is only in a recent reference from Germany that the Court has been directly asked to rule on the compatibility of a Member State's rules on loss of nationality with Community rules on citizenship of the Union. The case concerns Janko Rottmann, a former Austrian national, who after exercising his Treaty right to free movement, naturalized in Germany. Because he has acquired a new nationality, he lost his original Austrian citizenship. The German authorities are trying to revoke his naturalization as he has failed to inform them of certain criminal charges pending in Austria at the time of his naturalization. If deprived of his German nationality, he would become stateless as well as lose European Union citizenship.

The referring court asked the ECJ whether 'Community law precludes the legal consequences of the loss of Union citizenship resulting from the fact that a revocation, lawful as such under national (German) law, of a naturalization as a national of a Member State (Germany) acquired by intentional deception has the effect, in combination with the national law on nationality of another Member State (Austria) that statelessness supervenes'.[63] Secondly, the German court enquired which of the two Member States in question should either adjust its nationality laws or suspend its application as to prevent statelessness.

---

law must be in line with international conventions, thus transposed to the Community legal order this can only mean in line with the EC Treaty (now TFEU). See Jessurun d'Oliveira 1995, 63. The bottom line remains that the exact restrictions that the Treaty can imply are not clearly spelled out.

62 Evans 1995, 100.

63 Case C–135/08, *Janko Rottmann v. Freistaat Bayern*, reference for a preliminary ruling, OJ 5.7.2008. In order to be naturalized in Germany, the applicant has had to renounce his former Austrian nationality, as Germany does not, as a general rule, allow dual nationality. In case his German nationality would be revoked, his former Austrian nationality would not be automatically revived, thus leaving him stateless.

This case raises a series of provocative questions regarding the manner in which national citizenship legislations intersect with Community law.[64] On the basis of the international standards existing with respect to nationality, a state is allowed to revoke naturalization in case of fraud or deception. Both the UN conventions dealing with statelessness,[65] as well as the European standard in this field, the European Convention on Nationality allow for this possibility even if the person would consequently become stateless. Stephen Hall has argued that any withdrawals of nationality that the Member States might try to operate have to conform to the human rights standards protected by the Court of Justice as general principles of Community law.[66] His argument is that 'a national measure which, in violation of the fundamental human rights protected by the Court of Justice, deprives a Union citizen of his nationality is either unenforceable by national authorities, including national courts or is ineffective to deprive the person involved of his Union citizenship'.[67]

The first issue that the Court had to tackle was whether or not the situation falls within the ambit of Community law. Without attempting to establish a link between the exercise of a Treaty freedom and Mr. Rottmann's current situation, the Court has stated that

> It is clear that the situation of a citizen of the Union who, like the applicant in the main proceedings, is faced with a decision withdrawing his naturalization, adopted by the authorities of one Member State, and, placing him, after he has lost the nationality of another Member State that he originally possessed, in a position capable of causing him to lose the status conferred by Article 17 EC [now Article 20 TFEU] and the rights attaching thereto falls, *by reason of its nature and its consequences*, within the ambit of European Union law.[68]

Moreover, it claimed authority over the interpretation of the status of European citizenship and its loss and went on to remind the Member States that Union citizenship is intended to be the fundamental status of the nationals of the Member States, that when exercising their powers in the sphere of nationality must have due regard to Community law. The limit of Member States' powers in this field is the principle of proportionality, which must be respected as a matter of Community law, even in case of a withdrawal of naturalization because of fraud. The ECJ

---

64 Mantu forthcoming 2010.

65 The 1954 Convention relating to the Status of Stateless Persons and the 1961 Convention on the Reduction of Statelessness.

66 The topic of human rights protection in the Community legal order has generated a vast literature. In this chapter I am interested only in the manner in which fundamental rights protected as general principles of Community law can enhance the protection against denationalization for Union citizens.

67 Hall 1996, 129.

68 Case C–135/08, judgment delivered on 2 March 2010, paragraph 42.

has set down the general contours of proportionality in case of loss of nationality but left their practical application to be ultimately judged by the national court. Nevertheless, it would seem that the Court has abandoned its reluctance to enter the core areas of nationality attribution, although for the time being, the full implications of its decision remain to be clarified by future case law.

Conclusions

This chapter has looked at the function of Member State nationality in the EU context, not least as regards the right to labour migration which the state is prohibited from trying to control. The traditional understanding of this concept tells us that it is the finest expression of the relationship between an individual and a state. The desirability of holding such a status is evidenced among others by the national's right to enter freely his/her state without being the subject of immigration controls. In the case of the EU, holding the 'right' nationality brings even more advantages as one gets access to the territories of the other Member States and their labour markets. While it may not have been the most obvious manner of controlling migration, nationality has been an avenue of confining access to this space only for a certain well defined category of individuals, the nationals of the Member States. For as long as the attribution of nationality takes place at the national level and, outside the scrutinizing powers of the Union's institutions, the possibility of keeping this area of freedom, security and justice free of undesirable elements seems real. It is interesting to note that the only cases in which the Court has been asked to review the criteria used by the Member States for nationality acquisition, *Chen* and *Kaur* have clear labour migration related implications. The introduction of Union citizenship with its programmatic destiny as fundamental status of the nationals of the Member States, challenges the agreed *staus quo* as it opens up the possibility of curtailing the power of the Member States in the area of nationality attribution and application of labour migration rules.

State narratives of labour migration control presuppose a world structured by territoriality and nationality. The state is presented as controlling its territory, clearly demarcated by borderlines, and the population contained within these limits. Only certain individuals will be allowed to cross the state border, and in today's world one's capacity of crossing such borders is correlated with one's economic capacity and viability. The European Union has premised the accomplishment of its goals on the idea of free movement, which has required the abandonment of control over the movement of the labour factor. The departure from the conceptualization of movement in terms of control has nevertheless been incomplete, as nationality has continued to play an important part in the identification of those entitled to enjoy free movement. The fact that European citizenship remains formally linked to state nationality impacts upon the manner in which national sovereignty finds its expression in the context of migration, and labour migration even more so. And yet, the EU project and the establishment of EU citizenship are evidence of the fact that it is possible to imagine and construct a version of labour migration that is premised on mobility and free movement without compromising the legitimacy of such an endeavour.

Bibliography

Alston, P. (ed.) 1999. *The EU and Human Rights*. Oxford: Oxford University Press.

Besson, S. and Utzinger, A. 2007. Introduction: Future Challenges of European Citizenship – Facing a Wide-Open Pandora's Box, *European Law Journal*, 5.

Carlier, Y. 2005. Case note on Chen, *CMLRev* 42, 1121–31.

Carrera, S. 2005. What does the Free Movement Mean in Theory and Practice in an Enlarged EU?, *European Journal of Law*, 11(6), November.

Condinanzi, M., Lang, A. and Nascimbene, B. 2008. *Citizenship of the Union and Free Movement of Persons*. Leiden: Nijhoff.

d'Oliveira, H.U. Jessurun. 1995. Union Citizenship: Pie in the Sky?, in *In Search of a New Order*, edited by A. Rosas and E. Antola. London: Sage Publications, 58–84.

Evans, A. 1995. Union Citizenship and the Equality Principle, in *In Search of a New Order*, edited by A. Rosas and E. Antola. London: Sage Publications, 85–112.

Hailbronner, K. 2005. Union Citizenship and Access to Social Benefits, *CML Rev* 42, 1245–67.

Hall, S. 1996. Loss of Union Citizenship in Breach of Fundamental Rights, *ELRev* 21.

Kochenov, D. 2004. Pre-Accession, Naturalization and Due Regard to Community Law, *Romanian Journal of Political Sciences*, 4, 74.

Kunoy, B. 2006. A Union of National Citizens: The Origins of the Court's Lack of Avant-Gardisme in the *Chen* case, *CMLRev* 43, 179–90.

Mantu, S. 2008. *The Boundaries of European Social Citizenship*. Nijmegen: Wolf Legal Publishers.

Mantu, S. 2010. Case C–135/08 *Janko Rottmann v. Freistaat Bayern*: The End of Nationality Legislation as We Know It?!, *Journal of Immigration, Asylum and Nationality Law*, forthcoming.

O'Leary, S. 1992. Nationality Law and Community Citizenship: A Tale of Two Uneasy Bedfellows, *Yearbook of European Law*, 12, 353–84.

O'Leary, S. 1998. The Options for the Reform of European Union Citizenship, in *Citizenship and Nationality Status in the New Europe*, edited by S. O'Leary and T. Tiilikainen. London: Sweet & Maxwell.

Olsen, E.D.H. 2006. *Work, Production, Free Movement and Then What? Conceptions of Citizenship in European Integration, 1951–71*. EUI Working Papers, SPS 08.

Peers, S. 2006. Human Rights in the EU Legal Order: Practical Relevance for EC Immigration and Asylum Law, in *EU Immigration and Asylum Law*, edited by S. Peers and N. Rogers. Leiden, Boston: Martinus Nijhoff, 115–37.

Rogers, N. and Scannell, R. 2005. *Free Movement of Persons in an Enlarged European Union*. London: Sweet and Maxwell.

Rostek, K. and Davies, G. 2007. The Impact of Union Citizenship on National Citizenship Policies, *Tulane European and Civil law Forum*, 22, 89–156.

Sassen, S. 2003. Citizenship Destabilized, in *Liberal Education*, available online at http://www.aacu.org/liberaleducation/le–sp03/le–sp03feature2.cfm.

Shah, P. 2001. British Nationals under Community Law: The *Kaur* Case, *EJML* 3, 271–8.

Withol de Wenden, C. 2002. European Citizenship and Migration, in *New European Citizenship and Identity*, edited by R. Leveau and K. Mohsen-Finan. Aldershot: Ashgate, 79–89.

Chapter 12
Migration Flows and Security in North America

Alexandra Délano and Mónica Serrano

In the course of nearly a century, the movement of Mexicans across borders has remained an essentially bilateral issue between Mexico and the US. The presence of a 2,000-mile shared border with the world's largest recipient of migrants has involved both risks and opportunities for both countries. Over this period, the movement of people across this frontier not only mushroomed well beyond most available predictions, but the nature of observed patterns shifted from temporary and circular trends towards sedentary and one-way flows. By the turn of the century the movement of people across the US–Mexico border had turned the Mexican population in the US into the largest component of the growing Hispanic population in that country. Seven years later Mexico had not only emerged as one of the largest sources of legal migrants to the US – between 5 and 6 million people – but also as a leading source of undocumented migrants, estimated at 6.2 million in 2008. The intensity and the magnitude of such flows of people illustrate only too clearly the role that migration has played as a major driver of regionalization in North America.[1]

This chapter starts by considering the security dimensions of migration flows which have long occurred between Mexico and the US. The first section describes the impact of the North American Free Trade Agreement (NAFTA) on wider efforts to regulate regional economic integration and intensified cross-border flows, including the movement of people. It then reflects on the impact of the 2001 terrorist attacks on both regional border controls and on the broader regional security environment in which labour migration takes place. The next section explores the shifting goals that have informed US and Mexican efforts to regulate labour migration. We examine the evolution of US, and more specifically Mexican responses to the changing character of migratory flows, first in the context of NAFTA and then in a post-9/11 environment where security concerns

---

1 The presence of Mexicans in US territory can be traced back to the mid-19th century. But today Mexico is the country of origin of the largest community (about 11 million) of foreign-born residents in the US. Adding to this number an estimated 19 million Mexican Americans, the 30 million Mexican-origin population constitutes 64% of the 46.9 million Hispanics in the country. Aleinikoff 2005, 4. See also US Census Bureau 2009 and CONAPO 2008.

about violence and illicit flows along Mexico's northern and southern borders have become more prominent. This is followed by a brief concluding section that delves into some of the main security dimensions that have accompanied migration movements between the US and Mexico.

The North American Free Trade Agreement and Movement of People

For over a century, the movement of people, goods, traditions and culture across the US Mexican border has, on the whole, taken place in an unregulated manner. In the early 1990s increasing levels of integration led Canada, Mexico and the US to negotiate and ratify the North American Free Trade Agreement (NAFTA) in an effort to establish an institutional framework that could help channel and regulate economic relations in North America. The entry into force of the North American Free Trade Agreement in 1994 established a slim governance framework for regional economic integration, one that was deliberately intended to remain as a limited enterprise and that explicitly ruled out the free movement of people. At the time, supporters of NAFTA in both the US and Mexico proceeded along the unreserved assumption that the agreement would contribute to contain the flow of migrants to the US by promoting economic development in Mexico. By no means was the light institutional architecture of NAFTA intended to modify, much less regulate, the movement of people across borders.[2]

The inauguration of NAFTA prompted many to foresee a new era for trilateral relations and more specifically for US–Mexico relations, one that would help Mexico establish a solid basis for economic growth and development. Intensified free trade was expected to work to bring about economic and, according to some, political progress in the junior NAFTA partner. Yet, emphasis on free trade, rather than on the conditions in which economic exchanges take place, led all three parties to discard issues related to assistance, compensation or structural distributive justice. NAFTA was intended to promote free trade, not to alter the landscape in which economic relations were to be conducted.

Before long, the persistent flow of undocumented migrants and illicit commodities raised doubts about the capacity of the trade agreement to close the development and dependency gap among NAFTA's partners and more specifically between Mexico and its North American neighbours. One the one hand, the unrelenting pace of undocumented migration suggested the resolute search among migrants for better economic prospects that were simply not available in Mexico. And on the other, the political expectations that had been attached to NAFTA's

---

2   Although at the opening of the NAFTA negotiations Mexican representatives tried to include a chapter on the free movement of people, these proposals were eventually withdrawn owing both to the evident lack of support among US and Canadian delegations and fear that it would potentially increase the pressures over Mexico's energy sector.

impact on improved US–Mexico relations failed to materialize as old thorny issues continued to strain the bilateral relation.

By the time NAFTA turned ten years old, its initial success in terms of investment and export promotion paled into an anxious doubt about its future viability. Notwithstanding this, the material and security realities underpinning relations between the US and Mexico, and the dynamics underlying the wider regionalization process in North America made clear the urgent need for some measure of institutional forms of governance. By the turn of the century, regional trends on the ground suggested that NAFTA and regional processes had taken the three partners, but more specifically the US and Mexico, a considerable distance from their original and modest plans for trade and investment. At that juncture, the tidy free-trade scheme that both Ottawa, Washington and Mexico had at first envisaged was far from sight. In its place, a complex web of economic and non-economic connections materialized, tying the three countries closer together.

The recognition of the need to address the governance and the politics of the borders in North America was the direct result of the magnitude and intensity of ever-rising trans-border flows. By the end of the century, 200 million crossings of people were registered at the US–Canada border and 300 million legal crossings at the US southern border with Mexico. The volume of containers and merchandise arriving into the 301 US ports of entry had also increased dramatically.[3] Yet, while the density of integration had brought the three countries closer together, the vast inequalities that had long underpinned relations among the US and its neighbours continued to obstruct the emergence of more formal institutional mechanisms. The prospects for a sound system of regional governance remained distant.[4] Moreover, the record of security cooperation accumulated over the previous decade did not offer scope for realistic regional collaboration. In the period between 1994 and 2001 security cooperation had proceeded on an entirely bilateral basis: Ottawa and Washington had started tackling rising traffic congestion at the border, while the US and Mexican governments continued to engage in efforts to stem an increasingly copious undocumented migration and a massive overflow of illicit drugs.

9/11, Border Controls and Shifting Migration Flows

In the course of a decade both Canada and Mexico had gradually appreciated the particular way in which tighter integration had altered the traditional patterns that had long structured and characterized their bilateral relations with Washington. Through the NAFTA years asymmetric interdependence had clearly deepened, making both Ottawa and Mexico more aware of their exposure and vulnerability *vis a vis* the US. Without warning 9/11 both transformed and heightened regional security concerns. If economic dependence had already constrained Mexico's

---

3   See MacFarlane and Serrano 2005, 229.
4   Hurrell 2006, 546.

and Ottawa's available political choices, the terrorist attacks further narrowed the room for regional aloofness.

9/11 compelled policymakers in all three countries to pay attention to their regional security environment. There is no doubt that security considerations and border controls long predated 9/11. However, it would be difficult to deny that the terrorist attacks of September 2001 unleashed a new period of regional security cooperation with immediate effects for regional dynamics, including migration.

The resulting security paradigm re-emphasized the control of national borders and national territory at the expense of alternative frameworks for regional security aimed at reconciling regional competitiveness and security needs. But perhaps most significantly, as such, the post-9/11 security response did not represent a radical departure from prevailing security logics as it clearly intensified existing trends and tendencies. If through the late 1980s the war on drugs had rolled up counter-narcotic measures with immigration control, at the turn of the century, 9/11 and the war on terror rolled up counter-narcotic measures and immigration control policies up with counter-terrorist measures.

The framework of cooperation for border control and 'smart' border management actively promoted by security brokers after 9/11 was swiftly adapted to the existing security 'infrastructure' which had been erected around illicit drug flows and undocumented migration. In Ottawa policymakers sought to protect Canada's interests and its standing in Washington through the administrative approach of the Manley/Ridge smart border declaration. Yet, once US security concerns were extrapolated to the US–Canada border, the risk of the 'Mexicanization' of Canada–US border relations became increasingly clear. Canada, like Mexico, shares a long and porous border with the US, but the contrast between the two borders has been significant. For decades the US–Canada border remained fairly unattended, while the US–Mexican border had long been a conspicuous factor in US–Mexican relations. However, through the 1990s the pressures associated to heightened cross border flows congregated to make the US–Canada border ever more visible. Already in 1999 the Ressam affair, which involved the detention of an Algerian national carrying explosives into the US, had signalled a shift in the politics of the US–Canada border. In the post-9/11 period, the fear that terrorists could enter the US via the US–Canada border heightened perceptions in Washington – not far removed from prevalent views of the Mexican line – of the porosity of the US–Canada border as a security danger.[5]

Within a rapidly changing security environment not only did border relations between the US and Canada become ever more securitized, but they showed increasing convergence with US policies toward its southern flank. Nowhere were the parallels more evident than in Washington's decision to deploy National Guard troops, and to triple the number of border agents positioned along the northern border. Indeed, Washington's decision to tighten the surveillance of the northern

---

5   Andreas 2005, 453–4.

border brought with it echoes of the enforcement paradigm that had long informed its policies on the southern line.[6] In the case of the US 2000-mile southern flank, for over two decades successive US administrations had sought to deter undocumented migration and the flow of illicit commodities through intensified enforcement. Predictably, the idea of a greater freedom of movement in North America was first called into question by the hardening of regional borders and the tightening of border controls along the US–Mexican border. Thus, through the NAFTA years a 75-mile-long metal fence was put in place, and the size of the border patrol enlarged and tripled to reach 11, 106 agents in 2005. Washington's determination to tighten the border was also reflected in unremitting efforts to improve the sophistication of surveillance and apprehension technology.[7]

In a brief space of time, the same arguments that had been marshalled to justify the tightening of the border to stop the flow of illicit drugs were articulated together to validate US responses against undocumented migration. Just as border controls had sought to prevent illegal drugs from entering the US, so a parallel process was deployed to interdict undocumented migrants. Starting in 1993, the enforcement paradigm that has shaped US immigration control policies has shared some important tenets with the central assumptions that have long informed drug control policies. The underlying premise has been that tighter enforcement would help deter illegal crossings along the US–Mexican border. Hence, in the period between 1993 and 2009, the operating budget of the Border Patrol increased from 203 million to 1.4 billion US dollars, and its workforce from approximately 5,000 in 1995 to 12, 700 employees in 2009, of whom 11,120 are agents assigned to patrol the US land borders.[8]

Similarly to what has been the case with drug control measures, muscular enforcement has no doubt increased the risks attendant upon undocumented migrant flows, and has markedly contributed to 'redistribute illegal crossings', shifting migration routes towards ever more dangerous crossings, but has clearly failed to stop the flow. Powerful economic incentives – which include the prospect of salaries eight to ten times those earned south of the border and the prospects of family re-unification – have clearly outweighed considerations about potential risks and costs.[9] Indeed, there is no evidence to suggest that

---

6   In the period starting in 2002, not only border controls, but also migratory controls and visa harmonization were both tightened and increasingly brought into line among all three NAFTA partners. McFarlane and Serrano 2005, Andreas 2005, 456.

7   In 1993 the size of the border patrol was estimated at 3,965 agents. In the period between 1993 and 2005 the total expenditure in border enforcement grew six-fold. Cornelius 2007, 2.

8   See Andreas 2000, 89. The most recent figures can be found at http://www.cbp. gov/xp/cgov/about/ organization/assist_comm_off/.

9   On salary differentials see Cornelius 2007, 6. The interaction between economic and non-economic and personal considerations in migrants' decision to relocate has also been emphasized by Zolberg 2006, 64.

widespread awareness of the life threatening risks that now come with border crossings – with over 4,000 reported migrant fatalities in the period between 1995 and 2008[10] – has influenced migrants' behaviour or fundamentally altered decisions to embark in an increasingly uncertain trans-border journey. In contrast, what is conspicuously clear is that punitive enforcement has pushed migrants to increasingly rely on the services provided by people smugglers. In other words, robust enforcement may have failed to deter border crossings, but has succeeded in altering the characteristics of undocumented crossings, and encouraged the consolidation of an illicit human cross-border market.[11]

In that order, tighter enforcement has also had an impact on decisions concerning longer sojourns within the US. Expert studies have confirmed impressionistic assessments pointing to the reduced frequency of returns. Thus, in the period between the early 1980s and the beginning of the 2000's, the likelihood that an undocumented migrant would return to Mexico within a year after entry fell from about 45% to around 25%.[12] Similarly, interviews carried out both in Mexico and the US suggest that while intensified enforcement has indeed increased the risk of apprehension, the proportion of arrested migrants has remained comparatively low, at around 23%.[13] Research carried out at both ends of the migrant flow also suggests that rather than reducing the propensity to head north, tighter enforcement has encouraged migrants to remain in the US, inducing in turn a shift towards sedentary trends. Moreover, the analysis of migration movements taking place in the last two decades also indicates that the risks attendant upon tighter enforcement have encouraged migrants to relocate their relatives and to decide to settle with their families in the US.

There is no doubt that family and social networks have played a key part in the calculations underpinning migrants' decisions to embark on this precarious route, but the great expectation of economic and social opportunities can make the risk worthwhile. In short, studies conducted at both ends of the migration flow seem to suggest the failure of the border enforcement strategy inaugurated in 1993 by 'Operation Gatekeeper'.[14]

---

10   See statistics published by Conapo, 'Cuadro IV.3.6. Muertes en la frontera México-Estados Unidos, 1995-2006', www.conapo.gob.mx/MigrInternacional/Series/04_03_06.xls. See also *Reforma,* December 19, 2007.

11   Although the tighter enforcement strategy effectively raised the probability of apprehension, smugglers' services typically include up to three 'free' attempts. Cornelius 2007, 3, 5.

12   Cornelius 2007, 6.

13   Cornelius 2007, 11.

14   Cornelius 2007, 7–10.

Migration Policies Before and After 9/11

The changes in the characteristics of Mexico–US migration flows since 1986 with the passage of the Immigration Reform and Control Act in the United States (IRCA), and particularly after 1993 with the US government's implementation of stricter border controls along the US–Mexico border, have had a significant impact in both countries' migration policies. Viewed from Washington's standpoint the growth of the migrant population, in the context of the IRCA's process of regularizing the status of approximately two million Mexican migrants, was a consequence of loss of control of the border. This assumption prompted the US government to pursue a number of corrective policies aimed at the strengthening of border controls, and at dissuading and limiting undocumented migration in the mid-1990s. As mentioned above, the growing difficulties and costs of crossing the border disrupted the circularity that previously existed with migrants returning to Mexico after a period of time working in the US. The result was a significant growth of the Mexican community in the US; a trend that was accompanied by xenophobic reactions in the US.[15]

Whether as a result of the initial effects of NAFTA on Mexico's economic development –particularly the displacement of many sectors such as agriculture – or due to sluggish economic reform, the lack of economic alternatives was an important factor in explaining the growth of the Mexican immigrant population in the mid-1990s.[16] Equally significant, particularly through the economic boom experienced by the US economy in the 1990s, was the rising demand for low and semi-skilled labour in the US. The trade and investment dynamics reinforced by NAFTA generated a strong demand for foreign labour which was met both by large numbers of documented temporary workers and undocumented migrants, including a noteworthy proportion of Mexican workers.[17]

Not surprisingly, the growing salience of migration raised attention to the issue in both the US and Mexico. What is clear is that under the new conditions, Mexico could no longer remain passive, and ignore the magnitude of such migratory reality. By the late 1980's the Mexican government began to consider possible responses to the realities of such dense migration flows. Accordingly, Mexico gradually transitioned from a position of limited engagement or 'a policy of no policy' with regards to the management of migration and border issues and began to recognize its responsibility in the causes and the effects of migration to, from

---

15   According to some experts, while in the 1970s the estimated number of Mexicans who stayed in the US oscillated around 30,000; two decades later this figure increased to approximately 400,000. See Verea 2007.

16   See Delgado Wise and Márquez Covarrubias 2008.

17   In the period between 1994 and 2005 the total number of documented temporary workers admitted in the US increased from 205,794 to 726,036. Mexican documented workers clearly dominated two categories: agricultural seasonal workers and temporary or seasonal non-agricultural workers. Verea 2006.

and through its territory. As most sending states, Mexico faces the challenge of addressing the root causes of migration and effectively controlling the borders in a context where humanitarian and security concerns are high on the agenda. But unlike other countries, Mexico faces the additional challenge of sharing a 2,000-mile land border with the world's largest recipient of migrants and its most important trading partner.

Thus, since the first periods of emigration, Mexico has had to balance its own interests of maintaining a level of emigration as a safety valve to economic and political pressures in the country and protecting migrants' rights while sustaining a good relationship with the United States. In some cases, the stability of the relationship with the US has been prioritized over the need to protect migrants' rights and respond to policies that affect them. However, this has changed in recent years due to the combination of a number of factors. These include: political and economic developments in Mexico; changes in the characteristics of migration and migrants' activities; and equally important, the evolution of the bilateral relationship in the NAFTA context.

Mexican scholars recognize that these policies are part of a fundamental change of Mexico's position on migration and reflect a wider shift in foreign policy discourse and strategies. As Mexican historian Lorenzo Meyer describes it: 'Times are changing ... In the past, when Mexico's foreign policy was based on a principle of non-intervention, it was a taboo for Mexican leaders to talk about internal affairs of other countries, especially the United States'.[18] Still, the extent to which Mexico should promote its immigration agenda in the US is a matter of controversy and the issue of 'non-intervention' is strongly present in discussions about what Mexico can or should do. It is not clear yet whether Mexico has more to gain by being outspoken on these issues and lobbying for immigration reform, even though keeping silent has not produced any positive results either.[19] Moreover, Mexico's position is vulnerable to changes in the international and bilateral context, as was evident after 9/11.

In Mexico, transition to democracy prompted a serious rethinking and reorganization of foreign policy goals and priorities. Thus, at the beginning of Vicente Fox's government (2000–2006), the Minister for Foreign Affairs, Jorge G. Castañeda, described the new 'axes' on which Mexican foreign policy would be based in order to adapt to the most recent national and international transformations. These included the democratization process in Mexico, the depth of economic integration with the US and the pressures of globalization. This new foreign policy approach would entail a more active presence in multilateral fora a consistent defense of human rights at both the national and international levels, and a deepening of the North American integration process. This foreign policy review logically included a more comprehensive bilateral agenda with the US.

---

18   As quoted by reporter Manuel Roig Franzia in *The Washington Post*, January 8, 2008.

19   Castañeda 2007, 160.

The goal of regulating migration flows through the negotiation of an ambitious migration agreement between Mexico and the US was a major turning point in the new foreign policy strategy.[20] The logic behind this initiative can best be captured by a migratory flow of almost 400,000 people a year, and the presence of nearly 10 million first-generation Mexican migrants in the US in 2000 (of which, close to 5 million were undocumented migrants).[21] Viewed from this standpoint, the need to establish broader cooperation mechanisms, including a migration agreement, was perceived as a sensible route to face the challenges of copious migration flows.

The decision to elevate migration as a top priority in the bilateral agenda and Fox's promise to govern for 120 million Mexicans, including the migrant 'heroes' (as he referred to them) represented a decisive shift from the Mexican governments' traditional attitude of 'no policy' on this issue. In the first months of 2001, the Mexican government distanced itself from the traditional passive and reactive attitude to US migration policies that had long characterized the approach of previous administrations. Consequently, the Fox government opted for a pro-active and assertive course of action, proposing an agenda for bilateral cooperation on these issues. The new agenda crystallized in a an ambitious proposal for a 'migration agreement' between Mexico and the United States that encompassed five points: 1) regularization of undocumented workers who were already in the US; 2) more visas for Mexican immigrants; 3) broadening the scope of temporary worker programs; 4) increasing border safety; and 5) targeting development initiatives to areas of high out-migration and strengthening the Mexican economy in order to reduce emigration pressures.

The incipient bilateral dialogue that Mexico and Washington had initiated on migration issues was abruptly interrupted by the tragic 2001 terrorist attacks. In the aftermath of 9/11, US government's foreign and domestic policy priorities were swiftly adjusted to the inescapable challenges posed by Al Qaeda and the new expressions of terrorism. Although migration issues were not dropped completely from the bilateral agenda, they were approached in a very different manner by the Bush administration. As Gustavo Mohar, a high Mexican migration official explained, 'the ability of the terrorists to elude the controls, regulations, and scrutiny aimed at foreigners arriving in the US sparked a re-conceptualization of how to protect US borders and prevent the entry of any foreign nationals who would pose a new threat'.[22] Thus, after 9/11, immigration was viewed through a

---

20   Castañeda 2001, 288.

21   According to some estimates, nearly two thirds of the estimated 12 million undocumented population currently living in the US have remained in the country ten years or less, which coincides with the economic boom and the NAFTA period. According to Deborah W. Meyers, 80% of undocumented migrants are from Latin America and 60% of these from Mexico; 60% entered without inspection, 40% overstayed visas or entered on fraudulent documents. Meyers 2007, quoted in Verea 2007. See also Grieco 2003.

22   Mohar 2004.

security lens and cooperation with Mexico was limited to control of the borders and related security issues.

Although there was no progress on the 'migration accord', the post-9/11 security imperative brought Mexico and the US to closely collaborate on the basis set out by the 22-point 'Mexico–US Border Partnership Action Plan', also known as the 'Smart Borders Initiative', signed in 2002. The new framework for cooperation included agreements in areas of infrastructure and secure flow of people and goods. In addition to this, the three NAFTA partners subsequently signed the 'Partnership for Prosperity' which included proposals to promote foreign and domestic investment in Mexico's marginal areas. Viewed from the standpoint of migration, this was, of course, a limited initiative that appeared 'to stand little chance of raising Mexican living standards significantly, and thereby reducing pressures to migrate'.[23] From then on, and until the end of the Fox administration, the idea of a migration agreement was no longer formally discussed at the bilateral level. Nevertheless, the goal of some version of reform kept an important place in Mexico's strategic calculus on migration. Indeed, the Mexican government maintained this proposal as a guideline for its position and activities on immigration.

Considering that the US agenda became focused on security issues, the Mexican government accordingly fine-tuned its proposal, arguing that the shared management of migration flows through formal cooperation mechanisms and the regularization of undocumented immigrants in the US would contribute to the country's security by 'bringing them out of the shadows'.[24] Mexico also focused on giving the US guarantees of its commitment for security at the border. For example, on April 23, 2003, Secretary of Homeland Security Tom Ridge and Secretary of Government Santiago Creel issued a joint statement on enhanced bilateral cooperation to create a 'smart border' that facilitates the transit of goods and people while protecting against crime and terrorism. On May 6, 2003, the day before a meeting with Secretary of State Colin Powell in Washington, D.C., Minister Derbez indicated in a speech at the Centre for Strategic and International Studies that security was the number one priority for Mexico.[25] On June 3, 2003, US and Mexican officials announced the launch of 'Operation Desert Safeguard', to save migrants' lives by deploying more and better-equipped Border Patrol agents west of Nogales, Arizona, increasing the number warnings (in Spanish) of the dangers, and taking more forceful measures against smugglers.[26]

At the same time, in an effort to address concerns about security and violence along Mexico's southern border, the Fox administration launched the 'Plan Sur'. Moving away from a traditional position of facilitating cross-border markets

---

23   Alba 2004.
24   See for example, *Reforma*, July 11, 2003.
25   Storrs 2005, 6.
26   Storrs 2005, 7.

and family interactions along the southern border,[27] this program was designed to strengthen migration controls and surveillance in the border region with Belize and Guatemala, and to improve infrastructure in detention centres for undocumented migrants. As Castillo and Toussaint have argued, the notion of migration control was profoundly influenced by a shift in policy that in the post-9/11 context emphasized security. Although the thrust of these changes reflected a greater degree of convergence with Washington's views on migratory controls, the securitization of Mexico's southern border entailed negative consequences for the country's international standing on these issues. Not only did Mexican authorities lack a clear vision of what security meant in this context, but more profoundly, the potential contradictory effects of securitizing migratory controls were overtly overlooked.[28] As a result, the participation of security forces in migration controls soon became the target of intense disapproval. Indeed, the incapacity of the security agencies to differentiate migrants from gangs or criminals operating along the border region only added momentum to rising concerns about human rights violations. Notwithstanding this, Mexico's shift in policy towards its southern border remained shaped by other considerations. Although responses to the flow of migrants from Central America were clearly incompatible with the actions pursued by the Mexican government towards its own undocumented migrants in the US, the shift in policy reflected an attempt to adjust to rising security pressures in the bilateral relation with its northern neighbour. Indeed, an important motivation in this policy shift was Mexico's determination to demonstrate to Washington both its commitment and its capacity to control flows along both borders and to remain as a reliable partner in North America's security agenda.

Despite Mexico's efforts, this focus on security on both of its borders did not render any results in terms of reviving the bilateral discussions over a migration agreement. As the signs of Washington's return to a unilateral position on the management of migration gathered force, the Mexican strategy gradually adjusted. Mexico's policies refocused and again moved towards the idea of promoting a comprehensive immigration reform, including the five points on which the proposal for the migration agreement had been based, and lobbying in favour of the bills that coincided with Mexico's position (e.g. the McCain-Kennedy initiative). The Mexican government, in turn, expressed its concern regarding other bills such as the Sensenbrenner Bill, as it focused mainly on border security measures (such as extending existing fences at the US–Mexico border) and criminalized undocumented immigration, and those who provided aid to immigrants under such status. Despite Mexico's lobbying and diplomatic efforts, on October 26, 2006, President Bush signed Congress's Bill HR 6061 'to establish operational control over the international land and maritime borders of the United States', which included extending the fence along the US–Mexico border and allocating more resources for Border Patrol operations.

---

27   Castillo 2006.
28   Castillo and Toussaint 2009, 79–80.

Notwithstanding these setbacks, Mexico continued promoting a 'shared responsibility' agenda and, for the first time, formally detailed its position through the document 'Mexico and the Migration Phenomenon' (published in English and Spanish). The main points of the report emphasized that the current situation regarding migration flows and policies required a new approach from the Mexican government, assuming its responsibility as a migrant-sending, receiving and transit country. It also recognized the linkage between migration, borders and security and Mexico's commitment to a regional approach and cooperation with the neighbouring countries – in particular with Central America. The document made no specific mention of a migration agreement with the US but rather stressed the need for general collaboration between the countries as the only way to manage migration effectively and make any new legislation in the US workable.[29]

This last point represented a fundamental shift from the position maintained in 1986 during the process leading to the passage of IRCA when the Mexican government chose not to get involved in the debates over the content of the legislation, and did not take an explicit position on the issue. It was also a much stronger stance than the one assumed in 1996 when the government simply expressed its concern about a number of laws that limited migrants' access to public services, imposed more controls at the workplace and restrictions for family reunification and allocated resources for border controls (i.e. the *Personal Responsibility and Work Opportunity Reconciliation Act* (PRWORA); the *Antiterrorism and Effective Death Penalty Act* (AEDPA) and the *Illegal Immigration Reform and Immigrant Responsibility Act* (IIRIRA)).[30]

The change in Mexico's position of limited engagement was also evident in its increasing activism regarding its relationship with the population of Mexican origin in the United States. In the period between 1988 and 2000 the dynamics of gradual democratization had prompted political parties in Mexico, and in particular the left wing party (PRD), to reach out to Mexican communities in the US. By the turn of the century, President Vicente Fox, the first democratically elected opposition candidate after 70 years of one-party rule, explicitly sought to cultivate and institutionalize the relationship with the Mexican-origin communities in the US. The Fox administration made this a priority in the national agenda. This was done mainly by creating the Presidential Office for Mexicans Abroad (OPME) in December of 2000, which was later integrated into the Institute of Mexicans Abroad (IME), officially established in April 2003. By promoting an agenda that gave migrants access to channels for direct political participation in Mexico and

29   The document is available at: http://www.sre.gob.mx/eventos/fenomenomigratorio/docs/mexicofrentealfenommig.pdf (last viewed May 31, 2007). See also Derbez 2006.

30   The laws included favourable measures such as greater cooperation between the INS and local and state authorities to facilitate naturalization processes, but their main effects were negative in terms of reducing migrants' access to certain health services, education and social services, as well as eliminating the legal process of having the right to a hearing before deportation (Garcia y Griego and Verea 1998).

tools for empowering and strengthening their organizations in the US through the IME and its Advisory Council (CCIME), the Mexican government also moved away from a limited and cautious position regarding its consular activities and the protection of migrants' rights.

Rather than focusing merely on the customary practices regarding the defence of migrants' human rights (i.e. aid in legal affairs, repatriations, supporting migrant organizations and providing health, education and cultural services), the Mexican government also adopted a set of new policies to improve its services for migrants (i.e. the promotion of matrículas consulares[31]), to provide opportunities for the exercise of migrants' political rights in Mexico (i.e. the passage of the legislation regulating absentee voting); and, finally, to promote the development of migrant leadership networks, offering them direct channels to communicate their views to the Mexican government (i.e. through the creation of the CCIME, an Advisory Council within the Institute of Mexicans Abroad integrated by migrant leaders).

Although these initiatives triggered negative reactions amongst certain quarters in the US, the studied silence of prominent circles, including the banking sector and some state authorities pointed to their tacit acquiescence. As policymakers and economic actors in both the US and Mexico considered their approaches to the Mexican communities they kept in mind the increasing economic and political weight of the Hispanic population in the US.

By the end of his administration in 2006, it was clear that Fox's main objective in the bilateral agenda – i.e. establishing a comprehensive migration agreement with the United States – would not be achieved. Nonetheless, the priority of migration in the national agenda was not set back. For example, in the first years of his government, President Felipe Calderon increased the consulates' budgets and announced plans to add two more consular representations to the existing 48 offices. In the context of the US presidential campaigns, President Felipe Calderón, Minister of Foreign Affairs Patricia Espinosa, and other high-level Mexican officials protested against the harsh discourse on immigration used by many presidential candidates and the lack of recognition of immigrants' contributions.[32] Taking a forceful position on Mexico's capacity to lobby in favour of Mexicans living in the US, Calderón also instructed Mexican diplomats to participate more actively in

---

31 Although Mexican consulates have offered this form of ID since 1871 – based on a practice recognized by the Vienna Convention on Consular Relations, it was only after the terrorist attacks of September 11, 2001 and the increase in detentions, raids and security measures that affected Mexican immigrants, when the Mexican government considered it necessary to issue a new secure version and widely promote the acceptance of this form of ID in US financial institutions and government offices. It was mainly intended for Mexicans living abroad who could not obtain a Mexican passport or any form of official ID in the US, or simply needed a more 'portable' identification card that included their address in the US (the *matrícula* does not provide any information on the person's migratory status and is mainly intended as a form of ID for daily activities).

32 See for example, *Associated Press,* December 5, 2007 and Schwartz 2007.

public debates, liaise with NGOs, and develop a strong, unified public position on immigration.[33] In addition, Mexico continued its efforts to expand the discussion of migration issues and the development of mechanisms for its management at the regional and multilateral level. For example, Mexico actively participated in the draft of the '*Montevideo Declaration*' and the '*Montevideo* Commitment on *Migration and Development*' signed by the Heads of State and Government at the XVI IberoAmerican Summit of November 2006. This document emphasized the protection of migrants' rights, the need to move away from unilateral approaches to migration management and to decriminalize undocumented migration. In November, 2007 the UN General Assembly passed a resolution presented by Mexico on the need to protect immigrants' rights.

The changes observed in Mexico's emigration policies through the 1990s, have not been exempt of contradictions and setbacks. However, in a context characterized by growing interdependence, where most issues are closely linked and have an effect on one another, a return to the traditional policy of limited engagement on immigration issues was simply not an option. Under the new conditions, the traditional justification of limited responses to US policies that affect Mexican immigrants based on principles of 'non-intervention' came at a far higher political cost than before. Moreover, the Mexican government faces growing pressures from domestic and transnational actors regarding the need to address the causes of emigration, provide adequate channels for the exercise of emigrants' political and economic rights in their home country and effectively protect their rights in their host country. As well, a humanitarian approach to the southern border and the protection of rights of Central American immigrants in Mexico is increasingly considered part of this comprehensive approach to migration.

There are obvious limits to the success of Mexico's actions both in terms of its own institutional capacities as well as in terms of exerting pressure on the US to change its unilateral policies or directly influencing policy reform. The push to establish formal institutions between the countries on issues of immigration and expand the framework of regional integration to include the management of flows of people between the NAFTA countries has also found obstacles. This not only has to do with the differences in capabilities and vulnerabilities between Mexico and the United States, but is also explained by the particularity of migration as an issue that touches upon debates about national identity, sovereignty and security.

Migration, Security and US–Mexican Relations

Migration movements and flows embody a key part of the equation of US–Mexico relations as well as of ascendant dynamics in North America. As is the case in other regional latitudes, the causes of Mexican migration to the US remain the object of intense debate. Some have emphasized economic incentives and the weight of

---

33   López 2007.

structural inequalities which continue to underpin economic interactions between the US and Mexico. In their view, the role of foreign migrant labour, whether in Europe or in North America, has long been a feature that has accompanied Western capitalist dynamics. Observers have also pointed to the role played by demographic forces and balances, while others have underlined the weight of agency and individual decisions linked to personal preferences and considerations. Whilst the lengthy debate about pull and push factors has failed to yield definitive answers to these questions there is indeed the view that a multiplicity of factors shape migration flows and these include not only the individual decisions of migrants, but also the actions of those who continue to solicit and request their services.[34] Whatever the relative importance of the various factors that have fostered this wave of migration, what is already clear is that its magnitude and intensity has meant that the issue is no longer confined to academic circles and discussions, and it has obviously gained public relevance. Indeed, the ripples produced by this phenomenon now travel across cultural and social norms, embedding them in local and national politics and political processes at both ends.

At century's dawn, efforts to control undocumented migration and the illicit movement of drugs and arms between the US and Mexico had in themselves testified to their transnational dimension. Indeed, in Mexico, as in other places, the impact of technological innovations in transport and communication was reflected in the ever greater density and dynamism observed in migration flows, and ultimately in the emergence of a transnational Mexican community in the US bringing the two countries closer together in unprecedented ways.[35] Over the years, these changes, which were also accompanied by the extraordinary rise of remittance flows, led observers to raise questions about their implications for both countries. As has been the case elsewhere, the dense movement of people across the US–Mexican border forced attention to focus on their consequences at both the recipient and the sending points and at the regional level. In Mexico, in the period between 2000 and 2006, the volume of remittances increased from US\$ 6.6 billion to more than US\$ 24 billion, approximately 3% of Mexico's GDP, turning the flow into the second most important source of hard currency after oil revenues.[36]

While in the course of the last two decades, the persistent movement of people across the border has generated significant tensions in relations between the US and Mexico, such dense flow has also called into question the capacity of both countries to stem the stream of people. As has often been the case in other

---

34　Portes and DeWind 2004, 838.

35　Although the consolidation of a true Mexican diaspora in the US is still an open question, particularly in terms of its ability to effectively maximize the available economic and political opportunities at both ends and to establish and manage a truly transnational public space, the more salient political visibility of the Hispanic and Mexican communities is beyond doubt. See R.C. Smith 2003, 299.

36　In the year 2006, the total amount of remittances moved by migrant workers across regions amounted to more than US\$ 300 billion. *The Economist*, 6 October 2007.

experiences, the tension that we observe in North America between the sending and the receiving state has been a direct consequence of the diverging goals that have repeatedly underlay their efforts to regulate migration flows. What is clear is that both the intensity and the volume of migration movements pointed to a widening gap between what Washington, in particular, attempted to achieve and what its record of control showed it could deliver.

Throughout this period, the tension between US efforts to impose effective controls and the dynamism of the mechanisms that activate and help sustain migration flows become more acute. At the general level, the reduced capacity of the US to contain the flow has been linked to a number of factors, among which two deserve special attention. The first and most obvious relates to the long lasting role of business interests in maintaining the constant flow of labour migrants. The second factor is linked to the trend by which organizations including churches, social communities and political interests have more often engaged with the fortunes of undocumented migrants.

In the US, as has been the case in post-industrial Europe, the rise of a dual labour market has been accompanied by an acute sensibility and heightened public indignation against the inhuman conditions, and hideous discrimination imposed upon labour migrants.[37] Over the course of half a century, not only did the constant movement of people across the US–Mexican border play a part in the configuration of a Hispanic community in the US, but has also contributed to important shifts in the political realm north of the border. In many corners of the US, the assault on Hispanic migrants that has accompanied efforts to locally enforce migration laws has also provided the foundations for new political alliances and coalitions. Indeed, it is not difficult to imagine how the targeting of ethnic migrants may have mobilized the Hispanic community and helped consolidate alliances with progressive liberals and with organizations like churches and unions that have a 'clientelist interest in migrants'.[38]

Evidence of the new political relevance of the migrant community in both the US and Mexico has been provided both by Mexico's efforts to more actively engage with these communities in the US, and by the attempts first of President Bush, and more recently of the Obama administration to woo Hispanic voters through pledges of immigration reform.[39] Indeed, the heated debate that took place

---

37   The Southern Poverty Law Center released a study in 2009 showing that Latino immigrants in the South 'are routinely cheated out of their wages and denied basic protections in the workplace. In their communities, they are subjected to racial profiling and harassment by law enforcement – and frequently forced to prove themselves innocent of immigration violations, regardless of their legal status. And they are, increasingly, targeted for violent hate crimes' (Southern Poverty Law Center, April 2009: http://www.splcenter. org/sites/default/files/downloads/UnderSiege.pdf).

38   Zolberg 2006, 76.

39   Although the actual political weight of these communities remains a matter of debate, their political salience has become particularly clear in the context of close

in the US Senate in 2006, and the more recent pledge by President Obama to again embark upon immigration reform, suggest the recognition of a new political reality. Hispanics and black Americans, who collectively represented 12% of the vote in 1980, accounted for 22% of the electorate in 2008. In the same period, white voters saw their share of the electorate shrank from 88% to 74%.[40]

At the heart of recent discussions of migration movements across the US–Mexican border is the question of security. At the more general level, migration experts have long debated the security implications of migration flows for both the sending and the receiving state. In North America, for over a century, undocumented migration has taken place between two sovereign territorial states and two distinct legal jurisdictions. Although recent developments seem to suggest that migration now moves within the confines of one emerging social space, the movement of people between Mexico and the US has created important security challenges at both ends, including Canada and Central America. As is the case in other latitudes, the history of migration flows between Mexico and the US has shown that while it can bring economic benefits it can also prove to be socially problematic; strong migration flows can have important consequences for both the recipient and sending countries. Unless assisted by proactive measures, in the medium and long term, migration flows can alter the face and character of both the sending and the recipient societies. The vivid images of migrant Mexican communities in the US, as well as the desolate landscape of villages left to women, children and in many cases to the elderly bear witness to this.[41]

Not surprisingly, the intricate effects of such processes can easily influence the ideas and concepts underpinning security thinking amongst US and Mexican political experts and policymakers. In the US, questions about the capacity of Mexican migrants to adapt and integrate, and to do so without altering the political and institutional landscape, soon surfaced. Although efforts to preserve cultural boundaries have perpetually been part of the calculus of immigration policies, debates about integrative concerns have come with an unconcealed racist edge. The arguments about national cohesion and identity propelled by Samuel Huntington and right-wing politicians in the light of the Hispanic flow are reminiscent of the opinions voiced by George Kennan and earlier xenophobic views.[42]

---

electoral competition. According to some experts, even in the aftermath of 9/11 the Hispanic vote determined the result of the mayor's election for the city of New York. See Mitchell 2002, 32.

40   While in 1980, Ronald Reagan defeated Jimmy Carter by winning 55% of the white vote, in 2008 John McCain again matched that percentage but lost decisively to Barack Obama. Hardwood 2009.

41   Cornelius 2007, 9.

42   Zolberg 2006, 70; Schoultz quotes Kennan: 'it seems unlikely that there could be any other region on earth in which nature and human behaviour could have combined to produce a more unhappy and hopeless background for the conduct of human life than in Latin America'; see Schoultz 1998, 331.

Meanwhile, at the Mexican end the implications of such an exodus raise serious questions about its longer-terms implications for the texture and health of the social fabric across villages and communities. From the Mexican perspective, the apparent benefits of migration flows in releasing pressures from the labour market and generating additional financial flows may have seemed attractive in the first place. Yet, the longer-term costs of tearing apart the social fabric could not be easily disregarded. According to some observers, such costs have included the gradual desolation of villages and in some extreme cases a reduced capacity among communities to protect themselves from drug trafficking and organized crime. From a transnational point of view, the intensification of migration flows has further contributed to the blurring of the national-international divide. This has, of course, long been the case, but the density of migration flows now woven into the fabric of both US and Mexican societies testifies to the transnational configuration of this phenomenon.[43]

Changes in the institutional environment in which migration flows now occur have also brought to the surface the potential links between security and peoples' movements. The analysis of such links suggests a fundamental tension between migration enforcement and regional security. The tightening of border controls and migration policies through the implementation of the twin smart border agreements has brought with it harmful effects on at least two fronts. On the one hand, the implementation of these policies had an unambiguous negative effect on the economic competitiveness of North America. On the other, the massive institutional border security reform unleashed by 9/11 brought illicit flows closer together. As mentioned earlier, tighter border enforcement may have failed in its efforts to deter undocumented migration, but has significantly contributed to reconfigure the organization of the illicit market.

In an important sense, the propensity of undocumented migration, illicit drugs and potentially terrorists too, to flow together in one 'black' stream or network

---

43 An important indicator of the potential vulnerability of social groups and communities *vis-à-vis* migration flows concerns their increased dependence towards remittances. According to the national poll on household income and expenses, in 2006 a total of 1,858,758 families received remittances from the US. In some states, including Michoacán, some estimates calculate that at their peak remittances represented 12% of the local economy. Over the past two years, the impact of the financial crisis has been detected in a reduced flow of remittances that has cut down by 14% the number of recipient families. Between 2006 and 2008 more than 275,000 families living in urban districts and 225,000 in rural areas were cut from the remittance flow. Among urban families this represented a reduction of 19% in the household income, whereas among rural families the drop in the household income has been estimated at around 27%. *The Economist*, 6 October 2007; Mexico: número de hogares que reciben remesas disminuye 14.8%, según estudio, available at http://www.infolatam.com/entrada/mexico_numero_hogares_que_reciben_remesa-15190. html, last viewed July 28, 2009.

has been closely associated to the impact of tighter enforcement at the borders. This enforcement shift and ensuing institutional reform has rested largely on a renewed emphasis on prohibition and prohibitionist policies. Without a doubt, unilateral priorities forcing the amalgamation of anti-migration, anti-drug and anti-terrorist policies into a single infrastructure have been deployed in the context of bilateral frameworks. Yet, the result at the US southern border has been the perceptible convergence of flows of undocumented migrants and illicit drugs, and the diversion of undocumented migration bound to the US via Canada. Clearly tighter enforcement has entailed negative implications for the way in which these flows organize and coordinate their movements.

Although experts have long questioned the wisdom of such approaches to undocumented migration flows, the core features of US migration control policies remain practically unchanged. It may be the imperative of post-9/11 security that accounts for the more aggressive unilateral nature of US migration policy, of which the decision to expand the existing fence along the border is the most hostile expression. The difficulty with this approach is not whether it is socially or politically justified. From an analytical point of view the problem lies in the disproportionate relation between realistic attainability and inordinate costs. The massive resources invested in these policies have failed to secure the much expected results, while the collateral damage has been evident both in the tragic fatality rate at crossing points and in the greater risk of convergence of illicit flows.

Notwithstanding this, Mexico's initial readiness to contest the virtue of these policies has gradually given way to greater alignment with US approaches. Indeed, the unilateral impulse from Washington did not prevent the continuing cooperation between US and Mexican border patrols and security agencies in border control operations. Thus in December 2007, the Mexican and US governments established the *International Transborder Police* focused on fighting organized crime and drug traffic, human smuggling networks, reducing violence at the border and combating international terrorism.[44] The new 'comprehensive' bilateral approach to transnational illicit flows was clearly reaffirmed by the negotiation of the Merida Initiative. Within the framework of this initiative the US government committed itself to provide Mexican authorities with financial aid and expertise to combat drug traffic and organized crime, and to foster tighter cooperation between the National Institute for Migration and the Department of Homeland Security in relation to border controls and verification of migratory documents.

Such joint initiatives may have provided policymakers in Mexico with a sense of purpose and direction, but the accumulated record of failure should not be forgotten. Moreover, beyond the tangible record of failure, Mexico now risks reproducing on its southern border the very same policies that it has long condemned on its northern border.[45] Within the context of intensified US–Mexico cooperation, the Mexican government was bound to reinforce controls over its southern border.

---

44 Fernández 2007.
45 See Castillo and Toussaint, in Serrano, forthcoming, 2010.

Thus, plans to strengthen controls over Mexico's southern border now include the use of electronic chips to track Central American immigrants who cross the border regularly for work or tourism.[46] With a logic that should come as no surprise, the tightening of the southern border prompted human rights groups to express outrage at the treatment of Central American migrants in Mexico's territory. Under the pressure of human rights activists, the Mexican Congress passed legislation on April 2008 removing criminal penalties for undocumented immigrants in Mexico. The legislation also introduced possibilities for regularization and emphasized the respect of immigrants' human rights. Mexico is now trapped in a game of double standards. As Mexico seeks simultaneously to engage with its diaspora in the US and to cooperate with Washington's security agenda it must navigate the complex and conflicting relation between two clearly opposing agendas.

Concluding Remarks

Over the past decades, integration and globalization have undermined the boundaries of political communities in North America. Although the recent financial and economic crises may have slowed down the pace of regional integration and cross border movements there is little doubt that the relationship between Canada, Mexico and the US is now bigger than the sum of its parts. Indeed, not only do security dynamics lock Canada, the US and Mexico all together, but the social and political logics of regionalism have developed a momentum beyond the power of either party to arrest.

This chapter has discussed the role that migration flows have played in regionalization processes in North America, and more specifically in regional integration between Mexico and the US. Although migration flows between these two countries have a century-long history, they have expanded dramatically in the course of the last few decades. In the period between the mid-1980s and the present, migration movements between Mexico and the US countries evolved from a seasonal trickle of agricultural workers to an increasingly dense and one-way flow of undocumented migrants. While this transformation owed much to the suppressive policies deployed by successive US administrations, it also took place in a rapidly changing security environment that forced governments in Mexico and Washington to adjust their policy responses.

As this chapter has tried to show, migration and security are complex, multiple interconnected processes. Although there is often a perceived threat to the cultural identity of the host country, relocation imposes considerable and unavoidable challenges of adaptation to the outgoing population. Whether legal or illicit, what is clear, however, is that if dense migration flows are not accompanied by policies aimed at helping migrant communities to acclimatize and integrate, the risk of intolerance and discrimination can only go up. But beyond the most visible and

---

46   *The Associated Press*, December 28, 2007.

contentious manifestations of migratory flows at the recipient end, there is now a considerable body of evidence that accounts for their negative consequences at the dispatching end. While earlier studies revealed that migrant groups were not necessarily the least privileged, the more recent consensus is that depopulation has left villages more vulnerable to a number of social disorders including the risk of take-over by criminal organizations.

For a long time, the disengaged approach to migration pursued by both Mexico and the US allowed migration flows to attain their own homeostatic equilibrium along economic trends and forces. Out of this spontaneous adjustment to changes in the marketplace came the seasonal and circular movement through the border. Yet, the shift to ever more restrictive policies to stop migration at crossing points disturbed this natural balance, pushing undocumented migrants towards more sedentary and clandestine patterns awakening in turn resentment, chauvinistic sentiments and ultimately freezing hostile stereotypes.

In contrast to other experiences in which regional decisions and policies have not only enabled but over time adjusted to demographic and market trends, regional policies in North America have confined migration flows to the condition of an intractable problem. In the course of the last decades, policy priorities in Washington set the dial between risk-free migration and obdurate movements, contributing to turn migration into a truly regional security challenge at both the departing, crossing and recipient stages.

Putting things in a wider perspective, if we compare say the regional setting for Spain in its transition years to Mexico's, then the following conjectures may be offered. While Spain was able to benefit from an encouraging and favourable regional environment in its transition to democratic institutional stability, Mexico has had to navigate increasingly hostile currents. Beginning with the anti-drugs policy, followed by the tightening of migratory controls, along with a studied indifference to Mexican proposals to deepen regional integration and to regulate migration, successive administrations in the US have done little to offer viable solutions to shared and regional problems. To the contrary, US securitization of first its anti-narcotic and then migration policies have actively contributed to Mexico's descent into drug-driven instability. This owes less to market dynamics than to the unintended effects of the criminalization and enforcement policies so passionately pursued by security maximizers. What is beyond doubt is that by failing to provide Mexico with a more stable setting, both the US and Canada have contributed to eroding their own security. Without more nuanced responses, the US will find, as it is already experiencing, that a faltering and violent situation south of the border can quickly jump and travel across borders. Notwithstanding its efforts to remove itself from NAFTA's southern flank, in the medium and long term, mounting instability on NAFTA's southern border is likely to impose a burden on regional security dynamics.

On their voyage to integration, the three NAFTA partners designed a free trade plan, but little beyond that. And yet, whether they like it or not, all three countries are now enmeshed in a thick web of social, political and security dynamics from which they cannot easily escape. The dynamics unleashed by regional integration have locked both Canada and Mexico into an organic relationship with the US, while the security of the US is inescapably tied to that of its neighbours, including Mexico.

Bibliography

Alba, F. 2004. Política migratoria: un corte de caja, *Nexos*, 317, 31–7.

Aleinikoff, A. 2005. No Illusions: Paradigm Shifting on Mexican Migration to the United States in the Post-9/11 World, *US–Mexico Policy Bulletin*, Woodrow Wilson International Center for Scholars, Mexico Institute Issue 5, 4.

Andreas, P. 2000. *Border Games: Policing the US–Mexico Divide*. Ithaca, NY: Cornell University Press.

Andreas, P. 2005. The Mexicanization of the US–Canada border', *International Journal*, LX(2), 453–4.

The Associated Press, 2007. Mexican President Accuses US Candidates of Being Anti-Mexican. December 5.

The Associated Press. 2007. Mexico to Track Migrations over Border. December 28.

Castañeda, J.G. 2001. Los Ejes de la Política Exterior de Mexico, *Nexos,* 288.

Castañeda, J.G. 2007. *ExMex: From Migrants to Immigrants,* New York: The New Press, 2007.

Castillo, M.Á. 2006. Mexico: Caught Between the United States and Central America, *Migration Information Source*, Migration Policy Institute, April 1.

Castillo, M.Á. and Toussaint, M. 2009. *Diagnóstico sobre las migraciones centroamericanas en el estado de Chiapas y sus impactos socioculturales.* México: Agencia Española de Cooperación Internacional para el Desarrollo (AECID).

Castillo, M.Á. and Toussaint, M. 2010. Seguridad y Migración en la frontera sur de México, in Mónica Serrano, forthcoming.

CONAPO. 2008. 11.8 millones radican en EU, Press Release no. 26, August 20.

Cornelius, W.A. 2007. Introduction: Does Border Enforcement Deter Unauthorized Immigration? in *Impacts of Border Enforcement on Mexican Migration: The View from the Sending Communities*, edited by W.A. Cornelius and J.M. Lewis. La Jolla: Center for Comparative Immigration Studies, UCSD.

Delgado Wise, R. and Márquez Covarrubias, H. 2008. The Mexico–United States Migratory System: Dilemmas of Regional Integration, Development and Emigration, in *Migration and Development: Perspectives from the South*, edited by S. Castles and R. Delgado Wise. Geneva: International Organization for Migration, 113–42.

Derbez, L.E. 2006. México ante el fenómeno migratorio, *Reforma,* May 1.

The Economist. 2007. Counting the Cash-Remittances to Latin America. 6 October.

Fernández, H. 2007. México y EU concentran policía transfronteriza. *El Universal,* December 2.

Garcia y Griego, M. and Verea, M. 1998. Colaboración sin concordancia: la migración in la nueva agenda bilateral México-Estados Unidos, in *Nueva agenda bilateral in la relación México–Estados Unidos*, edited by M. Verea, R. Fernández de Castro and S. Weintraub. México: Fondo de Cultura Económica, 112–19.

Grieco, E. 2003. The Foreign Born From Mexico in the United States, *Migration Information Source*, Migration Policy Institute, October.

Hardwood, J. 2009. Republicans Rethinking the Reagan Mystique, *International Herald Tribune*, 13 June.

Hurrell, A. 2006. Hegemony in a Region that Dares Not Speak Its Name, *International Journal*, LXI(3).

López, M. 2007. Instruye FCH diálogo con EU, *Reforma,* December 8.

MacFarlane, N. and Serrano, M. 2005. Security Regulation or Community? Canada, Mexico, and the borders of identity, in *Regionalism and Governance in the Americas*, edited by L. Fawcett and M. Serrano. Basingstoke: Palgrave, 2005

Meyers, D.W. 2007. *Key Data and Policy Points: US Immigration Fundamentals.* Paper presented at Instituto Nacional de Migración, Secretaría de Gobernación, June 20 2007, quoted in Verea 2006.

Mitchell, C. 2002. The Significance of September 11, 2001: Terrorist Attacks for United States-Bound Migration in the Western Hemisphere, *International Migration Review*, 36(1), Spring.

Mohar, G. 2004. Mexico–United States Migration: A Long Way To Go, *Migration Information Source*, Migration Policy Institute, March 1.

Portes, A. and De Wind, J. 2004. A Cross Atlantic Dialogue: The Progress of Research and Theory in the Study of International Migration, *International Migration Review*, 38(3), Autumn.

Reforma. 2003. Ofrece Creel seguridad por migración, July 11.

Reforma. 2007. Muere en la frontera un mexicano al día, December 19.

Roig Franzia, M. 2008. Mexico Rebukes US Candidates on Migrant Issues, *The Washington Post*, January 8.

Schwartz, J. 2007. Mexico's Frustration with US Immigration Policy Builds, *Austin American Statesman*, November 17.

Schoultz, L. 1998. *Beneath the US: A History of US Policy Towards Latin America.* Cambridge: Harvard University Press.

Smith, R.C. 2003. Migrant Membership as an Instituted Process: Transnational-isation, the State and the Extra-territorial Conduct of Mexican Politics, *International Migration Review*, 37(2), Summer.

Southern Poverty Law Center. 2009. *Under Siege: Life for Low-Income Latinos in the South*. April.

Storrs, L.K. 2005. *Mexico–United States Dialogue on Migration and Border Issues, 2001–2005.* Report for Congress, Congressional Research Service (CRS), June 2.

US Census Bureau, Hispanic heritage month 2009: September 15–October 15, *News Release,* July 15, 2009.

Verea, M. 2006. *Temporary and clandestine labor mobility to the US (1996–2006), versus the increasing restrictive migration policies.* Paper presented at the Latin American Studies Association, Montreal, mimeo, 1–21.

Verea, M. 2007. A 12 años del TLCAN = + migración, in *Desafíos de la migración: saldos de la relación México–Estados Unidos,* edited by E. Cabrera. México D.F.: Editorial Planeta, 339–74.

Zolberg, A.R. 2006. International Migration in Political Perspective, in *The Migration Reader: Exploring Politics and Policies,* edited by A. Messina and G. Lahav. Boulder, Colorado: Lynne Rienner.

Chapter 13

Equivocal Claims: Examining Labour Migration Regimes with Ambivalent Control Claims – Central Asian States' Policies on Migration Control

Lilia Ormonbekova

Central Asia, a region geographically including five countries – Kazakhstan, Kyrgyzstan, Tajikistan, Turkmenistan and Uzbekistan – is rather new to global population movements, when compared to old migrant destinations such as Europe and North America. Labour migration policies in these states, be it with regard to outward or inward migration, have nevertheless undergone dramatic changes in less than a decade. In the early 1990s, with the dissolution of the Soviet Union, migration was mainly of ethnic origin and of a permanent type, characterized by populations' movements to historic homelands (e.g. former Soviet Germans moving permanently to Germany, ethnic Russians to Russia, etc.). In the mid-1990s, economic disparities between former soviet countries began to grow and started to act as a push-pull factor for people seeking employment abroad. Correlating with migration push-pull theory, movements obtained a 'strong economic dimension'[1] and became a 'function of demand-pull and supply-push factors.'[2] In the early 21st century labour migration has definitely taken a leading role in all population movements within the Commonwealth of Independent States (CIS) by outnumbering ethnic migration.

As in every migration system, Central Asian labour migrants tend to choose the same destination – a country with higher wages, where there is a shortage in inexpensive labour. Due to the rapid development of lucrative industries, Russia and (later) Kazakhstan became the main recipients of labour migrants. Prospective economic benefit was not the only pull factor for persons seeking employment abroad: historic, cultural and often family ties served as incentives to migration, as well as *lingua franca* – Russian – still widely spoken by all former soviet citizens.

---

1   Hollifield 1998, 596. See Cornelius, Martin and Hollifield 2003; Brettell and Hollifield 2008; and Castles and Miller 2003, for more details on migration push-pull theory.

2   Ibid.

With these developments in view, Central Asian governments, and to a greater extent Kazakhstan's authorities, faced the very important challenge of responding to migration issues. It is important to note that there were attempts to regulate labour force movements at regional (CIS) levels in the mid-1990s; agreements, however, required commitment from dozens of newly independent states to protect other CIS citizen-migrants undertaking economic activities in their respective territories, whereas the post-dissolution economic crisis shifted the attention of the CIS members to their own challenges and citizens. Later attempts to reach consensus within smaller organizations (e.g. Eurasian Economic Community) have been delayed due to growing self-determination of migrant-receiving countries as regards the fact that migration might become a matter of trade-offs between the latter and the sending countries, and due to the lack of political will of Central Asian leaders who were unwilling to prioritize labour migration issues.

This chapter will focus more on the countries' individual policies and analyse how Central Asian states control labour migration. Kazakhstan is discussed as a country of destination,[3] whereas Tajikistan, Uzbekistan and Kyrgyzstan as sending countries.[4]

In the first paragraph I will analyse how and why Central Asian states elaborate their entry and exit rules, what internal considerations and transformations in a country are taken into account during implementation of migration policies, and how an individual migrant is impacted by the latter in his home country and abroad. The second paragraph will provide tentative definitions of control mechanisms in Central Asia.

Labour Migration Control in the Central Asian Context

Before starting with an analysis of the development of labour migration control in individual Central Asian states, one should note that these countries had never been independent before joining the Soviet Union in the 1920s–1930s. Upon gaining independence in the early 1990s, they had to develop their individual legislative bases from scratch; moreover, as they had never witnessed emigration or immigration, they had no experience in tackling these issues. Thus, many expectations were related to development of regional CIS framework in areas of migration and freedom of movement.

In the early 1990s, the leaders of newly independent states – former soviet republics – anticipated that people who had developed close ties during the soviet

---

3   While many reports add to these formulations, the World Bank Report is the most recent one on this issue: Mansoor and Quillin 2007, 3. http://siteresources.worldbank.org/INTECA/Resources/257896-1167856389505/Migration_FullReport.pdf.

4   Though Kazakhstan is the second largest receiving country in the CIS (after Russia), control over Central Asian labour migration to Russia will not be explored in this chapter, as it deserves a separate study. Turkmenistan will neither be covered, as there are no important and visible migration processes in the country, due to the quasi-totalitarian regime.

era, and could travel freely within the USSR,[5] would like to avail themselves of this right along with their republics gaining independence and the emergence of new borders between them. Thus, in 1992, 12 newly independent states signed the Bishkek Agreement on Free Movement of Citizens of CIS States, which guaranteed the freedom to travel to all co-signatories' territories, provided a person was a citizen of one of the parties to the Agreement.[6] Later, many factors, the main ones concerning security, led to the withdrawal of several states from this agreement, which I will explain in this chapter.

Immediately after the dissolution of the Soviet Union, many ethnic returnees were considered labour migrants, which led to adoption of the 1994 Agreement on Co-operation in the Field of Labour Migration and Social Protection of Migrant Workers.[7] The document, based on ILO principles, concerned only *legal* migrant workers and members of their families. The Agreement contained provisions on mutual recognition of diplomas and years of experience, on rules of employment in the receiving country and elimination of double taxation. As for equal treatment, only the medical care provisions dealt with this requirement. Migrant workers were also entitled to social security and to free transfer of their savings in accordance with the legislation of the receiving country.

Nevertheless, the leaders ignored the importance of further concluding bilateral agreements between CIS member-states. Although this was an essential condition for the Agreement's fulfillment, it was not put into practice, undermining the entire system. Until the beginning of the 21st century, labour migration movements remained dominated by ethnic, and not economic incentives, suggesting that the 1994 CIS Agreement was well ahead of its time. Therefore, when labour migration became more distinct, with clear preferences as to destinations, and most importantly, *predominantly irregular*, the 1994 CIS Agreement proved to be out of date[8] and insufficient in order to respond to challenges.

---

5   The most important means of prohibiting long-term movement was, however, the residential registration of citizens (*propiska*), which required that the place of residence be recorded in the citzen's passport and with the local authority.

6   Soglashenie o bezvizovom peredvizhenii grazhdan gosudarstv SNG po territorii ego uchastnikov ot 9 octyabrya 1992 goda (The Agreement on Visa-free Movement of Citizens of the CIS Members within the CIS, 9 October 1992), http://www.zatulin.ru/institute/sbornik/010/07.shtml#Приложение.

7   Soglashenie o sotrudnichestve gosudarstv uchastnikov SNG v oblasti trudovoy migrazii i sozial'noy zashity trudovyh migrantov, 14 aprelya 1994 goda (The Agreement on Co-operation of the CIS Member States in the Field of Labour Migration and Social Protection of Migrant Workers, 14 April 1994), http://www.cis.minsk.by/main.aspx?uid=7742.

8   An example is a labour migration agreement between Kyrgyzstan and Azerbaijan, which has been of no use to the signatories, as there was no large-scale labour migration from Kyrgyzstan to Azerbaijan and *vice versa*. This fact demonstrates that many CIS agreements were concluded in line with a reciprocal political will of former soviet republics, in order to simply 'follow the common path', without taking into account the actual situation.

The inability of multilateral and bilateral agreements to regulate labour migration flows and the urgent need to provide for individual legislative bases led to a gradual development of migration laws in Central Asian states. Nevertheless, this took place only at the beginning of the 21st century, almost ten years after these states had gained independence.

Taking into account the ability of a state with a long migration history to control inward and outward movements, the following questions are important in defining Central Asian states' progress in establishing control over labour migration:

- Is there an effective law on migration and other legislative framework on relevant issues?
- Is there a government body acting in a ministerial rank on issues of migration?
- Is there a migration policy, based on international law?
- Is there an elaborated and well-known procedure for entry, exit, labour migration, social benefits, social protection, tax payments and change of migrant's status?
- Is the country party to international conventions on migration issues?
- Do government bodies actively cooperate with non-governmental agencies and civil society in managing migration?

I will examine these factors separately for Central Asian states and start with Kazakhstan, the main recipient of Central Asian labour.

Kazakhstan: Destination Country of Central Asian Migrants'

According to a World Bank Report, Kazakhstan is the 9th largest migrant-receiving country in the world, and the 3rd largest destination country among former soviet republics (after Russia and Ukraine).[9] Taking into consideration that Ukraine is mainly a transit country for migrants heading to the West, Kazakhstan may be indeed considered the second largest recipient of labour migrants in the CIS and the country of first destination in Central Asia.

Statistics demonstrate that in 2007, about 6.8 million foreigners entered Kazakhstan, while only 4.9 million left.[10] With regard to migrants from other Central Asian countries, Uzbek citizens accounted for about 2.2 million persons in total of those entering Kazakhstan, with only half of them returning to Uzbekistan. About 1.5 million Kyrgyz citizens came to Kazakhstan in 2007 and only 0.6 million of them left for Kyrgyzstan. Out of 89,000 Tajiks that entered Kazakhstan, about 10,000 stayed. These calculations show that about 2 million

---

9   Migration Could Yield a 'Triple Win' For Migrants And Sending And Receiving Countries, Says World Bank Report, http://web.worldbank.org/WBSITE/EXTERNAL/NEWS/0,,contentMDK:21183567~pagePK:34370~piPK: 34424~theSitePK:4607,00.html.

10   The Statistics Agency of the Republic of Kazakhstan, www.stat.kz.

Central Asian citizens (most of which are believed to be in irregular situation) stayed in Kazakhstan, whereas the population of the country totals approximately 16 million people.

In 1997, long before responding to significant labour migration flows, Kazakhstan adopted the Law on Population Migration. The law resulted from an intention to define who can be considered a migrant and was essentially devoted to Kazakh repatriates (*oralmans*).[11] Other laws and regulations concerning migration issues, to name the most important, are the Constitution of the Republic of Kazakhstan (1995), the Law on Citizenship (1991), the Decree on Legal Status of Foreign Citizens in the Republic of Kazakhstan (1995), Rules of Entry and Stay of Foreign Citizens in the Republic of Kazakhstan and their Departure from the Republic of Kazakhstan (2000), and Conceptions of Migration Policy (1997, 2000). The adoption of this rather extensive legislative framework, which mostly occurred in the 1990s, demonstrates that the documents were not a consequence of labour force influx. Rather, they were introduced in order to add to the newly found independence and the sensitive issue of the re-establishment of national values lost during the soviet era.

The creation of the Committee for Migration in 1997 may also be regarded as one of the means used to implement the idea of re-founding national identity: the Committee's main task is implementation of immigration policy, and mainly, assistance to ethnic returnees. Among other duties of this government body that has the rank of ministry is the drafting of proposals as for quotas on labour migration. To add to the significance of this organ, the Committee analyses migration processes and fulfills financial duties related to allocations for repatriates.

With regard to the implementation of the abovementioned regulations, and starting with entry rules, Kazakhstan has a visa-free regime with all CIS countries, except Turkmenistan, and eased visa regime (although not reciprocal) for most of the highly developed Western countries, as well as for highly developed countries of South-East Asia and Oceania. As for citizens of CIS countries, most of these relations are based on a freedom of movement of persons within regional frameworks.[12] Other countries enjoy this regime due to economic considerations and an intention of Kazakh authorities to attract foreign investment.

A particular feature with regard to control over entry is the introduction of a 'migration card' in 2003. It serves as a tool for counting the number of persons entering the country and as a means of foreigners' registration at local internal

11 The return of the *oralmans* is very important for the Kazakh authorities, mostly due to the fact that in Kazakhstan, Kazakhs did not constitute the majority of the population after the dissolution of the Soviet Union. The *Oralmans'* repatriation is considered a way to increase number of Kazakhs in the country and to contribute to conservation of national values.

12 Under the 1992 Bishkek Agreement on Free Movement of citizens of CIS States and the 2005 regulation under Eurasian Economic Community (EurAsEC), with Belarus, Russia, Kazakhstan, Kyrgyzstan and Tajikistan, as member-states.

authorities. Foreigners leaving Kazakhstan must submit the cards to Kazakh border guards.

Depending on their country of origin, foreign citizens are allowed to stay for up to 90 days without registering at a local representation of the Ministry of Interior.[13] This recent increase in the number of days is linked to the fact that many Central Asian citizens entered Kazakhstan on false purposes while really focusing on finding work opportunities. In the past, five days was a very limited period for attainment of this goal, and it is argued that the increase gives irregular migrants more time and consequently allows them to regularize their status as labour migrants in Kazakhstan.[14]

The penalty for violating the allowed period of stay is a fine and deportation. The identity document of a person illegally staying in Kazakhstan is marked thus hindering further entry into the country.

In the case of foreign citizens for whom an invitation is required for obtaining a Kazakh visa, full responsibility regarding the foreigner's stay is put upon the inviting side in Kazakhstan. If the period of a foreigner's stay is violated, the host is subject to reimbursement of deportation costs to the state. While this measure is in line with tightening control over irregular migration, it is evident that it aims at increasing the number of nationals at Kazakh work places, whereas irregular migrants are again left to shadow market and to dishonest employers. Moreover, control over irregular migration in Kazakhstan is not yet developed to the point where all inviting sides are checked; many criminal groupings create firms that often become bankrupt and disappear in order to avoid prosecution.

Since late 2009 there have been various announcements in the media about the adoption of a new migration law in the spring 2010.[15] The law is supposed to introduce a sector-, and a country-based approach to selecting migrant workers, and labour migration would continue to be quota-based. Human rights activists have urged the government to revise the draft law because in its current form the migrant's right to enter the country is made dependent on having a signed contract with an employer, which limits considerably the possibility of finding legal employment and increases the number of irregular migrants.[16]

The social protection of migrants is another challenge faced by the Kazakh government: while the 1994 CIS Agreement guarantees such protection, it only concerns legal migrants. It goes without saying that irregular migrants do not receive any guarantees during their work in Kazakhstan, nor do they usually have a written contract with their employers. The question of allocations is currently the most problematic item on the agenda of regional organizations.[17]

---

13 Website of the Kazakh Ministry for Foreign Affairs, www.mfa.kz.

14 From an interview with a representative of the Committee on Migration of Kazakhstan, 20 November 2008.

15 See OSCE 2009 and Eurasianet 2009.

16 From an interview with a Human Rights Watch staff member, November 2009.

17 From an interview with a representative of the EurAsEC, November 2008.

Evidently, a receiving state would not be willing to pay allocations, such as pensions, to foreign citizens, of whom the most part is in irregular situation. While the 'social block' issues do not directly relate to control mechanisms, it derives from the abovementioned that where there is no willingness to accept the fact that migrants should be entitled to a minimum of protection, there is consequently a reluctance to acknowledge the significant number of shortcomings in control over irregular labour migration.

However, Kazakhstan warmly accepts international assistance in regulating migration issues. It hosts a regional ILO office and an IOM mission. Many regulations related to migration were introduced following advocacy and technical assistance programmes provided by these international organizations. One negative aspect is that Kazakhstan, like many other destination countries, abstains from signing main international conventions, such as ILO Convention Concerning Migration for Employment (C97), and Convention Concerning Migrations in Abusive Conditions and the Promotion of the Equality of Opportunity and Treatment of Migrant Workers (C143). There is, in addition, low participation from civil society and NGOs in the elaboration of migration policies, which might be explained by tough control over the latter by Kazakh authorities.

Why is labour migration control in Kazakhstan equivocal? First of all, despite the existence of a relatively developed legislative framework, Kazakh authorities focus more on repatriates, while fighting against irregular labour migration requires more targeted actions. For instance, due to rampant corruption within migration police, border guards, road police and even customs officers, irregular migrants on a large scale bribe those who apprehend them and continue their stay in the country.[18] Secondly, the issuance of quotas in Kazakhstan is ambivalent, as it does not take into account the high demand for inexpensive labour in the country,[19] and it remains to be seen whether the new law would be different in this regard. Thirdly, it can be argued that Kazakhstan's current migration policy is extremely client-oriented: many civil servants in government and legislative bodies have their unannounced financial interests in lucrative industries, and are, therefore, interested in maintaining the *status quo* with regard to the management of labour migration policy. Finally, as A. Zolberg states, 'control includes not only the erection of more or less restrictive barriers to free movement across state boundaries, but also a policy of permissive indifference or benign neglect...'.[20] In case of Kazakhstan, indifference is often the reason for the equivocal nature of labour migration control, with both irregular migrants and those who implement migration policy obtaining certain benefits from the situation.

---

18   The amount of bribe equals 3–4,000 tenge (around 30–40 US$). From an interview with an Uzbek irregular migrant in Kazakhstan, November 2008.

19   The official quota allowed for 16,000 to 17,000 working places in 2005, while there were allegedly about 2 million irregular migrants in Kazakhstan (this data was relevant before the recent 2008 financial crisis).

20   Zolberg 1981, 8.

Tajikistan: A Pool of Inexpensive Labour Force

Tajikistan, the country with the lowest GDP per capita among former soviet republics, sends about one million migrants abroad yearly (out of a population of 6 million).[21] Without them, the country would probably find it difficult to survive economically, because migrant remittances account for approximately one third of its GDP.[22] While in the past most Tajik migrants chose Russia as their main destination in the CIS, their number is now growing in Kazakhstan, which is closer geographically and unlike Russia does not yet witness many cases of xenophobia against migrants.

It is noteworthy that in the 1990s a civil war in Tajikistan was the main factor for emigration. When peace was restored in the late 1990s, it was lack of work opportunities that forced Tajik citizens abroad. In this regard, the adoption of the Law on Migration in late 1999 demonstrates mainly two phenomena: first, that this war-torn country has not been able to consider any legislative framework on migration before peace was established. Secondly, it makes clear that the law was used by the Tajik authorities as an incentive to legalize their citizens' willingness to go abroad in order to earn a living for those who stayed in a devastated country, thus easing social tensions. Another issue that adds to the encouragement of labour emigration from Tajikistan by authorities is drug trafficking from neighbouring Afghanistan: Tajikistan lies on main drug transit route towards the west, and enabling Tajik people with legal bases to exit the country freely was most probably a better means to maintain order in the country than to let them engage in drug-related crime.

Together with the adoption of the Law on Migration, the State Migration Service was established within the Ministry of Labour and Social Protection of the Population. Its duties mainly include analyses on migration, issuance of licences to foreigners wishing to work in Tajikistan, assistance to repatriates. This government body has been rather active regarding joint implementation of international technical assistance programmes, on a regional level. The Tajik State Migration Service was a pioneer in experimenting with the best foreign practices in labour emigration. Many of the programmes regarding assistance to prospective labour migrants in Tajikistan are currently mirrored in the Kyrgyz Republic, which demonstrates that there are some positive developments in the matter.

It is evident that the Tajik authorities are willing to encourage labour emigration as long as it provides for a very important remittances' share in the country's GDP. When it comes to control and particularly exit from the Tajik territory, regulations oblige Tajik citizens leaving the country for more than three months to inform local representation of the Ministry of Interior on their intentions. There is, however, no evidence that returning labour migrants faced problems with the Ministry of Interior due to violation of this obligation, which again adds to encouraging the

---

21   Mansoor and Quillin 2007, 5.
22   Ibid., 6.

government's labour emigration policy or, to quote A. Zolberg, the government's 'benign neglect'.[23]

Tajikistan's pioneer experience in assisting its citizens wishing to work abroad contributed to its ratification of the main ILO conventions with regard to labour migrants in 2007.[24] The Tajik government's openness to international aid also resulted in creation of sustainable non-governmental organizations that work closely with international organizations and the State Migration Service in order to better address labour migration challenges. It is likely that this close interaction often encourages Tajik officials to speak freely at regional level together with Kyrgyz colleagues on matters of advocacy towards their migrant-citizens, as Kyrgyzstan currently experiences similar processes with regard to open dialogue with civil society.

Returning to the main subject of this chapter, however, labour migration control in Tajikistan is equivocal from two points of view: first, the Tajik government currently seems to be mainly interested in migrant remittances as a means of maintaining peace in the country and easing social tensions; it has little control over the number of departing citizens and would not be able to assist labour migrants with investing their remittances in the country without international assistance. If one might consider advocacy for migrant-citizens' rights abroad as a matter of control, Tajikistan has regularly insisted on more actions from destination countries, but it lacks political instruments or trade-off proposals in order to achieve any progress in the field.[25] Secondly, migration control in Tajikistan is biased by the country's geographical situation and lack of experience in border management: its border with Afghanistan serves as a leak for irregular migrants from South Asian countries, while Tajik border management is not enough developed to allow for the immediate identification of forged documents, visas and invitations.

Kyrgyzstan: Another Pool of Labour Migrants in Central Asia

Kyrgyzstan is another economically devastated Central Asian country, with a population of 5 million people, of which around 1 million are reportedly engaged in labour migration abroad.[26] The main reason for emigration is lack of employment opportunities in the country. The country's economy is highly dependent on migrant remittances, which amount to about one fourth of Kyrgyz GDP.[27]

As in the case of Tajikistan, the adoption of the Law on External Migration by Kyrgyz authorities as late as 2000 is thought-provoking. It coincided with

---

23   Zolberg 1981, 8.

24   ILO Conventions No. 97 and No. 143.

25   Kyrgyz and Tajik PM Call for More Favourable Regime for Their Citizens Working in Other EuAsEC Countries, *Daily Developments in Central Asia*, 19 April 2007, EC Delegation to Kazakhstan, 1.

26   Mansoor and Quillin 2007, 15.

27   Ibid., 9.

the beginning of a visible labour emigration to Russia, Kazakhstan and western countries. Again, one might argue that there has been an unofficial encouragement of the process by state authorities.

The adoption of the special law on external migration led to the establishment of the abovementioned State Committee on Migration and Employment of the Kyrgyz Republic in 2000. Its main duties implied developing initiatives for migration policy, protection of Kyrgyz migrants abroad, assistance to foreign citizens in the country, and cooperation with other government bodies and international donors in the area of migration. Launched in 2009, the reform of the state administration led to new developments in this area, namely the creation of a fully-fledged ministry on migration – the Ministry on Labour, Employment and Migration. According to state officials, the transformation of the committee into a ministry is related to the global financial crisis, which despite contrary predictions has not forced Kyrgyz migrants to return home.[28] Moreover, they argued that it was high time to take into consideration the interests of Kyrgyz migrants working abroad.[29] While it is too early to evaluate the progress achieved by the Ministry in protecting Kyrgyz migrants abroad, it should be noted that there are no migration ministries in other CIS states, which gives Kyrgyzstan an opportunity to be an example in managing labour migration.

Returning to the former State Committee on Migration and Employment, it was an active player at the regional level as regards negotiation and advocacy on Kyrgyz migrants' situation in CIS destination countries, although it faced challenges domestically. According to an IOM expert, there were no interaction between government bodies dealing with migration issues; moreover, another authority, the Department of Migration Service under the Kyrgyz Ministry of Foreign Affairs, often competed with the Committee thus creating duplication of activities.[30]

There have been positive developments for the control of labour emigration from Kyrgyzstan and assistance to labour migrants: a government Regulation on Activity of Individuals and Legal Entities in the Kyrgyz Republic Dealing with Employment of Kyrgyz Citizens Abroad is regarded as a response to human trafficking by individuals or companies allegedly inviting Kyrgyz citizens to work abroad in service industries (i.e. as waiters, baby-sitters, dancers, etc.). With international assistance, the State Committee on Migration has created SOS and help-lines for prospective migrants and initiated a media campaign inviting Kyrgyz citizens to check the inviting individual's or the company's legal status at specially created centres of assistance.[31] Due to the fact that migrants, who were mistreated by an inviting side, may report these facts to the centres of assistance, the database

---

28   See also OSCE 2009.

29   Channel 5 news, 22 October 2009.

30   From an interview with an IOM expert, October 2008.

31   Mission of the International Organization for Migration in the Kyrgyz Republic, www.iom.elcat.kg.

of dishonest companies is currently being enlarged and human trafficking cases are treated with more attention.

Another intention of the State Committee on Migration was to encourage the establishment of private employment agencies following the Philippines' example.[32] However, local experts question this intention, due to the fact that prospective migrants would be required to pay for the services offered by these agencies.[33]

Coming back to questions of exit control, the Kyrgyz Republic has also maintained the tradition of registering its citizens' residence and the *de jure* obligation for citizens to inform local representations of the Ministry of Interior about their intentions to leave the country. As in the case of Tajikistan, there is no evidence that returning Kyrgyz citizens faced problems with the Ministry of Interior.

With regard to foreign citizens entering Kyrgyzstan, there is a visa-free regime with all CIS states, except Turkmenistan, and an eased visa regime for citizens of highly developed countries.[34] These entry rules result from the country's efforts to attract foreign investment, and, in case of a visa-free regime with CIS states – from an intention to maintain soviet era legacies of free movement.

The eased control over entry, however, is challenging for the country. The increase in number of foreign citizens is visible, and one might suggest that most of them are in irregular situation. The government's actions regarding the fight against illegal immigration to Kyrgyzstan is biased by the high level of corruption among law-enforcement agents, a lack of detention facilities for apprehended illegal migrants (many are freed due to lack of financial means at temporary facilities), and the low level of penalties and sanctions towards foreigners.

Labour migration control in Kyrgyzstan is therefore ambivalent: while many efforts are made by the government to assist Kyrgyz labour migrants abroad, to provide them with opportunities of vocational training and legal advice,[35] the country seems to be mainly interested in migrant remittances and ways to avoid social discontent. For instance, due to the recent financial crisis there is a fear among state officials that migrant remittances will decrease and thus make it impossible to plan many development projects in the country.[36] On the other hand, a representative of the former State Committee on Migration and Employment of the Kyrgyz Republic once declared that the objective of the Committee (i.e. of the Kyrgyz Republic) had been changed to contain returning labour migrants

---

32   From an interview with an IOM expert, October 2008.

33   From an interview with an OSCE representative in Bishkek, December 2008.

34   Website of the Kyrgyz Ministry for Foreign Affairs, www.mfa.kg.

35   From an interview with a representative of the State Committee on Migration and Employment of the Kyrgyz Republic, December 2008.

36   From an interview with a representative of Ministry of Economic Development of the Kyrgyz Republic, October 2008.

within the country.[37] This is the example of an equivocal policy, as it remains to be seen how the state intends to employ this important number of returning nationals. The creation of the Ministry on Migration in late 2009 was likely to show the government's determination to take a more efficient control over the issue, which remains to be seen. Moreover, Kyrgyzstan lacks political instruments at the regional level, and sometimes has to cede to more powerful regional actors in exchange of trade-offs with regard to its migrants.[38] The Kyrgyz government is also likely to be inactive in the short-term towards increasing number of irregular foreigners on its territory, as many law-enforcement agents have financial interest in obtaining bribes from the latter.

Uzbekistan: The Denying Labour Migrants Sender

There are reportedly 2 million Uzbek migrants working outside the country (out of 25 million citizens).[39] Approximately, 60% of Uzbek labour migrants head to Russia, and 25% to Kazakhstan.[40] The initial large-scale outward migration in Uzbekistan started in the late 1990s, like in Tajikistan and Kyrgyzstan, although the country has not yet adopted any law on migration. This might be mainly explained by two phenomena: first, Uzbek authorities who strive in vain to ascertain the country's leading role in Central Asia, and find it difficult to acknowledge its poor economic situation; secondly, the country's authoritarian regime has on several occasions been threatened by religious extremists, and therefore, Uzbekistan has repeatedly limited its citizens' exit from the country.

While there is a government body dealing with migration issues – the Agency for External Labour Migration Affairs under the Ministry of Labour and Social Protection, it only deals with *legal* labour migration, without considering the illegal one. The Agency operates in two directions: it negotiates labour migration agreements with foreign countries and examines individual labour contracts between a foreign employer and an Uzbek citizen before a final decision is taken by the Minister on whether the person may leave the country. It also issues regulations on labour migration abroad and licences to foreigners wishing to work in Uzbekistan. In order to question the efficiency of this Agency's work, the example of labour immigration in Uzbekistan is revealing: according to an Uzbek

---

37   From an interview with a representative of the State Committee on Migration and Employment of the Kyrgyz Republic, October 2008.

38   During the Soviet era, many Soviet republics owned resorts at a Kyrgyz lake Issyk-Kul. It has been reported by a Russian media that recently Kyrgyzstan agreed to cede to Kazakhstan with regard to 50-year rent of four such resorts, in exchange of Kazakhstan's more favourable attitude towards Kyrgyz migrants. See *Nezavisimaya Gazeta*, 18 April 2008.

39   Uzbekistan to Send Labour Migrants to New Zeeland (in Russian), 11 December 2008, http://news.trend.az/index.shtml?show=news&newsid=1368505&lang=RU.

40   Ibid.

NGO, no work permit was issued to foreign citizens since this country became independent.[41]

Naturally, with regard to exit control, leaving citizens are free to leave the country and do not in general report on the reasons of their exit, although during security threats[42] the border with Kazakhstan and Kyrgyzstan was closed on several occasions. Moreover, when it comes to traveling to countries with which Uzbekistan has a visa regime, an exit permit must be obtained from the authorities, reminiscent of the tough controls over movements outside the Union during the Soviet era.

Uzbek authorities have not been cooperative with international organizations in the field of migration, nor have they signed the most important international conventions on migration issues. It is evident that there is no participation of civil society in elaboration of migration policy, due to the sole fact that even such influential international NGOs, such as the Human Rights Watch, are forbidden in the country. Probably, one of the explanations for this policy of denial are Uzbekistan's constant foreign policy shifts from the CIS to Western countries and *vice versa:* Uzbekistan has developed very close ties with the US government in security and the fight against terrorism since it gained independence; in 2005 the Andijan massacre took place in the country, with allegedly a few thousand people killed for their ties to religious extremists; the international community, except for CIS countries, and mainly, Russia, all condemned it. It led to Uzbekistan's 'return' to the CIS activities in 2005–2008, which might explain the fact that in 2007 the country signed a labour migration agreement with the Russian Federation. Recent suspension of Uzbekistan's membership in the EurAsEC, an 'ineffective organization'[43] (according to the president), however, hindered many regional initiatives within this regional organization, and again turned the country towards the West. It is unclear, though, whether recent 2008 activities of the Agency for External Labour Migration Affairs with regard to sending Uzbek migrant-apprentices to Malaysia, Japan, and United Arab Emirates, account for the country's foreign policy shifts.

As for control over entry in Uzbekistan, there is a visa-free regime with some of CIS countries, while visas have repeatedly been introduced for Kyrgyz and Tajik citizens.[44] Visa regimes within highly developed countries are not eased, unlike in Kyrgyzstan and Tajikistan, and mainly reflect foreign policy priorities at a certain period of time.

Very strict rules apply in Uzbekistan to illegal entry and lack of registration at the Ministry of Interior: a foreigner's passport is stamped and the person is

41　From an interview with a representative of an Uzbek NGO, September 2008.

42　Uzbekistan introduced a visa regime with these countries in 2003–2004 due to concerns on religious extremists entering the country from Kyrgyz and Kazakh neighbouring regions.

43　Uzbekistan Suspends EurAsEC Membership, Moscow Unruffled, November 2008, http://en.rian.ru/world/20081112/118264022.html.

44　Website of the Turkmen Ministry for Foreign Affairs, www.mfa.tm.

deported immediately (with a fine from two to 100 minimum wages, or from one to three years of imprisonment). The same applies for an Uzbek citizen, who fails to ensure the timely departure of a foreign visitor invited to Uzbekistan: the host faces a fine, corrective labour measures or imprisonment.

The abovementioned developments in Uzbekistan's labour migration policy create an image of a controlling state, although control is mainly exercised on paper and with regard to legal labour migrants. It is likely that bureaucratic procedures introduced by the state with regard to legal emigration result in high numbers of irregular labour migrants, whom Uzbek authorities found difficult to acknowledge in order not to accept its weak position in the region. On the contrary, the country's tough control over foreigners' stay (mainly due to security concerns) is impressive and reflects an intense focus on the defense of national interests.

Attempts to Define Labour Migration Control in Central Asia

While considering rules on entry and exit as direct tools of migration control, the typology of rules proposed by M. Weiner is also helpful in trying to define labour migration control in this region.[45] Based on his arguments, Central Asian states have 'unwanted entry rules', e.g. they are unwilling or unable to prevent illegal entry. The result is that the irregular migrants are often unprotected and harassed by legal authorities. As for exit rules, Central Asian countries, and mainly the sending ones – Kyrgyzstan and Tajikistan (with slight derivation of Uzbekistan, which allegedly tends to 'prohibition exit rules') – are characterized by *promotional exit rules*. Citing Weiner again and considering especially Kyrgyz and Tajik governments, the latter 'encourage citizens to seek employment abroad in order to *relieve unemployment or to increase remittances*. They create vocational opportunities for a prospective migrant in order to enhance the latter's chance of finding work opportunities abroad.' As it may be seen from the abovementioned country cases, migration control claims with regard to entry and exit in Central Asian countries have more or less defined features.

Taking into account J.F. Hollifield's definition that 'the more liberal and democratic a society is, the greater the likelihood that migration control will be an issue, and that there will be some level of 'unwanted migration',[46] one might come to think that migration control is rather an issue in Kazakhstan, particularly with regard to irregular migration; as well as in Kyrgyzstan and Tajikistan, essentially when it concerns labour migrants – citizens of these countries. While the international community does not consider these three countries purely liberal and democratic, comparing their regime with the Uzbek one, where migration issues have been mostly ignored, one undoubtedly realizes that Kazakhstan, Kyrgyzstan and Tajikistan are less authoritarian when it concerns labour migrants.

---

45   Weiner 1985, 445.
46   Hollifield 2008, 190.

One therefore might conclude that in general labour migration control claims in Central Asia are characterized by unwanted entry rules and promotional exit rules (the latter with exception of Kazakhstan – destination country), whereas declared migration policies are often ambiguous: although the governments elaborate rather extensive legislative mechanisms (Kyrgyz, Tajik and Kazakh cases), control over implementation of the regulations and laws is hindered in many ways (e.g. by rampant corruption). Uzbekistan's policy of denial is, in this regard, the most equivocal: while creating many bureaucratic procedures for its migrant-citizens in order to seemingly control their exit for purposes of legal labour emigration (prohibition exit rules), the government indirectly encourages Uzbek citizens to illegal migration, while not taking actions with regard to their protection abroad.

All in all, it is noteworthy, that Central Asia is a young region, where migration processes emerged less than two decennia ago. Its migration dynamics have not yet stabilized and they are most likely to be influenced by political and socio-economic factors, such as the recent global financial crisis. Moreover, one should bear in mind that with regard to international migration studies, where mostly *liberal* states are explored, Central Asia has to be approached differently, as its democratization processes are at their earliest stages. Shifts in labour migration control in Central Asian states, are therefore likely to happen often, until the overall stabilization of the region occurs.

Bibliography

Brettell, C.B. and Hollifield, J.F. (eds) 2008. *Migration Theory: Talking Across Disciplines*. New York and London: Routledge.

Castles, S. and Miller, M.J. 2003. *The Age of Migration: International Population Movements in the Modern World*, Third Edition. New York and London: Guilford Press.

Cornelius, W., Martin, P. and Hollifield, J.F. 2003. *Controlling Immigration: A Global Perspective*, Second Edition. Stanford, CA: Stanford University Press.

Eurasianet, *Watchdog Group Calls on Astana to Enhance the Rights of Migrant Workers*, available online at: http://www.eurasianet.org/departments/insight/ articles/eav120209.shtml.

Hollifield, J.F. 1998. Migration, Trade and the Nation–State: The Myth of Globalization, *UCLA Journal of International Law and Foreign Affairs* 3(2), 596.

Hollifield. J.F. 2008. The Politics of International Migration, How Can We 'Bring the State Back In'?, in *Migration Theory: Talking Across Disciplines*, edited by C.B. Bretell and J.F. Hollifield. New York: Routledge.

ICMPD. 2005. *Re-direction of the Budapest Process towards the CIS Region (Third Meeting Final Conclusions)*, Almaty, Kazakhstan, 19–20 May.

IOM. 2006. *Migration Perspectives: Eastern Europe and Central Asia*.

IOM. 2007. *Migration Initiatives – 2007*, 69–72.

IOM in Eastern Europe and Central Asia, 2004–2007.

Mansoor, A.M. 2007. *Migration and Remittances: Eastern Europe and the Former Soviet Union*, Washington DC: World Bank.

Mansoor, A.M. and Quillin, B. 2007. *Migration and Remittances: Eastern Europe and the Former Soviet Union*. Washington DC: World Bank. Available online at: http://siteresources.worldbank.org/ INTECA/Resources/257896-1167856389505/Migration_FullReport.pdf.

Massey, D.S., Arango, J., Hugo, G. and Taylor, J.E. 1993. Theories of International Migration: A Review and Appraisal, *Population and Development Review*, 19.

Nezavisimaya Gazeta. 2008. Nazarbayev Promised to Support Bakiev, 18 April (in Russian), available online at: http://www.ng.ru/cis/2008-04-18/9_nazarbaev. html.

OSCE. 2006. *Handbook on Establishing Effective Migration Policies in Countries of Origin and Destination*.

OSCE. 2009. *Impact of the Global Financial Crisis on Labour Migration From Kyrgyzstan to Russia: Qualitative Overview and Quantitative Survey*, available online at http://www.osce.org/bishkek/item_1_41548.html.

OSCE. 2009. *Kazakhstan's New Migration Law Discussed at Workshop in Astana*, available online at: http://www.osce.org/astana/item_1_41050.html.

OSCE/ICMPD. 2006. *Workshop on Labour Migration in Central Asia (Consolidated Summary)*, Almaty, Kazakhstan, 31 January–1 February.

Sadovskaya, E. 2001. *Nezakonnaya migraziya v Kazakhstane (Illegal Migration in Kazakhstan)*, available online at: www.demoscope.ru/center/fmcenter/ sadovsk.html.

Sadovskaya, E. 2006. Labor Migration in Regional Context: Kazakhstan as Centre of Central Asian Migration System, *Central Asia's Affairs*, 3, Kazakhstan Institute for Strategic Studies, available online at www.kisi.kz.

Weiner. M. 1985. On International Migration and International Relations. *Population and Development Review*, 11(3).

Zolberg, A.R. 1981. International Migration in Political Perspective, in *Global Trends in Migration: Theory and Research on International Population Movements*, edited by M.M. Kritz et al. New York: Center for Migration Studies.

Chapter 14

Reflections on Immigration Controls and Free Movement in Europe

Didier Bigo

Summary

Effective control of cross-border practices in market-economy regimes whose borders have to remain open to goods, capital and services if those regimes are to remain viable, is nearly impossible. The article shows the tensions between a legal system predicated on openness and a groundswell of security-driven rhetoric justifying coercive and ostracizing practices against foreigners.

The Principle of Free Movement: A Core Value of the European Union

From the outset, the crucial role of the free movement of goods, capital, information and services in what is now the European Union was enshrined in the Treaty of Rome. Free movement of services supposes free movement of labour. As a result of the important legal changes introduced by the Treaty on the Single European Act of 1992, which set out to make Europe something more than a common market, and in keeping with the constant case-law of the European Courts on Article 14, the concept of free movement was explicitly defined as free movement of persons. They were defined as all individuals, living on the territory of the European Union, i.e. citizens of the Member States of the Union and, in addition, all third-country nationals residing legally within Europe's borders.[1]

This conception of free movement of persons has obliged to distinguish between internal and external European Union borders, i.e. borders between European Union countries and borders that are at once national and Union borders. The 1985 Schengen Agreement and its implementation treaty of 1990, when they came into force in 1995, officially instituted this distinction by providing for controls to be lifted at internal borders within the Union and concomitantly reinforced at the Union's external borders.[2] However, this simple idea is not always reflected in practice. And although we are seeing the advent of a form of 'policing at a distance' mechanisms aimed at blocking foreigners upstream before they leave their own

---

1   Guild and Niessen 1996.
2   Bigo and Guild 2003; Hreblay 1994; Pauly 1994.

countries, tracking systems that pick up the traces left by people moving from one country to another, and even, in some countries, moves towards expulsion and forced return involving cooperation at inter-State level with countries of transit and origin, there has been no significant dip in cross-border flows of persons.

The proliferation of laws on immigration has given rise to enormous legislative efforts, some virulent debates, a degree of legal uncertainty as to the law applicable to the facts in a given case, and procedural ambiguities that give police considerable latitude, but it has not changed the demographic and economic realities.[3] There have doubtless been serious consequences for the legal status of individuals living on the territory, but it should be clearly stated that the legal measures and public policies adopted by politicians have not had the intended impact. The political will to curb immigration, buoyed up as it has been by popular sentiment, has had next to no impact in terms of effective control of cross-border practices in market–economy regimes whose borders have to remain open to goods, capital and services if those regimes are to remain viable.[4]

Free Movement of Persons Called into Question?

The speeches of the French Minister of immigration, integration and identity Brice Hortefeux and of his successor Eric Besson, stating the government's will and ability to effectively send home all illegal migrants and to prevent the entry of new ones, seemed to call into question the very principle of free movement of persons to share with our neighbours and the world, and to restrict its understanding to a 'European only' free movement, even if it is already a critic of the previous 'zero immigration' argument. And many NGOs have reacted strongly to this new wave of populist argument played out in France, Italy, Austria, but, in any case, beyond the modulations of discourses by politicians, it is central to understand that this symbolic politics calling for opening or closure, and playing always with a very narrow construction of what is a European cultural identity, has de facto no effect on the reality of illegal entries and re-entries into the territory. There is a veritable abyss between the politicians' willingness to control more or less tightly borders by discourses and law making, and the effective practices of bordering the EU, as demonstrated by the Eurostat and Frontex statistics on passages across the Union's borders.[5] The swiftness with which the government attempts to send people home gives rise to arbitrary treatment of certain individuals but does nothing to solve the problem. Detention and expulsion of foreigners are not effective solutions and raise issues of legitimacy and fundamental rights.[6] Immigration policy based on policing is a massive failure, albeit not yet recognized as such, and as far as possible

---

3   Bigo 1996.

4   Anderson and O'Dowd 1999; Andreas and Snyder 2000; Bigo 2004; Castles 2002; Mohar and Alcarz 2000.

5   Statistics on border crossings in Europe. Eurostat. Frontex.

6   Kobelinsky and Makaremi 2008.

this failure is being kept under wraps. This approach is the clumsy application to a non-Federal entity of an American policy that, even in its own context, is not particularly effective.

As pointed out by several reports to the European Parliament and Commission, Member States' intention to go no further along the path to 'communitarization' than the institution of police measures relating to entry at borders, stays of less than three months, visas, document fraud and possibly expulsions, creates an almost farcical situation. Checks are rigorously applied in some places such as airports where it is easy to institute them, but are totally lacking along thousands of kilometres of land or sea borders which cannot be policed except at a prohibitively high cost.[7]

It is vital to have a long-term economic and social policy on migration that provides for decent conditions of family unification, equal wages and pension rights, and cross-border movements facilitated by international agreements. Free movement of persons definitely entails problems in terms of fraud, but a prohibitionist policy creates more problems than it solves inasmuch as it is does not prevent fraud but causes it to become professionalized. This type of policy always costs the tax-payer more than alternative approaches and has a highly deleterious effect on the way foreigners are treated. There is therefore a knock-on effect in terms of foreign and even security policy. But the package of proposals currently in the pipeline turns its back on the results of research and perpetuates belief in the dogma of a border that is open but totally controlled (smart border) and would allow each State to act more or less as it sees fit.

Pact on Immigration

The Pact on Immigration as put forward by the French presidency[8] and adopted in 2008 aimed at remedying some of these aberrations by calling for a longer-term policy. It partially dissociates itself from the policing and security vision, or perhaps it would be more accurate to say that it presents that vision as a necessary step on the way to a further goal in the form of a compromise between the various Member States on expulsion rationales and their impact on human rights and the Union's image abroad. But even if it is reinterpreted in that light, the Pact is far from being a solution. It again aims to divest the Commission of its powers at a time when it might finally be able to use them, and seeks to give the Council and Member States the means to undermine the principles of free movement and move towards 'Eurosurveillance', in other words systematic control of foreigners entering the territory of the Union and even control of EU citizens within the Union's borders, in the name of the fight against terrorism and illegal immigration.

---

7   Centre for European Policy Studies (CEPS).

8   Adopted by the Council of the European Union, 24 September 2008, see http://register.consilium.europa.eu/pdf/en/08/st13/st13440.en08.pdf (visited on 10 August 2009).

In particular, the system seeks to prevent illegal immigration arising as a result of people overstaying legally obtained three-month tourist visas. At the same time, the borders would be opened up to a larger number of (qualified) people entering through legal immigration channels.[9]

A tiny group within the European Commission in charge of technical systems is playing into the hands of a handful of Members States that wish to call into question the free movement of persons and propose in its place, a speedy movement of persons under high surveillance with no physical obstacles (as in the special access corridors in airports for those who have accepted before hand to give all their personal data and to submit themselves to multiple biometric identifiers) that would then create the impression that there is still freedom, because of that speed. There is a tendency to align the Union's policy on Australian and American practices despite the fact that they have been almost unanimously criticized by jurists and international courts, at risk of setting up extremely expensive systems that will be condemned by national and European courts as soon as they come into effect.

This trend is extremely worrying, as the previous European Union regime drew its very strength and legitimacy from the promotion of the values of free movement of persons that other regional groups of States, including the NAFTA made up of the United States, Canada and Mexico, had restricted to the utmost. By making free movement a key value in its relations with neighbouring countries and promising that they too will be able to share in these great freedoms of movement in the future even if they do not join the Union's political institutions, the European Union has raised hopes beyond its borders. However, if it follows the example of

---

9   On 13 February 2008, the European Commission presented a 'border package' containing three communications on EU external border management. Two of these documents, namely the papers on assessment and future development of Frontex – European Commission (2008a). Report on the evaluation and future development of the FRONTEX Agency.

Brussels, COM(2008) 67 final – and on the creation of a European border surveillance system (Eurosur) – European Commission, Communication on examining the creation of a European border surveillance system, COM(2008) 68 final – propose major developments as regards the role of the Frontex agency and the future direction of EU integrated border management (IBM). The assessment of Frontex carried out by the Commission's services is timely. Since the start of its operational phase in 2005, the agency has expanded its activities considerably in all its fields of competence, and EC subsidies to its budget more than tripled over the period from 2006 to 2008. However, the assessment does not offer any analysis of the compliance of Frontex with the fundamental values of the EU. It therefore seems important to recall that Frontex is a Community agency belonging to the first pillar. As such, it must not only respect fundamental European values in its activities but also promote them, particularly in an area that impacts on essential questions linked to migration and free movement. Note by Julien Jeandeboz for the European Parliament's LIBE Committee. http://www.statewatch.org/news/2008/aug/pe408295_en1.pdf, http://www.libertysecurity.org/auteur284.html.

the other regional blocs which focus almost exclusively on the security dimension, it will sow the seeds of discontent and transform its neighbours into potential enemies. Coercive measures ostensibly justified by security concerns are often the first to foment insecurity and the very violence they purport to combat. It is therefore necessary to think hard before launching into a technological regime that primarily benefits the security industry and does not necessarily help the citizens of the Union.

Free Movement of Persons: The End of a European Specificity?

This openness policy advocated by the Commission, particularly in those units linked to the first pillar, emphasizes the role of borders as meeting points rather than as barriers. It is worth noting that in their public communications, when seeking to differentiate Europe from George Bush's America and its ultimatum in the war against terrorism, both the Commission and the Council refer to free movement of persons and extol the Union's values. However, these statements have not prevented them from adopting projects within the third pillar that will 'normalize' the Union as part of a transatlantic security area.

For the time being, Eurosur and the European Entry-Exit system are still under consideration. They have not yet been accepted and a keen struggle is going on around them. The European Commission and Parliament take the view that the principle of free movement of persons is not just empty rhetoric that could be disavowed in the name of the fight against illegal migration. According to their arguments, which are based on law and the interpretations of the courts, the post-Amsterdam European governance system has so far constrained governments to abide by their previous undertakings. In so doing it has prevented certain powerful States from reneging on their European and international commitments notwithstanding promises by their governments to close borders, better control illegal immigration by all possible means, challenge family unification, put an end to the 'asylum-seeker scandal' and, more generally, protect their citizens from 'foreigners'. On the other side of the argument, Member States and the Council are seeking to free themselves from what they perceive as the trammels created by the lobby of fundamental rights lawyers and pro-Federalists who, they claim, have not grasped the significance of the state of emergency Europe faces and of popular calls for protection.

Focus on State Security

In earlier deliberations on the European concept of Integrated Border Management, the Council stated unequivocally that '[b]order management is a security function in which all Member States have a common interest that stems from the Schengen arrangement. First and foremost, border management is an area of policing, where security interests have to be met while fully recognizing the commitments in the field of international protection and human rights'.[10] Only the last part of the sentence pays lip service to human rights, while the first part focuses on operational measures. This attempt by several governments to whitewash their real intentions is not merely a symptom of the post-11 September security syndrome.[11] It is a manifestation of the populism or 'government xenophobia' that has affected many political parties, including ones on the left, and has made huge inroads into the tabloid press distributed by a handful of major international press groups. It has flourished by taking advantage of human-interest stories featuring crimes perpetrated by foreigners, illegal entry of foreigners into the country, their plight and their perceived role as scroungers taking advantage of the bounty of a welfare state to which they have made no contribution.[12] Following a sort of watered down McCarthyite logic, minority parties outside national parliaments – or in some cases even within coalitions – have attacked governments for their inability to resolve the problem of illegal immigration and stem the flow of foreigners into the country or the naturalization of their children. Some have even advocated procedures that would 'clarify' (i.e. screen for) allegiance based on identity, claiming that a citizen's bond with his country has a quasi-sacred quality that goes beyond territorial links and cultural integration.

The Self and the Other

There is scarcely a country in Europe – be it Austria, Denmark, the Netherlands, France, the United Kingdom, Hungary or Bulgaria – that, over the past 15 years, has not experienced this temptation to indulge in the rhetoric of rejection of the Other in the name of protection of the Self. The focus may be on the State's national security interests, on economic growth supposedly threatened by foreigners' cheating the system, or on the threatened identities of majorities under the impression that they are becoming minorities in their own countries and alarmed by the eclipse of their own values as central and quasi-monopolistic values in the society in question.[13]

A host of individual voices pointing to specific dangers and linking them to the arrival of foreigners or their presence in the country link up to form a network and refer to one another as portents of an overarching truth. The word 'immigrant', which may refer to 'others' already in the country and those entering it, has generally been ethnicized and 'racialized' by association with the idea of the non-Community immigrant or third country national. The concept of a 'third' country almost invariably conjures up in the imagination images of the poorer countries of the South and almost never of countries like the US, Japan or Australia. The immigrant of the popular imagination, who comes from the South and does

10   Council of the European Union 2006a, 3.
11   Bigo, Bonelli and Deltombes 2008; Bigo and Tsoukala 2008.
12   Valluy 2008.
13   Appadurai 1998.

not have sufficient resources to be a good consumer, has become the scapegoat for many of society's ills. He is held responsible for organized crime and trafficking in drugs.

We have tried to show in detail how transfers of legitimacy may operate, semantically and organically, between instruments used in the fight against terror and organized crime as well as against drugs, hooliganism, money-laundering, trafficking in goods, works of art and money, trafficking in persons, petty transfrontier crime, delinquency and unruly behaviour in the inner cities, protests accompanied by violence and hate rhetoric, or even computer piracy, the use of encrypted software on the internet and access to certain sites. For these transfers to operate (who would not favour the arrest of dangerous terrorists?), all it takes is generally for the communications of public or private security agencies to connect up these phenomena (techniques of enquiry developed to combat terrorism or organized crime will also be used against a person using a prohibited software programme) and focus on individuals or 'target groups' whose profile suggests that they may move from harmless to more dangerous categories.

Insecurity Continuum

At European level, emphasis is placed on the fact that the acts in question take place across at least one State border. We have referred to this as an insecurity continuum, whose focus is often the migrant and which sets out to feed the impression that we are threatened by insecurity on a world scale in which crime, war and political violence are inextricably bound up and force the police, the army and the intelligence services to work together both at national level and internationally.[14] Anastassia Tsoukala and Alessandro dal Lago have also demonstrated how this insecurity continuum is propagated in the media and how it is implicitly echoed even by pro-migrant communications.[15]

The European Players of Control Policies

It is tempting to ascribe these opposing tendencies to specific groups according to their ideological colouring (populist right, pro-open-borders left) or institutional affiliations, with some Members States and the Council taking a pro-sovereignty stance while the Commission advocates an open policy and the European Parliament and the courts (the Court of Justice of the European Communities and the European Court of Human Rights) position themselves as guardians of the rule of law and free movement. However, although the empirical studies carried out over the past few years do not fundamentally call these assumptions into question, they nevertheless reveal a much more complex picture. In many cases, past outcomes

---

14   Bigo 2002; Boswell 2007.
15   Dal Lago 1999; Tsoukala 1999.

of struggles between these different groups, including some compromises, have not been the fruit of in-depth discussions on European migration policy. On the contrary, almost all these groups have avoided addressing the subject in all its ramifications and have deeply sectorized the debate.

'Three-month' Policy, Myopia on Migration

For many years, in their public statements, policy-makers at national and European level responsible for police and border issues have focused almost exclusively on illegal border crossings, people smugglers and all the consequences of the 'three-month' policy. The matter of people entering legally and outstaying tourist visas seemed too complex to mobilize opinion, and would not always have drawn attention to the population groups who were the primary targets...even though experts were fully aware that those people represented almost 75% of so called unlawful migration flows. Those responsible for asylum matters on the other hand preferred to focus on the idea of fraud and 'asylum shopping' instead of discussing contemporary conditions of persecution and the status of camps. And their counterparts in charge of criminal justice policy have given the media their head when it came to reporting on insecurity in the inner cities and the correlation between crime and foreigners, despite the fact that overall levels of homicide and robbery have dropped and that, when it comes to violence, criminological studies have shown that we should be more afraid of our spouses or ex-spouses than of foreigners.

Particularly in the early days, in order to justify their role, the European agencies often tended to overstate the cross border dimension of crime and talk about international drug or organized crime rings on a world scale. However, arrest patterns have rather tended to indicate the presence of local pools of criminals circulating within a 50-mile radius but crossing for example the borders between France, Belgium, the Netherlands and Luxembourg.

Police-driven Approach

Heads of State have often acknowledged that migration policy is almost exclusively the preserve of their home affairs and justice ministries. The labour, industry and trade ministries have remained on the periphery while security and identity issues and, more recently, integration from an assimilationist standpoint, have remained at the heart of the debate. The justice and home affairs ministries, either at home or collectively within the Council or particular groups (Schengen in its early days, now Prum) see themselves as 'laboratories': in practice, they or the officials they have seconded to the Directorate-General (DG) for Home Affairs, which subsequently became the DG for Justice and Home Affairs and is now the DG for Justice, Freedom and Security, will always favour a police-driven approach to activities linked to free movement and crossing of borders. This approach supposes a degree of respect for individual rights but where compromises are necessary, it will always favour efficient policing over other considerations.

Often, within the different directorates, officials' allegiances to their origins give rise to differences of sensibility when it comes to the degree of latitude police forces should be allowed. Within Europol, the point of view of those police forces who support a strict 'criminal investigation' approach, in which the information gathered is validated by magistrates and which consequently allows for a high degree of trust between the various stakeholders, has been undermined by those who seek to maximize proactive intelligence gathering, even where the information is of doubtful origin and unconfirmed, on the grounds that it may help when it comes to suspects or groups of people whose profiles are similar to those of others who have committed crimes, even if there is no evidence that they are guilty of criminal conduct.

Faith in the ability to detect 'high-risk' individuals using technological means and profiling techniques based on expert systems combining human police knowledge and psycho-sociological criteria, or GPS systems built into mass screening software, has led to a merging of intelligence and prevention concerns with the traditional police concerns of investigating crime and punishing the guilty. The fact that the current Director of Europol and his predecessor are both Germans has probably heightened this trend. Both were influenced by their experiences at the German Federal Criminal Police Office, which has limited operational powers but has been able to gain recognition by developing this type of expertise.

Collection of data on individuals who cross borders or on foreigners with criminal records has been considered a priority since 1996. The proposal to harmonize criminal law at European level (*corpus juris*) and create a European prosecution service has been dropped in favour of a more intergovernmental vision of 'mutual trust in each other's rules' rather than harmonization of categories. The upshot of this will be a Eurojust that will fall far short of a real European justice system and will improve the prosecution's procedural options without any corresponding Europeanization of the right to defence. As a result, the justice and freedom panels of the triptych will remain sketches, while the security panel has come to focus more and more on an investigative, forward-looking vision embracing surveillance of the movements of foreigners who enter the European Union and are liable to remain there illegally, and even of their children born in an EU country, where they have retained their parents' faith or continued to identify with it.[16]

Anti-terrorist Measures

It would therefore be inaccurate to refer to 11 September 2001 as *the* critical juncture. Moves to step up of security around immigration and the association of immigration with terrorism go back considerably further than that. However,

---

16 Bigo et al. 2007.

the US decision of 13 September to give the President powers of emergency plainly sped up procedures in Europe and was grist to the mill of all those who were already calling for a proactive approach based on prevention, technological intelligence gathering and more intrusive and comprehensive surveillance.

The list of antiterrorist measures that have an impact on migration flows is impressive. The fight against terrorism has clearly served as a justification for strengthening control mechanisms whose efficacy in combating clandestine organizations is far from proven but which 'help' the police in their surveillance and control of foreigners living in the Union. However, it should be pointed out that communications specific to migration policy or asylum have not necessarily used the argument of terrorism per se. It has never been said in so many words that migrants and their children or people who profess the Moslem religion were potential terrorists. Rather, at national and European level, the ploy has been a stepped up call for allegiance on the part of these groups, requiring of them that they shout from the rooftops their rejection of the terrorism of Al Qaeda.

Several governments have tried to mobilize criminology and political sciences to help them distinguish between good and bad Islamists (the latter are often called Salafists, although analyses of the way perpetrators of terrorist attacks in Europe do not reveal any serious correlation between any specific tendency within political Islam and recourse to violence). These governments have vigorously condemned certain imams for terrorism apologia, giving many Muslims the impression that profession of their faith had become a suspicious sign and causing defenders of fundamental rights to fear for freedom of opinion. The integration tests policy has not helped to create an image of openness, particularly where it has been accompanied by a visa policy increasingly linked to biometric identification technologies.

Fortress Europe ...

Many analysts have spoken about Fortress Europe, an electronic walls policy, a tendency to cling to a white nationalist identity tending towards racism, a war on immigrants viewed as a negligible human surplus that can be thrown out if the needs of the economy so require, or a militarization of the European borders via the States of the southern Mediterranean and the support operations of the Frontex agency. Some localized events like those in Lampedusa, Ceuta and Melilla show that at times national political games and European support mechanisms come into play that unfortunately reinforce the tendency towards coercion disproportionate to the circumstances, highly reminiscent of the old colonial practice of deterrence by group punishment with no concern for individual cases.

... Within the Rule of Law

At the same time, we have seen massive protest movements against this type of practice. Governments have pulled back from their initial projects for fear of condemnation. International obligations of non-refoulement and the prohibition on mass expulsions have, on the whole, been complied with. The 'exceptionalist' rhetoric used to justify coercive actions by intelligence services and military special forces, so in vogue in the United States, has been largely contained. There has been no resort to policies prohibiting ships from landing like the one applied by the US to Haitians and Australia to Indonesia.

Still more importantly for the future, in a new institutional structure in which the immense majority of governments recognize the role of the courts and the importance of the European Human Rights Convention, there are number of factors that may change the balance of power and limit the impact of the rejectionist populism vehicled by certain press groups and its instrumentalization by politicians or the European institutions and agencies. Among these factors are the dismantling of the pillar systems despite the fact that the new restrictions concerning police and national security matters will remain in place, the extension of the powers and obligations of the European Parliament to areas where it previously had no role, the growing role of the European data-protection controller and its links with national data-protection offices, and the role of the Agency for Fundamental Rights and even that of mediators.

The complexity of the mechanisms, which cannot be reduced to a simple opposition between two sides, means that we should beware of hasty conclusions. The opening up of Europe was always ambiguous, even among its advocates in the 1950s (with their idea of 'European preference'), and, despite efforts after the fact to ensure that the status of European citizens does not become too disparate, the failure of a positive concept of European citizenship applicable to all those living on the territory was doubtless a key moment. The development of sectoral policies within the so-called 'pillars' has undoubtedly had an even more negative impact on migration policies and has been one reason for their gradual shift towards the security and crime-fighting vision. Other negative factors include the mounting climate of insecurity worldwide, and the gradual erosion of State power, including the monopoly on even large-scale forms of violence.

Tension between Legal System and Security Driven Rhetoric

Moreover, European (in)security professionals, be they European agencies, informal networks and their national affiliates, or private groups taking part in police work or providing police forces with technologies, have played on widespread fears and threats to justify a vision of Europe, but often one that is not compatible with free movement. They have also constituted powerful and convergent networks of interests, despite internal disputes as to the threats that need to be combated on a priority basis, and it would not be an exaggeration to speak of these (in)security professionals as a 'field of forces'.

At the same time, other sectors have been active in resisting these trends, opposing them by legal means, for example by mobilizing social and political pressures among foreigners, their children or groups that support them as in the case of the demonstrations by the '*sans papier*', by setting constitutional mechanisms in motion, and by tapping into people's desire for a richer political life and a smaller democratic deficit at European level and more binding obligations on national governments in terms of the rule of law and respect for international treaties and fundamental rights.

At the same time, the process of affirming the rights and guarantees to which foreigners are entitled, the reform-treaty process, and the increase in avenues of appeal all help to contain national political dynamics of rejection and often impose minimum standards and good practices. In the current context, the important thing to grasp is this tension between a legal system predicated on openness and a groundswell of security-driven rhetoric justifying coercive and ostracizing practices against foreigners. It is of course always tempting to look only at one side, and the aim of this brief overview is to provide some additional parameters in order to enable everyone to form a judgement on the basis of a more complete picture.

The absorption of migration issues into policy responses to security concerns is the result of a broad gamut of actions by professional politicians, security professionals and some media outlets, but it is not necessarily linked to any strategic intention.[17] Moreover, because of the success of resistance efforts based on fundamental rights, legal cohesiveness and social and political mobilization and the real scope of the issues subsumed under the terminology of migration, those most affected in practice are the most vulnerable foreigners, second-generation immigrants and Muslims who are most visible in the practice of their faith, as well as people blocked in their countries because they are refused a visa. At the same time, the flows continue unabated and the will to control borders and screen foreigners on an individual basis remains an unrealistic technological dream that could become a nightmare for us all. The result is arbitrariness in some places and some areas, and a total failure to meet the broader challenges effectively.

Bibliography

Anderson, J. and O'Dowd, L. 1999. Borders, Border Regions and Territoriality: Contradictory Meanings, Changing Significance, *Regional Studies*, 33(7).

Andreas, P. and Snyder, T. (eds) 2000. *The Wall Around the West: States, Borders and Immigration Controls in North America and Europe*. Lanham, Boulder, New York and Oxford: Rowman and Littlefield.

Appadurai, A. 1998. Dead Certainty: Ethnic Violence in the Era of Globalization. *Public Culture*, 10(2), 225–47.

---

17   A shorter version of this chapter was published in the Europe section of the journal *Migration et Societé* under the title *Phagocytage des questions migratoires par les enjeux de sécurité*.

Bigo, D. 1996. *Polices en réseaux: L'expérience européenne*. Paris: Presses de Sciences Po.

Bigo, D. 2002. Security and Immigration: Toward a Critique of the Governmentality of Unease, *Alternatives*, 27.

Bigo, D. 2004. Criminalisation of 'Migrants': The Side Effect of the Will to Control the Frontiers and the Sovereign Illusion, in *Irregular Migration and Human Rights: Theoretical, European and International Perspectives*, edited by R. Cholewinski, B. Bogusz, A. Cygan and E. Szyszczak. Leiden: Martinus Nijhoff Publisher.

Bigo, D. and Guild, E. 2003. *La Mise à l'Ecart des Etrangers: Le Visa Schengen, collection Cultures et Conflits*. Paris: L'Harmattan.

Bigo, D. and Tsoukala, A. 2008. *Terror, Liberty, Insecurity: Illiberal Practices of Liberal Regimes, Liberty and Security*. London and New York: Routledge.

Bigo, D. et al. 2007. *The Field of the EU Internal Security Agencies, Cultures et Conflits*. Paris: L'Harmattan.

Bigo, D., Bonelli, L. and Deltombes, T. 2008. *Au nom du 11 Septembre, les démocraties à l'épreuve de l'antiterrorisme*. Paris: La découverte.

Boswell, C. 2007. Migration Control in Europe after 9/11: Explaining the Absence of Securitization, *Journal of Common Market Studies* 45(3), 589–610.

Castles, S. 2002. Migration and Community Formation under Conditions of Globalization, *International Migration Review*, 36(4).

Council of the European Union. 2006a. *Integrated Border Management; Strategy Deliberations*. 13926/06, FRONT 207/COMIX 826. Brussels: Council of Europe.

Guild, E. and Niessen, J. 1996. *The Developing Immigration and Asylum Policies of the European Union*. The Hague/London: Kluwer Law International.

Hreblay, V. 1994. *La libre circulation des personnes: les accords de Schengen, Politique d'aujourd'hui*. Paris: Presses universitaires de France.

Kobelinsky, C. and Makaremi, C. 2008. Confinement des étrangers: technologies et acteurs, *Cultures et Conflits*, 71.

Lago, A.D. 1999. *Non-persone: l'esclusione dei migranti in una società globale, Interzone*. Milan: Feltrinelli.

Mohar, G. and Alcarz, M.-E. 2000. US Border Controls: A Mexican Perspective, in *The Wall around the West: States Borders and Immigration Controls in North America and Europe*, edited by P. Andreas and T. Snyder. Lanham, Boulder, New York and Oxford: Rowman and Littlefield.

Pauly, A. (ed.) 1994. *Schengen en panne*. Maastricht: European Institute of Public Administration.

Tsoukala, A. 1999. The Perception of the 'Other' and the Integration of Immigrants in Greece, in *The Politics of Belonging: Migrants and Minorities in Contemporary Europe*, edited by A. Geddes and A. Favell. Aldershot, Brookfield, Singapore and Sydney: Ashgate.

Valluy, J. 2008. Xénophobie de gouvernement, nationalisme d'Etat, *Cultures et Conflits*, 69.

Index